On This Day SHE MADE HISTORY

For permissions requests or inquiries, please contact:

Emma J. Rosen

EMMA.ROSEN.BOOKS@GMAIL.COM

On This Day SHE MADE HISTORY

366 Days With Women Who Shaped the World

Emma Josephine Rosen

CONTENTS

Dear Reader,

Have you ever wondered why it often appears as though women haven't made as significant an impact throughout history? In the textbooks we perused during our school days, the pages were predominantly filled with the names of men – rulers, explorers, villains, warriors, scientists... Occasionally, a remarkable woman would make a fleeting appearance, almost as an exception to the rule, reinforcing the notion that history is predominantly a male domain.

But is this truly the reality? Were women disinterested, lacking in skills, or simply incapable of participating in the pivotal events of their communities? Did they shy away from creating, shaping, and changing the world surrounding them? Or it's not about them but about the historians who decided which stories were worthy of ink in their pens and space on their websites.

In truth, women have always been dynamic forces in every facet of human existence. They've assumed roles as rulers and rebels, creators and criminals, innovators, warriors, teachers, leaders, dreamers, and doers. They've helped shape our world, even when some (male) historians seemed determined to erase them from the annals of history.

I envisioned this project as a collection of historical snapshots, each capturing what women were up to on a particular day. However, I must admit that this idea has a built-in limitation. Some remarkable women whose stories lack precise dates may not have found their place within these pages. I must also confess that I've occasionally presented a minor event with an exact date solely to introduce you to their names and not because that was the most critical thing they have ever done. When even that proved impossible, I strived to include them in the anniversary lists in the second section of this book.

I've crafted this book as an invitation for further exploration. The entries are concise and modest, designed to serve as a springboard for your research and discovery. I almost hear you thinking, "Oh, that's fascinating; I need to find out more."

This book is a valuable resource for educators looking to diversify their curricula and infuse them with stories too often overlooked. It offers a multitude of narratives that can breathe life into classrooms, serve as the foundation for extra credit projects, or spark the curiosity of students eager for more.

I must also acknowledge that while I've made every effort to include women from diverse cultural backgrounds and corners of the globe, the data available online and in my reference materials inevitably reflects a Western bias. Much work remains to ensure that the remarkable lives of women from all parts of the world are fully appreciated and recognized.

During my year-long research journey, I delved into countless websites, books (thank you, libraries, for scanning books and making them available to the broad public!), academic articles, photographs, images, scans, news outlets worldwide, encyclopedia entries, and more. Every minute of this detective work was an adventure, and I owe my inquisitive mind a debt of gratitude for savoring every moment of it.

However, despite my careful efforts, I acknowledge that mistakes may have crept into this work. After all, I am but human, prone to imperfections. Thus, I invite you, dear Reader, to join me in the quest for accuracy. If you know of an overlooked occurrence or a remarkable deed by a woman deserving of inclusion, please do not hesitate to reach out. Should your contribution earn its place in the next edition, your name will proudly grace the acknowledgments section.

This book is written for those who yearn to broaden their horizons, are eager to learn, and are open to new experiences and intellectual adventures (I believe the term "nerds" might also fit). It is a testament to the indomitable spirit of women who have shaped our world, often against all odds.

Divided into two parts, the first section of this book presents a wide array of events tied to specific days throughout the year. The second section provides birth and death anniversaries for each day, alongside a comprehensive list of female Nobel Prize laureates.

I sincerely hope this book will inspire you to explore more stories of women who were overlooked, erased, forgotten, or unfairly dismissed as unimportant, hysterical, dangerous, uppity, or too intelligent for their own good.

Welcome to "On This Day She Made History." Let's embark on this nerdy adventure together.

With warm regards,

Emma Josephine Rosen

emma.books@gmail.com

❧ ❧ ❧

JANUARY

❧ ❧ ❧

January 01

1007: Imperial Princess Shushi of Japan was granted the esteemed title of *Ippon Shinno* (First Rank Princess), solidifying her position within the royal hierarchy.

1818: Mary Shelley's novel *Frankenstein* was anonymously published in London, becoming the first science-fiction book.

1850: Worcester, Massachusetts, hosted the inaugural National Women's Rights Convention, attracting over 1,000 participants.

1877: Queen Victoria of the United Kingdom was proclaimed Empress of India, a title that lasted until India gained independence on June 22, 1948.

1902: The German Association for Women's Suffrage (*Deutscher Verein für Frauenstimmrecht*, later: *Deutschen Verband für Frauenstimmrecht*) was founded. The founding members included Anita Augspurg and Lida Gustava Heymann, who became chairwoman and vice-chairwoman, Minna Cauer, Charlotte Engel-Reimers, Agnes Hacker, Käthe Schirmacher, Helene Stöcker, and Adelheid von Welczeck.

1939: Stanisława Paleolog, a Polish official, and military and political activist, gained the rank of commissioner in the Women's Police. During her tenure, Paleolog specialized in combating crimes like human trafficking, sexual exploitation, and juvenile delinquency. Her primary role involved fighting crimes against women and children addressing the trafficking of women sent to escort agencies in South America.

1947: The Proceedings of the Cambridge Philosophical Society published an article by Phyllis Nicolson and John Crank, introducing the Crank-Nicolson method for the numerical evaluation of heat-conduction equations.

1953: Esther Lederberg published details of her isolating the λ (*lambda*) bacteriophage in the article "Genetic Studies of Lysogenicity in Escherichia Coli," published in the *Genetics Journal*. She first reported the discovery in 1951 while still a PhD student. Her studies showed that λ had a typical lifestyle in which the phage rapidly made many copies of itself before bursting out of the E. coli host and an alternative lifestyle in which the phage existed quietly within E. coli as just another genetic marker.

1959: Caroline Klein Simon became the second woman to hold the N.Y. Secretary of State position.

1972: Women were officially welcomed into the United States Polo Association, with Sue Sally Hale becoming the first female member.

1977: Jacqueline Means became the first woman ordained to the priesthood in the Episcopal Church.

1994: Comandante Ramona led the occupation of San Cristóbal de las Casas as part of the Zapatista Army of National Liberation's uprising.

2002: Evelyn M. Witkin received the National Medal for Science from President George W. Bush for her contributions to

DNA mutagenesis and repair research.

2011: Dilma Rousseff was inaugurated as Brazil's first female President.

2016: Fabiola Gianotti became the first woman Director-General at CERN (European Organization for Nuclear Research) in Switzerland.

2016: Reports emerged of over 1,200 women subjected to sexual assault during the 2015-2016 New Year's Eve celebrations in Germany, sparking widespread concern.

2019: Same-sex marriage became legal in Austria.

2022: France initiated free birth control for women aged 18 to 25 to reduce unwanted pregnancies and offer enhanced contraceptive access.

January 02

1817: Martha Christina Tiahahu, a Moluccan (Indonesia) freedom fighter against the Dutch colonizers, died on a ship in the Banda Sea. She was captured twice and was sent to Java for enslaved work at a coffee plantation. After she fell ill, she refused to eat or take medicine and soon died. She was buried at sea. To honor her memory, January 2 was designated Martha Christina Tiahahu Day, during which the people in Maluku spread flower petals over the Banda Sea in an official ceremony. She was also declared a National Heroine of Indonesia.

1946: Ruth Seid, writing under the gender-ambiguous pen name Jo Sinclair, was awarded the prestigious Harper Prize for her novel *Wasteland*.

1975: Elisabeth Domitien became the Central African Republic's first female prime minister. She served until April 4, 1976. She was the first woman to serve as prime minister of a country in Sub-Saharan Africa.

1991: Sharon Pratt Dixon became the first African-American woman to serve as the Mayor of a major city. Additionally, Dixon was the first woman to serve as the Mayor of the District of Columbia in the United States.

2001: Sila María Calderón became the first woman elected as the governor of Puerto Rico.

2004: The emergency contraception became available for the first time without a prescription in Australia.

2016: Gisela Mota Ocampo, the newly inaugurated Mayor of Temixco, Mexico, was assassinated at her home shortly after assuming office. The incident, occurring less than a day after her inauguration, was attributed to organized crime, although no specific drug cartel or gang was mentioned.

2022: U.S. Representative Marjorie Taylor Greene faced the permanent suspension of her Twitter account due to alleged violations of the company's policies on COVID-19 misinformation.

January 03

1913: Rosina Ferrario became the first Italian woman to gain a pilot license. During World War I, she strived to form a Women Aviators Volunteer Squadron for evacuating wounded soldiers by air. Still, the Italian High Command rejected the idea due to their reluctance to deploy women near the battlefront.

1918: The Woman Suffrage Committee initiated its hearings, providing a platform for witnesses to present arguments for and against the Voting Rights Amendment.

1933: Minnie D. Craig became the first woman elected Speaker of the North Dakota House of Representatives. Her accomplishment made her the first female Speaker in the state's history.

1949: The Abeokuta Women's Revolt, also known as the Egba Women's Tax Riot, reached a triumphant end. Led by Funmilayo Ransome-Kuti, the Abeokuta Women's Union spearheaded this resistance movement against unjust taxation imposed by the Nigerian colonial government.

1949: Margaret Chase Smith, a Republican from Maine, began her tenure in the Senate, serving until 1973. She was the first woman to serve in both the House and the Senate, having served in the House from 1940 to 1949.

1987: Aretha Franklin was inducted as the first woman in the Rock & Roll Hall of Fame.

2013: Elizabeth Ann Warren assumed office as the first female U.S. senator from Massachusetts, securing victory by defeating the incumbent Republican, Scott Brown.

2018: Iceland enacted a new law aimed at promoting gender equality. The legislation mandated that government agencies and companies with over 24 full-time employees demonstrate equal pay between men and women.

2019: Sharice Davids, a member of the Ho-Chunk Nation, made history by becoming the first openly LGBT+ Native American elected to the U.S. Congress. Additionally, she became the first openly lesbian person elected to the U.S. Congress from Kansas. She was one of the first two Native American women elected to Congress, alongside Deb Haaland of New Mexico, a member of the Laguna Pueblo.

2021: Nancy Pelosi secured her re-election as the Speaker of the House in the 117th United States Congress with a narrow seven-vote majority (216–209).

January 04

1490: Anne of Brittany made a significant proclamation, declaring that anyone who aligned themselves with the king of France would be deemed guilty of the crime of *Lèse -majesté*.

1851: Ann Preston, a pioneering figure in medicine and a student in the first class of the Female Medical College of Pennsylvania (later known as the Woman's Medical College of Pennsylvania), expressed her excitement and satisfaction in a letter to her friend Hannah Darlington. She described the joy of exploring new knowledge, the respite from everyday responsibilities, the motivation of competition, and the allure of embarking on a different way of life.

1972: Dame Rose Heilbron became the first female judge to preside over cases at the Old Bailey, the Central Criminal Court of England and Wales in London.

2007: Nancy Pelosi became the first woman elected Speaker of the United States House of Representatives. Pelosi served as Speaker from 2007 to 2011 and then again from 2019 onwards.

2011: Kathryn Aurora Gray, a 10-year-old Canadian prodigy, became the youngest person to discover a supernova.

2013: Protests against sexual violence erupted across Asia following the heinous Delhi gang rape incident. The demonstrations spread to countries such as Nepal, Sri Lanka, Pakistan, and Bangladesh.

2023: Olivia Hussey, renowned for her role as Juliet in the 1968 film adaptation of William Shakespeare's *Romeo and Juliet*, filed a lawsuit alongside her co-star Leonard Whiting against Paramount Pictures in the Los Angeles County Superior Court. The case sought damages of US$500 million, alleging sexual abuse, sexual harassment, fraud, and the unauthorized filming of the actors in the nude without their knowledge. During filming, Hussey and Whiting were 15 and 17 years old, adding further weight to their claims.

January 05

1850: Dame Sidney Jane Browne, a notable figure in British nursing leadership, became the first president of the Royal College of Nursing. Recognized for her remarkable service in four military wars and campaigns, she received numerous honors, including a peerage.

1912: Sun Yat-sen, the inaugural provisional President of the Republic of China, met with women's suffragist Lin Zongsu, during which he pledged his support for women's suffrage in the newly established republic.

1925: Nellie Tayloe Ross from Wyoming assumed office as the first female governor in the United States.

1945: Four Jewish women involved in the *Sonderkommando* revolt on October 7, 1944, in Auschwitz-Birkneau Nazi Camp - Ala Gertner, Regina Safirsztajn, Rose Grunapfel Meth, and Roza Robota, were publicly hanged in Birkenau. They were all tortured for months before the execution.

2012: Mae Jemison, the first female African-American astronaut, was appointed to lead the DARPA and NASA-sponsored 100-Year Starship project.

2015: An archaeological team from the Czech Republic unearthed the tomb of Khentakawess III, an ancient Egyptian queen previously unknown to historians. This remarkable discovery shed light on the life and legacy of this influential queen during the Fifth Dynasty, offering valuable insights into Egypt's rich history.

2022: Kimberlé Williams Crenshaw received the 2021 Triennial Award for Lifetime Service to Legal Education and the Legal Profession from the Association of American Law Schools (AALS). In her thought-provoking acceptance speech, Crenshaw emphasized the responsibility of the legal academy to combat the suppression of antiracist frameworks. She called on legal educational institutions to confront their historical apathy towards racial subordination and champion the freedom to teach and learn Critical Race Theory, countering concerted efforts to undermine its profound legacy.

January 06

1745: Elizabeth Montagu, an English social reformer and writer, organized the inaugural gathering of the Blue Stockings Society, which was crucial in fostering stimulating conversations and promoting education among its members.

1896: The first-ever women's 6-day bicycle race commenced at Madison Square Garden in the United States.

1907: Maria Montessori, a groundbreaking figure in education, established her first school and daycare center for working-class children in Rome, Italy. She was one of the first women to attend medical school in Italy, and her innovative approach to education would have a lasting impact worldwide.

1919: The National Woman's Party erected a symbolic Watchfire for Freedom. Positioned directly in front of the White House, an urn was employed to burn the disingenuous words of President Woodrow Wilson regarding democracy.

1920: Three Japanese feminists, Hiratsuka Raichō, Ichikawa Fusae, and Oku Mumeo, met at Hiratsuka's residence with other activists to draft two petitions, one to grant women citizenship and the ability to be politically active, while the other to protect women and require men to get tested for syphilis before getting married. The second petition also would have granted wives the ability to divorce their husbands and receive compensation in these cases.

1975: The International Women's Year (IWY) Conference commenced in Mexico City, representing a significant global gathering focused on advancing women's rights and advocating for gender equality.

2006: Ellen Johnson Sirleaf assumed office as the President of Liberia, making history as the first elected female head of state in Africa.

2011: The body of Susana Chávez, a Mexican poet and human rights activist, was found at her home in Ciudad Juárez. Susana was fighting for the plight of women to end the wave of femicide that plagued the city since 1993. At first, the police tried to blame her for the death, claiming she was partying with the wrong crowd. Norma Ledezma, Justice for our Daughters coordinator, linked Susana Chavez's death to Juarez's prevailing culture of impunity. Marisela Ortiz, founder of May Our Daughters Return Home, condemned the intolerance and impunity perpetuating crime.

2013: Colleen LaRose, known by her alias Jihad Jane, received a 10-year sentence for her involvement in a failed al-Qaeda-linked plot to assassinate Swedish artist Lars Vilks. Vilks had depicted the head of the Muslim Prophet Mohammed on a dog, which sparked controversy and drew international attention.

2013: Janet Yellen secured confirmation from the U.S. Senate to become the new chair of the Federal Reserve - the first woman to hold this esteemed position.

2023: Swati Mohan, an accomplished Indian-American scientist, assumed the role of mission commentator during NASA's DART (Double Asteroid Redirection Test) mission.

2023: After serving a 20-year sentence, Ana Montes, a former senior analyst at the Defense Intelligence Agency in the United States, who had spied on behalf of the Cuban government for 17 years, was released from the FMC Carswell facility in Fort Worth, Texas.

January 07

1483: Catherine became the Queen of Navarre after the death of her brother, Francis. Her mother, Magdalena of Valois, was her regent until 1494.

1837: The first letter from Sarah Moore Grimké to her friend, Mary S. Parker, was signed on this date. The collection of letters by Grimké relating to women and their roles in society, especially within the church, was later compiled into a book called *Letters on Gender Equality and Women's Status*. She was an American abolitionist widely held to pioneer the women's suffrage movement.

1839: Georgia Female College, now known as Wesleyan College, opened its doors in Macon, Georgia, USA. It was the first college specifically chartered to grant bachelor's degrees to women.

1896: Fanny Farmer's first cookbook, *The Boston Cooking-School Cook Book*, was published. She standardized cooking measurements, revolutionizing culinary practices and making recipes more accessible and consistent for home cooks.

1939: Marguerite Perey, a French physicist and student of Marie Skłodowska-Curie, made a groundbreaking discovery by identifying Fr (*francium*), the last naturally occurring element.

1948: Fanny Blankers-Koen, a Dutch track and field athlete, set a new world record in the 60-meter hurdles.

1955: Marian Anderson, an acclaimed African-American contralto singer, made history as the first person of color to perform at the Metropolitan Opera, performing in Giuseppe Verdi's *Un Ballo in Maschera*.

1963: Ruth Jessen, an American golfer, emerged victorious in the Women's Western Open, a prestigious and longstanding golf tournament for women.

1979: Sadako Ogata, a Japanese diplomat, assumed the role of United Nations High Commissioner for Refugees (UNHCR), becoming the first woman to hold this position.

1985: Kay Cottee, an Australian sailor, completed a solo circumnavigation of the world, making her the first woman to achieve this remarkable feat non-stop and unassisted.

2002: Mosadi Seboko became the first woman *Kgosikgolo* (hereditary leader/chief) of the Balete people in Botswana. She also became chairperson of the *Ntlo ya Dikgosi* (an advisory body to the parliament) on February 28, 2002, and was crowned on August 30, 2003.

2020: Tsai Ing-wen secured her re-election as the President of Taiwan, making her the first female President to win a second term in office.

2022: A study led by Nicole Schanche of the Center for Space and Habitability CSH at the University of Bern was published in *Astronomy & Astrophysics*. The study reported the discovery of an eccentric exoplanet named TOI-2257 b orbiting a nearby red dwarf.

January 08

1499: Anne, the Duchess of Brittany, entered into a marriage with Louis XII of France following the death of her previous husband, King Charles VIII. She was the only woman to have been the queen consort of France twice.

1816: Marie-Sophie Germain, a notable mathematician, physicist, and philosopher, made history as the first woman to receive a prize from the Paris Academy of Sciences. She was honored for her paper titled *Recherches sur la théorie des surfaces élastiques* (*Research on the Theory of Elastic Surfaces*).

1868: Susan B. Anthony, Elizabeth Cady Stanton, and Parker Pillsbury published the first issue of The Revolution, indicating the beginning of women's political journalism.

1870: The American Woman Suffrage Association released the inaugural edition of the *Woman's Journal* in Boston. The journal was edited by prominent activists Lucy Stone, Mary Livermore, and Julia Ward Howe, and it served as a platform to promote women's suffrage and gender equality.

1896: The first issue of *La Voz de la Mujer* (*The Woman's Voice*) was published. It was Argentina's first Anarcha-feminist and feminist newspaper. It circulated in Buenos Aires from 1896 to 1897 and in Rosario in 1899. In addition to proposing an anarchist feminism in opposition to the reformist feminism of the period, the newspaper defended the ideals of anarchist communism. The newspaper's motto was *"Ni dios, ni patrón, ni marido"* ("Neither god, nor boss, nor husband"). The newspaper advocated women's rebellion against male oppression and supported the proletariat's fight, critiquing various forms of authority. It aimed to establish anarchist communism, target the institution of marriage, and promote free love and flexible unions.

1977: Anna Pauline "Pauli" Murray became the first African-American woman ordained as an Episcopal priest at the Washington National Cathedral in Washington, D.C. In 2018, Murray was honored by being included in the Episcopal Church's calendar of saints.

2001: President Bill Clinton awarded Helen Rodríguez Trías the Presidential Citizen's Medal, the second-highest civilian honor in the United States. The recognition was in tribute to her tireless advocacy and work for women, children, individuals with HIV and AIDS, and impoverished communities.

2011: Icelandic Member of Parliament Birgitta Jónsdóttir expressed her strong disapproval of the United States' attempts to access her private information, deeming it "completely unacceptable." She demanded a meeting with the U.S. ambassador and initiated legal action.

2011: U.S. Representative Gabrielle Giffords from Arizona became the target of an assassination attempt when she was shot during a public event. The incident sparked widespread concern and renewed discussions on gun violence and public safety issues.

2023: American alpine skier Mikaela Shiffrin was able to equal Lindsey Vonn's record of 82 wins in the FIS Alpine Ski World Cup. Shiffrin secured the record after winning the giant slalom event in Kranjska Gora, Slovenia, solidifying her status as one of the most accomplished female skiers in history.

January 09

400: Aelia Eudoxia, the wife of Emperor Arcadius, was granted the title of *Augusta*. This prestigious honor allowed her to wear the revered purple *paludamentum* (a cloak) and be depicted in Roman currency, signifying her elevated status.

1431: The trial of Joan of Arc commenced in Rouen, France. Joan of Arc, a young peasant girl who claimed divine guidance, had played a pivotal role in the Hundred Years' War and was accused of heresy and other charges.

1811: The first recorded women's golf tournament occurred at Musselburgh Golf Club in Scotland. The match was organized for the town fishwives.

1954: The Bollingen Prize for Poetry was jointly awarded to Louise Bogan and Leonie Adams. The Bollingen Prize, established by philanthropist Paul Mellon, is a prestigious literary award recognizing outstanding poetry achievements.

1965: Claudia Jones, a Communist, feminist, and Black nationalist activist, was buried alongside Karl Marx's tomb in Highgate Cemetery, North London. She was called the "Godmother of modern Black Britain" due to her activism after she was deported from the U.S. Her dedication led to the establishment of the first newspaper in the Black British press, *The West Indian Gazette And Afro-Asian Caribbean News*, which debuted in 1958.

2017: Acclaimed American actress Meryl Streep delivered a powerful speech critiquing President-elect Donald Trump at the 74th Golden Globe Awards.

2022: MJ Rodriguez made history by becoming the first transgender actress to win a Golden Globe for Best Actress in the television series Pose.

2023: The National Women's Soccer League (NWSL) in the United States imposed lifetime bans on several former coaches following an investigation into allegations of abuse during the 2021 season. Richie Burke of Washington Spirit, Rory Dames of Chicago Red Stars, Christy Holly of Racing Louisville, and Paul Riley of North Carolina Courage were banned from participating in the league due to their alleged misconduct.

January 10

1917: National Woman's Party members began picketing outside the White House, holding banners with messages demanding women's suffrage. The pickets, known as suffrage sentinels, maintained a constant presence with hourly shift changes, advocating for equal voting rights for women.

1918: Jeannette Rankin, the first woman elected to the U.S. House of Representatives, played a leading role in advocating for the passage of the women's suffrage amendment on the House floor.

1918: The Representation of the People Bill was approved by the House of Lords in the United Kingdom. This bill extended voting rights to women over 30 with specific property qualifications. While it enfranchised approximately 8.5 million women, it still fell short of universal suffrage for all women in the U.K.

1949: The television adaptation of Gertrude Berg's popular radio program, *The Goldbergs*, premiered. The show portrayed the daily life of an upwardly mobile American Jewish family and was one of the earliest successful sitcoms on television.

1980: The Bartolina Sisa National Confederation of Campesino, Indigenous, and Native Women of Bolivia (*Confederación Nacional de Mujeres Campesinas Indígenas*

Originarias de Bolivia "Bartolina Sisa"; CNMCIOB-BS; informally, the Bartolina Sisas) was founded thanks to the efforts of Lucila Mejía de Morales (who became the first executive), Irma García, Isabel Juaniquina, and Isabel Ortega. Their mission was to empower native and indigenous peasant women by defending their human rights, promoting participation in decision-making, eliminating discrimination and violence, enhancing their role in food security, and strengthening their presence in peasant organizations. The name *Bartolina Sisa* refers to the Aymara peasant leader of the 18th century, the wife of Túpac Katari, reflecting the influence of the Katarista movement in peasant politics.

2020: Iranian human rights lawyer Nasrin Sotoudeh received a sentence of 11 years in prison and a 20-year ban on practicing law or traveling. The conviction was widely criticized, with France condemning it as "deeply shocking." Another activist, Shiva Nazar-Ahari, was sentenced to four years in prison and 74 lashes. Calls for the release of Sotoudeh and Nazar-Ahari were made by human rights organizations and governments concerned about their rights and well-being.

January 11

1055: Theodora Porphyrogenita was crowned empress of the Byzantine Empire at 74. She was the last ruler of the Macedonian line, which had been in power for over two centuries.

1827: Aimata Pōmare IV Vahine-o-Punuatera'itua became the Queen of Tahiti. She ascended to the throne at 14 following the death of her brother, Pōmare III.

1897: Martha Hughes Cannon, an American physician, suffragist, and advocate for women's rights in Utah, took her seat as a State Senator in the 2nd Utah State Legislature. She became the first woman to hold such a position in the United States, defeating her own husband, who was also running for the seat.

1912: The Lawrence Textile Strike, also known as the Bread and Roses Strike, began. Wage cuts and reduced work hours for women and children in the Lawrence, Massachusetts, textile mills sparked it. The strike, led by diverse immigrant, primarily female, workers, lasted more than two months and drew attention to poor working conditions.

1919: The U.S. Senate voted on the 19th Amendment to grant women the right to vote. However, the vote fell two votes short of the required two-thirds majority to pass.

1935: Amelia Earhart completed the first solo flight from Hawaii to North America, landing in Oakland, California.

1971: Janis Joplin's second and final solo album, *Pearl*, was released posthumously. The album succeeded, reaching No. 1 on the Billboard 200 chart and remaining there for nine weeks.

1984: The Women of Faith conference brought together religious women from diverse backgrounds to share their faith experiences and perspectives.

2011: British television presenter Miriam O'Reilly won an employment tribunal case against the BBC for ageism and victimization. She had been removed from the program *Countryfile* when it was rescheduled to an evening slot in 2009, and she alleged victimization.

2016: Carli Lloyd, a professional soccer player from the USA, received the FIFA Women's World Player of the Year title, while Jill Ellis, the coach of the USA women's national team, was honored as the FIFA World Coach of the Year for Women's Football.

2021: Pope Francis issued an apostolic letter modifying the canon law, officially opening the ministries of lector and acolyte to women within the Catholic Church.

January 12

1305: Uljay Qutlugh Khatun, the 7-year-old daughter of the late Ghazan Khan, married Bastam, the 8-year-old son of Oljaitu Khan, ruler of the Ilkhanate in Iran. This marriage alliance aimed to consolidate power and strengthen relations between the two factions.

1609: The Basque witch trials began in Spain. The Inquisition court in Logroño received a letter from the village commissioner of Zugarramurdi, leading to the arrest of four women, including María de Jureteguía and María Chipía de Barrenetxea. These trials were part of a broader wave of witch trials across Europe during the Early Modern period.

1915: The U.S. House of Representatives voted on the federal woman suffrage amendment for the first time, but the measure was defeated.

1920: The Wafdist Women's Central Committee (WWCC) was established in Egypt, with Huda Sha'arawi serving as its first president. The WWCC was crucial in advocating for women's rights and social reforms in Egypt during the early 20th century.

1932: Hattie Caraway, representing Arkansas, became the first woman elected to the United States Senate. She served in the Senate from 1931 to 1945, breaking barriers for women in American politics.

1935: Amelia Earhart completed a solo flight from Hawaii to California, covering 2,408 miles.

1999: Britney Spears released her debut solo album, *...Baby One More Time*. The album became a commercial success and launched Spears' career as a pop icon.

2016: The Saudi Arabian government arrested Samar Badawi, a prominent human rights activist. Badawi was honored with the International Women of Courage Award by the United States in 2012 for her advocacy work. Her arrest highlighted ongoing concerns about human rights in Saudi Arabia.

January 13

47 BCE: Queen Cleopatra VII of Egypt elevated her younger brother, Ptolemy XIV, to co-ruler. This move was likely a political strategy to consolidate power and maintain stability in Egypt.

1001: Empress consort Fujiwara no Teishi, also known as Sadako, died in childbirth. Her life and courtly experiences were chronicled in *The Pillow Book* by her contemporary, Sei Shōnagon, providing valuable insights into the cultural and social dynamics of the Heian period in Japan.

1900: The first annual convention of the Alabama Equal Suffrage Association took place in Selma, Alabama. The convention brought together Birmingham, Huntsville, Montgomery, and Selma delegates to advocate for women's suffrage. Alabama ratified the 19th Amendment, granting women the right to vote, on September 5, 1953.

1913: Delta Sigma Theta Sorority was founded by twenty-two women at Howard University. These women participated in the historic 1913 Women's Suffrage March in Washington, D.C., making Delta Sigma Theta the only Black women's organization to walk in the march.

1970: The United States Court of Appeals for the Third Circuit made a significant decision in the *Schultz v. Wheaton Glass Co.* case. The court ruled that the Equal Pay Act protected jobs that were "substantially equal" in terms of job requirements, even if they had different titles or descriptions—this decision aimed to address wage disparities based on gender.

2021: Lisa Marie Montgomery was executed by lethal injection by the U.S. federal government for the 2004 murder of Bobbie Jo Stinnett. Montgomery's execution followed the lifting of the last stay on her execution by the Supreme Court. She became the first woman to be executed by the federal government since 1953.

January 14

1794: Elizabeth Hog Bennett became the first woman in the United States to give birth to a child via Cesarean section successfully.

1893: Queen Lili'uokalani, the last reigning monarch of the Kingdom of Hawaii, nullified the U.S. law and proclaimed a pro-Hawaiian constitution. This act led to her arrest and subsequent dethronement as the Hawaiian monarchy was overthrown and replaced by a provisional government.

1914: Mary A. Blagg, Ella K. Church, A. Grace Cook, Irene Elizabeth Toye Warner, and Fiammetta Wilson were elected as the first female Fellows of the Royal Astronomical Society.

1919: Charlotte Adelgonde Elisabeth Marie Wilhelmine became the Grand Duchess of Luxembourg after her sister, Marie-Adélaïde, abdicated the throne. She ruled until 1964 when she abdicated for her son Jean. Charlotte was the last agnatic member of the House of Nassau.

1970: Diana Ross and the Supremes held their final concert together. Diana Ross, the group's lead singer, pursued a successful solo career while the Supremes continued with new members.

1972: Queen Margrethe II of Denmark, born Margrethe Alexandrine Þórhildur Ingrid, ascended the throne, becoming the first Queen of Denmark since 1412.

2019: Over 31,000 teachers, nurses, counselors, and librarians in Los Angeles went on strike demanding higher pay after failed negotiations for improved compensation and work conditions. Most striking professionals were women, highlighting the gender dynamics within these professions and the fight for equitable treatment.

January 15

1559: Elizabeth I, often called "The Virgin Queen," was crowned Queen of England in Westminster Abbey, London. She was the last monarch of the House of Tudor and is remembered as one of England's most influential and successful rulers.

1560: The first works of Anne Locke were published, including sonnets based on biblical Psalms and her translation of John Calvin's sermons. The book was reprinted multiple times in the following years.

1913: Britain's Royal Geographical Society members voted to admit women, ending 82 years as an all-male organization.

1919: Rosa Luxemburg and Karl Liebknecht, prominent figures in the German communist movement, were murdered in Berlin by the right-wing paramilitary Freikorps. Their deaths significantly impacted the political landscape of post-World War I Germany.

1951: Ilse Koch, known as the "Witch of Buchenwald" and the wife of the commandant of the Buchenwald concentration camp, was sentenced to life imprisonment for the atrocities she committed during the Holocaust.

1968: Jeannette Rankin, the first woman elected to the U.S. Congress, led a march of more than 5,000 female peace activists in Washington, D.C., to protest the Vietnam War.

1973: Golda Meir, the Prime Minister of Israel, became the first Israeli Prime Minister to visit the Pope.

1997: Princess Diana called for an international ban on landmines during her visit to Angola, where she witnessed the impact of landmines on civilians. Her advocacy for this cause drew attention to the humanitarian consequences of landmines and led to increased efforts for their eradication.

2009: Gabourey Sidibe made her acting debut in *Precious*. Her powerful performance earned her critical acclaim, including an Independent Spirit Award for Best Female Lead and nominations for the Golden Globe and Academy Award for Best Actress.

2016: Yingluck Shinawatra, the former Prime Minister of Thailand, appeared in court to face corruption charges, a significant event in the political turmoil and legal proceedings surrounding her administration.

2023: Former lawmaker Mursal Nabizada, a vocal critic of the Taliban, and one of her bodyguards were shot and killed in Kabul, Afghanistan.

January 16

27 BCE: Livia Drusilla became a Roman empress as the wife of emperor Augustus, serving as his trusted confidante, and was rumored to be involved in the deaths of several of Augustus' relatives, including his grandson, Agrippa Postumus. Livia became the role model for the noble Roman matron, with modest attire, homemaking skills, and unwavering loyalty to her husband.

1864: Anna E. Dickinson, an American abolitionist and orator, became the first woman to address the President of the United States, Abraham Lincoln, the First Lady, members of the Supreme Court, and a joint session of Congress at the U.S. House of Representatives.

1904: Dewi Sartika, a Sundanese advocate for and pioneer of education for women in Indonesia, opened a school named *Sakola Istri* at Bandung (Java), which later was relocated to Jalan Ciguriang and the school name changed to *Sekolah Kaoetamaan Isteri* (Wife Eminency School). By the year 1920, all of the cities and regencies had one *Sekolah Kaoetamaan Isteri* school, which later changed its name to *Sekolah Raden Dewi*.

1920: Five African-American women from Howard University founded Zeta Phi Beta sorority, focusing on social causes and community service. Zeta Phi Beta became influential in promoting education, leadership, and empowerment among African-American women.

2005: At age 66, Adriana Iliescu became the world's oldest recorded birth mother when she gave birth to a daughter through IVF treatment. Her case sparked discussions and debates regarding the ethical and medical considerations surrounding advanced maternal age and assisted reproductive technologies.

2006: Ellen Johnson Sirleaf was sworn in as the 24th President of Liberia, making her the first female elected head of state in Africa. She played a significant role in stabilizing Liberia after years of civil war and promoting women's rights and empowerment during her presidency.

2016: Tsai Ing-wen, a member of the Democratic Progressive Party (DPP), was elected as the first female President of Taiwan. Her election marked a historic moment in Taiwanese politics, and she focused on maintaining stability in cross-strait relations while promoting Taiwan's democratic values.

2016: Milagro Sala, a Tupac Amaru neighborhood association leader and a prominent figure in the *Movimiento piquetero* of Argentina, was arrested on charges of allegedly inciting public disturbances.

2019: Theresa May's government survived a no-confidence vote by a majority of 19 in the British Parliament. The vote was held in the context of ongoing negotiations and debates surrounding Brexit and the United Kingdom's withdrawal from the European Union.

2023: Metropolitan Police Parliamentary and Diplomatic Protection officer David Carrick pleaded guilty to 49 offenses, including 24 rapes, at Southwark Crown Court in London, UK. His crimes spanned from 2003 to 2020, primarily in Hertfordshire, where he lived.

January 17

1314: Queen Oljath married Qara Sonqur, the Governor of Maragheh, in what is now the East Azerbaijan province of Iran. A dowry of 30,000 dinars was exchanged as part of the marriage agreement.

1690: Elizabeth Moore of Leicestershire was granted a medical and surgery license in Coventry and Lichfield, Lincoln, and Peterborough dioceses. Her expertise and skill in healing were acknowledged through multiple testimonials.

1893: The government of Queen Lili'uokalani and the Kingdom of Hawaii was overthrown by the Citizens' Committee of Public Safety with the assistance of the United States Marine Corps.

1933: Miriam "Ma" Ferguson became the first female Governor of Texas. Shortly after taking office, she decided to dismiss all 44 Texas Rangers.

2018: Helen G. James, a former United States Air Force enlistee, upgraded her discharge status to "honorable" after being arrested and discharged as "undesirable" during the Lavender Scare campaign. This change in status allowed her, at the age of 90, to access veterans' benefits and services.

January 18

1223: Rusudan (daughter of Tamar the Great) became the Queen of Georgia and ruled until 1245.

1486: Elizabeth of York, daughter of Edward IV, married King Henry VII of England, bringing together the House of Lancaster and the House of York and marking the end of the War of Roses.

1777: Mary Katherine Goddard, an American newspaper publisher and postmaster, printed the first copy of the *United States Declaration of Independence* in Baltimore, Maryland.

1977: Actress Julie Newmar was granted a U.S. Patent for her invention Pantyhose with a Shaping Band for Cheeky Derriere Relief.

2014: The Screen Actors Guild Awards took place, and Cate Blanchett won the Screen Actors Guild Award for Outstanding Performance by a Female Actor in a Leading Role for her performance in *Blue Jasmine*.

2022: Salima Mukansanga from Rwanda became the first woman referee to officiate an Africa Cup of Nations game. She took charge of the match between Zimbabwe and Guinea in Cameroon.

January 19

1920: The American Civil Liberties Union (ACLU) was founded by a committee that included Crystal Eastman, Helen Keller, Jane Addams, Elizabeth Gurley Flynn, and Rose Schneiderman. It was initially focused on freedom of speech for anti-war protesters.

1933: Mary, Lady Bailey, a British aviator, was rescued after being missing for four days in the Sahara Desert. She made an emergency landing southwest of Tahoua, Niger, French West Africa, and was found dehydrated and exhausted but without injuries.

1953: The episode "Lucy Goes to the Hospital" premiered and became one of the most-watched TV events in history.

1966: Indira Gandhi became the head of the Congress Party and the Prime Minister of India, becoming the country's first female head of government.

1977: Iva Toguri, also known as "Tokyo Rose," was pardoned by President Ford. The Japanese government ordered her and other women to broadcast sentimental American music and false announcements to demoralize Allied soldiers during World War II.

2009: Anastasia Baburova, a Ukraine-born journalist for *Novaya Gazeta* and a journalism student at Moscow State University, was murdered alongside human rights lawyer Stanislav Markelov in Moscow. For a few months before the murder, Baburova was investigating Russian neo-Nazi groups. She was also active in the anarchist environmentalist movement.

2021: Emily Onyango was appointed the first woman bishop of the Anglican Church of Kenya.

2023: Sierra Leonean President Julius Maada Bio signed a gender equality bill into law, which mandates the employment of at least 30 percent of women in all businesses. The law also guarantees at least 14 weeks of maternity leave and equal pay.

2023: Jacinda Ardern announced her intention to resign as the Prime Minister of New Zealand by February 7.

January 20

842: On his deathbed, Theophilus named his wife Theodora as regent for their two-year-old son Michael III and designated a selection of advisors to assist her. Theodora ruled in her own right until her son deposed of her on March 15, 856, and sent her to a convent.

1236: Eleanor of Provence was crowned the queen consort of England. She was known for her intelligence, poetic talent, and beauty. She led fashion trends by importing French clothing. When she was queen dowager, she expelled all Jews in her lands in 1275.

1343: Joanna I became the queen of Naples and ruled until 1382.

1374: Floreta of Santa Coloma de Queralt was issued the first license *in arte Medicine*—to practice medicine in Catalonia and became the doctor of Leonor de Sicilia.

1869: Elizabeth Cady Stanton became the first woman to testify before the United States Congress.

1873: Susan B. Anthony, Matilda Joselyn Gage, and Elizabeth Cady Stanton of the National Woman Suffrage Association referred a petition to the Committee on the Judiciary at the U.S. House of Representatives.

1961: An African-American contralto, Marian Anderson, sang during President John F. Kennedy's inauguration.

1978: Indira Gandhi, leader of the Congress Party, assumed office as the Prime Minister of India once again.

2014: Israel made revenge porn illegal.

2021: Kamala Harris became the first female, African-American, and Asian American Vice President of the United States.

2022: Zara Rutherford, at 19, completed her trip and became the youngest woman to fly solo around the globe in a 155-day journey, surpassing the previous record set by Shaesta Waiz, who was 30 years old at the time of her adventure.

2023: The Burkina Faso Armed Forces rescued 62 women and four babies kidnapped by jihadists in Arbinda, Sahel Region, on January 15.

January 21

1859: Sarah Parker Remond, an American lecturer, activist, and abolitionist campaigner, delivered her first anti-slavery lecture at the Tuckerman Institute in Liverpool, England. She traveled throughout the British Isles over the next three years, captivating audiences with descriptions of the inhumane treatment of enslaved people in the United States and highlighting the discrimination faced by free African Americans.

1908: The Sullivan Ordinance, a municipal law passed by the board of aldermen in New York City, made it illegal for women to smoke publicly.

1971: Annie Leibovitz's photograph of John Lennon graced the cover of *Rolling Stone* magazine, starting her artistic career.

2001: German rally driver Jutta Kleinschmidt became the first woman to win the Paris-Dakar Rally, a grueling off-road race covering thousands of kilometers.

2010: Norwegian adventurer Cecilie Skog, accompanied by American Ryan Waters, achieved the first unassisted and unsupported crossing of Antarctica, covering a distance of 1,800 kilometers.

2012: Starting from April 30, clinics in the United Kingdom offering pregnancy services, including abortions, were permitted to advertise on radio and television. The Broadcast Committee of Advertising Practice ruled that there was no justification for prohibiting such clinics from promoting their services.

2017: On Donald Trump's first full day as President of the United States, more than 500,000 people gathered in Washington, D.C., and millions more participated in women's rights marches across the U.S. and worldwide. The demonstrations were held to advocate for women's rights and equality. A total of 408 demonstrations were reported in the U.S., with 168 protests in other countries.

January 22

906: Empress Dowager He, the wife of the late Emperor Zhaozong and mother of the reigning Emperor Ai, was secretly executed by the warlord Zhu Quanzhong. She was strangled and posthumously demoted to the rank of a commoner to defame her reputation.

1913: Anna Ancher, a celebrated visual artist from Denmark, received the *Ingenio et Arti* medal from King Christian X. This Danish medal recognizes notable achievements in science and art and is a personal honor bestowed by the monarch.

1930: The drama film *Anna Christie,* starring Greta Garbo, premiered at the Criterion Theatre in Los Angeles. This marked Garbo's first speaking role, and the film was promoted with the tagline "Garbo Talks!"

1941: Margarete Schütte-Lihotzky, an Austrian architect mostly remembered today for designing what is known as the "Frankfurt kitchen," was arrested by the Gestapo when contacting a communist resistance contact. She was sentenced to fifteen years and sent to prison. American troops liberated her on April 29, 1945.

1973: In the landmark case of *Roe v. Wade,* the U.S. Supreme Court ruled that the Constitution protects a woman's constitutional right to abortion. However, in June 2022, the Supreme Court overturned this ruling.

1992: Roberta Bondar became the first Canadian woman and neurologist to travel into space aboard the Discovery space shuttle.

1996: Judy Blume received the Margaret A. Edwards Award for Outstanding Literature for Young Adults, recognizing her exceptional contributions to young adult literature.

2020: Zeina Akar became the first female defense minister in Lebanon and the entire Arab world.

2020: Byun Hui-Su, a transgender soldier in South Korea, announced her intention to sue the armed forces after being discharged. She expressed her determination to pursue her case to the Supreme Court.

January 23

1678: Sultan Inayat Zakiatudin Syah became the sixteenth monarch of the Acèh Darussalam (modern-day Indonesia) and the third *sulṭāna* regnant to rule in succession. She ruled for ten years.

1849: Elizabeth Blackwell became the first female doctor in the United States. She faced numerous rejections from medical schools, but eventually, Geneva Medical College in western New York accepted her application after a vote among the student body, who initially thought it was a joke.

1870: The Marias Massacre occurred in Montana, where 173 members of the Blackfoot tribe, primarily women and children, were killed by the United States Army.

1911: Marie Curie narrowly missed becoming the first woman member of France's Académie des Sciences by two votes. Edouard Branly secured the majority with 29 votes in the subsequent round, and Curie did not pursue membership again.

1997: Madeleine Albright was confirmed by the United States Senate and became the first female Secretary of State in the country's history.

2012: Felicity Aston accomplished a remarkable feat by becoming the first person to ski alone across the Antarctic landmass using only personal muscle power. She also became the first woman to cross the Antarctic mainland alone.

2013: Yad Vashem, Israel's official memorial to the victims of the Holocaust, posthumously honored Mary Elmes as Righteous Among the Nations. Elmes had saved the lives of at least 200 Jewish children during World War II.

January 24

1948: Maria Mandl, an Austrian *SS-Helferin* ("SS helper") and a top-ranking official at the Auschwitz-Birkenau extermination camp, where she is believed to have been directly complicit in the deaths of over 500,000 prisoners, was executed for war crimes after a trial in November 1947 in Kraków, Poland.

1978: Indira Gandhi, the former Prime Minister of India, publicly apologized for the mistakes and excesses committed during the Emergency. She took full responsibility for these actions, acknowledging the burden of those mistakes.

1985: Penny Harrington became the first female police chief of the Portland Police Department in Portland, Oregon, and the first woman to hold such a position in a major city in the United States.

2005: Yulia Volodymyrivna Tymoshenko became Ukraine's first female prime minister.

2011: Adele released her second studio album, *21*, which became the best-selling album of the 21st century, with over 31 million copies sold worldwide.

2013: The United States military lifted the ban on women serving in combat positions, allowing them to take on a wider range of roles within the armed forces.

January 25

1700: The last pregnancy of Anne, Queen of Great Britain, ended in a stillbirth. She was pregnant 17 times over 12 years, experiencing miscarriages and stillbirths. Out of her five liveborn children, four passed away before turning two. Experts speculate on what medical issues could have caused such problems with carrying a pregnancy to term.

1777: After being rejected by the University of Turin, Maria Pellegrina Amoretti graduated at 21 in *Iure utroque* (civil and canon Law) at the University of Pavia, defending her doctoral theses. She was the author of a treatise on dowry law entitled *Tractatus de jure Datium apud romanos*. She is considered the third woman with a doctoral degree and the first with a degree in Law.

1851: Sojourner Truth, a prominent American abolitionist and women's rights leader delivered a powerful speech at the first Black Women's Rights Convention in Akron, Ohio.

1858: Queen Victoria's daughter, Victoria, married Friedrich of Prussia, accompanied by the famous *Wedding March* composed by Felix Mendelssohn, which later became a popular wedding processional.

1868: Mary Putnam Jacobi made history by entering the medical amphitheater of Paris's Ecole de Medicine as the first woman ever. Although she had to use a side entrance and sit in a specially designated chair, her achievement was significant.

1890: Nellie Bly, an American journalist, completed her journey around the world in just 72 days, setting a new record.

1961: President Kennedy acknowledged Alice Dunnigan as the first African American White House correspondent after two years of being ignored. She became the first Black woman in the Senate and House of Representatives press galleries.

1971: The U.S. Supreme Court ruled in *Phillips v. Martin Marietta* that employers cannot discriminate against women with pre-school-age children unless they also refuse to hire men with young children under Title VII of the Civil Rights Act of 1964.

1972: Shirley Chisholm became the first major-party African-American candidate for President of the United States and the first woman to run for the Democratic presidential nomination.

2011: English poet Jo Shapcott received the 2010 Costa Book Awards for her poetry collection *Of Mutability*, which was poetry's second consecutive win in the prize.

2016: Belgium expressed support for a proposal by Dutch minister Lilianne Ploumen to establish a fund to compensate for the impact of the reinstated Mexico City policy, which restricted U.S. federal funding for NGOs involved in abortion-related activities. President Joe Biden later rescinded the policy in January 2021.

2021: President Biden signed an executive order overturning the ban on transgender individuals serving in the military.

2021: Malka Leifer, a former Melbourne school principal facing numerous charges of child sexual abuse, was finally deported to Australia after a six-year delay and being a fugitive in Israel.

2021: Janet Yellen was confirmed as Treasury Secretary by the U.S. Senate, becoming the first woman to lead the Treasury Department.

2021: Kaja Kallas became the first woman to hold the position of Prime Minister of Estonia after winning the support of the Riigikogu.

2023: UNESCO designated January 25 as the International Day of Women in Multilateralism, recognizing women's crucial role in promoting human rights, peace, and sustainable development within the multilateral system.

January 26

1966: Annabelle Rankin, an Australian government official and diplomat, became the Minister for Housing, making her the first woman in Australia to be appointed to a cabinet position. Before that, she served as a Senator for Queensland (1947-1971) and Government Whip in the Senate (1951-1966).

1987: Chandanaji became the first Jain woman to receive the title of *Acharya*, a significant religious and spiritual role in Jainism.

2000: Blu Greenberg was honored with the Woman Who Made A Difference award from the American Jewish Congress Commission for Women's Equality during a ceremony at the Israeli *Knesset* in Jerusalem.

2005: Condoleezza Rice was confirmed by the U.S. Senate as the first female African-American Secretary of State. Before her nomination, she also served as the first woman to hold the position of National Security Advisor.

2009: Nadya Suleman gave birth to the world's first surviving octuplets, making headlines globally.

2013: Kathleen Wynne was elected as the leader of the ruling Ontario Liberal Party and became the first female Premier of the Canadian province of Ontario. She also became the first openly gay Premier in Canadian history.

2015: Libby Lane was consecrated as the Bishop of Stockport, becoming the first woman appointed by the Church of England as a bishop following the July 2014 decision by the general synod to allow women to become bishops.

2018: Jamitha Teacher, a female Imam, led the Friday prayer of Jumu'ah Namaz in Malappuram, Kerala, becoming the first woman Imam in India to lead the ceremonial prayer.

2020: Billie Eilish achieved a remarkable feat at the 62nd Annual Grammy Awards, sweeping the major categories and winning Song of the Year, Record of the Year, Album of the Year, and Best New Artist.

2022: The National Assembly of France voted to criminalize conversion therapy to protect LGBTQ+ individuals. Violators could face up to three years in prison and fines of up to €45,000.

January 27

1687: In a notorious case in 17th century England, midwife Mary Hobry murdered her abusive husband, Denis Hobry, after enduring repeated assaults. Mary dismembered his body and scattered the remains in various locations. Despite her defense of justifiable homicide, Mary was convicted of murder and burned at the stake.

1961: Leontyne Price, a celebrated soprano, debuted at the Metropolitan Opera in New York City. She became the first African-American to open a concert season there, performing the role of Leonora in Verdi's opera *Il Trovatore*.

1964: U.S. Senator Margaret Chase Smith announced her candidacy for the Republican presidential nomination, becoming the first woman to do so.

2000: Zadie Smith published her debut novel, *White Teeth*, which received critical acclaim and won numerous awards, including the 2000 James Tait Black Memorial Prize for fiction, the 2000 Whitbread Book Award for best first novel, the Guardian First Book Award, the Commonwealth Writers First Book Prize, and the Betty Trask Award.

2016: Hilda Heine was elected as the President of the Marshall Islands by Parliament, becoming the country's first female President. She also became the first woman to hold the position of President in any Micronesian country.

2022: Xiomara Castro was officially inaugurated as the 56th President of Honduras, making her the first female President in the country's history.

January 28

1591: Agnes Sampson, the Wise Wife of Keith, was executed for witchcraft in Edinburgh, Scotland.

1813: Jane Austen anonymously published her novel *Pride and Prejudice* in London, which went on to become one of her most famous works.

1908: Julia Ward Howe, an American poet, peace advocate, abolitionist, and feminist, became the first woman elected to the American Academy of Arts and Letters.

1912: Opika von Méray Horváth, a Hungarian figure skater, won the gold medal at the Ladies World Figure Skating Championships in Davos, Switzerland, the first of her three consecutive victories.

1914: Nellie McClung, a Canadian suffragist, organized a satirical play at the Walker Theatre in Winnipeg, Manitoba, to mock the opposition of Manitoba Premier Rodmond Roblin to women's suffrage. The play contributed to the advancement of the women's suffrage movement, and Manitoba granted women the right to vote in 1916.

1917: Carmelita Torres, a domestic worker, initiated the Typhus Bath Riots in El Paso, Texas, by punching a USPHS medical officer. The incident arose from the mistreatment and inspection of Mexican immigrants suspected of carrying diseases, subjecting them to fumigation, vaccinations, and other invasive procedures.

2008: Adele released her debut album, *19*, named after her age at the time of release. The album garnered critical acclaim and earned Adele multiple awards, including Best New Artist at the Grammy Awards.

2013: Queen Beatrix of the Netherlands announced her abdication in favor of her son, Prince Willem-Alexander, who would ascend to the throne as the new King of the Netherlands on April 30, 2013.

2014: Mamphela Ramphele, a former anti-apartheid activist, joined the main opposition party, Democratic Alliance (DA), in South Africa and became their presidential candidate for the 2014 general election.

2019: Naomi Osaka, a professional tennis player, became the first Asian player to achieve the No. 1 ranking in women's singles tennis.

2022: Laurie Leshin, a geochemist and space scientist, was appointed the first female Director of NASA's Jet Propulsion Laboratory.

January 29

1007: Murasaki Shikibu, a renowned writer and lady-in-waiting, was granted a prestigious position directly below Empress Shōshi in the palace. Murasaki Shikibu is best known as the author of *The Tale of Genji*, often considered the world's first novel.

1688: Madame Jeanne Guyon, a French mystic, was arrested and imprisoned for seven months in France. She was accused of advocating Quietism, a spiritual practice deemed heretical at the time, following the publication of her book *A Short and Very Easy Method of Prayer*.

1848: Ernestine Rose, an American suffragist, abolitionist, and social reformer, delivered a speech at the annual Thomas Paine dinner, emphasizing the role of knowledge in liberating women from ignorance and dependency.

1891: Lili'uokalani, also known as Lydia Lili'u Loloku Walania Kamaka'eha, began her reign as the last monarch and the only queen regnant of the Kingdom of Hawaii.

1912: Anna LoPizzo, an Italian immigrant striker, was killed during the Lawrence Textile Strike, also known as the Bread and Roses Strike. The strike, led chiefly by immigrant women, aimed to protest poor working conditions and wage reductions. LoPizzo's death further galvanized the workers' fight against injustice.

1913: Alpha Kappa Alpha, the first African-American sorority, was officially incorporated, providing a supportive network and promoting educational opportunities for African-American women.

1926: Violette Neatly Anderson became the first Black woman to practice law before the U.S. Supreme Court, breaking barriers in the legal profession.

1943: The United States Marine Corps Women's Reserve (MCWR) was established, allowing women to serve in the Marine Corps during World War II. Ruth Cheney Streeter was commissioned as a major in the U.S. Marine Corps and appointed director of the U.S. Marine Corps Women's Reserve, making her the first woman to hold that position.

1951: Henrietta Lacks, a patient at Johns Hopkins Hospital, unknowingly had samples taken from her cervix during her treatment for cervical cancer. These samples led to the development of the HeLa Immortal Cell Line, which has been instrumental in biomedical research.

1998: The New Woman clinic in Birmingham, Alabama, was bombed by an anti -abortion domestic terrorist, resulting in the death of a security guard and severe injuries to a nurse.

2009: President Obama signed the Lilly Ledbetter Fair Pay Act into law, amending the Civil Rights Act of 1964 to combat discriminatory compensation practices. It was the first bill signed into law by President Obama. The act aimed to promote equal pay for equal work and provide more avenues for addressing pay discrimination.

January 30

1942: The United States Congress established the Women's Reserve of the United States Naval Reserve, commonly known as WAVES (Women Accepted for Volunteer Emergency Service). Over 86,000 women served in active duty during World War II as part of WAVES.

1962: An outbreak of mass hysteria known as the "laughter epidemic" began at a girls' mission school in Kashasha, Tanganyika (now Tanzania). The phenomenon spread to 14 schools and affected over 1,000 people, causing uncontrollable laughter and fainting spells.

2003: Belgium became the second country in the world to legalize same-sex marriage, following the Netherlands. This landmark decision granted same-sex couples the right to marry and enjoy marriage's legal benefits and protections.

2011: Natalie Portman won the Outstanding Performance by a Female Actor in a Leading Role award at the 17th Screen Actors Guild Awards for her captivating performance in the movie *Black Swan*.

2015: The Women's Mosque of America, claimed to be the first female-only mosque in the United States, opened its doors in Los Angeles. It aimed to provide a space for women to lead prayers and engage in religious activities in an inclusive and supportive environment.

2016: Over 2,100 pregnant women in Colombia were infected with the Zika virus, a mosquito-borne disease. The Zika virus outbreak raised concerns due to its potential association with severe congenital disabilities, particularly microcephaly, in infants born to infected mothers.

January 31

1659: Giovanna De Grandis was arrested in Rome and charged with trafficking the lethal *Aqua Tofana* poison. This arrest led to the *Spana Prosecution* case, in which she implicated the mastermind, Gironima Spana, resulting in the arrest and trial of 40 individuals involved in the poisoning scheme.

1675: During the Salem Witch Trials, Cornelia (Dina) Olfaarts was found not guilty of witchcraft - a rare outcome that resulted in the wrongful accusations and executions of numerous individuals, mostly women.

1912: The play *Rutherford and Son* by Githa Sowerby premiered at the Royal Court Theatre in London. The play explores themes of gender roles, family dynamics, and industrialization in early 20th-century England.

1924: Herma Szabo of Austria won the ladies figure skating gold medal at the first Winter Olympics in Chamonix, France. This event marked the only women's event at the Games that year.

1938: Emma Tenayuca organized and led the San Antonio pecan shellers strike involving 12,000, primarily Mexican-American, workers. During the strike's duration, the police arrested and detained numerous protesters and picketers, among them Tenayuca. Finally, it ended successfully on March 8, with improved wages.

2012: In Afghanistan, a woman was killed by her husband and mother-in-law three months after giving birth to her third daughter, as she had not produced a son.

2013: Icelandic teenager Blaer Bjarkardottir won a legal fight to use her given name, which the Icelandic Naming Committee had deemed inappropriate for a female.

2015: Lydia Ko of New Zealand, who was not yet 18, became the youngest golfer, regardless of gender, to achieve the world number 1 ranking in golf. She surpassed the previous record held by Tiger Woods by nearly four years.

2017: Susan Kiefel was sworn in as Australia's first female Chief Justice.

❦ ❦ ❦

FEBRUARY

❦ ❦ ❦

February 01

1587: Queen Elizabeth I of England authorized the signing of her cousin Mary, Queen of Scots' death warrant. Mary had been implicated in a plot to assassinate Elizabeth. Seven days later, Mary was executed by beheading at Fotheringhay Castle, following the directive of Elizabeth's privy council.

1862: Julia Ward Howe published the *Battle Hymn of the Republic* in the *Atlantic Monthly*. With its powerful and patriotic lyrics, the song became a widespread anthem during the American Civil War and served as a call to action against slavery.

1864: The Collar Laundry Union was formed in New York, led by Kate Mullany. It was the first women's union in United States history. The union was crucial in advocating for improved working conditions and higher wages for female laundry workers. Over the next few years, the organization increased weekly wages from $2 to $14.

1979: Patricia Era Bath published an article titled "Rationale for a Program in Community Ophthalmology" in the *Journal of the National Medical Association*. In the article, Bath highlighted the high incidence of eye abnormalities among Black individuals and the limited availability of ophthalmic services, which led to excessive rates of preventable or curable blindness.

2002: Tina Sjögren from Sweden became the first woman to complete an unsupported journey to the South Pole, traveling with her husband, Thomas Sjögren. They journeyed from the Hercules Inlet, covering the distance in 63 days.

2003: The Space Shuttle Columbia disintegrated during reentry into the Earth's atmosphere, resulting in the tragic loss of all seven astronauts on board. Among them were female astronauts Kalpana Chawla and Laurel Clark.

2009: Jóhanna Sigurðardóttir formed the first cabinet in Iceland, becoming the country's first female prime minister. She also became the world's first openly gay head of government.

2019: The Boy Scouts of America officially changed its name to Scouts BSA, opening up membership to young women for the first time—this decision aimed to promote inclusivity and provide equal opportunities for boys and girls in scouting activities.

2021: Aung San Suu Kyi, the leader of Myanmar's National League for Democracy (NLD) party and a prominent political figure, was arrested and ousted by the country's military.

February 02

962: Pope John XII crowned King Otto I as Holy Roman Emperor at the Old St. Peter's Basilica in Rome. This event marked the end of Rome's feudal anarchy and the unification of the East Frankish Kingdom and the Kingdom of Italy into a common realm known as the Roman Empire. Otto's wife, Adelaide, was anointed empress, and her coronation played a significant role in establishing her divine authority within the empire.

1901: The United States Congress established the United States Female Army Nurse Corps as a permanent corps within the United States Army Medical Department. Dita H. Kinney was named the first superintendent of the Corps when it was launched in March of the same year.

1935: Kirsten Malfrid Flagstad, a Norwegian dramatic soprano singer, debuted at the Metropolitan Opera as Sieglinde in *Die Walküre*. Her performance was broadcast nationwide on the Met's weekly syndicated radio program and garnered widespread acclaim.

1960: Loretta Lynn signed her first contract with Zero Records, indicating the beginning of her legendary six-decade-long career in country music. Known for her powerful vocals and poignant storytelling, Lynn achieved great success with hits such as "You Ain't Woman Enough (To Take My Man)," "Don't Come Home A-Drinkin' (With Lovin' on Your Mind)," and "Coal Miner's Daughter."

1973: Tonie Nathan and Sharon Presley founded the Association of Libertarian Feminists (ALF) on Ayn Rand's birthday. They aimed to "provide a libertarian alternative to those aspects of the women's movement that tend to discourage independence and individuality." In the paper *Government is Women's Enemy*, Sharon Presley and Lynn Kinsky opposed state health and safety rules in child-care institutions and public education, saying that public schools

> "not only foster the worst of traditionalist sexist values but inculcate docility and obedience to authority with sterile, stifling methods and compulsory programs and regulations."

1988: Four lesbian women, Olivia Butler, Rachel Cox, Angela Nunn, and Sally Frances, climbed the building of the U.K. House of Lords to protest and disturb an ongoing debate over the Section 28 law, which was to come into force in May. The law prohibited schools and local authorities from sponsoring any "promotion of homosexuality" and teaching "the acceptability of homosexuality as a pretended family relationship."

2005: The Government of Canada introduced the Civil Marriage Act, which would later become law on July 20, 2005. This legislation legalized same-sex marriage in Canada.

2015: Sheila O'Donnell, an Irish architect (together with her colleague John Tuomey), received the 2015 Royal Gold Medal for Architecture. The award, personally approved by Queen Elizabeth II, recognizes individuals who have made significant contributions to the advancement of architecture.

February 03

1625: Francesca Caccini's opera, *La liberazione di Ruggiero*, premiered in Florence, Italy. This opera is notable for its longevity, as it continued to be staged for almost 400 years, with performances witnessed as late as 2018.

1871: Mary Ann Shadd graduated from Howard University's Law Department, becoming the first African-American woman to obtain a law degree in the United States. Shadd was a prominent abolitionist, suffragist, journalist, and educator who advocated for equal rights and opportunities for African Americans.

1956: Autherine Lucy, an African-American student, was admitted to the University of Alabama. However, her enrollment sparked widespread racial tensions, and white mobs rioted for days until she was suspended and ultimately expelled from the university.

1995: Astronaut Eileen Collins became the first woman to pilot the Space Shuttle for the STS-63 mission.

2011: The Day of Rage occurred in Yemen, organized by Tawakkol Karman, a Nobel Peace Prize winner and journalist. The protests aimed to bring attention to human rights abuses, corruption, and political repression in Yemen as part of the broader Arab Spring movement.

2015: Harper Lee, an American author, announced her plans to publish her second book, a long-awaited sequel to *To Kill a Mockingbird*. The novel, *Go Set a Watchman*, was completed in the 1950s but remained misplaced for several decades. It was eventually released on July 14, 2015, and provided readers with further insights into the characters and themes explored in Lee's iconic first novel.

2018: Celebrating Buchi Emecheta event occurred in London, organized by her son, Sylvester Onwordi. The Buchi Emecheta Foundation was launched as a charitable organization to promote literary and educational projects in the U.K. and Africa during the event. Buchi Emecheta, a Nigerian-born novelist, settled in the U.K. in 1962. She wrote novels, plays, an autobiography, and works for children. Some of her most famous works include *Second Class Citizen* (1974), *The Bride Price* (1976), *The Slave Girl* (1977), and *The Joys of Motherhood* (1979).

2020: The Hospital Authority Employees Alliance (HAEA), a Hong Kong labor union representing Hospital Authority staff, launched a five-day strike under the leadership of Winnie Yu Wai-ming, demanding full border closure in response to the COVID-19 outbreak.

February 04

1838: Rebecca Gratz founded the first Jewish Sunday School. Her initiative aimed to provide education and religious instruction to Jewish children in Philadelphia, Pennsylvania, fostering a sense of community and preserving Jewish traditions.

1901: Giacomo Puccini's opera *Tosca* premiered in the United States at the Metropolitan Opera House in New York City. The opera, featuring the talented soprano Milka Ternina in the lead role of Floria Tosca, became widely acclaimed for its dramatic storyline and beautiful music.

1974: Patricia Hearst, the 19-year-old granddaughter of newspaper publisher William Randolph Hearst, was kidnapped from her apartment in Berkeley, California. The abduction was carried out by a group associated with the radical-terrorist organization, the Symbionese Liberation Army. Hearst's subsequent involvement with the group and her controversial actions during captivity garnered significant media attention.

1981: Gro Brundtland became the first female Prime Minister of Norway. Brundtland, a member of the Norwegian Labour Party, served as Prime Minister on three separate occasions, making notable contributions to social welfare, sustainable development, and global health issues.

1983: Karen Carpenter, an American singer and musician renowned as the lead singer and drummer of the duo The Carpenters, passed away at 32 due to complications related to anorexia nervosa. Her death increased awareness of eating disorders and their impact on mental and physical health.

1987: Meena Keshwar Kamal, an Afghan activist who founded the Revolutionary Association of the Women of Afghanistan (RAWA), was assassinated in Quetta, Pakistan, by either the agents of the Afghan

Intelligence Service KHAD, the Afghan secret police, or fundamentalist Mujahideen.

1997: Madeleine Albright, the United States Secretary of State, publicly disclosed that she had recently discovered her Jewish heritage. Albright's grandparents, three of whom were killed in the Holocaust (Shoah), had kept their Jewish identity hidden from her. This revelation had a profound impact on Albright's personal and professional life.

2014: The Scottish Parliament legalized same-sex marriage in Scotland with an overwhelming majority vote of 105–18, extending marriage rights to all couples, regardless of gender or sexual orientation.

February 05

1894: In Amsterdam, women from various religious and political backgrounds established the *Vereeniging voor Vrouwenkiesrecht* (Society for Women's Suffrage). This organization advocated for women's right to vote and played a crucial role in the Dutch suffrage movement.

1975: Isabel Perón, the President of Argentina, decreed *Operativo Independencia* to address what she considered "subversive elements" in the province of Tucuman. Exploiting the situation, she staged a self-coup and assumed extraordinary powers, leading to a period of authoritarian rule.

2009: Jennifer Figge became the first woman to swim across the Atlantic Ocean. Starting from the Cape Verde Islands off the coast of Africa, she embarked on a journey of nearly 4,000 kilometers and reached Trinidad in the Caribbean on January 10.

2009: The Sudanese cabinet decided to remove an article from the draft Children's Act of 2009 that sought to ban female genital mutilation (FGM) along with other harmful customs and traditions affecting children's health. The government distinguished between "circumcision or infibulation" and "circumcision of Sunna," considering the latter a less extensive procedure. This decision was condemned by women's rights activists who advocated for eradicating FGM.

2013: An extensive investigation into Ireland's Magdalene asylums exposed significant state collusion in the admission of numerous "fallen women" to these institutions. These women endured abuse and were subjected to unpaid labor in conditions resembling slavery. The asylums were eventually closed less than two decades ago.

2019: Stacey Abrams became the first African-American woman to deliver a State of the Union response. As a politician and activist, Abrams provided the Democratic Party's rebuttal to President Donald Trump's State of the Union address, making her a prominent figure in American politics.

February 06

1694: Dandara, an Afro-Brazilian warrior and leader of enslaved people in Quilombo dos Palmares, Brazil, was captured. Rather than be returned to a life of slavery, she chose to commit suicide, becoming a symbol of resistance against oppression.

1902: The Young Women's Hebrew Association was established in New York. This organization aimed to provide young Jewish women with educational, cultural, and social opportunities.

1935: Turkey held its first national elections in which women were allowed to vote and run for office. Eighteen female candidates were elected to Turkey's parliament, marking an important step toward women's political participation.

1957: Doria Shafik, an Egyptian feminist, poet, editor, and one of the principal leaders of the women's liberation movement in Egypt, entered the Indian Embassy in Cairo after announcing to the government and the media that she was undertaking a second hunger strike (see: March 12, 1954) over President Gamal Abdel Nasser's dictatorial regime. She was put under house arrest by Nasser, her name was banned from the press, and her magazines were banned from circulation, which ended her political activism.

2003: Stella Obasanjo, Nigeria's First Lady and the spokesperson for the Campaign Against Female Genital Mutilation delivered the official declaration for "Zero Tolerance to FGM" in Africa. The announcement was made during a conference organized by the Inter-African Committee on Traditional Practices Affecting the Health of Women and Children (IAC). Subsequently, the UN Sub-Commission on Human Rights recognized and adopted this as an international awareness day.

2006: Rosalyn Higgins was elected president of the International Court of Justice (ICJ) in The Hague, becoming the first woman to hold this position. The ICJ is the principal judicial organ of the United Nations.

2011: A former Israeli soldier, Anat Kamm, reached a plea bargain in Tel Aviv District Court. She pleaded guilty to leaking over 2,000 secret military documents to the Haaretz newspaper. The leaked documents revealed potentially illegal Israeli assassination operations against Palestinians in the West Bank. Kamm believed she had discovered evidence of war crimes.

2012: Queen Elizabeth II celebrated the 60th anniversary of her reign as the monarch of the United Kingdom and other Commonwealth realms. The Diamond Jubilee events were held throughout the year to honor this significant milestone.

2017: Queen Elizabeth II celebrated her 65th anniversary as the sovereign, observing a Sapphire Jubilee. She became the first and only British monarch to commemorate such a moment.

2020: Christina Koch returned to Earth from the International Space Station after spending a continuous 328 days in space, setting the record for the longest single spaceflight by a woman.

2021: French religious sister Nathalie Becquart was appointed by Pope Francis as one of the Undersecretaries of the Synod of Bishops. She became the first woman to hold this position, granting her the right to vote in the Synod.

2022: Berta Soler, the leader of the activist group Ladies in White, and her husband were violently assaulted in Havana, Cuba, by pro-government groups, including the Rapid Response Brigade and officers of the Cuban State Security.

2022: New Zealand snowboarder Zoi Sadowski-Synnott won a gold medal in women's slopestyle at the Winter Olympics, securing New Zealand's first-ever gold medal.

February 07

1884: Elizabeth Hamilton Cullum and others established the New York Cancer Hospital, the first cancer hospital in the United States.

1916: Lady Hardinge Medical College was established in New Delhi, India, to provide women with opportunities to study medicine. The college was named after Lady Winifred Sturt, also known as Lady Hardinge, who envisioned a place where women could pursue medical education.

1961: Jane Fonda made her acting debut in the NBC drama *A String of Beads*, which was the starting point of her successful acting career, earning her numerous accolades in the years to come.

1969: Diane Crump, the first professional female jockey in the United States, participated in her first race at the Hialeah Park Race Track in Florida. Her participation faced opposition and required a police escort due to the abuse she encountered.

1971: Switzerland adopted women's suffrage with a majority vote, granting

Swiss women the right to vote. Previous attempt to secure women's voting rights in 1959 failed.

1976: The movie *Taxi Driver* was released, featuring Jodie Foster as a child prostitute. Foster's portrayal earned her critical acclaim and a nomination for the Academy Award for Best Supporting Actress.

2006: Uma Thurman was awarded the title of Knight of the *Ordre des Arts et des Lettres* in France for her achievements.

2011: American skier Lindsey Vonn was honored as the Sportswoman of the Year at the Laureus World Sports Awards, recognizing her exceptional performance in skiing.

2017: Russian President Vladimir Putin signed a law decriminalizing domestic violence in Russia.

2019: Alexandria Ocasio-Cortez, a U.S. Representative, submitted her first piece of legislation, the Green New Deal, to the House of Representatives—the proposal to address climate change through a comprehensive economic and infrastructure overhaul.

2019: Vanessa Tyson, a professor from California, accused Lieutenant Governor of Virginia Justin Fairfax of sexually assaulting her in 2004.

2021: Sarah Thomas became the first female NFL official to officiate a Super Bowl game.

February 08

1587: Mary, Queen of Scots, was beheaded on the orders of her cousin, Queen Elizabeth I of England. The execution ended a long-standing conflict between the two queens and their respective claims to the English throne.

1765: Frederick the Great, King of Prussia, issued a decree abolishing the historic punishments inflicted on unmarried women in Germany for "sex crimes." The order ended the *Hurenstrafen*, a practice of public humiliation aimed at shaming women.

1926: Edith Clarke became the first woman to deliver a paper at the American Institute of Electrical Engineers (AIEE) annual meeting. In her presentation, Clarke discussed using hyperbolic functions to calculate the maximum power capacity of electrical lines without experiencing instability.

1976: The Women's Rabbinical Alliance (WRA) was formed by fifteen pioneering female rabbis and rabbinical students from various institutions. The WRA aimed to provide mutual support, communication, and collaboration among women in the rabbinate and address their challenges.

1985: Jane Ramsey, the Executive Director of the Jewish Council on Urban Affairs (JCUA) in Chicago, was arrested along with three other protestors for protesting against apartheid in South Africa at the South African consulate in Chicago. The protest aimed to draw attention to the injustices of the apartheid system.

2013: Nine women engaged in a polio vaccination campaign were fatally shot in Kano, Nigeria. The attack was believed to be orchestrated by the Islamist movement Boko Haram, which had previously issued threats against those involved in vaccination efforts.

2013: The cover of the latest edition of Lucy Maud Montgomery's novel *Anne of Green Gables* sparked controversy. The original depiction of the character Anne, with red hair and freckles, was changed to a blonde, buxom farm girl with a seductive look. This alteration, similar to the controversy surrounding the cover of Sylvia Plath's *The Bell Jar*, drew criticism from readers.

2022: Daria Serenko, a Russian feminist activist and artist, received a 15-day jail sentence for an Instagram post backing tactical voting with symbols from the banned FBK (Alexei Navalny's' Anti-Corruption Foundation).

February 09

999: The *Mogi* Ceremony of Fujiwara no Shoshi took place in Japan. This initiation ceremony marked the transition of noble Japanese girls into adulthood. The practice of the tradition spanned from the Heian period to the Azuchi-Momoyama period, and it continued in the imperial family until the Meiji period.

1864: The Women's National Loyal League petitioned the U.S. Congress to outlaw slavery in all states. This petition was part of the ongoing efforts by women's organizations to support the abolitionist movement and advocate for the end of slavery.

1907: The Mud March, organized by the National Union of Women's Suffrage Societies (NUWSS) in the U.K., became the first large procession of the suffrage movement. Thousands of women marched through the streets of London to advocate for women's right to vote.

1935: Sonja Henie from Norway won the ladies' World Figure Skating Championships for the ninth consecutive year. The competition took place in Vienna, Austria, and Henie's continued success established her as one of the most dominant figure skaters of her time.

1984: *The Rink*, a musical by John Kander and Fred Ebb, premiered on Broadway starring Chita Rivera and Liza Minnelli as mother and daughter. The story revolved around their family's roller-skating rink. Chita Rivera won her first Tony Award for her role in the show, successfully running 204 performances at the Martin Beck Theatre.

2012: The United States Department of Defense issued new guidelines that removed restrictions on the use of women in combat.

2013: Annette Schavan resigned as Germany's Minister of Education following allegations of plagiarism in portions of her 1980 doctoral dissertation. The controversy surrounding her academic work led to her stepping down from her position.

2019: Elizabeth Warren, a U.S. Senator from Massachusetts, announced her candidacy for the 2020 United States presidential election at a rally in Lawrence, Massachusetts, which holds historical significance as the site of the 1912 Bread and Roses strike.

February 10

1628: Margareta i Kumla, a religious visionary, faced an order from King Gustavus Adolphus of Sweden to end what he considered "foolishness and insanity" associated with her visions. The order prohibited Swedes from making pilgrimages to see Margareta, and she was threatened with imprisonment if she continued to preach about her angelic visions.

1840: Queen Victoria of the United Kingdom married Prince Albert of Saxe-Coburg and Gotha. Their marriage would be happy and influential, and they had nine children together.

1870: The Young Women's Christian Association (YWCA) was formed in New York. The organization aimed to provide support, education, and empowerment for young women, and it has since grown into a global movement advocating for women's rights and social justice.

1919: The Inter-Allied Women's Conference was held to voice women's concerns during the Paris Peace Conference following World War I. Despite not being allowed to participate in the official conference, women organized their own gathering to ensure their perspectives were heard and to advocate for gender equality and peace.

1966: Jacqueline Susann published her best-selling novel, *Valley of the Dolls*. The book, which explores the lives of three women in the entertainment industry, became a cultural phenomenon and one of the best-selling novels of all time.

2012: A Ugandan lawmaker who proposed the Anti-Homosexuality Bill removed the proposed death penalty clause from the bill. The bill still contained severe penalties for homosexuality, but removing the death penalty was seen as a positive development.

2018: Kay Maree Goldsworthy became the first female archbishop in the Anglican Church of Australia.

2019: United States Senator Amy Klobuchar announced her candidacy for the 2020 United States presidential election. Klobuchar sought the Democratic nomination, emphasizing her experience and pragmatism as crucial qualities for effective leadership.

2021: Fulton County District Attorney Fani Willis initiated a criminal investigation into former U.S. President Donald Trump for his efforts to overturn Joe Biden's victory in Georgia. This investigation included Trump's phone call with Secretary of State Brad Raffensperger, in which he pressured Raffensperger to "find enough votes" to change the election outcome.

2021: Women's rights activist Loujain al-Hathloul was released by the Saudi government after imprisonment for nearly three years. While her release was a positive development, she still faced travel bans and probationary measures that limited her freedom.

February 11

1858: In Lourdes, France, Bernadette Soubirous, a 14-year-old miller's daughter, experienced her first visions of the Virgin Mary. These visions eventually led to the establishment of the Our Lady of Lourdes devotion, which became an important pilgrimage site for Catholics worldwide.

1916: Emma Goldman, an activist and advocate for women's rights and social justice, was arrested for lecturing on birth control. Her arrest was based on violating the Comstock laws, which banned the dissemination of "obscene" material, including information about contraception.

1936: Dame Laura Knight, an English painter, became the first woman ever appointed to the Royal Academy. This appointment significantly recognized her artistic talent and contributed to breaking gender barriers in the art world.

1958: Ruth Carol Taylor became the first African-American woman hired as a flight attendant. She was employed by Mohawk Airlines, although her career was short-lived, lasting only six months due to discriminatory practices such as banning married flight attendants.

1975: Margaret Thatcher became the first woman leader of the British Conservative Party. She became the first female Prime Minister of the United Kingdom in 1979, serving in that position for eleven years.

1989: Barbara Harris was consecrated as the first woman in the Anglican Communion to serve as a suffragan bishop. Her consecration as the Episcopal Diocese of Massachusetts suffragan bishop was met with controversy and threats due to her gender and being an African American.

2015: Özgecan Aslan, a Turkish university student, was murdered while resisting attempted rape. Her murder sparked widespread outrage and led to mass protests across Turkey. These protests, which involved thousands in several provinces, were Turkey's first significant mass movement for women's rights.

February 12

1502: Isabella I, Queen of Castile, issued an edict outlawing Islam in the Crown of Castile. This edict forced most of her Muslim subjects to convert to Christianity, indicating a significant religious and cultural shift in the region. Before this, in 1492, Isabella I had banished or forced the conversion of the Jewish population in the Crown of Castile.

1554: Lady Jane Grey, also known as the "Nine Days Queen," was beheaded at the Tower of London at the age of 16. Lady Jane Grey briefly held the title of Queen of England for nine days in 1553 before being overthrown by Mary I.

1870: Women in the Utah Territory gained the right to vote, granting suffrage to women in that region 50 years before the passage of the 19th Amendment to the United States Constitution in 1920, which gave women's suffrage nationwide.

1873: After Queen Teri'i-maeva-rua II died childless, her niece succeeded to the throne, taking the name Teri'i-maeva-rua III. The new queen was still only a child, so Prince Temauriari'i (husband of the late queen) acted as regent until her majority.

1902: The First Conference of the International Woman Suffrage Alliance began in Washington, D.C., United States, aiming to explore the feasibility of organizing an International Woman Suffrage Association. National associations from Canada, Germany, Great Britain, Norway, Sweden, and the United States were represented, along with individual delegates from Australia, Chile, Russia, and Turkey.

1909: The National Association for the Advancement of Colored People (NAACP) was founded. Notable charter female members of the NAACP included Ida B. Wells-Barnett, Mary Church Terrell, Anna Garlin Spencer, and Mary White Ovington. The NAACP has played a crucial role in advocating for civil rights and equality for African Americans.

2004: Del Martin and Phyllis Lyon, a couple since 1952, known for their feminist and gay-rights activism, married in the first same-sex wedding in San Francisco after Mayor Gavin Newsom allowed marriage licenses for same-sex couples. However, it was voided by the California Supreme Court on August 12, 2004. They married again on June 16, 2008, following the California Supreme Court's decision in In re Marriage Cases, which legalized same-sex marriage in the state.

2007: Rigoberta Menchú, an Indigenous activist from Guatemala and Nobel Peace Prize laureate, announced the formation of an Indigenous political party called *Encuentro por Guatemala.* She became the first Indigenous Maya woman to run in a Guatemalan presidential election in 2007.

2011: Julie Andrews and Dolly Parton were among the recipients of the prestigious Grammy Lifetime Achievement Awards, recognizing their significant contributions to the music industry.

2012: The British singer Adele won multiple Grammy Awards for her hit songs. She received awards for Song of the Year and Record of the Year for "Rolling in the Deep" and Album of the Year for *21*.

2012: Tenzin Choedon, a teenage Tibetan Buddhist nun, died after setting herself on fire in protest against Chinese rule in Tibet.

2016: Mariam Mosque, Scandinavia's first female-led mosque, was founded in Copenhagen, Denmark, by Sherin Khankan. The mosque aimed to provide a space for Muslim women and promote gender equality within the Muslim community.

2017: Adele won more Grammy Awards, including Record of the Year and Song of the Year for her song "Hello" and Album of the Year for *25*.

2019: Finnish writer and poet Tua Forsström was elected as a new member of the Swedish Academy. The Swedish Academy is responsible for deciding the annual winner of the Nobel Prize in Literature.

February 13

106: After the death of Emperor He of Han, Empress Dowager Deng assumed control and placed her infant son, Han Shangdi, on the throne of China. This event marked the beginning of the Yanping era, which lasted only one year.

1863: A tragic incident involving a 14-year-old kitchen maid named Margaret Davey was reported. Her dress, inflated by a crinoline (a stiffened petticoat), caught fire as she stood on the fireplace fender. She suffered extensive burns and ultimately died. During the late 1850s and late 1860s in England, it is estimated that around 3,000 women died in fires related to crinolines. Florence Nightingale estimated that at least 630 women died from their clothing catching fire in 1863-64.

1913: Mary Harris Jones, also known as "Mother Jones," was arrested at 83 in Charleston, West Virginia. She led a group of miners to confront Governor William E. Glasscock during conflicts between striking coal miners and company police. She was taken to an area of Charleston under martial law and later faced a military court trial on charges of conspiracy to commit murder. Jones was convicted and sentenced to three years in prison but was released after 85 days under the new Governor.

1917: Dutch exotic dancer Mata Hari was arrested in Paris on suspicion of being a German spy. She gained notoriety during World War I and was accused of espionage. Mata Hari was tried, found guilty, and executed by firing squad.

1953: Christine Jorgensen, a transgender woman, returned to New York after undergoing successful gender reassignment surgery in Denmark. She became widely known as the first person to undergo gender affirming surgery and significantly raised awareness and understanding about transgender issues.

1969: Members of the Redstockings, also known as the Redstockings of the Women's Liberation Movement, a radical feminist nonprofit, stormed the New York State Joint Legislative Committee on Public Health hearing considering changes in the abortion law. They questioned why there were 14 men and only one woman among the speakers, who happened to be a nun. The committee chair defended the lineup, claiming they were experts. This only fueled the Redstockings' anger as they expressed that women were the actual authorities on abortion, advocating for the law's repeal rather than reform.

1972: The musical film *Cabaret*, starring Liza Minnelli and Michael York, was released. It became a critical and commercial success, earning numerous awards and accolades, including eight Academy Awards.

2010: The American premiere of Lera Auerbach's *Double Concerto for Violin, Piano, and Orchestra, Op. 40*, composed in 1997, was performed by the Fort Wayne Philharmonic Orchestra, conducted by Andrew Constantine, with violinist Jennifer Koh and pianist Benjamin Hochman as soloists.

2011: Jazz artist Esperanza Spalding became the first jazz musician to win the Best New Artist award at the Grammy Awards.

2011: Nationwide protests took place in 200 cities across Italy as tens of thousands of women vehemently expressed their opposition to Italian Prime Minister Silvio Berlusconi. They accused him of tarnishing the reputation of women through a series of sex scandals.

2012: Washington governor Christine Gregoire signed a bill into law legalizing same-sex marriage in the state of Washington, making it the seventh state in the United States to recognize same-sex marriage at that time.

February 14

1855: Elizabeth Cady Stanton, an American women's rights leader and suffragist, became the first woman to appear before a joint judicial committee in the New York State Legislature.

1863: Anna Henryka Pustowójtówna, an activist in the Polish independence movement, disguised herself as a male soldier and went by the alias "Michał Smok" to fight in the January Uprising. She took part in multiple battles, working as a commander's adjutant. She was later involved in the Paris Commune.

1870: Esther Hobart Morris began her tenure as a justice of the peace in South Pass City, Wyoming, making her the first woman justice of the peace in the United States. The Sweetwater County Board of County Commissioners appointed her to the position after the previous judge resigned in protest of Wyoming Territory's passage of the women's suffrage amendment in December 1869.

1920: The League of Women Voters was founded at the Victory Convention of the National American Woman Suffrage Association in Chicago, USA. The league was formed to continue the fight for women's suffrage and to help newly enfranchised women become informed and engaged citizens.

1957: Chien-Shiung Wu, a Chinese-American physicist, published her paper describing the Wu Experiment titled "Experimental Test of Parity Conservation in Beta Decay" in *Physical Review*. Her groundbreaking experiment demonstrated a violation of the principle of parity conservation in the weak nuclear force, challenging a fundamental assumption in physics.

1985: Whitney Houston, an American singer and actress, released her self-titled debut studio album, *Whitney Houston*. The album became one of the best-selling debut albums of all time and launched Houston's successful music career.

1998: The first V-Day benefit performance of Eve Ensler's play *The Vagina Monologues* took place in NYC, raising over $250k for local anti-violence groups. It became a movement to end violence against women and girls, with events organized worldwide on February 14 and around that date.

2009: Noor Al-Fayez was appointed to the Saudi Council of Ministers in a new position as the deputy minister for women's education.

2009: In Malaysia, about 300 Muslim activists representing 47 countries gathered to launch *Musawah* ("Equality" in Arabic), a global movement for equality and justice in the Muslim family and family laws to promote progressive interpretations of sacred texts, called "feminist tafsir." Sisters in Islam, a Malaysian Muslim feminist group, organized the event. The conference, planned for two years, started a campaign to secure Muslim women's rights within an Islamic framework.

2012: One Billion Rising, a worldwide movement, was established by Eve Ensler (known for her play *The Vagina Monologues* and initiator of the V-Day movement) to eradicate rape and sexual violence directed towards women. Events are held yearly in more than a hundred countries to demand action and justice.

2013: Around 30 Burmese garment workers employed by the Century Miracle Apparel Manufacturing Company in Jordan went on strike for better pay, improved conditions, and an end to racial discrimination. The strike quickly gained momentum, with over 1,200 female and 100 male workers joining. Burmese workers were earning approximately $155 per month, compared to the up to $200 paid to non-Burmese workers. Finally, on March 7, management met with the workers and announced the implementation of a new salary structure.

2020: A court in Istanbul, Turkey, declared novelist Aslı Erdoğan not guilty of charges related to terrorist group membership and "undermining national unity." Erdoğan, along with other employees of the pro-Kurdish newspaper Özgür Gündem, had been accused of having connections to Kurdish militants. The ruling was considered a victory for freedom of expression and human rights.

February 15

1848: Sarah C. Roberts, a 5-year-old African American girl, was barred from attending a Boston Public School due to her race. In response, her father, Benjamin Roberts, filed the nation's first school integration lawsuit on her behalf, known as *Roberts vs. the City of Boston*.

1879: U.S. President Rutherford B. Hayes signed a bill into law allowing female attorneys to argue cases before the United States Supreme Court.

1898: The U.S. House Judiciary Committee met to hear representatives from the National Woman's Suffrage Association (NWSA) advocating for a constitutional amendment granting women the right to vote. Susan B. Anthony, NWSA's president, expressed concern about the Fifteenth Amendment, which was to give voting rights regardless of race, seeing it as a "humiliation" for white American women. Anthony drew comparisons between the struggles of women and formerly enslaved individuals,

> "the ballot ...is put in the hands of every man outside the State Prison, whether they have sufficient sense to cast their ballots or not, yet the women of the country were compelled to humiliate themselves in pleading for rights that should have been accorded them long ago."

A few days later, Helen App Cook, in a letter in *The Washington Post*, responded "with a pained surprise" to Anthony's testimony on women's rights. She recognized Anthony's influence and encouraged her to prioritize universal suffrage before negative views about Black men's voting rights spread further.

1912: More than 70 women's organizations gathered in the U.S. Capitol rotunda to unveil the Portrait Monument statue to honor Lucretia Mott, Elizabeth Cady Stanton, and Susan B. Anthony. The monument served as a tribute to these prominent suffragists and their contributions to the women's rights movement.

1946: The first electronic digital computer, ENIAC (Electronic Numerical Integrator and Calculator), was demonstrated for the first time at the University of Pennsylvania. A team of programmers consisting of six women—Kathleen McNulty, Jean Jennings Bartik, Frances Snyder Holberton, Marlyn Wescoff Meltzer, Frances Bilas Spence, and Ruth Lichterman Teitelbaum—played a vital role in programming the ENIAC and contributing to early computer science. Adele Goldstine wrote the computer manual and helped improve its usability.

1982: Agatha Barbara became the first woman to serve as the President of Malta. She also holds the record for being the longest-serving woman Member of Parliament in Maltese political history.

2016: Taylor Swift's album *1989* won the Grammy Award for Album of the Year. With this achievement, Swift became the first female artist to win the award twice, solidifying her impact and success in the music industry.

February 16

1883: *Ladies' Home Journal*, a popular magazine targeting women readers, began publishing in the United States. It played a significant role in shaping women's interests, discussing women's issues, and providing a platform for female writers and journalists.

1919: The first elections since the establishment of the Republic of German-Austria (later Austria) were held, allowing Austrian women to participate for the first time.

Eight women were elected to the Austrian Constituent Assembly, namely Anna Boschek, Emmy Freundlich, Adelheid Popp, Gabriele Proft, Therese Schlesinger, Amalie Seidel, Maria Tusch, and Hildegard Burjan.

1919: The Democratic Republic of Georgia held its first free elections and established the inaugural Constituent Assembly of Georgia. Notably, this marked the historic participation of Georgian women in national voting for the first time, highlighting their growing role in the country's political landscape.

1935: German baroness Benita von Falkenhayn was sentenced to execution by beheading for her involvement in assisting her lover, Jerzy Sosnowski, in espionage activities on behalf of Poland. Her case drew attention due to her privileged background and the nature of her crimes.

1963: Hannah Arendt's article "Eichmann in Jerusalem" was published in *The New Yorker*. The report explored the trial of Adolf Eichmann, a high-ranking Nazi official responsible for organizing the Holocaust. Arendt's writings sparked intense debates and discussions regarding the nature of evil, responsibility, and the role of bureaucracy in the Holocaust.

2022: Cristina Calderón, the last full-blooded Yahgan and the last native speaker of the Yahgan language, passed away in Chile. Her death marked the end of an era for the Yahgan people and their language, highlighting the importance of language preservation and cultural heritage.

February 17

1870: Esther Hobart Morris became the first American woman to serve as a Justice of the Peace in South Pass City, Wyoming.

1933: Nina Mae McKinney became the first Black American to appear on television during a London broadcast by John Logie Baird.

2007: Angela McRobbie published an article, "Post-Feminism and Popular Culture," in *Feminist Media Studies Journal*, in which she confronted the undermining feminist gains of the 70s and 80s as if equality had been achieved and feminists could direct their attention elsewhere.

2016: The South Dakota legislature passed a bill that required students, including transgender students, to use school restrooms based on their assigned sex at birth rather than their gender identity. This legislation sparked controversy and debate surrounding transgender rights and discrimination.

2017: Leila de Lima, a senator and prominent critic of the Philippine Drug War, was charged with alleged drug-related crimes by Philippines Justice Secretary Vitaliano Aguirre II. The charges were widely seen as politically motivated and an attempt to silence de Lima's opposition to the government's drug policies. Her case garnered international attention and raised concerns about human rights and due process in the Philippines.

February 18

1641: Putri Sri Alam, after the death of her husband, ascended the throne of the Kingdom of Aceh Darussalamand (modern-day Indonesian province of Aceh) and took the title *Sulṭāna Taj ul-Alam Safiatuddin Syah* ("World crown, purity of the faith"). She became the first of four queen regnants or *sultanas* who sat on the throne from 1641-1699.

1890: The National Woman Suffrage Association (NWSA) merged with the American Woman Suffrage Association (AWSA) to form the National American Woman Suffrage Association (NAWSA). This merger united two significant women's suffrage organizations in the United States and unified their efforts to advocate for women's right to vote. Notable suffragists such as Susan B. Anthony, Alice Stone Blackwell, Elizabeth Cady Stanton, and Lucy Stone played significant roles in forming the NAWSA.

1898: Mary Church Terrell delivered a speech titled "Advancing Women of Color" at the National American Woman Suffrage Association session in Washington, D.C., where she urged NAWSA to support Black women's rights. Terrell also addressed the "double burden" faced by African-American women, highlighting that they had to overcome both gender bias and the impact of racism, setting them apart from their Euro-American counterparts.

1932: Sonja Henie, a Norwegian figure skater, won her sixth consecutive World Women's Figure Skating title in Montreal. Henie's dominance in the sport during the 1930s made her one of the most celebrated figure skaters of her time.

2012: Pope Benedict XVI announced the canonization of several new saints, including Kateri Tekakwitha, the Lily of the Mohawks. Kateri Tekakwitha became the first Native American saint from the United States. She was born in what is now New York and lived in the 17th century, embracing Christianity despite facing persecution.

2013: Artist Ruth Stage, known for using the ancient egg tempera painting technique, won the 2013 Lynn Painter-Stainers art prize for her artwork titled *The Isabella Plantation*.

2016: Pope Francis made statements suggesting contraceptives could be considered "morally acceptable" in certain circumstances, such as preventing the Zika virus. He referenced a historical case in which Pope Paul VI allowed nuns in Africa to use contraceptives in cases of rape.

February 19

1897: The Women's Institute was founded in Ontario, Canada, by Adelaide Hoodless. The Women's Institute aimed to provide educational opportunities and support for women in rural areas. It became a network of organizations across Canada and internationally, empowering women and addressing issues related to agriculture, home economics, health, and community development.

1910: Mary Mallon, known as "Typhoid Mary," was released from confinement at the North Brother Island Hospital in New York City. Mallon was a carrier of typhoid fever but showed no symptoms herself. She was quarantined to prevent further transmission of the disease. However, she was returned to isolation in 1915 and remained there until she died in 1938.

1913: An act of arson occurred when a house under construction for British cabinet minister David Lloyd George was firebombed near the Walton Heath Golf Club in Surrey, England. Suffragists were believed to be responsible for the attack. Suffragist leader Emmeline Pankhurst claimed responsibility for this incident and other arson attacks during a speech in Cardiff.

1958: Ellen Fairclough, Canada's first female cabinet minister, became the Acting Prime Minister when Prime Minister Diefenbaker and several senior cabinet ministers were away from Ottawa campaigning for re-election.

1963: Betty Friedan published her influential book *The Feminine Mystique*, which is often credited with sparking the modern feminist movement in the United States. The book challenged prevailing notions about women's roles and catalyzed women's rights activism.

1985: Val Plumwood, an Australian philosopher and ecofeminist known for her work on anthropocentrism, survived a saltwater crocodile attack which drastically altered her worldview from the "individual justice universe," where humans were predators, to the "Heraclitean universe," which was a world that was indifferent to her and would continue without her, where

> "being in your body is—like having a volume out from the library, a volume subject to more or less instant recall by other borrowers—who rewrite the whole story when they get it" (quote from *The Eye of the Crocodile*).

2002: Vonetta Flowers won a gold medal in the two-person bobsled event in Salt Lake City, becoming the first African American to win a gold medal in the Winter Olympics.

2014: Nadezhda Tolokonnikova and Maria Alyokhina, former members of the Russian punk rock band Pussy Riot, were arrested and later released after protesting during the 2014 Winter Olympics in Sochi.

2021: Mya Thwe Thwe Khaing, a young protester in Myanmar, died from a gunshot wound to the head. She was shot during anti-coup demonstrations, becoming the first reported death since the opposition to the military coup began in Myanmar. Her death sparked further outrage and intensified the ongoing protests in the country.

February 20

1731: Louise Hippolyte became the second woman to serve as Princess of Monaco. She ascended to the throne upon the death of her father, Prince Antonio. However, her reign was short-lived, as she died of smallpox nine months later on December 29.

1869: Ranavalona II, the Merina Queen of Madagascar, was baptized. She played a significant role in promoting Christianity in Madagascar during her reign.

1912: The Women's Suffrage Alliance (*Nǚzǐ cānzhèng tóngménghuì*), the first national women's suffrage organization in China, was founded. Among its founding members were Zhang Hanying, Lin Zongsu (chair of the Shanghai Women's Political Consultative Conference), Wang Changguo (promoter of Hunan Changsha Women's National Association), Shen Peizhen (chair of the Shanghai Women's Shangwu Association), Chen Hongbi (chair of the Shanghai Aihua Company), Wu Mulan (chair of the Shanghai Women's League), Zhang "Sophie" Zhaohan, He Xiangning and Cai Hui, with Tang Qunying as its president.

1914: Rosa Luxemburg, a Polish-Jewish socialist activist, stood trial at the Frankfurt Criminal Court in Germany. She was charged with encouraging public disobedience through her anti-war speeches. Luxemburg passionately argued against war during her trial, highlighting its destructive nature. She was sentenced to one year in prison, which she served during the early years of World War I.

1930: Habiba Msika, a talented Tunisian-Jewish artist, was attacked by an obsessed fan who broke into her apartment in Tunes and set her on fire. She passed away the next day at just 27 years old.

1935: Norwegian explorer Caroline Mikkelsen became the first woman to set foot on Antarctica. She accompanied her husband, Captain Klarius Mikkelsen, on an Antarctic expedition.

1985: The Irish government approved the sale of contraceptives, defying the influence of the Catholic Church. This decision came after the Irish Supreme Court recognized a constitutional right to marital privacy that included access to contraceptives in 1973. The change in laws took several years due to conservative pressures.

1998: Tara Lipinski, at the age of 15, became the youngest Olympic figure skating gold medalist in history. She won the gold medal at the Winter Olympics in Nagano, Japan.

2007: Zille Huma Usman, the Punjab Minister for Social Welfare in Pakistan, was shot dead by a man who disagreed with her for not observing the Islamic dress code and held the belief that women couldn't become rulers in Islam. Her assassination highlighted the challenges faced by women in positions of power in some societies.

2021: Naomi Osaka, a Japanese tennis player, defeated Jennifer Brady in the Women's Singles final to win the Australian Open. With this victory, Osaka became the first player since Maria Sharapova in 2012 to win a fourth Grand Slam singles title.

February 21

1838: Angelina Grimké, an American abolitionist and women's rights advocate, made history by addressing the Massachusetts state legislature about the 20,000 anti-slavery petitions submitted by women. She became the first woman to speak before a legislative body.

1866: Lucy Hobbs Taylor, an American dentist, became the first woman to earn a doctorate in dentistry.

1915: Nellie McClung, a prominent Canadian suffragist and women's rights activist, presented a petition to the Alberta Legislature advocating for women's right to vote.

1920: The New Women's Association (NWA, also known as New Women's Society, *Shin-fujin kyokai*), a Japanese women's rights organization, held its first meeting in Tokyo.

1962: Margot Fonteyn, an esteemed British ballerina, and Rudolf Nureyev, a renowned Russian dancer, debuted their first performance in the Royal Ballet's production of *Giselle* in London. Their partnership would become one of the most legendary in ballet.

1996: Zahra Rajabi, an activist for refugee rights and a member of the People's Mojahedin Organization of Iran (PMOI), was tragically killed by assassins. She fought for the rights and well-being of refugees and significantly contributed to the cause.

2014: In Sudan, a married Ethiopian woman was imprisoned after being gang-raped because she waited before reporting the assault. She faced the death penalty for adultery under Sudanese law.

2019: Hoda Muthana, an Alabama woman who had joined the Islamic State (ISIS), was barred from reentering the United States. Muthana's decision to join the extremist group and subsequent attempt to return to the U.S. sparked a significant legal and public debate regarding citizenship and individuals' responsibilities in terrorist activities.

February 22

705: Empress Wu Zetian, who had reigned for 15 years, was removed from power in a coup organized by her chancellor, Zhang Jianzhi, leading to the restoration of the Tang dynasty in China, with Wu Zetian's son, Zhong Zong, being reinstated as emperor.

1680: Catherine Deshayes Monvoisin, a French fortune teller, was involved in the notorious "Affair of the Poisons." She led a group of killers and was ultimately convicted of witchcraft. Catherine and 36 others were executed for their involvement in poisonings.

1942: Three members of the White Rose, a nonviolent anti-Nazi group in Germany, were executed by beheading in Munich. Sophie Scholl, her brother Hans, and Christoph Probst paid the ultimate price for their resistance against the Nazi regime.

1974: Barbara Allen Rainey, an American aviator, received her wings of gold, becoming the first designated female aviator in the U.S. Navy and the first woman to qualify as a naval jet pilot.

2001: The International Criminal Tribunal for the former Yugoslavia (ICTY) recognized wartime sexual violence as a war crime for the first time. Three Bosnian Serb soldiers were sentenced to prison, symbolizing an important step in acknowledging and addressing such atrocities.

2009: Penélope Cruz became the first Spanish-born actress to win an Academy Award. She received the Best Actress in a Supporting Role award for her performance in the film *Vicky Cristina Barcelona*.

2014: Yulia Tymoshenko, the former prime minister of Ukraine, was freed from prison after more than two years of detention on politically motivated charges. Her release was part of the Euromaidan events that unfolded in Ukraine.

2014: Marit Bjørgen, a Norwegian cross-country skier, became the most successful female Winter Olympian by winning her sixth gold medal in the Women's 30-kilometer freestyle event. She would go on to win ten Olympic medals in her career.

2015: Julianne Moore, an American actress, won the Academy Award for Best Actress for her role in the film *Still Alice*.

2017: Chan Yuen-ting, the manager of Eastern Sports Club, became the first woman to coach a male football club in a top-flight continental competition. She led her team against Guangzhou Evergrande in the AFC Champions League.

2019: The Americana folk group Our Native Daughters, consisting of Rhiannon Giddens, Amythyst Kiah, Leyla McCalla, and Allison Russell, released their debut album *Songs of Our Native Daughters*. The album explored themes of history, race, and womanhood, showcasing the talent and collaboration of these talented singer-songwriters.

February 23

1789: María Pascuala Caro Sureda, who was the second Spanish woman to be a doctor of philosophy (from the University of Valencia), entered the Dominican convent of Santa Catalina de Siena in Palma de Mallorca to become a prioress.

1902: American Protestant missionaries Ellen M. Stone and Katerina Stefanova Tsilka were released by Bulgarian rebels in the Ottoman Empire after more than five months of captivity. They had been kidnapped on September 3, 1901. During their detention, Miss Tsilka, pregnant then, gave birth to a daughter while being held for ransom near Bansko, Bulgaria.

1909: The Socialist Party organized the first National Women's Day (later International Women's Day) in New York. Meetings were held at Murray Hill Lyceum in New York City and at the Brooklyn Labor Lyceum.

1911: Socialist and suffragist activists held a joined march in Boston celebrating International Women's Day.

1952: Lydia Wideman of Finland became the first female Olympic cross-country skiing champion. At the Winter Olympics, she won the inaugural 10-kilometer event in Oslo, Norway.

1956: Norma Jean Mortenson legally changed her name to her stage name, Marilyn Monroe. She was a renowned American actress, model, and sex symbol of the 1950s and early 1960s.

1972: Angela Davis, a prominent American activist and scholar, was released from jail on bail. Davis had been charged with murder, kidnapping, and conspiracy during a high-profile trial.

February 24

1386: Elizabeth of Bosnia, the mother of Queen Mary of Hungary and Croatia, orchestrated the assassination of Charles III of Naples, the ruler of Hungary, Naples, Achaea, and Croatia, resulting in the reinstatement of Queen Mary as the ruler of Hungary and Croatia.

1389: Queen Margaret of Norway and Denmark won over King Albert of Sweden in battle, establishing herself as the ruler of all three kingdoms. King Albert was subsequently deposed from the Swedish throne and taken as a prisoner.

1863: During the Polish January Insurgence against Russian rule, Maria Piotrowiczowa (24), a patriot and social activist, died in the battle near the village of Dobra. At first, she was on auxiliary duty, collecting money for the troops and buying weapons, food, and supplies, but when the military situation deteriorated, she took on front-line duty. She rejected the surrender proposal and defended the troop flag donated by Łódź women killing and wounding Cossack soldiers. In the same battle, three more women were killed: Weronika Wojciechowska (19), Antonina Wilczyńska (20), and Katarzyna (surname unknown).

1864: Rebecca Lee Crumpler became the first African-American woman to earn a medical degree when she was awarded a doctoral degree from the New England Female Medical College in Boston, Massachusetts.

1871: The Danish Women's Society was established in Denmark to advance women's rights. It later officially adopted the name *Dansk Kvindesamfund* on December 15.

1912: Henrietta Szold founded Hadassah, the largest Jewish organization in American history. Hadassah focused on healthcare and education in the Land of Israel (now Israel) and the United States.

1917: In Turin, Italy, socialist women marked International Women's Day during World War I's hardships by posting posters with the message:

> "Hasn't there been enough torment from this war? Now the food necessary for our children has begun to disappear. It is time for us to act in the name of suffering humanity. Our cry is 'Down with Arms!' We are part of the same family. We want peace. We must show that women can protect those who depend on them."

1920: Nancy Astor became the first woman to speak in the House of Commons of the United Kingdom. She had been elected as a Member of Parliament three months earlier.

1932: Women in Brazil were granted the right to vote.

1968: Jocelyn Bell Burnell announced in Nature her discovery of a pulsar - a rapidly rotating neutron star she discovered in November.

2008: Jessica Klejka, a seventeen-year-old musher, won the 2008 Junior Iditarod, a sled dog race for young mushers between the ages of 14 and 17.

2010: The Pentagon lifted a longstanding policy prohibiting women from serving aboard U.S. Navy submarines.

2013: Quvenzhané Wallis became the youngest actress nominated for an Oscar in the Best Actress category. She was also the first person born in the 21st century to receive an Oscar nomination for her role as Hushpuppy in *Beasts of the Southern Wild*.

2017: The Guatemalan army blocked a ship from the Dutch NGO Women on Waves, which provides materials for abortions.

2020: Sabrina Ionescu, a college basketball player, became the first person in the history of college basketball to record 2,000 points, 1,000 rebounds, and 1,000 assists in her career.

2022: Russia invaded Ukraine, leading to millions of refugees, primarily women and children, fleeing to neighboring countries in the following months.

2022: In response to the Russian invasion of Ukraine, Russian activist Marina Litvinovich was detained by Moscow police after calling for anti-war demonstrations across Russia.

February 25

1570: Queen Elizabeth I of England was excommunicated by Pope Pius V for heresy and the persecution of English Catholics during her reign. The excommunication absolved her subjects from their allegiance to the crown.

1912: Marie-Adélaïde, the eldest daughter of Guillaume IV, became the first reigning Grand Duchess of Luxembourg.

1986: Corazon Aquino assumed the presidency of the Philippines, becoming the country's first woman president after Ferdinand Marcos fled the country.

1990: Violeta Chamorro was elected as the new president of Nicaragua, becoming the first elected woman president in the Americas. She succeeded Daniel Ortega.

1999: Radical feminist philosopher and theologian Mary Daly refused to allow male students into an advanced feminist theory course at Boston College despite an ultimatum issued by college officials. She explained that male students of feminist theory dominated the classroom with endless discussions about their own feelings, lack of understanding, or arguments. In response, female students adopted a stereotypical caregiving role and waste their energies trying to console and instruct the male students. Two male students threatened to sue her in the fall, arguing that Boston College violated Title IX by allowing Daly to refuse male students. The students received backing from the conservative Center for Individual Rights in Washington.

2012: Karen Kime was appointed as the first female Indigenous archdeacon in the Anglican Church in Australia. The appointment took place at a ceremony in Goulburn, New South Wales.

2013: Park Geun-Hye was inaugurated as the first female President of South Korea in the capital city of Seoul.

2021: Pamela Smith was named the new Chief of the United States Park Police (USPP) by the National Park Service. With this appointment, Smith, a 23-year veteran of the USPP, became the first Black woman to lead the 230-year-old federal law enforcement agency.

February 26

1730: Anna of Russia (Anna Ioannovna) became the reigning Empress of Russia following the death of her cousin, Emperor Peter II.

1783: A German astronomer, Caroline Herschel, discovered an open cluster known today as NGC 2360. She found 14 new nebulae, including NGC 205, the companion to the Andromeda Galaxy.

1936: Dolores Ibárruri, also known as La Pasionaria, was elected to the *Cortes Generales* as a deputy for Asturias, representing the Spanish Communist Party (PCE).

1944: Sue Dauser, the Director of the Navy Nurse Corps, became the first female Captain in the United States Navy.

2017: At the 89th Academy Awards, Viola Davis won the Best Supporting Actress award for her role in *Fences*, while Emma Stone won the Best Actress award for her role in *La La Land*.

2023: Shaina Vanessa Pretel, an Afro-Colombian trans woman and social leader, was tragically shot and killed inside her house in Santiago de Cali, Colombia. She had been actively defending the rights of

Afro-Colombian trans women at a meeting just hours before her death.

February 27

1559: Queen Elizabeth I of England instituted the Church of England by enacting the Act of Uniformity 1558 and the Act of Supremacy 1558. These acts established the Church of England as the official state church and made Elizabeth the church's supreme governor. The Oath of Supremacy, which recognized the monarch as the head of the church, was also reinstated.

1693: *The Ladies Mercury*, the first periodical explicitly dedicated to women, was published in London, England.

1922: The United States Supreme Court upheld the 19th Amendment to the Constitution, which guaranteed women the right to vote.

1943: During the *Fabrikaktion* in Berlin, where the Gestapo arrested the remaining Jews, around 1,800 Jewish men, most of whom were married to non-Jewish women, were temporarily housed at Rosenstraße. In response, hundreds of their wives began protests at the site, demanding the release of their husbands. After over a month of protests, the women were successful, and the Jewish men were released.

1970: The first national conference of the Women's Liberation Movement (WLM) was held in the United Kingdom, with over six hundred women in attendance. The conference discussed the WLM's first four demands: equal pay, equal educational and job opportunities, free contraception and abortion on demand, and free 24-hour nurseries.

1971: The first Dutch abortion clinic, *Mildredhuis* in Arnhem, began performing abortions.

2002: Lusia Harris-Stewart, a women's basketball legend, was honored by the James Family Foundation for her contributions to the game and her work in the community.

2012: Julia Gillard, the Prime Minister of Australia, won a leadership ballot within the Australian Labor Party, securing her position and prevailing over former Prime Minister Kevin Rudd.

2014: Arizona Governor Jan Brewer vetoed a bill that would have allowed businesses to discriminate against LGBTQ+ people based on their religious beliefs.

2022: The Feminist Anti-War Resistance (FAR or FAWR; *Feministskoye antivoyennoye soprotivleniye* (FAS)) was established by Daria Serenko and other activists to protest the 2022 Russian invasion of Ukraine. FAR rapidly gained popularity in its first month, amassing over 26,000 followers on Telegram. On December 23, 2022, Russia's Ministry of Justice designated the movement as a "foreign agent." In a manifesto, FAR called upon feminists worldwide to unite in opposition to the war initiated by Vladimir Putin's government:

> "Today, feminists are one of the few active political forces in Russia. For a long time, Russian authorities did not perceive us as a dangerous political movement, and therefore we were temporarily less affected by state repression than other political groups. Currently, more than forty-five different feminist organizations are operating throughout the country, from Kaliningrad to Vladivostok, from Rostov-on-Don to Ulan-Ude and Murmansk. We call on Russian feminist groups and individual feminists to join the Feminist Anti-War Resistance and unite forces to actively oppose the war."

February 28

1730: Tsarina Anna Ivanovna became the Empress of Russia. She ruled until 1740 and implemented several reforms during her reign.

1909: The first National Woman's Day was observed in the United States. It was organized by the Socialist Party of America to honor the 1908 garment workers' strike in New York, where women protested against poor working conditions and low wages.

1935: Contraceptives were prohibited in the Irish Free State. This ban remained in place until it was lifted in 1980.

2018: Dolly Parton, the renowned country music singer and philanthropist, donated her 100 millionth free book as part of her literacy program called Dolly Parton's Imagination Library. The presented book, *Coat of Many Colors*, was given to the Library of Congress in Washington, D.C.

2022: The United States House of Representatives voted to award the 6888th Central Postal Directory Battalion, also known as the Six Triple Eight, with the Congressional Gold Medal. During World War II, the Six Triple Eight was the only all-female, Black unit to serve in Europe. The medal is a recognition of their significant contributions during the war.

February 29

1692: The first warrants were issued for the arrests of three women, Sarah Good, Sarah Osborne, and Tituba, in the Salem Witch Trials. This event marked the beginning of a series of trials and executions related to accusations of witchcraft in Salem, Massachusetts.

1864: The strikes organized by the Collar Laundry Union in Troy, New York, ended with a victory when the remaining laundry bosses agreed to pay increases.

1940: Hattie McDaniel became the first African-American to win an Academy Award. She won the Best Supporting Actress award for her performance as Mammy in the film *Gone with the Wind.*

2016: During the 88th Academy Awards, Brie Larson won the Best Actress award for her role in the film *Room.* Her portrayal of a young woman held captive with her son received critical acclaim and the prestigious award. Additionally, Alicia Vikander won the Best Supporting Actress award for her role in *The Danish Girl.*

MARCH

March 01

1692: Sarah Good, Sarah Osborne, and Tituba were brought before local magistrates in Salem Village, Massachusetts, beginning the infamous Salem witch trials. Accusations of witchcraft spread, leading to several trials and executions in the region.

1864: Rebecca Lee became the first African-American woman to receive a medical degree in the United States. She earned her degree from the New England Female Medical College in Boston, Massachusetts.

1906: Emma Goldman, an influential anarchist and activist, published the first volume of *Mother Earth*, an anarchist journal that covered social science and literature.

1912: Suffragette leader Emmeline Pankhurst was among 148 suffragettes arrested in London for participating in a protest demanding women's right to vote. The suffragettes engaged in civil disobedience, including breaking windows in the West End of London, to draw attention to their cause.

1914: Margaret C. Anderson released the first issue of *The Little Review*, a literary magazine that aimed to offer a fresh approach to art criticism. Anderson emphasized the importance of appreciation in criticism and sought to provide a platform for emerging artists and writers.

1920: Probable date of publishing the first issue of *Sinyoja* (Korean: "New Woman") founded by Na Hye-sok, Kim Won-ju, Pak In-deok, Sin Chul-lyo, and Kim Hwallan. The journal focused on women's experiences in 1920s Korean society, aiming to strengthen feminist consciousness, fight patriarchal oppression, discuss colonial and political issues, and work for gender equality.

1932: Tikvah Alper, who graduated with distinction in physics from the University of Cape Town in 1929 (at age twenty) and then studied in Berlin with the nuclear physicist Lise Meitner in 1930–32, published a prize-winning paper on delta rays produced by alpha particles (*"Über die δ-Strahlen und die Beziehung zwischen Reichweite und Geschwindigkeit für langsame Elektronen"*) in the Journal *Zeitschrift für Physik*.

1945: Hannie Schaft and Truus Oversteegen, members of the Dutch resistance during World War II, executed Willem Zirkzee, a Nazi Dutch police officer, near the Krelagehuis in Haarlem. Schaft and Oversteegen played significant roles in the resistance movement and carried out acts of sabotage and assassinations against the Nazi occupiers.

1952: Dorothy M. Horstmann published a groundbreaking article titled "Poliomyelitis Virus in Blood of Orally Infected Monkeys and Chimpanzees" in the *Experimental Biology and Medicine Journal*. Her research challenged the prevailing belief that the poliovirus only grew in nerve cells and provided crucial insights for developing the polio vaccine.

2013: Privateers' owner and president Nicole Kirnan served as the team's coach for the first time, making her the first woman to coach a professional hockey team in the United States.

2016: South Dakota Governor Dennis Daugaard vetoed House Bill 1008, which aimed to enforce bathroom and facility usage based on gender assigned at birth for transgender students in state public schools. The governor's veto prevented the bill from becoming law.

2019: Sheila O'Donnell was named Architect of the Year at the Women in Architecture (WIA) awards.

2021: Ngozi Okonjo-Iweala became the Director-General of the World Trade Organization, making history as the first woman and African to hold that position.

March 02

1121: After the death of her husband, Floris II, Petronilla of Lorraine became the regent for Holland (Low Countries). Her 6-year-old son, Dirk VI, succeeded to the throne.

1882: Queen Victoria narrowly escaped assassination when a man shot at her while boarding a train in Windsor.

1942: The U.S. Department of War urged the Ford Motor Company to hire approximately 15,000 female employees at the Willow Run factory in the Detroit area to support the war economy. At that time, the location only employed 28 women.

1955: Claudette Colvin, a 15-year-old Black teenager, was arrested in Montgomery, Alabama, for refusing to give up her seat to a white woman on a public bus. Colvin's act of defiance preceded the more famous Montgomery bus boycott led by Rosa Parks.

2014: Lupita Amondi Nyong'o became the second African, first Kenyan, and first Mexican to win the Academy Award for Best Supporting Actress for her role in the film *12 Years a Slave*.

2016: Berta Cáceres, an environmental activist and indigenous leader from Honduras, was assassinated at her home. Cáceres co-founded and coordinated the Council of Popular and Indigenous Organizations of Honduras (COPINH) and had faced threats against her life for her activism.

2019: Bernardine Evaristo's novel *Girl, Woman, Other* was published. The book went on to win the 2019 Booker Prize jointly with Margaret Atwood's *The Testaments*.

2020: Minnesota Senator Amy Klobuchar suspended her presidential campaign and endorsed Joe Biden for president.

2021: All 279 schoolgirls who were abducted from a boarding school in Zamfara State, Nigeria, on February 26 were released by their armed kidnappers.

2021: Journalist Katsiaryna Barysevich was sentenced to six months in prison for reporting on the personal data related to the death of Raman Bandarenka during protests against Belarusian President Alexander Lukashenko.

2022: Hundreds of women protested in Abuja, Nigeria, after the National Assembly rejected several amendments to the Constitution to expand women's rights and autonomy. The amendments included reserving 35% of legislative seats and political party leadership positions for women and conferring citizenship to foreign husbands of Nigerian women, among other provisions.

March 03

895: Qatr al-Nada, the daughter of Khumarawayh ibn Ahmad, arrived in Baghdad to marry Caliph al-Mu'tadid. Her arrival, accompanied by a lavish retinue and a dowry of one million gold dinars, contrasted with the impoverished caliphal court.

1816: Juana Azurduy, a mestiza woman of Quechua descent from what is now Bolivia, led one of her anti-colonial military detachments, including a women's unit known as the Amazonas, to victory in a battle against Spanish troops near Villa.

1879: Belva Ann Bennett Lockwood became the first woman admitted to the U.S. Supreme Court bar. She played a prominent role in advocating for women's rights and ran for President of the United States in 1884 and 1888.

1887: Anne Sullivan began teaching Helen Keller, a 6-year-old girl who was both blind and deaf. Sullivan's teaching methods helped Keller become a renowned author and activist.

1913: Thousands of women marched in the National American Woman Suffrage Parade in Washington, D.C., organized by Alice Paul and Lucy Burns. The march took place the day before President Wilson's inauguration and aimed to demand the right to vote for women.

1957: Corry Brokken represented the Netherlands and won the 1957 Eurovision Song Contest in Frankfurt with her song *Net als toen* (*Just like then*). This victory marked the Netherlands' first win in the contest.

2012: Latonia Moore made an unexpected debut at the Metropolitan Opera, stepping in for an indisposed Violeta Urmana in the title role of the opera *Aida*. Moore's performance received acclaim and established her as a notable soprano.

2014: Evolutionary biologist Chantal Abergel, along with her colleague Jean-Michel Claverie, announced the discovery of pithovirus, the largest giant virus known at the time. The virus was revived from a 30,000-year-old sample of tundra, providing insights into ancient viruses and their survival mechanisms.

March 04

1852: Phi Mu sorority was established in Macon, Georgia. It is one of the oldest women's fraternal organizations in the United States and promotes personal development, academic excellence, and philanthropic service.

1906: The tsarist *Okhrana* arrested Rosa Luxemburg, a prominent revolutionary activist and Marxist theorist.

1910: The town of Spokane, Washington, yielded in its opposition to the Industrial Workers of the World (IWW), allowing the organization to hold meetings and events. Elizabeth Gurley Flynn, a labor leader, activist, and feminist, played a crucial role in advocating for free speech rights and challenging the opposition.

1917: Jeannette Rankin, a Republican from Montana, took her seat as the first female member of the United States Congress. Rankin was a committed pacifist and became known for her opposition to both World Wars while in office.

1933: Frances Perkins was sworn in as the Secretary of Labor, becoming the first female member of the United States Cabinet. She played a significant role in the New Deal era and implemented various labor reforms.

1945: Princess Elizabeth, who later became Queen Elizabeth II of the United Kingdom, joined the Auxiliary Territorial Service (ATS) as a truck driver and mechanic in London during World War II. She wanted to contribute to the war effort like many other women.

1969: The U.S. Supreme Court's landmark case *Weeks v. Southern Bell* challenged discriminatory practices that excluded women from higher-paying jobs traditionally held by men. Sylvia Roberts, a lawyer from the National Organization for Women (NOW), famously demonstrated the physical capability of women by lifting a heavy typewriter during the trial.

1975: A bomb was planted at the Federal Court of Justice in Karlsruhe, West Germany. It detonated in the evening when no one was in the building, causing significant material damage. The next day, editors of several West German newspapers and a publishing house in Berlin received envelopes with photocopies of a typed letter. The Women of the Revolutionary Cell claimed responsibility for the attack in the short text. The WoRC demanded the right to decide freely about their bodies and sexuality and criticized the position of judges, medics, and clerics who opposed the decriminalization of abortions. They called the Constitution a tool of oppression and were more aggressive in their views than most opponents of the abortion ban.

1982: Bertha Wilson became the first female puisne justice of the Supreme Court of Canada. She contributed significantly to Canadian jurisprudence and advocated for equality and justice throughout her career.

2002: Susan Howson, a British mathematician, became the first woman to win the Adams Prize, awarded annually by the University of Cambridge to a mathematician under 40. Howson was recognized for her contributions to number theory and elliptic curves.

March 05

1329: Joan became the Queen of Navarre when she and her husband, Philip of Évreux, were jointly crowned in Pamplona Cathedral.

1387: Na Pa, a Jewish woman and wife of Jehuda Gallipapa, was granted a license to practice medicine in Zaragosa, Spain - a notable achievement for a woman in medicine during that time.

1917: *The Poor Little Rich Girl*, a comedy -drama film starring Mary Pickford and directed by Maurice Tourneur, was released. Adapted from Eleanor Gates' play, the film was a box office success and became a trademark film for Pickford. The National Film Registry and Library of Congress later preserved it.

1935: Polly Adler, a well-known brothel keeper in America, was arrested. She gained fame after writing a best-selling memoir, *A House is Not a Home*, which depicted Jewish immigrant life in New York City and the underground world of the city's brothels.

1974: Helen Thomas became the first woman to cover the presidential beat as a UPI (United Press International) White House reporter. Before this, women were only allowed to cover the First Ladies. Thomas had a distinguished career as an award-winning reporter for 30 years.

2013: Journalist Christie Aschwanden, in an article in *Double X Science*, created the Finkbeiner Test, named for the science journalist Ann Finkbeiner, to help other journalists avoid gender bias in media articles about women in science. It suggests they avoided information such as that she is a woman, what is her husband's job, what are her childcare arrangements, how she nurtures her underlings, how the competitiveness in her field took her aback, how she is a role model for other women or how she's the "first woman to ..."

2021: NASA named the landing site of the Mars 2020 Perseverance rover within the Jezero crater on Mars in honor of Octavia E. Butler, a renowned American science fiction author. This recognition pays tribute to Butler's contributions to science fiction literature.

March 06

1875: Stefania Wolicka, a Polish woman, became the first woman to earn a Ph.D. from the University of Zurich in Switzerland. She also became the first woman to earn a Doctorate of Philosophy degree in Europe in the modern era.

1886: *The Nightingale*, the first American nurses' magazine, was published for the first time. This magazine provided a platform for nurses to share their experiences, knowledge, and advancements in the nursing field.

1901: In Dohnavur, a place in British India's Madras division, a seven-year-old girl named Preena found refuge at a Christian mission after escaping from being sold into prostitution. Preena informed missionary Amy Carmichael about the prevalent human trafficking and "temple prostitution," where young girls were held captive in Hindu temples. In response, Carmichael established the Dohnavur Fellowship, a sanctuary and school, to protect children from such exploitation. She rescued over 1,000 children from traffickers and wrote a bestselling book called The Gold Cord in 1932.

1913: Izabela Moszczeńska-Rzepecka, a Polish feminist and irredentist journalist, translator, suffragette, and the first Polish author to advocate sex education for both girls and boys, was freed from prison after a year-long incarceration. She was arrested for her anti-Russian activity and, in particular, for writing an article about unjust actions against the autonomy of Finland.

1922: Hasya Drori, an Israeli politician, made an aliya from Russia to Mandatory Palestine and started to live in a tent in Tel Aviv. She was a member of the Knesset from the Mapai from 1949-1951.

1923: The Egyptian Feminist Union was founded at the home of activist Huda Sha'arawi, who served as its first president until she died in 1947. It was known as the Wafdist Women's Central Committee before that. It published a periodical, *L'Egyptienne*, from 1925, and from 1937, the journal *al-Misriyyah* (*The Egyptian Woman*).

1931: Ruth Rowland Nichols set a women's altitude record by reaching 28,743 feet.

1953: Rosalind Franklin, a British scientist, sent her two manuscripts on A-DNA to *Acta Crystallographica* in Copenhagen. Franklin's work on X-ray diffraction played a crucial role in understanding the structure of DNA.

1967: Svetlana Alliluyeva, the daughter of Joseph Stalin, defected to the United States. She left the Soviet Union, seeking political asylum and a new life outside her father's shadow.

2014: Two members of the protest band Pussy Riot were attacked by a group of people in a McDonald's, resulting in chemical burns and head injuries. Pussy Riot gained international attention for their activism and critical stance against the Russian government.

March 07

1870: Wyoming became the first U.S. state to permit women to serve on juries when six women were seated. However, this right was later rescinded and then reinstated in the 1950s.

1911: Inez Millholland led her first suffrage parade, becoming a prominent figure in the suffrage movement. She held a sign with the words,

> "Forward, out of error,
> Leave behind the night,
> Forward through the darkness,
> Forward into light!"

Her passionate activism and leadership contributed to the fight for women's right to vote.

1919: Maria Dulębianka, a Polish artist and activist known for promoting women's suffrage and higher education, died. She was buried next to Maria Konopnicka in Lychakiv Cemetery. The funeral drew a significant crowd, uniting individuals from various walks of life in a display of patriotism. Women's rights activists, single mothers, shelter residents, and their dedicated guardians were among those in attendance. Dulębianka and Konopnicka (a writer and activist) lived together for two decades, although it was never confirmed if they considered themselves a same-sex couple.

1933: Eleanor Roosevelt, the First Lady of the United States, began conducting weekly press conferences exclusively for female reporters. This initiative provided a platform for women journalists to engage with the First Lady and cover important issues of the time.

1951: Lillian Hellman's play *Autumn Garden* premiered on Broadway in New York City. Hellman, a renowned playwright, tackled love, relationships, and disillusionment themes in this production.

2010: Kathryn Bigelow became the first woman to win the Academy Award for Best Director. She received the award for her film *The Hurt Locker*, a gripping war drama set in Iraq.

2013: Hilary Mantel, the acclaimed British author, was awarded the prestigious 2013 David Cohen Prize for literature. The prize recognized her outstanding contributions to the world of literature.

2015: The all-female Mizrachi Jewish band A-WA released their first song, *Habib Galbi* (*Love of My Heart*). The piece combined Hip Hop and electronic music elements with traditional Yemeni Arabic poetry lyrics, garnering global popularity and acclaim.

2015: Sayaka Osakabe, a Japanese women's rights activist and founder of the Matahara Net, received the U.S. State Department's International Women of Courage Award.

March 08

1702: Queen Anne ascended to the throne, becoming queen regnant of England, Scotland, and Ireland. Her reign lasted until May 1, 1707.

1838: Jenny Lind, known as the Swedish Nightingale, debuted as Agathe in Carl Maria von Weber's opera *Der Freischütz* at The Royal Theatre. Her exceptional talent and powerful voice made her a renowned opera singer.

1879: Aletta Henriëtte Jacobs became the first woman to attend a Dutch university and the first Dutch woman to receive a medical degree. She graduated with a medical doctorate and wrote a unique doctoral thesis on localizing physiological and pathological symptoms in the cerebrum.

1884: Susan B. Anthony addressed the U.S. House Judiciary Committee, advocating for an amendment to the U.S. Constitution to grant women the right to vote. Her efforts contributed to the ongoing fight for women's suffrage.

1908: Social Democratic Women's Society held a meeting on women's suffrage in New York. The gathered women called on the Socialist Party to actively pursue the fight for equal suffrage. Consequently, the Socialist Party dedicated the last Sunday of February as National Women's Day.

1910: Elise Deroche, also known as Baroness de Laroche, became the first woman to receive a pilot's license in the world, issued by the Aero Club de France.

1914: On the fifth annual International Women's Day, the first edition of the Workers' Dreadnought newspaper was published in the United Kingdom. It was initiated by Sylvia Pankhurst, Mary Patterson, and Zelie Emerson on behalf of the East London Federation of Suffragettes. The publication later transformed into Workers and served as the official weekly newspaper of the Communist Party.

1914: The Russian women's journal *Rabotnitsa* (*The Woman Worker*) was launched on International Women's Day. It became one of the longest-running and politically left-leaning women's periodicals.

1918: Women in Austria celebrated International Women's Day for the first time, using the occasion to protest against World War I.

1946: The Congress of American Women was established as the U.S. branch of the Women's International Democratic Federation. It was antifascist and leaned pro-Soviet. They advocated for women's rights and equality at home and work, supported labor and civil rights, and opposed anticommunist attacks on liberals. Membership included communists, popular front supporters, and liberal middle-class women. Eleanor Flexner led as executive director in 1946, with notable members like Gene Weltfish, Jacqueline Cochran, Mary van Kleeck, Charlotte Hawkins Brown, Muriel Draper, Elizabeth Gurley Flynn, Cornelia Bryce Pinchot, Susan B. Anthony II, and briefly, actress Jean Muir.

1964: The first occupation of Alcatraz took place, planned by Belva Cottier based on the 1868 Treaty of Fort Laramie. The occupation aimed to reclaim Native American land rights and draw attention to the mistreatment of Indigenous peoples.

1979: Thousands of women participated in the International Women's Day protests in Tehran, Iran, demonstrating against the introduction of mandatory veiling during the Iranian revolution.

1987: Salt-N-Pepa, the famous American hip-hop trio consisting of Cheryl James (Salt), Sandra Denton (Pepa), and Deidra Roper (DJ Spinderella), released their first song. It was initially the B-side of the *Tramp* single and later received a Grammy Award nomination.

2000: The first *Manifa* took place in Warsaw, Poland, to protest the police action against a woman arrested at an ob-gyn doctor's office suspected of aborting a fetus. She was forced to undergo a forensic examination. Additionally, it was a protest against other discriminatory laws and practices of the right-wing government. Since then, it has become an annual demonstration for women's rights.

2003: Shortly before the Iraq War, 26 persons, including authors Alice Walker, Maxine Hong Kingston, and Terry Tempest Williams, were arrested for crossing a police line at an anti-war rally outside the White House.

2011: Aya Virginie Touré organized peaceful protests across Côte d'Ivoire (Ivory Coast) with the participation of 45,000 women. The demonstrations were held to oppose President Laurent Gbagbo, who refused to step down after losing the presidential election to Alassane Ouattara.

2011: Mata Tuatagaloa Keli was sworn in as Samoa's first female judge.

2012: Sara Blakely, the inventor of Spanx, a popular shapewear brand, became the youngest self-made female billionaire on Forbes' list. Her innovative product revolutionized the undergarment industry.

2016: The World Health Organization (WHO) advised pregnant women against traveling to regions with active Zika virus transmission. This aligns with previous warnings issued by the U.S. Centers for Disease Control and Prevention (CDC) and other health organizations. The WHO Director-General, Margaret Chan, emphasized the increasing evidence of sexual transmission of the virus.

2017: The Day Without a Woman strike action took place on International Women's Day. Organized by the 2017 Women's March and the International Women's Strike movement, the strike called on women to refrain from work as a form of protest against the policies of the Donald Trump administration.

2018: A statue was unveiled in Govan, Glasgow, to honor the life of Mary Barbour, a key figure in the Red Clydeside movement of the early 20th century, a political activist and local leader. She is most renowned for organizing the women of Govan during the 1915 rent strikes.

2020: In response to the tragic death of Ingrid Escamilla, a woman killed by her boyfriend, women in Mexico City held protests on International Women's Day, demanding an end to violence against women. The march preceded a 24-hour female strike scheduled for the following Monday, emphasizing the urgent need for change and greater protection for women.

March 09

1325: Queen Isabella of England, wife of King Edward II and sister of King Charles IV of France, left England for Paris on a mission to mediate an end to the war between England and France.

1910: Mme. Ekaterina Breshkovskaya, known as the "Grandmother of the Russian Revolution," was convicted of conspiracy and sentenced to exile in Siberia. She played a significant role in the revolutionary movement in Russia.

1919: Italy passed a law that ended husbands' superiority in family law, granting women the right to control their property, have equal custody of their children, pursue careers, and run for public office.

1943: Rachela Auerbach, a Polish-Jewish writer, escaped from the Warsaw Ghetto and worked as a Polish secretary on the Aryan side, leveraging her non-Jewish appearance and German fluency. She recorded historical notes about the Jewish community at night. Responding to an underground Jewish committee's request, she penned *Yizkor*, a detailed essay on the 1942 Warsaw Ghetto deportation, along with another piece about Jewish writers, artists, and cultural activists in Warsaw. Both gained wide underground circulation. She was one of only three surviving *Oyneg Shabbos* (Oneg Shabbat; The Ringelblum Archive) group members.

1959: The first Barbie doll was unveiled and displayed at the American International Toy Fair in New York. Barbie, created by Ruth Handler, became an iconic and influential toy that has remained popular for decades.

1990: Antonia Novello was sworn in as the first Hispanic and female U.S. Surgeon General by Justice Sandra Day O'Connor.

1996: Subhana Barzagi Roshi became the first female *roshi* (Zen teacher) of the Diamond *Sangha* when she received transmission in Australia.

2019: Kane Tanaka, a Japanese supercentenarian, was officially recognized as the world's oldest living person at 116 years and 67 days old. She held the title until her passing at the remarkable age of 119 years and 107 days.

2021: Pope Francis appointed Núria Calduch as the first female Secretary of the Pontifical Biblical Commission.

2022: Russian airstrike destroyed a maternity ward and a children's hospital in Mariupol, Ukraine, resulting in the loss of lives and injuries. The attack caused devastation and highlighted the atrocities committed in the area by the Russian invaders.

March 10

1893: Lillian Wald opened The Nurses' Settlement in the Lower East Side of New York City. The establishment aimed to provide affordable healthcare to those in need, mainly focusing on serving immigrant communities.

1914: Suffragette Mary Richardson vandalized the painting *The Toilet of Venus* by Velázquez at the National Gallery in London. She used a meat chopper to damage the artwork as a protest to bring attention to the imprisonment of Emmeline Pankhurst, the prominent suffragette and founder of the Women's Social and Political Union in Great Britain.

1920: West Virginia ratified the 19th Amendment to the U.S. Constitution, granting universal women's suffrage. The state's ratification vote of 16 to 13 in favor followed a close vote of 47 to 40 in the state House of Delegates a week earlier.

1949: Mildred Gillars, also known as "Axis Sally," was found guilty of treason. Gillars was an American broadcaster employed by Nazi Germany during World War II. She used propaganda to undermine

American morale and spread Nazi ideology through her radio broadcasts.

1974: Shortly before the second and third readings of the abortion reform (Paragraph 218) in West Germany, doctors and women's groups joined forces against the abortion ban. In *Der Spiegel* magazine, 329 doctors and medical assistants declared that they "have performed abortions or assisted women in obtaining abortions and will continue to do so," signing it with their names.

1997: The American supernatural drama television series *Buffy the Vampire Slayer* aired for the first time. The show is considered to be part of a wave of television series from the late 1990s and early 2000s that feature strong female characters alongside *Xena: Warrior Princess*, *La Femme Nikita*, *Dark Angel*, and *Alias*. It also acquired attention from scholars and prompted the publication of some twenty books and numerous articles, delving into the show's themes through various academic lenses, including sociology, Speech Communication, psychology, philosophy, and women's studies.

2013: Aung San Suu Kyi was reelected as the leader of the Burmese National League for Democracy (NLD). Suu Kyi, a prominent pro-democracy advocate and Nobel Peace Prize laureate, played a crucial role in the political landscape of Myanmar (formerly Burma).

2017: South Korea's Constitutional Court upheld the impeachment of President Park Geun-hye, leading to her removal from office. Park was impeached following a corruption scandal involving abuse of power and bribery. Hwang Kyo-Ahn assumed the role of Acting President following her removal.

March 11

843: Empress Theodora II of the Byzantine Empire officially ended Iconoclasm by restoring the veneration of icons in Orthodox churches. This decision marked the genesis of the Feast of Orthodoxy, a commemoration of the restoration of the use of religious icons. Theodora II also ordered the persecution of the Paulicians, resulting in the massacre of approximately 100,000 followers in the Byzantine theme of Armenia.

1708: Queen Anne exercised her power by withholding Royal Assent from the Scottish Militia Bill, which was the final instance of a British monarch vetoing legislation, signifying the diminishing influence of the monarch in legislative matters.

1850: The Women's Medical College of Pennsylvania opened, becoming the second medical school for women in the United States.

1875: Jennie Kidd Trout became Canada's first licensed woman physician after qualifying as a medical doctor. She held this distinction until 1880, when Emily Stowe also became medical licensed.

1907: The women's club Colony opened on Madison Avenue in New York City. It was the first social club established by and for women in the city. Designed by Elsie de Wolfe, the first American interior designer, The Colony attracted several affluent and well-known women of the time.

1912: When the newly presented to the parliament Provisional Constitution did not include women's suffrage, the Chinese feminist activists left their seats in the gallery and stormed the parliamentary sets in a demonstration, after which they were banned from entering the building.

1959: Lorraine Hansberry's play, *A Raisin in the Sun*, debuted on Broadway, making her the first African-American female author to have a play performed on Broadway. The play explored racial and social issues and significantly impacted American theater.

2006: Michelle Bachelet was inaugurated as the first female president of Chile. She served as the president of Chile from 2006 to 2010 and then again from 2014 to 2018.

March 12

1857: Elizabeth Blackwell, the first woman to receive a medical degree in the United States, established the New York Infirmary for Indigent Women and Children, which aimed to provide healthcare services specifically for those who were destitute and in need of medical assistance.

1912: Juliette Gordon Low organized the first-ever Girl Scouts meeting in the United States. At that time, they were called the Girl Guides. The Girl Scouts is a renowned organization that empowers girls and young women through various educational and leadership activities.

1942: Irena Białówna, a Polish physician and public health professional, was arrested by the Gestapo for her work in the underground resistance. She was ultimately sent to Auschwitz Nazi Camp, where she worked in the medical section to support interned mothers and their children, often forging medical documentation to protect female prisoners. She was later moved to the camp in Ravensbrück, then to Gross-Rosen, and finally, to Neubrandenburg. She survived the war.

1946: Maria Ulfah Santoso became the first ever female cabinet member when she was selected as services minister in the Second Sjahrir Cabinet in Indonesia.

1954: Doria Shafik, an Egyptian feminist, poet, editor, and one of the principal leaders of the women's liberation movement in Egypt, started an eight-day hunger strike at the press syndicate in protest at the creation of a constitutional committee with no women on it. She ended her strike upon receiving a written statement that President Naguib was committed to a constitution that respected women's rights.

1959: Tibetan women protested against the Chinese government by surrounding the Dalai Lama's residence. The protest led to their arrest, and many were subjected to beatings and executions.

1993: Janet Reno became the 78th United States Attorney General, serving in that position until 2001. She was the first woman to hold the post and became the second-longest-serving Attorney General in U.S. history. Before her appointment, Reno also served as Florida's first woman State Attorney.

1994: Thirty-two women were ordained as priests in the Church of England - the first ordination of women in the history of the Church.

2009: The U.S. Food and Drug Administration (FDA) approved the FC2 Female Condom, a lower-cost alternative to existing female condoms. The FC2 Female Condom is a thin, flexible sheath worn by women inside the vagina as a contraceptive measure and to help prevent sexually transmitted infections, including HIV/AIDS.

March 13

1555: Louise Charlin Perrin Labé received from Henry II a *privilège* protecting her exclusive right to publish her works for five years. Her *Œuvres* include two prose works: a proto-feminist preface urging women to write and a dramatic allegory in prose entitled *Débat de Folie et d'Amour*.

1781: Gregoria Apaza, her sister-in-law Bartolina Sisa, and her brother Julian Apaza (known as Tupac Katari) initiated an indigenous revolt against Spanish colonial rule in Bolivia. They were members of the Aymara people and played significant roles in leading the resistance against the oppressive colonial forces.

1913: Archaeologist Katherine Routledge and her husband William began the Mana Expedition to Easter Island. The expedition aimed to study Easter Island's cultural and archaeological aspects, including its famous monumental stone statues known as Moai.

1942: Julia Flikke, a member of the Nurse Corps, became the first woman to attain the rank of colonel in the U.S. Army.

1967: Margaret G. Arnstein, an influential figure in nursing and public health, was appointed the Dean of the Yale School of Nursing. She held this position from 1967 to 1972 and made notable contributions to the field.

1986: Susan Butcher became the second woman to win the Iditarod, an Alaskan dog sled race known for its challenging terrain and harsh conditions.

2009: Lucy Shapiro, a prominent biologist and developmental geneticist, received the Canada Gairdner International Award for her significant contributions to biomedical science.

2012: Argentina's Supreme Court ruled that abortions resulting from cases of rape are not punishable.

2020: Breonna Taylor, a young African-American woman, was killed by police officers who forcibly entered her home in Louisville, Kentucky. Her death sparked widespread protests and ignited discussions about racial injustice and police reform.

2020: Katerina Sakellaropoulou was sworn in as the President of Greece, becoming the country's first woman to hold this office. She succeeded Prokopis Pavlopoulos and made history with her appointment as the highest-ranking official in the Greek government.

March 14

675: Princess Tōchi and Princess Abe of Japan visited the Ise Jingū shrine, a prominent Shinto shrine dedicated to the sun goddess Amaterasu. This visit holds cultural and religious significance in Japan.

1489: Catherine Cornaro, the Queen of Cyprus, sold her kingdom to the Republic of Venice, marking the end of her reign and the power transfer to Venice.

1889: Susan La Flesche Picotte graduated from the Woman's Medical College of Pennsylvania as the valedictorian of her class. She became the first Indigenous woman from the Omaha tribe to earn a medical degree, making significant strides for Indigenous women in medicine.

1902: The Irish Association of Women Graduates & Candidate Graduates was launched—the association aimed to promote equal opportunities for women in academia. Key organizers of this initiative included Agnes O'Farrelly, Mary Ryan, Mary Hayden, and Isabella Mulvany.

1908: Annie Besant and Beatrice Webb created The Fabian Women's Group to strengthen the bond between socialism and women's rights, advocating women's suffrage and equal unemployment benefits for women. Other female members included Emma Frances Brooke, a collectivist; Charlotte Wilson, an anarchist; Harriot Stanton Blatch, an American feminist; Katharine St. John Conway (Glasier), who was also involved with the Independent Labour party, and L. T. Mallet, a feminist lecturer and writer.

2000: Susan Solomon, an atmospheric chemist, received the President's National Medal of Science for her research on the global ozone layer. Her contributions helped advance our understanding of atmospheric chemistry and environmental issues.

2018: Angela Merkel was sworn in for her fourth term as the Chancellor of Germany. Merkel was a prominent political figure and the first woman to hold the office of Chancellor in Germany.

2018: One day after speaking out against extrajudicial killings by police and paramilitaries, Marielle Franco, an Afro-Brazilian socialist and feminist, was assassinated in Rio de Janeiro.

2022: Marina Ovsyannikova, a Russian state television journalist, interrupted a live news broadcast on Channel One Russia by holding a sign that read "No War" and "Stop the war. Do not believe the propaganda, they tell you lies here." She was subsequently arrested for her act of protest.

March 15

963: Emperor Romanos II of the Byzantine Empire passed away at the age of 25 under suspicious circumstances, with allegations of poisoning by his wife, Empress Theophano. Following his death, his infant son Basil II became the new emperor, with Empress Theophano assuming the role of regent and de facto ruler. She also appointed her three-year-old son, Constantine VIII, as co-emperor.

1626: Portugal declared war on Queen Nzinga of Ndongo, who ruled in present-day Angola, escalating the conflict between the Portuguese colonial forces and Queen Nzinga's kingdom.

1806: The Orphan Asylum Society in the City of New York held its inaugural meeting, thanks to the efforts of philanthropic women such as Isabella Graham, Joanna Bethune, Eliza Hamilton, and Sarah Hoffman. The society established Graham Windham, the first private orphanage in New York.

1906: Finland became the first European country to grant women the right to vote and run for political office.

1908: An article in The Sunday Paper in Rochester, New York, condemned female anarchists, claiming that

> "women anarchists have become the terror of the world's police."

The article suggested that emotional women lose their sense of fear and are often implicated in attacks against rulers.

1927: The first Women's Boat Race occurred on the River Thames in the United Kingdom between the University of Oxford and the University of Cambridge.

1966: Yad Vashem, Israel's official memorial to the victims of the Holocaust, recognized Ona Šimaitė as Righteous Among the Nations. She had assisted Jews in the Vilna Ghetto in Lithuania during World War II.

1971: Gloria Arellanes and Adelitas de Aztlán, both former female Brown Berets, opened *La Clínica Familiar del Barrio* in East Los Angeles, providing free medical services to the community.

1997: Arundhati Roy's debut novel, *The God of Small Things*, was published. The book went on to win the prestigious Booker Prize, establishing Roy as a celebrated author.

2012: Leanne Wood was elected as the new leader of the Welsh political party Plaid Cymru.

2019: Inspired by the Swedish activist Greta Thunberg, over a million people worldwide participated in the Strike for Climate or Fridays for Future movement, demanding action on climate change and environmental issues.

2021: Representative Deb Haaland of New Mexico was confirmed as the Secretary of the Interior in the United States, becoming the first Native American to lead a cabinet agency.

March 16

1781: Manuela Beltrán, a Neogranadine woman, led an anti-tax peasant rebellion that spread to the Andean Region of Colombia and the Llanos. This rebellion was a significant uprising against the Spanish colonial authorities and their oppressive taxation policies.

1876: Nelly Saunders and Rose Harland participated in the first recorded female boxing match in New York.

1883: Susan Hayhurst, an already pioneering American female physician, became the first woman to graduate from a pharmaceutical college in the United States - the Philadelphia College of Pharmacy.

1974: Women protest in many cities of West Germany against Paragraph 218 abortion ban.

2021: The Jack Daniel Distillery, the first registered distillery in the United States, announced the appointment of Lexie Phillips as Assistant Distiller, making her the first woman to serve officially as a distiller for the iconic Tennessee Whiskey brand.

March 17

659: Gertrude of Nivelles, daughter of Pepin of Landen, the mayor of the palace of Austrasia, requested to be buried in a plain linen shroud on her deathbed. This choice aligned with the traditional "furnished" grave practice with pagan origins.

1775: Catherine the Great of Russia issued a manifesto prohibiting freed serfs from being returned to serfdom.

1842: The Female Relief Society of Nauvoo was formally established as the precursor to the women's organization of the Church of Jesus Christ of Latter-day Saints (LDS Church).

1917: Loretta Perfectus Walsh officially became the first woman to join the United States Navy in a non-nursing role.

1969: Golda Meir became the first female Prime Minister of Israel. She served as the Prime Minister from 1969 to 1974 and played a significant role in Israeli politics and international diplomacy.

2000: Julia Roberts became the first female actor to earn $20 million for a single film, *Erin Brockovich*.

2019: U.S. Senator Kirsten Gillibrand of New York formally announced her candidacy for the Democratic Party's President of the United States nomination in the 2020 election.

2021: The Sapporo district court in Japan ruled that prohibiting same-sex marriage is unconstitutional. This decision represented a step towards recognizing and protecting the rights of same-sex couples in Japan.

2022: 151 feminists signed the *Feminist Resistance Against War: A Manifesto* in solidarity with the Russian Feminist Anti-War Resistance manifesto and Russian feminist anti-war efforts. Among the signatories were Ailbhe Smyth, Alba Flores, Amaia Pérez Orozco, June Fernández, Keeanga-Yamahtta Taylor, Nancy Fraser, Özlem Demirel, Teresa Rodríguez, Tithi Bhattacharya, Yayo Herrero, Carmen Magallón, Pamela Palenciano, Goretti Horgan, Lidia Cirillo, Zillah R. Eisenstein, Judy Rebick, Ofelia García, El Jones, Shahrzad Mojab, Maristella Svampa, Debora Diniz, Heloísa Helena, Luciana Genro, Sonia Guajajara, Piedad Córdoba Ruiz, Miriam Miranda, Mónica Baltodano, Daria Serenko, Diane Lamoureux, Pamela Philipose, Silvia Federici, and Talíria Petrone. The manifesto called for

> "a bold redirection of the situation to break the militaristic spiral initiated by Russia and supported by NATO."

By the end of March, the manifesto had collected over 2,500 signatures. However, the manifesto's name's similarity to the original Russian group confused their position, as the RAW activists advocate arming Ukraine rather than disarmament. Ukrainian activists critiqued the manifesto, accusing the signatories of denying Ukrainian women the right to self-defense.

March 18

218: Julia Maesa, the aunt of the assassinated Emperor Caracalla, who had been exiled to her residence in Syria by the self-proclaimed emperor Macrinus, proclaimed her 14-year-old grandson, Elagabalus, as the new emperor of Rome.

1554: Princess Elizabeth, who would later become Queen Elizabeth I of England, was imprisoned in the Tower of London during the reign of her half-sister, Queen Mary I. Elizabeth's imprisonment resulted from political and religious tensions.

1870: The Female Infanticide Prevention Act of 1870 was enacted in British India to address and prevent the murder of female infants. This legislation aimed to combat the practice of female infanticide, which was prevalent in some regions of India.

1921: Na Hye-sŏk, a Korean feminist, poet, writer, painter, educator, and journalist, had her first exhibition of paintings, the first exhibition by a Korean woman painter ever in Seoul.

1922: Judith Kaplan celebrated a Bat Mitzvah at twelve, which was the first known public celebration of this coming-of-age ceremony for Jewish girls. Her father, Rabbi Mordecai Kaplan, advocated for gender equality in religious opportunities and significantly initiated this change.

1936: The primarily female workforce of Semperit Factory in Krakow, Poland, an occupation-style strike started. The central demand was a 15% wage increase. By the order of local government officials, police brutally pacified the striking workers, and many women were beaten. A few days later, a mass solidarity strike was called across the city. During mass demonstrations, police opened fire, causing the death of eight workers and injuring dozens. Most striking workers' demands were accepted, and the mass solidarity strike was called off.

1965: Yad Vashem recognized Queen Mother Elisabeth of Belgium as Righteous Among the Nations. During the German occupation of Belgium from 1940 to 1944, she used her position and connections to aid in rescuing numerous Jewish children from deportation by the Nazis.

1970: Queen Sisowath Kossamak of Cambodia was placed under house arrest by General Lon Nol, while Prince Norodom Sihanouk was ousted from power. These events were part of the political upheaval and power struggles during the turbulent period in Cambodian history.

2020: The Abortion Legislation Bill 2019 passed its third reading in the New Zealand House of Representatives, legalizing abortion in New Zealand, which brought a significant change in the country's abortion laws, granting women increased reproductive rights and access to healthcare.

2021: Annemarie Jorritsma of the People's Party for Freedom and Democracy and Kajsa Ollongren of the Democrats 66 party were appointed as scouts (*informateurs*) for the next cabinet formation in the Netherlands. Their role involved exploring possibilities for forming a new government coalition after the elections.

March 19

1702: Princess Anne Stuart, daughter of King James II and sister of his successor Mary II, ascended to the thrones of England, Scotland, and Ireland following the death of William III. She became the queen regnant, ruling over the three kingdoms.

1907: Mary Mallon, also known as "Typhoid Mary," was sentenced to her first quarantine on North Brother Island. She was quarantined again in 1915 and remained there until she died in 1938. Sara Josephine Baker played a crucial role in tracking down Mary Mallon. She pioneered public health programs and worked to combat diseases like dysentery, smallpox, and typhoid.

1911: The first International Women's Day rallies took place in Austria, Denmark, Germany, and Switzerland, with over one million participating. The date for International Women's Day was officially changed to March 8 in 1913.

1975: In the case of *Weinberger v. Wiesenfeld,* the U.S. Supreme Court voted 8-0 to invalidate an outdated Social Security law that provided survivor benefits only to women, not men. Ruth Bader Ginsburg argued the case – her third at the Supreme Court.

1989: Maggie Smith received her fourth BAFTA award in the Best Actress in a Leading Role category for her performance in *The Lonely Passion of Judith Hearne*.

2009: Elena Kagan was confirmed by the U.S. Senate as the first female Solicitor General of the United States. This position is the third highest-ranking official in the Department of Justice.

2019: Karen Keskulla Uhlenbeck, a mathematician from the United States, became the first woman to receive the prestigious Abel Prize, which is awarded for outstanding achievements in mathematics.

2021: Samia Suluhu Hassan became the first female president of Tanzania following the death of President John Magufuli. She assumed office as the sixth president of Tanzania.

March 20

1852: Harriet Beecher Stowe's novel *Uncle Tom's Cabin* was published. The book became a powerful anti-slavery novel and significantly impacted the abolitionist movement in the United States.

1890: The General Federation of Women's Clubs (GFWC) was founded in the United States. The GFWC is one of the world's largest and oldest nonpartisan, nondenominational women's volunteer service organizations dedicated to community improvement and promoting the rights and well-being of women.

1982: Joan Jett's iconic song *I Love Rock 'n Roll* reached No. 1 on the Billboard charts. Joan Jett is considered a pioneer for female rock musicians and has significantly contributed to the industry.

1985: Libby Riddles became the first woman to win the Iditarod Trail Sled Dog Race. She completed the grueling race in 18 days, 20 minutes, and 17 seconds.

1990: Khaleda Zia became Bangladesh's first female prime minister, serving as the head of government for two non-consecutive terms.

1990: Imelda Marcos, the widow of former Philippine President Ferdinand Marcos, stood trial for bribery, embezzlement, and racketeering related to her husband's regime.

1991: The U.S. Supreme Court ruled unanimously in *UAW v. Johnson Controls* that excluding women from jobs that involve exposure to toxic substances that could harm a fetus was unconstitutional. The decision recognized that such policies violated women's rights and perpetuated gender-based discrimination.

2011: Huda al-Baan, the Yemeni Minister of Human Rights, resigned in protest after a sniper attack on anti-government demonstrators.

2021: Julia Letlow, the wife of the late Representative-elect Luke Letlow, won a special election and became Louisiana's first female Republican Representative. She succeeded her husband, who died from COVID-19 before being sworn into office.

March 21

1919: Universal suffrage was extended to women in the Socialist Federative Republic of Councils in Hungary. However, this right was short-lived, revoked when the Soviet Republic dissolved later that year. Women's suffrage in Hungary was not reinstated until 1945.

1922: Tadashi Hyōdō became the first woman aviator in Japan when she was licensed as a third-class airplane aviator (License No. 38)

1939: Kate Smith recorded the famous patriotic song *God Bless America*.

1970: Dana, representing Ireland, won the Eurovision Song Contest 1970 with the song *All Kinds of Everything*. The song, composed by Derry Lindsay and Jackie Smith, became a hit and launched Dana's successful music career.

1985: *Oranges Are Not the Only Fruit* by Jeanette Winterson was published by Pandora Press. It is a compelling coming-of-age tale set in an English Pentecostal community. It explores themes of youth, family dynamics, same-sex relationships, organized religion, and faith.

1986: Debi Thomas became the first African-American woman to win the World Figure Skating Championship.

1997: Film *Selena* was released based on the life of singer Selena Quintanilla-Pérez, starring Jennifer Lopez in her breakthrough role, directed by Gregory Nava

2012: Israel banned 'Underweight' Models. Israel's Knesset passed a law prohibiting models considered "malnourished" by World Health Organization standards from working within the country's fashion market. The WHO uses body mass index to determine malnutrition; anyone with a BMI below 18.5 falls within that category.

2021: Turkey became the first and only country to withdraw from the Council of Europe Convention for the Prevention and Combating of Violence against Women and Domestic Violence, commonly called the Istanbul Convention. It officially ceased to be effective in Turkey on July 1, 2021.

2022: Russian racewalker Elena Lashmanova received a two-year ban from the Olympics and was stripped of her gold medal from the 2012 Summer Olympics following doping allegations against her.

2022: Ketanji Brown Jackson's Supreme Court confirmation hearings began in Washington, D.C.

March 22

1544: The sisters Doña Gracia (Beatrice) and Brianda Mendes Nasi received a safe conduct from the Council of Ten, which permitted them to settle in Venice. Doña Gracia Nasi was a member of a wealthy crypto-Jewish family escaping from persecution in Portugal (through Antwerp). She became one of the wealthiest and most powerful women of her time in Europe and the Ottoman Empire. Gracia Nasi later moved to Ferrara, where she supported literary activities among its Jewish community and played a crucial role in funding and organizing the relocation of *conversos* from Portugal. In 1552, her family moved to Constantinople, where she became a leading figure in the Sephardi community of the Ottoman Empire, providing aid to needy Jews, backing scholars, and founding synagogues.

1638: Anne Hutchinson, a religious dissenter, was expelled from the Massachusetts Bay Colony on charges of heresy. She then escaped to Rhode Island, seeking religious freedom.

1962: Musical *I Can Get It For You Wholesale*, starring Barbra Streisand in her Broadway debut, opened at Shubert Theater, NYC, running for 300 performances.

1972: The United States Congress passed the Equal Rights Amendment (ERA), which aimed to grant equal rights to women. However, the required number of states did not ratify the ERA and did not become part of the U.S. Constitution.

1984: In the famous "Satanic Panic" trial, teachers at the McMartin preschool in Manhattan Beach, California - Virginia McMartin, Peggy McMartin Buckey, Ray Buckey, Ray's sister Peggy Ann Buckey, and teachers Mary Ann Jackson, Betty Raidor, and Babette Spitler were charged with 115 counts of child abuse, later expanded to 321 counts of child abuse involving 48 children as part of alleged "Satanic ritual abuse" of the children in the school. The charges are later dropped as completely unfounded.

1994: Iraqi-British architect Zaha Hadid became the first woman to win architecture's Pritzker Prize.

2009: Following the death of prison activist Katerina Goulioni on March 18, inmates at a women's prison in Thebes rebelled by refusing to return to their cells, causing fires and property damage. Demonstrators outside the prison clashed with riot police, and 200 inmates in Athens held a protest in support. Katerina Goulioni was an activist who had campaigned against inadequate facilities for disabled prisoners, suspicious prisoner transfers resulting in deaths, and degrading vaginal inspections, which she called "informal rape."

2012: Del Kathryn Barton, an Australian painter, won the 2013 Archibald Prize for her portrait of actor Hugo Weaving. The Archibald Prize is a prestigious art award in Australia focusing on portraiture.

March 23

59 CE: Emperor Nero of Rome ordered the murder of his mother, Agrippina the Younger. After failed attempts to eliminate her through a shipwreck, he had her executed, which was staged to look like suicide.

1858: Rani Lakshmibai of Jhansi, during the Indian rebellion against British rule, defended Jhansi against British troops. Her courageous efforts in resisting the British occupation became a symbol of resistance during that time.

1917: Virginia Woolf, a prominent writer and feminist, established the Hogarth Press with her husband, Leonard Woolf. The Hogarth Press became an influential publishing house known for publishing works by Virginia Woolf herself and other notable authors.

1968: Joni Mitchell, a Canadian singer-songwriter, released her debut album, *Song to a Seagull*. Mitchell's unique musical style and poetic songwriting would go on to make her a revered figure in the folk and rock music scenes.

2013: The Feminist Majority Foundation, a research and education organization founded in 1987 by Eleanor Smeal, Peg Yorkin, Katherine Spillar, Toni Carabillo, and Judith Meuli, with Peg Yorkin as the chair, hosted the 9th Annual National Young Feminist Leadership Conference in Arlington, Virginia, with speakers such as Dolores Huerta, Morgane Richardson, Monica Simpson, and Ivanna Gonzalez.

2016: The United States Supreme Court reviewed the case of *Zubik v. Burwell*, which involved a challenge to a provision of the Affordable Care Act related to contraceptive access. The case raised questions about religious freedom and the government's accommodation of religious organizations.

2017: Maria Teresa Ruiz, a renowned Chilean astronomer, received the L'Oréal-

UNESCO For Women in Science Award for discovering a new celestial body.

2020: The Feminist Impact for Rights and Equality Consortium (FIRE) was established as a feminist collective aiming to promote peace and security. The consortium comprised organizations such as the *Kvinna till Kvinna* Foundation and the Nobel Women's Initiative.

2021: Agnès Callamard, a Special Rapporteur appointed by the United Nations Human Rights Council, revealed that she had been threatened by a senior Saudi Arabian official while investigating the assassination of Jamal Khashoggi, a Saudi journalist and dissident.

2023: Two suicide bombers targeted a vehicle with politician Amina Mohamed Abdi in Beledweyne, Somalia. The attack resulted in the deaths of Amina Mohamed Abdi and 47 other people, with many more injured.

March 24

1831: Emilia Plater, a Polish-Lithuanian noblewoman, expressed her desire to join the uprising for Polish independence. She adopted a soldier's appearance, formed her own military unit, and led them in several battles, inspiring others in the fight for freedom.

1853: *The Provincial Freeman*, an anti-slavery newspaper, was published in Windsor, Ontario. It was edited by Mary Ann Shadd Cary, who became North America's first Black woman publisher. The newspaper played an important role in advocating for the abolition of slavery.

1919: The League of Women Voters, a nonpartisan political organization, was established at the National American Woman Suffrage Association convention in St. Louis.

1919: The Women's Royal Air Force (WRAF) deployed personnel to France - the first time WRAF members served overseas. Later that year, another contingent of WRAF members was sent to Germany.

1921: The Women's Olympiad, organized by Alice Milliat, took place in Monaco. It was the first international women's sports event, providing female athletes a platform to compete globally.

1974: The Coalition of Labor Union Women (CLUW) was founded. It is a nonprofit and nonpartisan organization representing trade union women's interests. CLUW aims to promote equal rights, social justice, and workplace equity for women.

1996: The U.S. space shuttle Atlantis docked with the Russian space station Mir, which was the first time a U.S. astronaut, Shannon Lucid, stayed for an extended period on the Mir. Shannon Lucid, an astronaut and biochemist, conducted experiments and spent 188 days aboard Mir, setting a new U.S. space endurance record and a world endurance record for women.

2002: Halle Berry became the first African American woman to win an Academy Award for Best Actress for her performance in the movie *Monster's Ball*.

2017: Marine Le Pen, the French National Front presidential candidate, met with Russian President Vladimir Putin and called for lifting European Union sanctions on Russia.

March 25

1888: The International Council of Women was convened for eight days by the U.S. National Woman Suffrage Association to commemorate the 40th anniversary of the Woman Suffrage Movement. The council aimed to promote women's rights and suffrage internationally, bringing together women from various countries to discuss common goals and strategies.

1898: Margaret Elizabeth Noble, also known as Sister Nivedita, was initiated by Swami Vivekananda into the vow of *Brah-*

macharya, a practice of self-discipline and celibacy. Sister Nivedita became one of India's most influential female figures, actively contributing to education, social work, and Indian nationalism.

1911: A devastating fire broke out at the Triangle Waist Company's factory near Washington Square in Lower Manhattan, New York. The factory employed around 500 workers, primarily women and girls. While some managed to escape through a rear exit, many were trapped inside due to locked doors and inadequate fire safety measures. The fire resulted in the deaths of 123 female and 23 male employees. This incident highlighted the dire working conditions and led to significant fire safety regulations and labor laws reforms.

1964: The Married Women's Property Act in England and Wales was revised, granting married women the right to retain half of any savings they had accumulated from the allowances provided by their husbands.

2021: Opposition leader Sviatlana Tsikhanouskaya called for a Freedom Day and renewed protests against President Alexander Lukashenko in Belarus. These protests aimed to pressure Lukashenko to resign following a disputed election held the previous year, which sparked widespread criticism and allegations of electoral fraud.

March 26

1918: Marie Stopes, a British author, released her influential book *Married Love* in the United Kingdom. The book discussed sexual health, contraception, and marital relationships. It played a significant role in promoting the importance of sexual education and reproductive rights.

1943: Elsie S. Ott became the first woman awarded the U.S. Air Force Medal.

1958: Miyoshi Umeki, an actress of Japanese descent, became the first East Asian-American woman to win an Academy Award for acting. She received the Best Supporting Actress award for her role in the film *Sayonara*.

1973: Susan Shaw became the first of ten women to be allowed on the floor of the London Stock Exchange.

2006: Maud Fontenoy from France became the first woman to row solo across the Pacific Ocean from Peru to Polynesia. She followed Norwegian explorer Thor Heyerdahl's route during his historic 1947 journey. Fontenoy completed the 8,000-kilometer (5,000-mile) trip, reaching the island of Hiva Oa one month ahead of schedule.

2017: Carrie Lam was appointed by the Hong Kong Election Committee as the first female Chief Executive of Hong Kong. Lam's appointment marked a historic moment, as she became the first woman to hold this high-ranking political position in Hong Kong.

March 27

1184: After serving as a co-ruler of Georgia with her father for six years, Tamar continued as the sole monarch after his death and was crowned a second time at the Gelati cathedral near Kutaisi. She ruled until she died in 1213.

1910: U.S. First Lady Helen Taft and the wife of Japan's Ambassador to the United States, Viscountess Chinda, planted two cherry blossoms in Washington D.C. It was the beginning of a tradition that would bring beauty to the American capital for years. This act established the National Cherry Blossom Festival, which celebrates the friendship between the United States and Japan.

1941: Allied naval forces won the Battle of Cape Matapan over the Royal Italian Navy during World War II. Mavis Batey, one of the female code-breakers at Bletchley Park, played a crucial role in the victory by deciphering the Italian Naval Enigma machine at 19.

1973: Sacheen Littlefeather, an Apache activist, spoke on behalf of Marlon Brando during the 45th Academy Awards to explain his boycott and refusal to collect his Best Actor Award for *The Godfather*. Brando's protest was aimed at raising awareness about the portrayal of Native Americans in Hollywood and drawing attention to the standoff at Wounded Knee.

1997: Pamela Gordon became Bermuda's first woman prime minister.

2007: *City of Bones*, the first novel in *The Mortal Instruments* series, was published by Cassandra Clare. The book succeeded significantly, captivating readers with its urban fantasy world and compelling characters.

2013: Patricia McCarthy won the 2013 National Poetry Competition, showcasing her talent and creativity in poetry.

2013: Kate Tempest received the 2013 Ted Hughes Award for innovation in poetry.

2017: The U.S. Food and Drug Administration (FDA) approved Niraparib, a drug developed by Tesaro, to treat ovarian cancer.

2022: During the 94th Academy Awards, Ariana Bose became the first Afro-Latina, the second Hispanic woman overall, and the first openly queer woman of color to win an Academy Award for Best Supporting Actress for her role as Anita in Steven Spielberg's *West Side Story*. Jane Campion won Best Director for *The Power of the Dog*, and Jessica Chastain won Best Actress for portraying Tammy Faye Messner in *The Eyes of Tammy Faye*.

2022: Russian artist Yevgenia Isayeva staged an anti-war protest in Saint Petersburg by dousing herself in fake blood. She was later detained by the police, highlighting the power of artistic expression as a form of activism.

March 28

1584: Irina Godunova became Tsaritsa of all Russia. Although her husband was the official ruler, she was the one who was really in charge. The couple couldn't produce a male heir, and after the Tsar's childless death, Irina's brother became the new Tsar on March 3, 1598.

1690: The University Viadrina (Frankfurt on Oder, Germany) certified the book *The Court Midwife* (*Die Kgl. Preußische und Chur-Brandenburgische Hof-Wehemutter*) by Justine Siegemund, a Silesian midwife. The book, organized as a dialogue between the author and her pupil Christina, offered a systematic, evidence-based approach to childbirth complications like poor presentations, umbilical cord issues, and placenta previa. Siegemund's innovative techniques include a two-handed intervention for correcting shoulder presentations and a method developed with François Mauriceau to address hemorrhaging in placenta previa by puncturing the amniotic sac. It was the first German medical text written by a woman.

1906: Mary Adela Blagg was elected to the British Astronomical Association, making her mark as a prominent figure in astronomy.

1907: The School for Girls advertisement appeared in the *Majles* daily newspaper. The School was opened at the residential home of Bibi Khatoon, an Iranian writer, satirist, and one of the pioneering figures in the Iranian women's movement in Tehran. It was open to young girls and their mothers and grandmothers who hadn't had the opportunity to obtain formal education before. The ad stated that

> "five female teachers have been appointed, each responsible for one subject, such as Writing and Calligraphy, History of Iran, Reading, Cookery book, Law, Religion, Geography, Science of Arithmetic.

Teaching will be adapted to the learning ability of each girl or woman. In addition, a location has been set aside for teaching manual arts, such as knitting, gold embroidery, silk embroidery, sewing, etc., and all these teachers are womenfolk and except for an aged porter, no other man will be in the School."

1915: Emma Goldman, a Jewish anarchist and feminist, was arrested in the United States for explaining birth control. Rather than paying a $100 fine, she spent 15 days in jail, demonstrating her commitment to reproductive rights and freedom of speech.

1927: Millicent Bryant became the first Australian woman to gain a pilot license.

1972: Elizabeth Holtzman announced her candidacy for the Democratic nomination for the United States House of Representatives from New York's 16th congressional district. She defeated the incumbent representatives Emanuel Celler and Robert O'Donnell in the primary. At 31, when she won the general election, she became the youngest woman ever elected to the United States Congress.

1982: The first NCAA women's college basketball national championship game occurred, with Louisiana Tech facing Cheyney. The game ended with a score of 76-62 in favor of Louisiana Tech.

2001: Hikaru Saeki became the first female star officer (admiral and general) in the Japan Self-Defense Forces (JSDF) with her promotion to Rear Admiral.

2006: Marthe (Hoffnung) Cohn, a Holocaust survivor who spied on the Nazis, published her memoir, *Behind Enemy Lines: The True Story of a French Jewish Spy in Nazi Germany*.

2007: *Aswat* - Palestinian Feminist Center for Gender and Sexual Freedoms, founded by Ghadir Shafie, organized its first public conference in Haifa, Israel. It revolved around the theme of "Exploring Home and Exile in the Queer Experience" and featured poetry readings and music. Approximately 250 people attended, with an estimated 10 to 20 Arab lesbians among them. However, the Islamic Movement strongly opposed the group, calling it "fatal cancer that should be forbidden from spreading out within the Arab society and from eliminating the Arab culture." Around 20 protesters gathered outside the event venue.

2009: Kim Yu-na, from South Korea, won the world figure skating championship, scoring 207.71 points overall. Her achievement was notable as she became the first female skater to surpass 200 points in the competition, solidifying her position as one of the sport's greats.

2016: The American Civil Liberties Union (ACLU) and Lambda Legal filed a federal lawsuit against a North Carolina law prohibiting transgender people from using bathrooms consistent with their gender identity.

2017: British Prime Minister Theresa May signed a letter invoking Article 50 of the Treaty on the European Union, formally initiating the United Kingdom's withdrawal from the European Union, a significant step in the Brexit process.

2021: Dianne Feinstein became the longest-serving U.S. Senator from California, surpassing Hiram Johnson. Her tenure in the Senate demonstrated her enduring impact and influence in California politics.

March 29

1667: Elisabeth of the Palatinate, a philosopher known for her correspondence with René Descartes, became the Princess-Abbess of Herford Abbey. Her critical views of Descartes' dualistic metaphysics and her work addressing metaphysical concerns anticipated the ideas of later philosophers.

1848: Queen's College in London was founded, becoming the first School worldwide to grant academic qualifications to young women.

1867: Queen Victoria gave the Royal Assent to the British North America Act, establishing Canada as a federal dominion. This act laid the foundation for the formation of modern Canada, with July 1 becoming Canada's national day.

1869: Idawalley Zoradia Lewis, an American lighthouse keeper known for her heroism, rescued two soldiers in a snowstorm after their small boat overturned.

1875: In the case of *Virginia Minor v. Happersett*, the U.S. Supreme Court ruled for the second time in two years that the 14th Amendment did not protect a woman's right to vote.

1914: Katherine Routledge and her husband William arrived on Easter Island for a one-year archaeological expedition. They focused on studying the island's giant Moai statues.

1951: Gertrude Lawrence starred in the Broadway opening of Rodgers and Hammerstein's musical *The King and I*. Lawrence's performance showcased her talents as a leading actress, and the musical enjoyed a successful three-year run.

2014: Same-sex marriages occurred in the United Kingdom after they were legally authorized to proceed in England and Wales from midnight UTC.

2019: The Cayman Islands legalized same-sex marriage following a court ruling that declared a law defining marriage as a relationship between a man and a woman unconstitutional. This decision granted equal marriage rights to same-sex couples in the Cayman Islands.

2021: Belarusian authorities charged opposition leader Sviatlana Tsikhanouskaya with terrorism, accusing her of attempting to stage false flag bombings in the capital, Minsk, and Barysaw. The charges against Tsikhanouskaya were seen by many as politically motivated and part of a broader crackdown on opposition figures in Belarus.

March 30

1834: Anne Lister and Ann Walker exchanged vows and rings and took communion together, considering themselves married, although their union did not have legal recognition. In 2018, Holy Trinity Church in Goodramgate, York, where the ceremony took place, was decorated with a commemorative plaque recognizing Anne Lister as a gender-nonconforming entrepreneur and their marital commitment.

1930: The League of Women Voters announced a 10th Anniversary National Convention to celebrate the victory of the 19th Amendment, which granted women the right to vote in the United States. The event honored veteran suffragists such as Alice Stone Blackwell and Carrie Chapman Catt.

1987: Marlee Matlin became the first deaf performer to win an Academy Award. She was awarded Best Actress for her acting debut in the film *Children of a Lesser God*.

2016: A study conducted by researchers at McGill University and the University of California, Los Angeles, revealed that extending the duration of paid maternity leave for women was associated with a decrease of over 10 percent in infant mortality rates. The study highlighted various factors contributing to this positive outcome, including reduced maternal stress, increased breastfeeding and infant care opportunities, and improved access to medical attention.

2017: Park Geun-Hye, the first female president of South Korea, was arrested as part of a corruption investigation. Her arrest marked a significant moment in South Korean politics, leading to her impeachment and removal from office.

2017: The state legislature of North Carolina repealed the Public Facilities Privacy & Security Act, commonly known as the "transgender bathroom bill." However, they also passed a law banning North Carolina cities from implementing civil rights protections for LGBTQ+ individuals until 2020.

2021: Three female polio vaccination health workers were killed by gunmen in Jalalabad, Nangarhar, Afghanistan.

2022: During the 2021–22 UEFA Women's Champions League knockout phase, 91,553 spectators attended the match between F.C. Barcelona and Real Madrid at Camp Nou in Barcelona, Spain. This attendance figure surpassed previous records, including the 1999 FIFA Women's World Cup Final, and showcased the growing popularity and support for women's football.

March 31

528: Empress Dowager Hu ordered the poisoning of her son, Emperor Xiaoming of Northern Wei, in an act of power consolidation.

1325: Queen Isabella of England, wife of King Edward II of England and sister of King Charles IV of France, negotiated a truce between the two kingdoms, effectively ending the War of Saint-Sardos.

1492: Queen Isabella of Castile issued the Alhambra Decree, also known as the Edict of Expulsion, which mandated the conversion of her Jewish and Muslim subjects to Christianity or their expulsion from Spain.

1888: Susan B. Anthony, Clara Barton, Julia Ward Howe, Sojourner Truth, and other prominent women organized The National Council of Women of the U.S., the oldest non-sectarian women's organization in the United States. The organization aimed to advocate for women's rights and promote social and political reforms.

1981: Sissy Spacek won the Best Actress Academy Award for portraying country singer Loretta Lynn in the film *Coal Miner's Daughter*.

1988: Toni Morrison's novel *Beloved* was awarded the Pulitzer Prize in Fiction. The book, known for its potent exploration of slavery and its impact on individuals and communities, received critical acclaim and cemented Morrison's legacy as a groundbreaking writer.

2016: Nguyễn Thị Kim Ngân was elected as the chairwoman of the National Assembly in Vietnam, becoming the first woman to hold this position in the country's history.

2016: Five players from the U.S. women's national soccer team, including Carli Lloyd, Becky Sauerbrunn, Alex Morgan, Megan Rapinoe, and Hope Solo, lodged federal wage discrimination complaints against the U.S. Soccer Federation (USSF) with the Equal Employment Opportunity Commission. The players highlighted the significant pay disparity between the women's and men's teams despite the women's team generating higher revenue.

2019: Zuzana Čaputová, an anti-corruption candidate representing the Progressive Slovakia party, won the second round of Slovakia's presidential election. With her victory, she became Slovakia's first female head of state.

2023: Whang-od Oggay, known as the last and oldest *mambabatok* (traditional Kalinga tattooist), appeared on the cover of *Vogue Philippines' Beauty Issue* at the age of 106 making her the oldest person ever to grace the cover of *Vogue* magazine.

APRIL

April 01

528: Empress Dowager Hu declared the 6-week-old daughter of Emperor Xiaoming of Northern Wei as the reigning Empress. However, she replaced her with the 3-year-old Yuan Zhao as the Emperor the next day.

1792: Etta Lubina Johanna Palm d'Aelders addressed the French Assembly, advocating for women's rights. She called for women to be admitted to civil and military roles, equal education for girls and boys, adulthood for women to be set at 21, and the promulgation of divorce laws.

1833: Prudence Crandall's School for Young Ladies and Little Misses of Color welcomed its first students. The school faced intense racism and legal challenges as it provided education for young African-American girls.

1868: Ranavalona II succeeded to the throne as the Sovereign of the Kingdom of Madagascar following the death of Queen Rasoherina.

1975: Lila Cockrell, a San Antonio city councilwoman, became the first female mayor of San Antonio, Texas. She served for four two-year terms, making her the first woman mayor of one of the top ten largest metropolitan cities in the United States.

2001: The Act on the Opening up of Marriage was enacted in the Netherlands, making it the first modern country to legalize same-sex marriage.

2005: Rev. Rosemarie Wenner became the first woman to be elected bishop of the United Methodist Church in Germany and the denomination's first female bishop outside the United States.

2007: Carrie Dann, a Western Shoshone elder and spiritual leader, was arrested with 38 other activists for trespassing at the Nevada Test Site during a Nevada Desert Experience event. The protest was part of her cultural, spiritual, and land rights activism.

2012: Leslie Feist, or Feist, won Artist of the Year at the Canadian Juno Awards, recognizing her musical achievements.

2016: Patricia Janet Scotland, Baroness Scotland of Asthal, assumed office as the sixth secretary-general of the Commonwealth of Nations. She was the first woman to be elected to this position.

2020: Reshma Kewalramani became the President and CEO of Vertex Pharmaceuticals, a biotechnology company based in Boston, Massachusetts. She became the first female CEO of a large U.S. biotech company.

April 02

1911: During the United Kingdom's census, suffragette Emily Davison hid in the crypt of the Palace of Westminster to be recorded as a resident of the House of

Commons on census night. This act was a symbolic protest for women's suffrage.

1911: In the wake of the Triangle Shirtwaist Factory fire, a meeting was held to discuss responsibilities and resolutions for future tragedy prevention. One of the speakers was Rose Schneiderman, a worker at the Triangle and a passionate labor union activist. She spoke to the gathered audience, among them Women's Trade Union League members. She said,

> "This is not the first time girls have been burned alive in the city. Every week I must learn of the untimely death of one of my sister workers. Every year thousands of us are maimed. The life of men and women is so cheap and property is so sacred. There are so many of us for one job it matters little if 143 of us are burned to death."

1912: Eleanor Trehawke Davies became the first woman to fly across the English Channel. She accompanied pilot Gustav Hamel as his passenger on this historic flight.

1914: The Irishwomen's Council was established in Dublin as an auxiliary organization of the Irish Volunteers. It comprised members from the Daughters of Ireland nationalist organization and was a paramilitary organization for Irish Republican women.

1917: Jeannette Rankin was sworn into the 65th U.S. Congress, becoming the first woman elected to serve in Congress. Her historic achievement predates the passage of the 19th Amendment to the Constitution, which granted women nationwide the right to vote.

1931: Jackie Mitchell, a 17-year-old baseball player, pitched in an exhibition game against the New York Yankees and struck out famous players Babe Ruth and Lou Gehrig. However, the next day, her contract was voided by the Baseball Commissioner, who claimed that baseball was too strenuous for women. This decision was later overturned in 1992.

2016: Women's rights activists in India were denied entry to the Shani Shingnapur temple despite a court ruling that granted them access. The high court in Mumbai recognized women's fundamental right to enter Hindu temples across Maharashtra and held the government responsible for protecting their rights. The police detained Activist Trupti Desai and 25 other supporters. The actions of the locals and authorities received criticism from women's rights advocates.

April 03

1871: Nanette B. Gardner cast her vote in Detroit, Michigan, after convincing city election officials that she should be allowed to vote as a woman without a husband to represent her. She expressed her astonishment at the commotion caused by such a simple act and questioned the unequal treatment of women compared to men in the voting process.

1913: Suffragette leader Emmeline Pankhurst was sentenced to three years in jail for her activism in the fight for women's right to vote in the United Kingdom.

1949: Seventy female students from nineteen universities gathered at Drexel Institute of Technology in Philadelphia and formed the Society of Women Engineers during a conference. The organization was officially organized in 1950 and has since become a significant advocate for women in engineering and technology, with over 40,000 members worldwide.

2011: Taylor Swift won the Entertainer of the Year award at the 2010 Academy of Country Music Awards, while Miranda Lambert received four awards, including Female Vocalist of the Year.

2014: Marie Louise Coleiro Preca was elected as the President of the Republic of Malta, becoming the second female President in 27 years.

2016: Thousands of people gathered for a pro-choice rally outside the Parliament of Poland in Warsaw in response to the ruling Law and Justice party leader, Jarosław Kaczyński, supporting a call by Polish Catholic bishops for a complete abortion ban. The rally was a demonstration of support for women's reproductive rights.

April 04

1731: Louise Hippolyte arrived in Monaco after her father's death to an enthusiastic reception. She crowned herself the sole regent of Monaco to preserve her own and her son's rights.

1887: Susanna M. Salter was elected as the first female mayor in the United States by the town of Argonia, Kansas.

1896: The first documented women's basketball game between two colleges occurred between Stanford and California.

1913: Suffragette Emily Davison ran onto the course of the Derby race in England, reaching for the reins of Anmer, King George V's horse. She was struck by the horse and sustained fatal injuries, becoming a martyr for the suffragette movement.

1938: Eleanor Roosevelt, the First Lady of the United States, organized the White House Conference on the Inclusion of African American Women and Children in Federal Welfare Programs. This conference addressed African-American women's and children's needs and challenges accessing welfare programs.

1970: *Bangladesh Mahila Parishad* (BMP, Women's Council of Bangladesh), a women's human rights organization, was established as the East Pakistan *Mahila Parishad* by Sufia Kamal. It was renamed after Bangladesh became independent.

2000: P!nk, the American singer, songwriter, actress, and dancer, released her debut studio album *Can't Take Me Home*. The album marked the beginning of her successful music career.

2007: The government of Eritrea issued a proclamation banning "female circumcision" (female genital mutilation; FGM).

2014: Anja Niedringhaus, a Pulitzer Prize-winning photojournalist, was shot and killed by an Afghan wearing a police uniform in Khost, Afghanistan.

April 05

1205: In the wake of her mother Isabella I's death, Maria of Montferrat succeeded her as queen of Jerusalem at thirteen.

1614: Pocahontas, the daughter of Chief Wahunsenacawh of the Powhatan tribe in Virginia, was forced into a child marriage with English colonist John Rolfe at Jamestown. Although she later traveled to England with Rolfe in 1616, she died before returning to Virginia.

1859: Martha Coston was granted a U.S. patent for a pyrotechnic (flare) night signal and code system. Her invention was significant in maritime safety and communication.

1911: Over 350,000 people participated in one of the largest labor demonstrations in U.S. history, marching along New York City's Fifth Avenue to commemorate the 146 Triangle Shirtwaist Factory fire (see: March 25) victims. This tragedy was crucial in advancing workers' rights and safety regulations.

1918: Sālote Mafile'o Pilolevu became the Queen of Tonga as Sālote Tupou III.

1922: The American Birth Control League was founded, which later evolved into Planned Parenthood. This organization has been instrumental in advocating for reproductive rights and providing healthcare services to women.

1947: Hisako Koyama, a Japanese artist, drew the largest sunspot of the 20th century. She created over 10,000 drawings of the

Sun's dark spots throughout her career, contributing to astronomical observations.

1962: The first successful kidney transplant between unrelated recipients (allotransplantation) took place using an anti-rejection regimen that included *azathioprine* and *prednisone*. *Azathioprine* was synthesized by Gertrude Elion and George Herbert Hitchings, leading to advancements in organ transplantation.

1971: The Manifesto of the 343 was published in the French news magazine *Le Nouvel Observateur*. It was a declaration signed by 343 women admitting having had abortions in France, demanding the freedom to have abortions and access to contraception.

1988: Tracy Chapman, an American singer-songwriter, released her self-titled debut album, *Tracy Chapman*. The album received critical acclaim and multiple Grammy Award nominations, establishing Chapman as a talented musician.

2016: Mississippi Governor Phil Bryant approved a new law that allowed religious groups and private businesses to deny services to gay and transgender individuals. The law sparked controversy and debates over LGBTQ+ rights and discrimination.

April 06

640: Lady K'awiil Ajaw began her reign as the queen regnant of the Maya city State of Cobá.

1340: Irene Palaiologina became the Empress regnant of Trebizond after probably poisoning her husband, Emperor Basil. Her rule was turbulent and ended with the arrival of her sister-in-law Anna, Basil's sister, on July 17, 1341, when Anna was acclaimed the Empress of Lazica

1896: The first modern Olympic Games were celebrated in Athens, Greece, after a ban of 1,500 years imposed by Roman Emperor Theodosius I. However, the participation of women was not allowed during these games as Pierre de Coubertin, the French aristocrat who revived the Olympics, believed it to be impractical and uninteresting.

1940: Khertek Amyrbitovna Anchimaa-Toka became the Chairwoman of Little *Khural* of the Tuvan People's Republic and is considered the first non-royal female head of state. The Tuvan People's Republic (the Tannu Tuva People's Republic) was a partially recognized state between 1921 and 1944. It was formally a socialist republic and de facto a Soviet puppet state.

1947: The first Tony Awards honoring American theater achievements were presented in the Grand Ballroom of the Waldorf-Astoria in New York City. The awards were established in honor of Mary Antoinette "Tony" Perry, an American co-founder and director of the American Theatre Wing.

1950: Bracha Zefira gave a farewell performance during her American tour in New York. She was a pioneering Israeli folk artist, songwriter, musicologist, and actress of Yemenite Jewish heritage. She played a pivotal role in merging Yemenite and other Middle Eastern Jewish music in Palestine. This fusion gave birth to a unique "Israeli style" and paved the way for the success of other Yemenite singers in the Israeli music scene. Her extensive repertoire, comprising over 400 songs, featured Yemenite, Bukharan, Persian, Ladino, and North African Jewish folk tunes alongside Arabic and Bedouin melodies.

1968: Barbara Castle was appointed the First Secretary of State in the United Kingdom, becoming the only woman to hold this position. Castle had a long political career, serving in various ministerial roles, including Minister of State for Overseas Development, Minister of State for Transport, and Secretary of State for Employment and Productivity.

2021: Arkansas became the first U.S. state to ban transitional care for transgender minors after the Legislature overrode Governor Asa Hutchinson's veto. **2021:** Võ Thị Ánh Xuân was elected as Vietnam's 15th Vice President by the National Assembly with 93.1% of the vote. She became the sixth consecutive woman to hold the position.

April 07

1141: Empress Matilda became the first female ruler of England, taking the title "Lady of the English."

1805: Sacagawea, a Native American woman, began her role as an interpreter and guide for the Lewis and Clark Expedition, contributing to the exploration of the American West.

1835: Charlotte Saunders Cushman, an American actress, made her first appearance on stage at Boston's Tremont Theatre, beginning a successful acting career that spanned four decades.

1848: New York State passed the Married Women's Property Act of 1848, which granted married women the right to control property they owned before marriage and expanded their legal rights and protections.

1894: Maud Powell, a prominent violinist, performed Dvořák's *Violin Concerto* with the New York Philharmonic under the supervision of the composer himself, Anton Dvořák, at Carnegie Hall.

1926: Violet Gibson, an Irish aristocrat and peace activist, attempted to assassinate Benito Mussolini, the fascist dictator of Italy, in Rome. Her assassination attempt was unsuccessful, and she was institutionalized until her death.

1957: The episode "The Marriage License" of the T.V. show *I Love Lucy* was reported to have been viewed in approximately 10 million homes on the evening it aired.

1978: The final national Women's Liberation Movement (WLM) conference was held in Birmingham, UK, which added a final demand related to ending violence against women and addressed issues of male dominance and aggression.

2009: Commander Josee Kurtz became the first woman to command one of Canada's major warships.

2010: Roza Otunbayeva became the President of Kyrgyzstan, becoming Central Asia's first female head of state.

2012: Joyce Hilda Banda, an educator and women's rights activist, became Malawi's first female President.

2013: Rehtaeh Parsons, a Canadian teenager, died after attempting suicide. Parsons had reported being raped and had experienced ongoing bullying. Her case brought attention to sexual assault, cyberbullying, and the treatment of victims.

2016: Planned Parenthood and the American Civil Liberties Union (ACLU) filed a lawsuit against Indiana, challenging the constitutionality of the state's new abortion law, which prohibited the procedure in cases of genetic abnormalities.

2017: Joan Baez, an influential folk singer and activist, was inducted into the Rock and Roll Hall of Fame for her significant contributions to music.

2021: Vera Bergkamp of the Democrats 66 party was elected Speaker of the House of Representatives in the Netherlands, becoming the first lesbian legislative Speaker in Dutch history.

2022: The Senate confirmed Ketanji Brown Jackson for a United States Supreme Court position. She became the first Black woman to be confirmed as a Supreme Court Justice.

April 08

1915: New York Governor Charles S. Whitman signed the Widowed Mothers Pension Act into law, thanks to the efforts of communal activist and reformer Hannah Bachman Einstein. The act provided financial assistance to widowed mothers, recognizing the challenges they faced as sole providers for their children.

1922: Teresa de Marzo performed all the required maneuvers using a *Caudron G-3* airplane and earned pilot license #76 as the first woman in Brazil.

1931: Amelia Earhart set the altitude record for an *autogiro*, an early type of helicopter, reaching 18,415 feet. She also completed the first transcontinental *autogiro* flight piloted by a woman.

1959: Grace Hopper led a gathering of computer manufacturers, users, and university professionals to explore the development of a programming language that would become known as COBOL. COBOL became one of the most widely used programming languages.

1968: BOAC Flight 712, a British Overseas Airways Corporation aircraft, caught fire shortly after takeoff. As a flight attendant, Barbara Jane Harrison assisted passengers in escaping the fire but died herself. For her courageous actions, she was posthumously awarded the George Cross, the highest award for bravery in the United Kingdom, making her the only woman to receive the George Cross in peacetime.

1993: Ellen Ochoa, an American astronaut, became the first Hispanic woman to go to space. She served on a nine-day mission aboard the Space Shuttle Discovery, during which the crew studied the Earth's ozone layer.

2002: Rebecca Diane McWhorter won the Pulitzer Prize in General Nonfiction for her book *Carry Me Home: Birmingham, Alabama, the Climactic Battle of the Civil Rights Revolution*. The book explores the pivotal events in Birmingham during the Civil Rights Movement and their impact on the larger struggle for racial equality in the United States.

April 09

1870: The *Senatus Academicus* of the University of Edinburgh ruled in favor of the "Edinburgh Seven," a group of women who were the first female medical students at the university. This ruling came after Edith Pechey, who had achieved the highest results in a chemistry exam, was denied a special scholarship and certificates of attendance for the chemistry classes, which were necessary for meeting the medical degree requirements. The university cited their attendance in separate classes as the reason for the denial.

1920: Marie Luhring, an early American female industrial designer and the first woman truck designer, became the first female member of the Society of Automotive Engineers.

1939: Marian Anderson, a renowned African American contralto singer, performed before a crowd of 75,000 people at the Lincoln Memorial in Washington, D.C. This concert was organized after the Daughters of the American Revolution (DAR) denied Anderson a show at Constitution Hall due to racism. Eleanor Roosevelt, then the First Lady of the United States, resigned her membership in the DAR in protest of their decision.

1939: Nora Ney (Sonia Najman), a Polish-Jewish actress, participated in her last production, the movie *Doktor Murek*. She survived the war deep inside the Soviet Union.

2002: The funeral of Queen Elizabeth, the Queen Mother, took place at Westminster Abbey in the United Kingdom. Queen Elizabeth, the Queen Mother, was the mother of Queen Elizabeth II and a beloved figure in British society.

2016: The Fourth African Feminist Forum, which unites activists to advance women's rights in Africa, started in Harare, Zimbabwe, under the theme: "African Feminism: Voice, Power and Soul." More than

170 feminists from across Africa gathered to participate in lectures, skill-sharing activities, debates, and art programming. During each of the three days, a Zimbabwean feminist pioneer was honored. On the first day, Chiwoniso Maraire; on the 2nd, Yvonne Vera; and on the 3rd day, Freedom Nyamubaya.

2018: U.S. Senator Tammy Duckworth of Illinois became the first senator to give birth while serving in office.

April 10

1864: Mary Walker, the first female surgeon in the U.S. Army, was captured by Confederate troops and arrested on charges of being a spy, which occurred right after she had finished assisting a Confederate doctor in performing an amputation.

1877: Rossa Matilda Richter, known as "Zazel," became the first human cannonball act in the British Isles and possibly the world. At 14, she performed this daring feat at the London Royal Aquarium, captivating audiences with her thrilling and innovative act.

1879: American painter Mary Cassatt presented her works at the Impressionist Show in Paris after receiving an invitation from Edgar Degas. Cassatt's participation in the exhibition helped establish her reputation as an influential Impressionist artist.

1946: Women in Japan got to vote for the first time, thanks to the efforts of the League for the Realization of Women's Suffrage, as well as numerous other women's advocacy groups and activists like Hiratsuka Raicho, Yosano Akiko, Kubushiro Ochimi, and others. While drafting the new constitution, two women, Beate Sirota Gordon and economist Eleanor Hadley were enlisted and assigned to write the section on civil rights and women's rights in Japan.

1951: Mufidah Abdul Rahman, one of Egypt's first female lawyers, represented Doria Shafik in court concerning her feminist activism and "storming the parliament." When the case went to trial, many *Bint al-Nil* (a feminist magazine founded by Doria Shafik) supporters attended the courtroom, and the judge adjourned the hearing indefinitely.

1959: Shōda Michiko, a commoner, married Crown Prince Akihito of Japan, becoming a member of the Imperial House of Japan. This marriage marked a significant departure from the tradition of Japanese imperial consorts from aristocratic or noble backgrounds.

1974: Golda Meir, the fourth Prime Minister of Israel, resigned from her position. Meir was a prominent political figure and a key leader during a critical period in Israeli history.

1986: Benazir Bhutto, the daughter of former Prime Minister Zulfikar Ali Bhutto, returned to Pakistan after years of self-imposed exile. She later became the first female Prime Minister of Pakistan.

1997: Gertrude B. Elion, a renowned biochemist and pharmacologist, received the 1997 Lemelson-MIT Lifetime Achievement Award. Elion's groundbreaking research led to the development of several life-saving medications, including treatments for leukemia, gout, organ transplant rejection, and viral infections.

2012: Jane Trumper became the first woman to run across central Australia's Simpson Desert at 51. Her remarkable achievement involved covering a distance of 660 kilometers in just 11 days.

2012: Chinese land rights lawyer Ni Yulan and her husband were sentenced by a Beijing court on charges of fraud and "provoking trouble." Ni Yulan, who was disabled, had been advocating for the rights of homeowners affected by forced evictions in China.

2017: The play *Sweat* by Lynn Nottage was awarded the Pulitzer Prize for Drama. The play explores the effects of industrial decline on a group of factory workers in

Pennsylvania and delves into themes of race, class, and economic struggle.

2019: Katie Bouman and scientists from the Event Horizon Telescope project unveiled the first-ever photograph of a black hole's event horizon.

2021: Irish jockey Rachael Blackmore became the first female winner of the Grand National, one of the world's most prestigious horse racing events.

April 11

1034: Emperor Romanos III (Argyros) of the Byzantine Empire was drowned in his bath on the order of his wife, Zoë Porphyrogenita. Zoë then married her chamberlain, who ascended the throne as Michael IV. This event marked a tumultuous period in Byzantine history known as the Byzantine Macedonian Dynasty.

1871: Nathalie Le Mel and Elisabeth Dmitrieff founded the Women's Union to Defend Paris and Care for the Wounded during the Paris Commune. The union aimed to advocate for women's equality and organized cooperative workshops for women. It attracted a significant membership of around a thousand women.

1881: Sophia B. Packard and Harriet E. Giles, a couple, established the Atlanta Baptist Female Seminary for African-American women, which later became known as Spelman College. In 1924, the institution received its collegiate charter, making it the second-oldest private historically black college or university (HBCU) for women in the United States, focusing on liberal arts education.

1913: The cricket pavilion at the Nevill Ground in England was intentionally destroyed in an arson attack. It was believed to be orchestrated by militant suffragettes as part of a coordinated campaign by the Women's Social and Political Union, a leading suffrage organization in the U.K.

1914: Margaret C. MacDonald, a Canadian military nurse, was appointed Matron-in -Chief of the Canadian Nursing Service. She became the first woman in the British Empire to achieve the rank of Major.

1953: Oveta Culp Hobby became the first United States Secretary of Health, Education, and Welfare, serving in President Dwight D. Eisenhower's cabinet. She was the second woman ever to hold a position in a presidential cabinet, playing a crucial role in shaping public health and education policies.

2000: Historian Deborah Lipstadt was vindicated in a libel suit brought against her by Holocaust denier David Irving. The court ruled in favor of Lipstadt, affirming the historical reality of the Holocaust and discrediting Irving's denialist claims.

2011: The ban on the *burqa* and *niqab*, face-covering garments worn by some Muslim women, officially came into effect in France. The controversial ban aimed to promote secularism and social cohesion but sparked debates regarding religious freedom and women's rights.

2013: In Bougainville, Papua New Guinea, two women were beheaded, and another woman and her two daughters faced the same fate. All women were accused of sorcery.

April 12

1879: Mary Baker Eddy established the Church of Christ, Scientist in Boston, Massachusetts. The church is known for its emphasis on spiritual healing and the teachings of Christian Science.

1896: Stamasia Portrisi became the first woman to win a marathon. She completed the marathon in Athens in 5 hours and 30 minutes.

1898: Marie Curie attended a French Academy of Sciences meeting where her teacher announced her discovery of more radioactive substances than uranium. Curie proposed that radioactivity was an atomic property independent of the physical or chemical state, which laid the foundation for her groundbreaking research in radioactivity.

1917: The Election Law Amendment Act was passed in Ontario, Canada, granting women the right to vote. Ontario became the fifth province in Canada to enfranchise women, following more than 50 years of activism by Canadian suffragists.

1976: Anne Rice's debut book *Interview with a Vampire* was published. The novel, exploring the life of a vampire named Louis de Pointe du Lac, gained significant popularity and began Rice's successful career as a gothic fiction author.

2012: BBC's journalist Natalia Antelava uncovered evidence of forced sterilization, often without their knowledge, of Uzbekistan's women as part of the government's population control. Interviews with survivors and medical professionals revealed the fear and secrecy surrounding this issue. During a meeting with Vladimir Putin in Moscow, the Uzbek president Islam Karimov said: "We are doing everything in our hands to make sure that the population growth rate [in Uzbekistan] does not exceed 1.2–1.3."

2015: Hillary Clinton announced her candidacy for the Democratic nomination for the U.S. President for the second time. Clinton previously ran for president in 2008 and served as the Secretary of State from 2009 to 2013.

2017: Marin Minamiya, a 20-year-old Japanese university student, was the youngest to complete the Explorers Grand Slam Challenge. The challenge involves ascending the highest peaks on each of the seven continents and reaching the North and South Poles.

2019: The comedy film *Little* was released, featuring Marsai Martin in the leading role and as an executive producer. At 13, Martin became the youngest person ever to be an executive producer for a major Hollywood film.

2022: Oklahoma Governor Kevin Stitt signed a law criminalizing most abortions in the state, with exceptions for cases where the mother's health was at risk. The law imposed severe penalties, including fines and imprisonment, on anyone performing an abortion, while the woman undergoing the procedure would not be penalized.

2022: Indonesia's Parliament passed a bill outlawing sexual abuse and forced marriage, strengthening protections for victims and survivors of such offenses.

2022: Alyssa Nakken, an assistant coach for the San Francisco Giants, became the first woman to coach on the field during a Major League Baseball regular season game. She made history during the team's matchup against the San Diego Padres, breaking barriers in professional baseball coaching.

April 13

1613: Pocahontas, an Algonquian princess, was captured by Samuel Argall in Passapatanzy, Virginia. The motive behind her capture was to use her as a bargaining chip to secure the release of English prisoners held by her father, Chief Powhatan. She was later taken to Henricus as a hostage.

1881: Rere-ao Te-hau-roa-ari'i was crowned Queen of Raiatea and Tahaa. She was the daughter of King Tahitoe of Raiatea and his second wife, Metua'aro. Her reign was marked by her efforts to minimize the influence of the French.

1920: President Woodrow Wilson appointed Helen Hamilton Gardener to the U.S. Civil Service Commission, making her the highest-ranking federal position held by a woman at that time. She served in this role until her death five years later.

1925: Women in the Dominion of Newfoundland obtained the right to vote. The bill granting suffrage to women over 25 was unanimously passed in the House of Assembly on March 9, 1925, and became law on April 13.

1933: Ruth Bryan Owen became the first woman to represent the United States as a foreign minister when appointed an envoy to Denmark.

1981: Elizabeth Becker Henley won the Pulitzer Prize for Drama for her play *Crimes of the Heart*. The play, set in Mississippi, explores the lives of three sisters and their relationships.

1985: During a neo-Nazi rally of the Nordic Reich Party, Danuta Danielsson, a Swedish woman of Polish-Jewish heritage whose mother survived the horrors of Shoah (Holocaust), hit one of them on the head with her handbag in Växjö, Sweden. The fascists were subsequently chased out of town. A photo taken of that moment became known as *The Woman with the Handbag* (*Kvinnan med Handvaskan*). The man who was hit with the bag was later convicted for the torture and murder of a Jewish gay person.

2018: Portugal's Parliament passed a law that simplified the process for individuals to change their legal gender. Portuguese citizens aged 16 and above can now modify their gender and name on official documents without requiring a medical report.

2022: The Kentucky legislature enacted a bill similar to Mississippi's legislation after overriding Governor Andy Beshear's veto. This bill prohibited abortions after 15 weeks of gestation and introduced restrictions on minors' access to the procedure.

April 14

972: Theophanu and Otto II were married, and she became the Queen consort of Germany. Following the death of her father-in-law, she assumed the role of Empress of the Holy Roman Empire on May 7, 973.

1714: Queen Anne of Great Britain performed the ritual of "touching" for the last time. This ritual was believed to cure the "King's evil," a form of mycobacterial *cervical lymphadenitis* known as scrofula.

1858: Harriet Tubman met abolitionist John Brown at a Constitutional Convention in Chatham, Ontario. Tubman played a significant role in the Underground Railroad, aiding enslaved individuals to escape to freedom.

1910: Elinor McGrath graduated from the Chicago Veterinary College, becoming the first female veterinarian in the United States.

1973: The West Coast Lesbian Feminist Conference took place, with about 1300 attending. The Conference became famous for the attacks on a transwoman, Beth Elliot, and the general anti-trans rhetoric during the keynote speech by Robin Morgan, who said, "I charge him as an opportunist, an infiltrator, and a destroyer—with the mentality of a rapist." The trope of "transsexual rapists" was often used to repeat violent attacks on transwomen. Among the most active anti-trans persons attending was the group the Gutter Dykes and Bev Von Dohre (BevJo).

2006: Kuwaiti women voted for the first time in their country's history. Two women, Jenan Boushehri and Khalida Khader, were among the candidates running for seats in the Salmiya district.

2018: Beyoncé became the first Black woman to headline the Coachella Music Festival, delivering a highly acclaimed performance celebrating Black culture and history.

April 15

42 BCE: Roman leaders taxed the property of 1,400 wealthy Roman women to fund a civil war. Hortensia, recognizing the injustice of taxation without representation, delivered a notable speech that led to a retreat by the leaders under the pressure of women's collective force.

1873: The Supreme Court ruling in *Bradwell v. State of Illinois* determined that Myra Bradwell's rights had not been violated when Illinois denied her the right to practice law because she was married.

1919: Julia O'Connor, an American labor leader, called for a strike by telephone operators across New England, demanding increased pay and recognition of collective bargaining rights. After five days, the Postmaster General agreed to negotiate an agreement between the union and the telephone company.

1919: British activist Eglantyne Jebb was arrested in London for distributing pamphlets to raise awareness and funds for German and Austrian children suffering from food shortages caused by the German blockade. Despite being found guilty of unlawful protest, Jebb's powerful speech during the trial impressed the prosecuting counsel, who offered to pay her fine. This experience inspired Jebb and her sister Dorothy Buxton to establish the Save the Children fund the following year.

1998: The Jewish Orthodox Feminist Alliance (JOFA), an organization promoting women's issues within the framework of *Halakha* (Jewish law), was incorporated. Blu Greenberg served as its first president.

2011: Four indigenous Purépecha women from Cherán in Mexico took illegal loggers hostage and initiated a rebellion against cartels, increasing autonomy for their community and successfully repelling them.

2016: Jeannie M. Leavitt became the first woman to take command of the 57th Wing at Nellis Air Force Base in the United States and was promoted to brigadier general.

2017: Emma Morano, the last person born before 1900, passed away at 117 years and 137 days.

2019: Aretha Franklin, the renowned singer, posthumously received the Pulitzer Prize Special Citation, making her the first individual woman to win this honor since 1930.

April 16

1912: Harriet Quimby became the first woman to fly an airplane across the English Channel.

1916: *Where Are My Children?*, a silent drama film directed by Lois Weber, premiered. The film explored the topic of illegal abortions and the societal hypocrisy surrounding the issue.

1943: Odette Sansom, a British spy operating in France during World War II, was captured by the Nazis. To protect the actual circuit leader, Peter Churchill, Sansom provided false information about her role, claiming to be the circuit leader herself.

2003: Makobo Modjadji VI was crowned the Rain Queen at age 25, making her the youngest queen in the history of the Balobedu tribe in South Africa. She was the sixth in a line of female rulers.

2014: The discovery of a protein called Juno, which plays a crucial role in mammalian fertilization, was published in the scientific journal *Nature*. Enrica Bianchi and Gavin J. Wright were credited with this discovery.

2022: Chinese astronauts Wang Yaping, Ye Guangfu, and Zhai Zhigang landed in Inner Mongolia after spending 183 days in space aboard the Shenzhou 13 spacecraft. Wang Yaping became the first Chinese woman to perform a spacewalk during the mission.

April 17

699: Lady Six Sky (Lady Wac Chanil Ahau or Wak Chanil Ajaw), a Maya queen of Naranjo, celebrated a military success as represented on a Stela 24, where she stands on a captive from the small polity of K'inichil Kab.

1732: Laura Maria Caterina Bassi Veratti publicly defended forty-nine theses before professors of the University of Bologna, for which she was awarded a doctoral degree on May 12 as the second woman in the world to obtain a doctoral degree (after Elena Cornaro Piscopia in 1678). A month later, she was appointed by the university as its first female teacher, albeit with the restriction that she was not allowed to teach all-male classes.

1878: In a slavery lawsuit, Henrietta Wood, a formerly enslaved person, sued Zebulon Ward, the man who had kidnapped and enslaved her 25 years earlier. The jury, consisting of twelve white men in Ohio, found in favor of Wood and awarded her $2,500 in damages, recognizing the injustice she had suffered.

1893: Alpha Xi Delta, a women's fraternity, was founded by ten young women at Lombard College in Galesburg, Illinois.

1912: Julia Lathrop became the first woman to head a U.S. federal government agency. President William Howard Taft appointed her to lead the United States Children's Bureau.

1954: Ray Alexander, Frances Baard, and Florence Matomela, trade unionists in South Africa, established The Federation of South African Women (FEDSAW) as a multi-racial women's organization and lobbying group to address women's issues directly.

1964: Jerrie Mock, an American aviator, became the first woman to fly solo around the world. At age 38, she flew a single-engine Cessna 180 named *Spirit of Columbus* on a 23,000-mile journey that took 29 days, starting and ending in Columbus, Ohio.

1969: Bernadette Devlin, a Northern Irish socialist and republican, became the youngest member of the British Parliament, taking her seat six days before her 22nd birthday.

1983: Alice Walker won the Pulitzer Prize for Fiction for her novel *The Color Purple*, which explores the lives of African American women in the early 20th century and addresses issues of race, gender, and identity.

April 18

1908: Jane Inglis Clark, her daughter Mabel, and Lucy Smith founded the Scottish Mountaineering Club, a climbing club for women in Scotland. The club aimed to bring together women passionate about mountain climbing and promote mountaineering in Scotland in summer and winter.

1925: The first Woman's World's Fair in the United States was officially opened in Chicago, Illinois, by the First Lady, Mrs. Calvin Coolidge—the fair showcased women's progress in seventy different industries and ran for over a week.

1954: After an inspiring visit by Margaret Singer, Shidzue Katō, a feminist and one of the first women elected to the Diet of Japan, co-founded the Family Planning Federation of Japan, which became affiliated with the International Planned Parenthood Federation. Several experts in medicine, hygiene, and psychology were part of the team working on the project, among them Haruo Mizuno.

1956: Maria Desylla-Kapodistria was elected mayor of Corfu, becoming the first female mayor in Greece.

1987: Annette Greenfield Strauss became the first elected female mayor of Dallas, Texas, making history in the city.

1995: Tina Rosenberg won the Pulitzer Prize for General Nonfiction for her book *The Haunted Land: Facing Europe's Ghosts After Communism.* The book explores the aftermath of communism in Europe and its impact on societies and individuals.

2019: Northern Irish journalist Lyra McKee was shot and killed by dissident republicans in the Creggan estate in Derry.

April 19

511: Lady of Tikal (also known as Woman of Tikal) began her rule of the Mayan city of Tikal (today Guatemala) at six.

797: Empress Irene of the Byzantine Empire organized a conspiracy against her son, Emperor Constantine VI, and declared herself *basileus*, a monarch.

1042: Emperor Michael V Kalaphates banished his adoptive mother, Zoë Porphyrogenita, accusing her of plotting to poison him, leading to a popular revolt, and the following day, Zoë and her sister Theodora were proclaimed co-empresses during a gathering at Hagia Sophia. Michael V was later captured, blinded, and castrated.

1539: After ten years of imprisonment, Katarzyna Weiglowa (Zelazowska) was burnt at the stake at 80 in Kraków, Poland. She converted from Roman Catholicism to either Judaism or Judaizing nontrinitarianism. Weiglowa refused to reject the "mistakes of the Jewish faith," embraced the unity of God, and denied the belief in the Holy Trinity.

1850: The first Ohio Women's Rights Convention occurred in Salem, Ohio. This convention was organized statewide and had women officers, with men not permitted to vote, sit on the platform, or speak during the convention.

1944: Hilda Thelander, an American pediatrician with expertise in contagious diseases, became the first physician in the U.S. Navy Medical Corps Reserve.

1967: Kathrine Switzer officially became the first woman to run the Boston Marathon. Before her participation, the marathon was considered a men-only event.

1977: Fifteen women members of the U.S. House of Representatives formed the Congressional Caucus for Women's Issues, aiming to address and advocate for women's rights and concerns.

1982: The United States announced that Sally K. Ride would become the first woman astronaut. Ride later became the first American woman to travel to space.

1994: Félicité Niyitegeka, the director of the Centre Saint-Pierre, a Catholic charity center in western Rwanda, helped hide and guide dozens of Tutsi refugees to the border with Zaire (now the Democratic Republic of Congo). She was murdered two days later, along with the Tutsis she had sheltered during the Rwandan genocide.

April 20

1240: Raziyyat-Ud-Dunya Wa Ud-Din (Razia Sultana), who was the first female Muslim ruler of the Indian subcontinent and the only Muslim woman to rule in Delhi, was overthrown after three and a half years of rule.

1740: The British were compelled to sign a treaty with the Jamaican Maroons, a community of formerly enslaved Africans who had gained their freedom under the leadership of Nanny of the Maroons, also known as Queen Nanny or Granny Nanny. Nanny was revered for her leadership and declared Jamaica's national hero in 1975.

1868: A group of women dined at Delmonico's restaurant in New York. It was the first deliberate instance of women eating in public without the company of men. This gathering was organized after journalist Jane Cunningham Croly was denied access to a dinner honoring Charles Dickens. Croly later established Sorosis, the first

American women's club to bring together women of intellect, culture, and humanity.

1919: Rose Finkelstein led a successful strike of 8,000 young women who worked as telephone operators at the New England Telephone and Telegraph Company. Known as the Boston Telephone Strike, the workers secured higher wages through collective action.

1933: Amelia Earhart, accompanied by First Lady Eleanor Roosevelt and a group of women reporters, took a nighttime airplane flight over Washington, D.C., and Baltimore during their visit to the White House—this flight aimed to promote women's achievements in aviation.

1939: Billie Holiday recorded *Strange Fruit*, a powerful protest song against the horrors of lynching, written by Abel Meeropol under the pen name Lewis Allan. The song became an iconic anthem of the civil rights movement.

2010: Fifty feminist experts and leaders gathered in Puerta Vallarta, Mexico, for a meeting organized by the Women's Initiative for Gender Justice and the Nobel Women's Initiative.

2012: Zanele Muholi, a photographer known for documenting Black lesbian life in South Africa, was robbed, resulting in the loss of over twenty external hard drives containing five years' worth of photos and videos, including documentation of the funerals of Black South African lesbians who were victims of hate crimes.

2015: Elizabeth Anne Fenn won the Pulitzer Prize for History for her book *Encounters at the Heart of the World: A History of the Mandan People*. Elizabeth Kolbert won the Pulitzer Prize for General Nonfiction for her book *The Sixth Extinction: An Unnatural History*.

April 21

1042: Zoë Porphyrogenita and her sister Theodora were crowned Byzantine co-Empresses after a popular uprising ousted Michael V. Zoë officially held the senior empress title, with her throne positioned slightly ahead of Theodora's during public events. However, Theodora was the primary driving force in their joint administration. Together, the sisters governed the empire, focusing on ending the sale of public offices and ensuring the fair administration of justice.

1702: Maria Margaretha Kirch, a German astronomer, discovered a comet known as the Comet of 1702 (C/1702 H1).

1944: Women in France gained the right to vote.

1969: Germaine Greer began writing her influential book *The Female Eunuch*. The book, published in 1970, became an international bestseller and a significant work within the feminist movement, exploring topics such as gender, sexuality, and women's liberation.

1972: Sweden became the first country to pass a law recognizing legal gender change. The amendment to civil registration rules allowed individuals who had undergone or applied for gender affirming surgery to update their birth registrations.

1977: The musical *Annie*, based on the popular newspaper comic strip *Little Orphan Annie*, premiered on Broadway. The musical achieved great success and has become a beloved and enduring production.

1978: Krystyna Chojnowska-Liskiewicz, a Polish naval engineer and sailor, completed her solo circumnavigation of the world, covering 31,166 nautical miles (57,719 km) in 401 days. She became the first woman to accomplish this feat.

2015: Mona Eltahawy's first book, *Headscarves and Hymens: Why the Middle East Needs a Sexual Revolution*, was published in the United States as a continuation of an article on the misogyny in Arab society entitled "Why Do They Hate Us?" which she wrote for *Foreign Policy* in 2012.

2018: Asma Al Thani, a mountaineer from Qatar, became the first Qatari to ski to the North Pole. She achieved this as part of an all-women Euro-Arabian expedition led by Felicity Aston.

April 22

1935: The horror film *Bride of Frankenstein* premiered in Los Angeles, starring Elsa Lanchester. It was a sequel to the original *Frankenstein* film and has since become a classic in the horror genre.

1969: Bernadette Devlin, the youngest woman ever to be elected to Westminster at the age of 21, delivered a controversial maiden speech in the House of Commons addressing the situation in Northern Ireland. Devlin was known for her activism and outspokenness on civil rights and Irish republicanism.

1976: Barbara Walters, a renowned reporter and co-host of the Today Show on NBC, accepted a contract to become the world's highest-paid newscaster and the first woman to anchor an evening news program for a major television network. She signed a five-year contract with a salary of $1,000,000 per year to serve as co-anchor, alongside Harry Reasoner, of the ABC Evening News, beginning in September.

1986: The New York Task Force on Women in the Courts released its report on gender equality. The two-year study revealed pervasive bias against women within the New York State court system, leading to unequal treatment and denial of equal justice for women.

1996: The Women's National Basketball Association (WNBA) was founded with an initial roster of eight teams. The Charlotte Sting, Cleveland Rockers, Houston Comets, and New York Liberty represented the Eastern Conference. At the same time, the Los Angeles Sparks, Phoenix Mercury, Sacramento Monarchs, and Utah Starzz formed the Western Conference.

April 23

1858: In a letter published in the *Liberator* on that day, Frances Ellen Watkins Harper described how she refused to give up her seat or ride in the city car in Philadelphia after a demand by the conductor. When she was to leave, the conductor refused to take her money, so she threw it on the floor and left when she intended to do so. She wrote,

> "all is not dark in Pennsylvania; but the shadow of slavery, oh how drearily it hangs!"

1872: Charlotte E. Ray became the first female African-American lawyer in the United States. She was admitted to the District of Columbia Bar and became an advocate for women's rights and civil rights.

1883: 245 women employed in a linen factory in Żyrardów started a five-day strike – the first in the Congress Kingdom of Poland. They protested the inhumane working conditions (14-hour workdays), meager pay, bad treatment from the male management, and child labor. Soon, more workers joined, and Russian soldiers brutally pacified the strike – three people were killed. Yet, their strike was successful.

2003: Leymah Roberta Gbowee, as a leader of the Women of Liberia Mass Action for Peace movement, spoke to Liberia's president and government officials, demanding an end to the war and advocating for peace. Her powerful speech reflected the women's exhaustion and determination to pursue a better future for their children.

2007: Barbara Hillary, a nurse and cancer survivor, became one of the oldest people, at the age of 75, to reach the North

Pole. She also made history as the first Black woman to achieve this feat. In 2011, at 79, she reached the South Pole, becoming the first African-American woman on record to do so and the first Black woman to reach both poles.

2015: Loretta Lynch was confirmed by the United States Senate as the Attorney General of the United States, making her the first African-American woman to hold this position. Lynch played a significant role in the U.S. justice system and advocated for civil rights and equal justice under the law.

2016: Leni Robredo, a human rights activist and lawyer, received endorsements from various groups as a candidate for vice president of the Philippines. Her campaign promoted human rights, labor rights, and social justice.

2021: SpaceX successfully launched astronauts K. Megan McArthur, Shane Kimbrough, Akihiko Hoshide, and Thomas Pesquet onboard a *Crew Dragon* spacecraft into low Earth orbit.

2022: In the Northern Ireland Assembly election, Hannah Kenney, a candidate from People Before Profit, was attacked by three men in east Belfast in what is considered a sectarian hate crime.

April 24

1885: Annie Oakley, a skilled American sharpshooter, was recruited by Nate Salsbury to join Buffalo Bill's Wild West show. She became one of the show's most famous and talented performers, showcasing her marksmanship skills and captivating audiences with her precision and showmanship.

1890: Sixty-three women's clubs nationwide officially established the General Federation of Women's Clubs by ratifying its Constitution. This organization aimed to unite women's clubs to promote education, social reform, and community service.

1966: Alma Thomas, an American artist, had her first retrospective exhibition at the Gallery of Art at Howard University. Curated by art historian James A. Porter, the exhibition showcased 34 of Thomas's works from 1959 to 1966, including her series of nature-inspired abstract paintings known as the Earth Paintings. One of her notable works, *Resurrection*, was later acquired for the White House collection in 2014.

1993: A day before The March on Washington for Lesbian, Gay, and Bi Equal Rights and Liberation, the first Dyke March took place, organized by the Lesbian Avengers, with over 20,000 women participating. During the March, a leaflet with a manifesto was handed out. It started with words,

> "Calling all lesbians! Wake up! It's time to get out of the beds, out of the bars, and into the streets. It's time to seize the power of dyke love, dyke vision, dyke anger, dyke intelligence, dyke strategy. It's time to organize and incite. It's time to get together and fight."

It also stated the "Top 10 Avenger Qualities" – compassion, leadership, no big ego, informed, fearlessness, righteous anger, fighting spirit, pro-sex, good dancer, and as the first one – access to resources (xerox machines).

2013: The 8-storey Rana Plaza in Dhaka, Bangladesh, collapsed, killing over 1,100 mainly female garment workers. The structure contained a shopping center on its lower levels, while five garment factories occupied the third through eighth floors. There were signs of cracks in the building's walls, but the poor workers were expected to come back or lose employment.

2015: Caitlyn Jenner, a former American Olympic Games champion, publicly announced her identity as a transgender woman.

2018: A statue of suffragist Millicent Fawcett was erected in Parliament Square, London, England. Fawcett was a leading figure in the women's suffrage movement in the United Kingdom and played a crucial role in securing women's right to vote.

2018: 22-year-old Eyvi Ágreda was severely injured in a fire attacked by a stalker (who knew her from work) on a bus and died more than a month later. Ten more people were injured in the attack. This incident gained significant media coverage, highlighting femicide and violence against women in Peru.

2022: Marine Le Pen, the leader of France's National Rally party, lost the presidential election to Emmanuel Macron. Le Pen's defeat marked a critical moment in French politics, as Macron was reelected for a second term as the President of France.

April 25

1228: Isabella II, Holy Roman Empress, and Frederick II's wife, died at 16 in Andria shortly after giving birth to her second child, Conrad IV. Her death marked an end to her short-lived reign as Empress.

1295: Queen María de Molina became Castile's regent following King Sancho IV's death. Her son, Ferdinand IV, ascended to the throne of Castile and León at 9, with Queen María acting as regent to govern on his behalf.

1942: Princess Elizabeth, who would later become Queen Elizabeth II of the United Kingdom, enlisted for war service during World War II. Like many other individuals during the war, she contributed to the war effort in various roles.

1965: A group of non-heteronormative people were denied service at Dewey's coffee shop in Philadelphia. Some were described as "feminine men," "masculine women," "persons wearing non-conformist clothing," or "homosexuals." Police made arrests, which triggered demonstrations and sit-ins. It was probably the first event of that kind in the U.S.

1978: St. Paul, Minnesota, repealed its gay rights ordinance, becoming the second U.S. city after Anita Bryant's successful anti-gay campaign in Miami-Dade County, Florida, in 1977. The ordinance's repeal was a setback for LGBTQ+ rights at the time.

1993: The March on Washington for Lesbian, Gay, and Bi Equal Rights and Liberation took place in Washington, D.C. An estimated 1,000,000 people attended, making it one of America's largest protests. Among the speakers and performers at the rally following the March were Indigo Girls, Judith Light, Melissa Etheridge, Nancy Pelosi, Madonna, Martina Navratilova, Eartha Kitt, Lani Ka'ahumanu, Urvashi Vaid, and Martha Wash.

2004: The March for Women's Lives occurred in Washington, D.C., drawing between 500,000 and 800,000 protesters, primarily advocating for reproductive rights and protesting the Partial-Birth Abortion Ban Act of 2003 and other abortion restrictions.

2012: Agnes M. Sigurðardóttir became the first woman appointed as the Bishop of Iceland, breaking new ground in the country's religious leadership.

2013: After the previous day's disaster in Bangladeshi factories, thousands demonstrate on the streets, and solidarity strikes are organized nationwide. Protesters were demanding the arrest of people responsible for the tragedy.

2017: Peggy Whitson, commander of the International Space Station (ISS), broke the record for the most total days spent in space by any NASA astronaut, surpassing 534 days.

2017: Despite its conflicts with women's rights, Saudi Arabia was elected as one of the twelve newly elected countries to the United Nations Commission on the Status of Women. This decision sparked discussions and debates regarding Saudi Arabia's stance on women's rights and its role within the commission.

2019: A federal district court in Washington State issued a preliminary injunction against the enforcement of an initiative by the Donald Trump administration known as the "gag order." The initiative aimed to restrict doctor-patient communications about abortion in family planning clinics receiving U.S. taxpayer funding.

2021: Chinese filmmaker Chloé Zhao became the first person of color to win the Academy Award for Best Director for her film *Nomadland*. South Korean actress Youn Yuh-Jung also became the first Korean to win in any acting category. She won the Best Supporting Actress award for her role in *Minari*.

April 26

1777: Sybil Ludington, at 16, rode 40 miles (64 km) through the night to warn American colonial forces of the approaching British soldiers. Her spirited ride, similar to that of Paul Revere, helped rally local militia to defend against the British during the American Revolutionary War.

1909: California became the second U.S. state to pass a eugenics law, allowing the state to sterilize convicted criminals and those deemed "feeble-minded" forcibly. The law permitted the castration of men and removal of women's ovaries, resulting in permanent sterilization and numerous health issues. The law was repealed in 1979, but California continued sterilizing some women in prison without their consent.

1912: Irish pilot Vivian Hewitt accomplished an airplane crossing of the Irish Sea, flying from Holyhead to Phoenix Park in Dublin.

1925: Edna Ferber, an American novelist, short story writer, and playwright, won the Pulitzer Prize for her book *So Big*. The novel explores the life of a widowed mother and her son, highlighting themes of love, sacrifice, and the pursuit of dreams.

2011: Nigerian author Chika Unigwe published her second novel, *On Black Sisters Street* (original title: *Fata Morgana*). The book delves into the lives of African women working in the red-light district of Antwerp, Belgium, and won the 2012 Nigeria Prize for Literature.

2017: The results of the WOMAN (World Maternal Antifibrinolytic) international study were published in *The Lancet* medical journal. The study revealed that tranexamic acid, a cost-effective and widely available drug, could save thousands of women dying from excessive bleeding during childbirth. Tranexamic acid has already been used in various contexts to control blood loss and can potentially significantly prevent maternal mortality. The study emphasized the importance of accessible and affordable interventions in reducing maternal deaths.

April 27

1903: Maggie L. Walker was named the President of Richmond's St Luke Bank and Trust Company, becoming the first African American woman to head a bank. She was a prominent businesswoman and community leader, advocating for African Americans' economic empowerment and social progress.

1992: Betty Boothroyd, a British Labour Member of Parliament for West Bromwich, was elected as the first and only female Speaker of the British House of Commons.

2005: The U.S. Senate passed a resolution recognizing the significance of African-American women in the scientific community. It honored five trailblazing Black women who contributed significantly to various scientific fields. These women included Ruth Ella Moore, Roger Arliner Young, Euphemia Lofton Haynes, Shirley Ann Jackson, and Mae Jemison.

2017: A congress of female Islamic clerics held in Cirebon, Indonesia, issued multiple fatwas (Islamic legal opinions), including one expressing opposition to child marriage. The Congress aimed to address women's rights and promote progressive interpretations of Islamic teachings.

2019: The official music video for Taylor Swift's song *Me!* premiered and broke Vevo's record for the biggest debut ever, garnering at least 56.9 million views within 24 hours. The colorful and whimsical video featured Swift and Brendon Urie and became a popular hit among her fans.

1993: The first Take Our Daughters to Work Day occurred, sponsored by the Ms. Foundation. The event aimed to introduce young girls to various career opportunities and inspire them to pursue their dreams.

2009: Sojourner Truth, a prominent African-American abolitionist, and women's rights activist, was honored by the National Congress of Black Women. After nearly a decade of effort, she became the first African-American woman to have a memorial bust in the U.S. Capitol, recognizing her significant contributions to American history and social justice.

April 28

1914: British suffragettes Hilda Burkitt and Florence Tunks set fire to the Felixstowe Bath Hotel in Suffolk, England, as part of their activism during the Votes For Women Campaign, which was empty at the time of the incident. However, their actions led to their arrest and subsequent imprisonment.

1915: The Women at the Hague International Congress of Women conference began in The Hague, Netherlands, with over 1,100 delegates. It aimed to promote peace and establish an International Committee of Women for Permanent Peace (ICWPP) with Jane Addams as its President. This conference played a significant role in forming the Women's International League for Peace and Freedom (WILPF).

1931: The program for women athletes was approved for the 1932 Olympics track and field events, allowing women to participate in a broader range of sports in the Olympic Games.

1949: Former First Lady of the Philippines, Aurora Quezon, was assassinated at 61 while en route to dedicate a hospital in memory of her late husband. Her daughter and ten other individuals were also killed in the attack.

April 29

1429: Joan of Arc entered Orléans in triumph, which was a significant turning point in the siege of Orléans during the Hundred Years' War. Joan toured the streets of Orléans to boost morale, distributed food to the people, and ensured the garrison received their salaries. She also sent messengers to the English bastions, demanding their departure, but the English commanders responded with jeers and threats.

1945: Marguerite Higgins, an American journalist, witnessed the opening of the German death camps towards the end of World War II. Her documentation of the atrocities she witnessed earned her a Pulitzer Prize in journalism in 1951.

1967: Aretha Franklin released her iconic single *Respect*, which became one of her signature songs and a symbol of the civil rights and feminist movements.

1976: Ana González de Recabarren's two sons, daughter-in-law, and husband were arrested and "disappeared" at the hands of Chile's secret police, the DINA, during the regime of Augusto Pinochet. This experience led her to become a prominent human rights activist, advocating for the families of the *Desaparecidos* (disappeared) in Chile.

2011: The Tribeca Film Festival in New York awarded the Best Narrative Feature prize to the Swedish film *She Monkeys*, directed by Lisa Aschan. The festival also honored the Israeli movie *Bombay Beach*, directed by Alma Har'el, with the Best Documentary prize.

April 30

1850: The Female Medical Education Society was incorporated to establish a medical school in Boston, including a teaching hospital, to provide women's education in midwifery and nursing. This initiative led to the establishment of the New England Female Medical College in 1852.

1937: The Commonwealth of the Philippines held a referendum allowing Filipino women to vote on whether they should be granted the right to suffrage. The referendum passed, giving women the right to vote in the country.

1974: Yvonne Madelaine Brill, a Canadian-American engineer, had her US-807657A patent granted for the dual thrust level monopropellant spacecraft propulsion system. The invention, also called the Electrothermal Hydrazine Thruster (EHT/Resistojet), is a fuel-efficient rocket thruster used in today's satellites.

1977: Azucena Villaflor and thirteen other mothers, including María Adela Gard de Antokoletz, gathered at the Plaza de Mayo in Buenos Aires, Argentina, initiating the regular weekly gatherings called the Mothers of the Plaza de Mayo. These gatherings were a form of protest demanding information about their "disappeared" relatives during the military dictatorship in Argentina.

1977: Synchronized marches under the banner of Take Back the Night occurred in various cities in West Germany, protesting against rape and violence against women—the demonstrations aimed to raise awareness and advocate for women's safety and rights.

2019: The state of Maine in the United States passed a bill called An Act to Ban Native American Mascots in All Public Schools. The bill, introduced by Maulian Dana, the Penobscot Nation Tribal Ambassador, aimed to prohibit Native American mascots in public schools to promote respect and eliminate stereotypes.

MAY

May 01

1505: Lady Margaret Beaufort, a prominent figure in English history, granted a charter for Christ's College in Cambridge, England, providing financial support for the college.

1846: Ida Pfeiffer, an Austrian explorer, travel writer, and ethnographer, embarked on a trip around the world, documenting her experiences and observations.

1855: Lucy Stone and Henry Browne Blackwell's marriage gained attention when Stone insisted on keeping her birth name, and the couple removed the word "obey" from their marriage vows. Their actions challenged traditional gender roles and advocated for equality in marriage.

1890: Virginia Bolten, an organizer in Argentina, led a group of thousands of workers in the first May Day demonstrations. Carrying the red flag, they emphasized the ideals of universal fraternity and the directives of the International Workers Committee of Paris.

1899: The first issue of women's magazine *al-ʿAila* (*The Family*) was published in Cairo, Egypt. It was created by Esther Moyal (al-Azharī), a Sephardic-Jewish journalist and women's rights activist born in Beirut, Lebanon. The magazine became a weekly newspaper, earning praise for its diverse content covering contemporary domestic issues, women's health, literature, and global news. Within *The Family*'s pages, she passionately advocated for women's rights, outlining her three core feminist principles: the inherent morality, free will, and active conscience of women; gender equality; and the unique qualities women possess, excelling in emotional refinement and perspective precision when provided with educational opportunities.

1921: The *Sekirankai* (Japanese: Red Wave Society), a Japanese socialist women's organization founded just a month before by members of an anarchist group, took part in the May Day celebrations by distributing copies of the *Fujin ni Gekisu* (*Manifesto to Women*) drafted by Yamakawa Kikue.

1925: María Cano, on Colombia's Labor Day, was named the "Labor flower of Medellín," an honorary title typically given to charity workers. Cano used the platform to engage in political activism and became a symbol for rebellious women.

1937: Jackie Ormes, the first African-American woman cartoonist, published her first comic strip, *Torchy Brown in Dixie to Harlem*, in the *Pittsburgh Courier*.

1950: Gwendolyn Brooks became the first African-American woman to win the Pulitzer Prize for Poetry and was appointed the Library of Congress's Consultant in Poetry (later called Poet Laureate).

1963: Gloria Steinem's exposé on the Playboy Club, titled "The Undercover Bunny," was published in *Show Magazine*, shedding light on the experiences of women working in the club.

1970: The Second Congress to Unite Women, organized by the National Organization for Women (NOW), occurred in New York City. The event sparked discussions and debates about lesbian rights within the feminist movement and eventually led to the recognition of lesbian rights as a legitimate concern for feminism.

1975: The first feminist conference occurred in Israel, in Beer Sheva, during which activists Amalia Bergman and Marsha Friedman announced the founding of ALF (Lesbian Feminist Organization) - the first lesbian organization in Israel.

2019: Fiona Onasanya, a member of the U.K. Parliament for Peterborough, was removed from her position following a successful recall petition. She had been convicted of perverting the course of justice, becoming the first M.P. in the country's history to lose their seat through this process.

May 02

1250: Shajar al-Durr became the new monarch of Egypt with her husband, Izz al-Din Aybak, as the *Atabeg* (commander in chief). She took on the royal name al-Malikah Ismat ad-Din Umm-Khalil Shajar al-Durr, along with titles like *Malikat al-Muslimin* (Queen of the Muslims) and *Walidat al-Malik al-Mansur Khalil Emir al-Mo'aminin* (Mother of al-Malik al-Mansur Khalil Emir of the faithful). She was revered in Friday prayers as *Umm al-Malik Khalil* (Mother of al-Malik Khalil) and *Sahibat al-Malik as-Salih* (Wife of al-Malik as-Salih).

1536: Anne Boleyn, Queen of England, was arrested and imprisoned on charges of adultery, incest, treason, and witchcraft.

1843: The "Mill Girls," predominantly female textile workers, went on strike in Massachusetts, demanding better working conditions.

1885: *Good Housekeeping* magazine was first published in the United States. It has since become a popular women's magazine focusing on home, lifestyle, and various topics of interest.

1915: Clara Immerwahr, a German chemist, pacifist, and women's rights activist, took her own life. Immerwahr was married to Fritz Haber, a Nobel Prize-winning chemist known for his work in developing chemical weapons. Her suicide has been linked to her opposition to her husband's involvement in chemical warfare.

1963: Audrey Faye Hendricks, a nine-year-old girl, became the youngest person arrested during the Civil Rights Movement.

2009: Queen Elizabeth II appointed Carol Ann Duffy as Britain's new poet laureate, making her the first woman and Scot to hold the prestigious position since its establishment 341 years earlier.

2011: Elizabeth May, an environmental activist, became the first Green Party of Canada member to be elected to Parliament. Her election symbolized a growing emphasis on environmental issues and sustainability in Canadian politics.

2022: A leaked draft opinion suggested that the U.S. Supreme Court was poised to overturn landmark cases such as *Roe v. Wade* and *Planned Parenthood v. Casey*, which have played crucial roles in establishing and protecting reproductive rights in the United States.

May 03

1856: Queen Victoria of the United Kingdom gave Norfolk Island to the population of Pitcairn Island, most of whom were descendants of the Mutiny on the Bounty. Pitcairn Island's practice of women's suffrage was extended to Norfolk Island, granting women the right to vote.

1933: Nellie Tayloe Ross, the first woman to be elected Governor of a U.S. state

(Wyoming), made history again by becoming the director of the United States Mint. She held this position until 1953.

1937: Margaret Mitchell won the Pulitzer Prize for her novel *Gone with the Wind*.

1955: Emma Rowena "Grandma" Gatewood, at age 67, began her solo thru-hike of the Appalachian Trail. She walked from Georgia to Maine, becoming the first woman to complete the trail.

1972: Seven women working for the women's health organization Jane were arrested and charged with multiple counts of abortion and conspiracy. They became known as the "Abortion 7." In a remarkable act of protecting patient information, one of the women swallowed index cards containing the contact information of their patients.

2016: Khadija Ismayilova, an imprisoned Azerbaijani journalist, received the UNESCO/Guillermo Cano World Press Freedom Prize for her exceptional dedication to upholding press freedom. Ismayilova's work and commitment to journalism made a significant impact despite facing challenging circumstances.

2023: Norwegian climber Kristin Harila became the fastest woman to climb all mountains above 8000 meters. By summiting Cho Oyu, she completed the ascent of the 14 highest peaks on the planet, becoming the seventh woman and the second fastest overall to accomplish this feat.

May 04

1912: The Women's Political Union suffrage parade occurred in New York City, organized by Harriet Stanton Blatch. Thousands of suffragists participated in the march, advocating for women's right to vote. The parade featured fifty-two women on horseback leading the way, accompanied by supporters and marching bands.

1914: Mary Ann Aldham, a suffragette, damaged a portrait of Henry James painted by John Singer Sargent at the Royal Academy Summer Exhibition in London using a meat cleaver. It was one of three attacks organized by suffragettes during that month.

1944: MGM released the film adaptation of *Gaslight*, starring Charles Boyer, Ingrid Bergman, and Angela Lansbury in her debut role. The film, a psychological thriller, garnered critical acclaim and became a classic of its genre.

1959: Ella Fitzgerald won the first Grammy Award. The renowned jazz singer was awarded Best Individual Jazz Performance for her song *But Not for Me*.

1979: Margaret Thatcher, a Conservative politician and Member of Parliament for Finchley from 1959 to 1992, became the first woman to serve as Prime Minister of the United Kingdom. Thatcher held the position until 1990, making her the longest-serving British Prime Minister of the 20th century. Known for her strong leadership and conservative policies, she earned the nickname "Iron Lady."

2011: Phoebe A. Cohen published a paper in *Geology*, suggesting that fossils found in Yukon may represent the earliest traces of biomineralization in eukaryotes. This research shed light on the early evolution of organisms capable of producing minerals within their tissues.

2016: The U.S. Justice Department notified North Carolina Governor Pat McCrory that the state's new law, restricting restroom access for transgender people, violated the U.S. Civil Rights Act. The department requested a response from the state regarding its intention to address the violations by May 9. However, the Governor's response did not specify the actions the state would take to address the concerns raised by the Justice Department.

May 05

1751: Cristina Roccati, at 19, earned a philosophy degree, becoming the third woman with doctoral qualifications. She continued her studies at the University of Padua, specializing in Newtonian physics, Greek, and Hebrew while nurturing her literary interests. In 1751, she started teaching physics at the Accademia dei Concordi di Rovigo and continued until at least 1777.

1809: Mary Kies became the first woman to receive an American patent. Her patent was granted for a technique of weaving straw with silk, which was used for making hats.

1921: Fashion designer Coco Chanel introduced her iconic perfume, Chanel No. 5. The fragrance became one of the world's most famous and bestselling perfumes, renowned for its luxurious scent and elegant packaging.

1927: English author Virginia Woolf published her novel *To the Lighthouse*. The book is considered one of Woolf's most successful works and is known for its use of the stream-of-consciousness narrative style.

1930: British aviator Amy Johnson started her solo flight from Croydon, England, to Port Darwin, Australia. Flying in an open cockpit *Gypsy Moth* plane, she completed the 11,000-mile journey on May 25, becoming the first woman to do so.

1938: Dorothy H. Andersen presented her research findings on cystic fibrosis disease at a meeting of the American Pediatric Association. Her work contributed to the understanding and diagnosing of this genetic disorder that primarily affects the lungs and digestive system.

1953: Virginia Schau, a photographer, won the Pulitzer Prize for Photography with her photograph titled *Rescue on Pit River Bridge*. She was the first woman to receive this prestigious award in photography.

1970: Nirmala Srivastava founded *Sahaja Yoga*, a religious movement, in the village of Nargol in Gujarat state, India. She claimed to have discovered a technique to open the *Sahasrara chakra*, an energy center located at the crown of the head, leading to self-realization. *Sahaja Yoga* centers were subsequently established worldwide, promoting meditation and spiritual practices.

1992: The first International No Diet Day was observed in the United Kingdom for the first time, initiated by a size-positive activist, Mary Evans Young. As it clashed with Cinco de Mayo celebrations in the U.S., the date was moved to the 6th. The day's goal was to raise awareness of weight discrimination and fatphobia, to raise questions about the safety and efficacy of commercial diets, to honor the victims of eating disorders and weight-loss surgery, and to avoid fixating on their body weight for the day.

2015: After a Royal Decree, Princess Pembayun received the new name Mangkubumi Hamemayu Hayuning Bawana Langgeng ing Mataram, which indicated her as the heiress presumptive to the throne of Yogyakarta. Before, only male heirs could become rulers.

May 06

1646: Anne Bradstreet, an American colonial poet, played a significant role in establishing Andover Parish in present-day North Andover, Massachusetts. She is considered one of the founding mothers of the parish.

1742: Elizabeth crowned herself Empress of Russia in the Dormition Cathedral in Moscow. She seized power through a coup on December 6, 1741, ending the regency of Anna Leopoldovna for the infant Ivan VI.

1913: The U.S. Senate investigating committee held four-day hearings to examine eyewitness testimony supporting Alice Paul's claim of police misconduct during the federal suffrage amendment parade on March 3, 1913. The testimony aimed to shed light on the mistreatment of suffragists during the parade.

1913: The United Kingdom's House of Commons rejected a proposed women's suffrage bill with a vote of 219-266 after the second reading. Notably, fifty Irish members of Parliament voted against the bill, including Prime Minister H. H. Asquith.

1939: Dorothy Garrod, an English archaeologist specializing in the Palaeolithic period, became the Disney Professor of Archaeology at the University of Cambridge. While this was seen as a significant moment for women, she was still excluded from speaking or voting on University matters as women were not full members of the University until 1948.

1943: Ayn Rand's novel *The Fountainhead* was published, presenting her philosophy of Objectivism. The book explores themes of individualism and independence through its protagonist, Howard Roark.

1945: Mildred Gillars, also known as "Axis Sally," delivered her last propaganda broadcast to Allied troops. She had been broadcasting Nazi propaganda throughout World War II, with her first broadcast occurring on December 11, 1941.

1949: The EDSAC, the world's first stored-program computer to operate a regular computing service, performed its first calculations using a program written by Canadian computer scientist Beatrice Worsley.

1956: The last episode of the T.V. show *I Love Lucy*, starring Lucille Ball, aired. The sitcom was immensely popular and considered one of television's greatest shows.

1975: Annie Dillard received the Pulitzer Prize for General Nonfiction for her book *Pilgrim at Tinker Creek*. The book is a memoir and reflection on nature and the author's observations while living in the Blue Ridge Mountains of Virginia.

1981: Maya Lin, an undergraduate architecture student at Yale University, won the competition for the design of the Vietnam Veterans Memorial. Her design, chosen out of 1,422 submissions, became a powerful and iconic symbol honoring the veterans of the Vietnam War.

2014: Monica Lewinsky, a former White House intern, published a book about her affair with President Bill Clinton titled *Monica's Story*. The book provided her perspective and personal account of the events during the scandal that captivated the nation in the late 1990s.

May 07

1973: Maxine Kumin, a poet, was awarded the Pulitzer Prize for her poetry collection titled *Up Country: Poems of New England*. The collection showcases her talent in capturing the essence of rural New England life.

1976: During an attack on Beirut, Lebanon, by 300 Palestinian Liberation Organization (PLO) fighters, Jocelyne Khoueiry, a Lebanese Christian militant, and a group of six other women defended a building in Martyrs' Square. Khoueiry's killing of the expedition leader forced the PLO militia to retreat. Her stand made her a revered figure in the Lebanese Christian community, leading to her eventual command of a women's militia of 1,000 individuals.

2009: The Şakirin Mosque officially opened in Turkey. The mosque's interior was designed by Zeynep Fadıllıoğlu, making her the first female interior designer of a mosque and the first woman to design a mosque in modern Turkey.

2022: In downtown Atlanta, United States, a demonstration took place supporting "pro-choice" policies following the leak of a draft opinion related to the U.S. Supreme Court case *Dobbs v. Jackson Women's Health Organization*. During the demonstration, an unidentified individual drove their car through the crowd. There were no reported injuries.

2022: The Taliban, who had regained control of Afghanistan, passed a law mandating that all women publicly cover their faces with a *burqa*.

May 08

1373: As Julian of Norwich, an English anchoress, was expected to die, last rites were administered to her. When she saw the cross, she experienced several spiritual visions. After recovering, Julian wrote them down. Over the years, she explored their theological meaning, which became the *Revelations of Divine Love* - considered the earliest surviving English language works by a woman.

1429: Joan of Arc, a French military leader and saint, lifted the Siege of Orléans during the Hundred Years' War. Her victory marked a turning point in the war and boosted French morale.

1557: Anne Locke arrived in Geneva, after leaving London with two of her children fearing religious persecution. It is believed that she used her time in exile to translate the works of John Calvin into English. She could return to England after Elizabeth I became a new queen.

1819: Ka'ahumanu, a Hawaiian queen consort, became *kuhina nui*, a position similar to a co-regent or prime minister. She was later recognized as Queen Regent of the Hawaiian Islands, wielding significant political power.

1860: Elizabeth Cady Stanton, a prominent women's rights activist, delivered a speech at the Cooper Institute's annual American Anti-Slavery Society meeting in New York. In her address, she denounced slavery, acknowledged the work of abolitionists, and highlighted the connection between slavery and women's rights.

1919: The Chemical Society decided that women should be admitted on the same terms as men, and the corresponding bylaw was passed in 1920. It came after many years of rejecting the idea. In 1904, after the election of Marie Curie as a Foreign Fellow, a petition was signed by nineteen British female chemists explaining why women should be accepted as Fellows. However, the motion was rejected when too few men showed up to vote. Among the cosigners were such great scientists as Lucy Boole, Katherine Alice Burke, Clare de Brereton Evans, Elizabeth Eleanor Field, Emily Fortey, Ida Freund, Mildred Gostling (Mrs. Mills), Hilda Hartle, Edith Humphrey, Dorothy Marshall, Margaret Seward (Mrs. McKillop), Ida Smedley (Mrs. Maclean), Alice Emily Smith, Millicent Taylor, M. Beatrice Thomas, Grace Toynbee (Mrs. Frankland), Martha Whiteley, Sibyl Widdows, and Katherine Isabella Williams.

1919: The constitution of Luxembourg was amended to grant universal suffrage to all citizens aged 21 and above, regardless of gender. This amendment took effect on May 15, allowing women to vote in national elections.

1950: Bernice Rosenthal Walters, an American physician and Lieutenant Commander, became the first female doctor assigned to duty on a U.S. Naval vessel. She served aboard the USSS Consolation hospital ship.

1953: Esther Lederberg, a renowned microbiologist, published a paper in *Genetics* detailing her discovery of the *λ bacteriophage*, a virus that infects bacteria.

1980: Farrokhroo Parsa, an Iranian physician, an outspoken supporter of women's rights, educator, and parliamentarian who served as minister of education under Amir Abbas Hoveida and was the first female cabinet minister, was executed by a firing squad at the beginning of the Islamic Cultural Revolution.

2012: Claire Lomas, a paralyzed British woman, became the first to complete a marathon using a bionic ReWalk mobility suit. She finished the London Marathon in 16 days, showcasing the potential of assistive technology.

2013: Megan Rice, an 83-year-old nun, and two accomplices were convicted of illegally trespassing into Tennessee's Y-12 National Security Complex nuclear facility as a protest against nuclear weapons.

2016: The Court handed down a verdict related to the Japanese artist Rokudenashiko (Megumi Igarashi) in her charge of "obscenity," finding her partially guilty for distributing the 3-D scanned data of her vulva data to encourage people to use it to make their own original genitalia artwork. The case drew international attention, prompting disputes about women's rights, artistic freedom, censorship, and double standards in Japan.

2019: Asia Bibi, a Christian woman acquitted of blasphemy charges after spending eight years on death row in Pakistan, left the country to reunite with her daughters in Canada.

2021: Natasha Asghar made history as the first woman from an ethnic minority to become a member of the *Senedd* (Welsh Parliament).

2022: U.S. First Lady Jill Biden made an unannounced visit to Uzhhorod, Ukraine, where she held a Mother's Day meeting with Ukrainian First Lady Olena Zelenska, emphasizing diplomatic relations and support between the two countries.

May 09

1914: In Glasgow, Scotland, suffragists fought with police attempting to raid a meeting on women's rights. The police faced resistance as flowerpots, tables, chairs, and other objects were thrown at them. Audience members and bodyguards trained in jiu-jitsu armed themselves with various makeshift weapons and fought off the officers. Barbed wire hidden in the stage decorations further impeded the police's attempts to arrest the speakers.

1914: U.S. President Woodrow Wilson declared the first national Mother's Day in the United States. He encouraged citizens to display the flag as a tribute to mothers who had lost sons in the war. The United States Congress had passed a law the previous day officially establishing the second Sunday in May as Mother's Day.

1922: The International Astronomical Union formally adopted Annie Jump Cannon's stellar classification system, which is still used today with minor modifications. Cannon's system categorized stars based on the strength of their Balmer absorption lines, providing a significant contribution to astronomy.

1960: The U.S. Food and Drug Administration (FDA) approved the world's first commercially produced birth control pill, Enovid-10. The research and development for this contraceptive pill were initially commissioned by birth control pioneer Margaret Sanger and funded by heiress Katherine McCormick.

1972: Workers from the Farah Manufacturing Company in El Paso, U.S., the vast majority of whom were Hispanic women (Chicanas), started a labor strike led by Sylvia M. Trevino. They protested against the lack of job security and union support, no benefits for workers, gender prejudices, low wages, raises based on favoritism, health and safety hazards, and unattainable quotas. The strike lasted almost two years and ended in favor of the female workers.

2017: Australian senator Larissa Waters became the first Australian politician to breastfeed during a parliamentary session. The House of Representatives had voted the previous year to allow breastfeeding and bottle-feeding in the chamber.

May 10

1849: Jenny Lind, a renowned opera singer, gave her last performance in the opera *Robert le Diable* in London. Queen Victoria and other members of the Royal Family were in attendance.

1854: Elizabeth Taylor Greenfield, born into enslavement in Mississippi, performed a concert for Queen Victoria at Buckingham Palace. She became the first African-American artist to perform before British royalty.

1872: Victoria Woodhull was nominated as the first woman candidate for President of the United States by the Equal Rights Party. Although she did not ultimately run an active campaign, her nomination was a significant achievement for women's political participation.

1922: Ivy Williams became the first female English barrister when she was called to the bar. While she did not practice law, she taught law at the Society of Oxford Home Students and became the first woman to be awarded the degree of DCL (Doctor of Civil Law) in 1923.

1967: Truus Menger-Oversteegen, a Dutch sculptor, painter, and member of the anti-Nazi Dutch Resistance, was recognized by Yad Vashem as Righteous Among the Nations, along with her sister Freddie Oversteegen and Hannie Schaft. Their brave actions during World War II saved the lives of many Jews.

2014: The song *Rise Like a Phoenix* by Austrian singer Conchita Wurst won the Eurovision Song Contest, capturing international attention and celebrating diversity.

2022: Katalin Novák assumed office as the first female President of Hungary.

2023: Joy Neville, an Irish referee, was announced as the first woman to officiate at a men's Rugby World Cup. She will take on this role during the tournament scheduled to be held in France in September.

May 11

912: Following the death of Emperor Leo VI, his brother Alexander III assumed the position of Emperor (*basileus*) of the Byzantine Empire. Alexander became the de facto ruler, ruling alongside Leo's young son, Constantine VII. Empress Zoe Karbonopsina, Constantine's mother, was expelled from the palace and exiled to a nunnery.

1685: In Wigtown, Scotland, five Covenanters, including Margaret Wilson, were executed for refusing to swear an oath acknowledging King James of England, Scotland, and Ireland as the head of the Church. They are remembered as the Wigtown martyrs.

1923: The First World Congress of Jewish Women took place in Vienna, Austria, providing a platform for Jewish women to discuss and address various issues of importance.

1929: Annie Webb Blanton established the Delta Kappa Gamma Society, an organization for professional women educators, in Austin, Texas.

1978: Margaret A. Brewer became the first woman in the United States Marine Corps to achieve the rank of general officer.

2009: Maya Saleh, a researcher from the Research Institute of the McGill University Health Centre and McGill University, published research in the *Proceedings of the National Academy of Sciences* demonstrating that women have a stronger immune system than men. The study suggested that the presence of estrogen in women could have a positive impact on the innate inflammatory response against bacterial pathogens.

2016: The Italian Parliament approved legislation recognizing civil unions of same-sex couples, granting legal recognition and protections to these relationships.

2022: Greece passed a law banning conversion therapy for minors and prohibiting the advertisement of such practices. This legislation aimed to protect the rights and well-being of LGBTQ+ individuals in the country.

May 12

1914: Suffragist Gertrude Mary Ansell vandalized a portrait of the Duke of Wellington by painter Hubert von Herkomer during its exhibition at the Royal Academy Summer Exhibition in London. This vandalism was the second attack of its kind and served as a protest by the suffragist movement.

1919: The Second International Women's Congress for Peace and Freedom took place in Zürich. During the congress, the attendees criticized the terms of peace presented at the Paris Peace Conference. They renamed their organization the Women's International League for Peace and Freedom.

1923: During the 9th Conference of the International Woman Suffrage Alliance in Rome, Italy, women from the Balkan and Eastern Europe (Bulgaria, Czechoslovakia, Greece, the Kingdom of Serbs, Croats and Slovenes - later Yugoslavia, Poland, and Romania) created the Little Entente of Women. It was an umbrella organization aiming to reunite women from the lands of the previous Austro-Hungary Empire. Romanian activist Alexandrina Cantacuzino became its first president, then a Serbian feminist Mileva Petrović, Greek Avra Theodoropoulou, and in 1927, a Polish physician Justyna Budzińska-Tylicka became the chair.

1949: Vijaya Lakshmi Pandit of India became the first foreign woman ambassador received in the USA.

1968: A Mother's Day march of "welfare mothers" was held in Washington, D.C. The protest was led by Coretta Scott King, wife of civil rights leader Martin Luther King Jr., and accompanied by Ethel Kennedy.

1985: Amy Eilberg became the first female Conservative rabbi when ordained by the Jewish Theological Seminary of America in New York. She later became the first woman appointed to serve on the Rabbinical Assembly's Committee on Jewish Law and Standards.

1989: Jennifer Anne Doudna and her colleagues published a landmark study titled "Stereochemical course of catalysis by the Tetrahymena ribozyme" in *Science*. In this study, they solved the crystal structures of two large RNAs, specifically the P4-P6 domain of the *Tetrahymena thermophila* group I intron ribozyme, which provided significant insights into RNA catalysis.

2014: Creating a Facebook page called My Stealthy Freedom gained significant attention. The page allowed women across Iran to post photos of themselves without the hijab, garnering over 130,000 likes within a week. The page served as a platform for women to express their desire for freedom and challenge the mandatory hijab laws in Iran.

May 13

1713: King Philip V of Spain issued a decree known as the *auto accordado*, which changed the order of succession for the Spanish throne, allowing a female descendant within the House of Bourbon to rule. This change paved the way for his great-great-granddaughter, Queen Isabella II, to ascend the throne in 1833.

1863: Rasoherina became the Queen of Madagascar. She ruled as queen consort alongside her husband, King Radama II, and later became the reigning queen following his assassination. Her reign was marked by political struggles and attempts to modernize Madagascar.

1888: Princess Isabel of Brazil, acting as regent, signed the *Lei Áurea* (Golden Law), abolishing slavery in Brazil. This historic law freed all enslaved people, making Brazil the last nation in the Americas to abolish slavery.

1908: An Act of Congress established the U.S. Navy Nurse Corps, officially recognizing women serving as nurses in the U.S. Navy. Before this, women had served unofficially on Navy ships and in Navy hospitals for nearly a century.

1995: Alison Hargreaves, a 33-year-old from Britain, became the first woman to conquer Mount Everest without using supplemental oxygen or the help of sherpas.

2016: The United States Education and Justice Departments issued guidance to U.S. public school districts nationwide, advising them to permit transgender students to use bathrooms aligned with their gender identity. This guidance aimed to promote inclusivity and equality for transgender students and was issued amidst the ongoing controversy surrounding North Carolina's "bathroom bill."

2016: Fatma Samoura, a Senegalese United Nations official, became the Secretary General of FIFA (*Fédération Internationale de Football Association*). She was the first woman and the first non-European to hold this position. Samoura's role focused on overseeing the administration and management of FIFA.

2017: Shaesta Waiz, born in a refugee camp and the first female certified civilian pilot born in Afghanistan, embarked on her solo flight around the world. The purpose of her journey was to inspire girls and young women to pursue education and careers in STEM (Science, Technology, Engineering, and Mathematics).

2019: Actress Felicity Huffman pleaded guilty to conspiracy and acknowledged paying $15,000 to change her daughter's SAT answers, a part of a larger college admissions scandal involving several high-profile individuals and highlighting issues of privilege and unethical practices in the education system.

May 14

1226: Isabella was crowned as the queen regnant of Armenia. Her father named her the heir upon his deathbed in 1219, when she was five, but it was contested.

1866: Teresa Carreño, a Venezuelan pianist, soprano, composer, and conductor, debuted at the Salle Érard in Paris. During her time in Europe, she had the opportunity to meet and collaborate with renowned musicians such as Gioachino Rossini, Georges Mathias, Charles Gounod, and Franz Liszt.

1913: The suffragettes, in their fight for women's voting rights, set fire to St. Catherine's Church in Hatcham, London, as part of a series of arson attacks.

1925: Virginia Woolf's novel *Mrs. Dalloway* was published. This novel is considered one of Woolf's most significant works. It is known for its innovative narrative style and exploration of themes such as identity, consciousness, and the complexities of social life.

1939: Lina Medina, a 5-year-old girl from Peru, gave birth to a baby boy, making her the youngest confirmed mother in medical history. This case raised significant ethical and medical concerns and remained a unique and rare occurrence.

1948: Golda Meir, an Israeli politician and stateswoman, was one of the signatories of Israel's Declaration of Independence. Meir later became the fourth Prime Minister of Israel, serving from 1969 to 1974. She was the first and, to date, the only woman to hold this position in Israel.

1970: Ulrike Meinhof, a German left-wing activist, assisted Andreas Baader in escaping and forming the Red Army Faction (RAF) in West Germany. The RAF, also known as the Baader-Meinhof Group, was a militant organization active from the 1970s until its dissolution in 1998.

1984: Jeanne Sauvé was sworn in as the first female Governor General of Canada, making history as the first woman to hold this position. She served as Canada's Governor General from 1984 to 1990 and played a significant role in representing the monarchy in Canada and promoting national unity.

2000: Cynthia Kenyon, a renowned biochemist and biophysicist, was presented with the King Faisal International Prize for Medicine in Riyadh, Saudi Arabia. Kenyon's groundbreaking research with *C. elegans*, a tiny roundworm, revealed insights into the genetic and molecular mechanisms of aging, particularly the role of the insulin receptor system.

2013: American actress Angelina Jolie publicly revealed that she had undergone a preventive double mastectomy due to her family's history of fatal breast cancer cases. Jolie's disclosure highlighted the importance of genetic testing, awareness of breast cancer risks, and personal choices regarding preventive measures.

2016: Jamala, representing Ukraine, won the 2016 Eurovision Song Contest held in Stockholm, Sweden. She delivered a captivating performance of the song *1944*, which highlighted the experiences of her Crimean Tatar ancestors during the mass deportation by the Soviet Union.

May 15

589: Authari, the King of Lombards, married Theodelinda, the daughter of Bavarian duke Garibald I. Theodelinda would exert significant influence at court and among the Lombard nobility.

1614: Marie de' Medici, the Queen Regent of France, convened the Estates General to suppress a rebellion organized by Henri II, Prince of Condé.

1851: Alpha Delta Pi sorority was established at Wesleyan College in Macon, Georgia, becoming the first secret society exclusively for women.

1869: Susan B. Anthony, Elizabeth Cady Stanton, and others founded the National Woman Suffrage Association (NWSA) in New York, advocating for women's suffrage in the United States.

1888: Louisa Lawson, under the pen name Dora Falconer, published *The Dawn: A Journal for Australian Women*. This monthly feminist journal was published in Sydney, Australia, from 1888 to 1905 and became the official publication of the Australian Federation of Women Voters.

1912: A labor activist, Emma Goldman, arrived in San Diego to support local Industrial Workers of the World members in their fight for public soapbox events. The soapbox campaigns were ultimately discontinued in September due to vigilantism.

1919: Single women over 20 were granted the right to vote in local elections on the Isle of Jersey.

1940: Nylon women's stockings were introduced in stores across the United States, and approximately five million pairs were sold on the first day.

1942: The Women's Army Auxiliary Corps (WAAC) was established in the United States with the signing of a bill into law.

1990: Édith Cresson became France's first female Prime Minister, serving in the role until 1992.

2014: Meriam Yehya Ibrahim, an eight-month-pregnant Christian woman, was sentenced to death by hanging for apostasy in Sudan.

2017: Players from the U.S. National Women's Soccer League whose salaries are not paid by a national federation have formed the NWSL Players Association to help "advance continued improvements in women's soccer." The union was formed under the leadership of Yael Averbuch and represented by lawyer and former Women's Professional Soccer player Meghann

Burke. The NWSLPA officially unionized in November 2018.

2019: Governor Kay Ivey of Alabama signed the Human Life Protection Act into law, which banned nearly all abortions in the state except in cases where the mother's health was at risk. The law classified abortion as a Class A felony and attempted abortion as a Class C felony.

2021: Tamika Catchings, a 10-time WNBA All-Star and four-time Olympic gold medalist, was inducted into the Naismith Memorial Basketball Hall of Fame, recognizing her significant contributions to the sport.

May 16

1568: Queen Elizabeth I of England arrested Mary, Queen of Scots, leading to Mary's imprisonment and eventual execution.

1678: Madame de La Fayette's La Princesse de Clèves, one of the first Western historical fiction and one of the earliest novels in literature, was published anonymously. Some sources state that it was published in March.

1728: Saint Margaret of Cortona, known as the patron saint of the falsely accused, homeless people, and those with mental illness, was canonized by the Catholic Church.

1910: The United States Court of Claims decided the case of *Liliuokalani v. United States*, ruling that the former Queen of Hawai'i, Liliuokalani, was not entitled to compensation for the "Crown Lands" seized during the overthrow of the Hawaiian monarchy in 1893.

1975: Junko Tabei from Japan became the first woman to reach the summit of Mount Everest, the highest peak in the world.

1991: Queen Elizabeth II became the first British monarch to address the United States Congress during a state visit to the United States.

1999: Angela Warnick Buchdahl became the first Asian-American cantor when the Hebrew Union College-Jewish Institute of Religion invested her. In 2001, she was ordained as a rabbi, making history as the first Asian-American female rabbi.

2013: British author Jenny Colgan received the 2013 Romantic Novel of the Year Award for her book *Welcome to Rosie Hopkins' Sweetshop of Dreams*.

2014: American journalist Barbara Walters retired after a career spanning 52 years. She had made significant contributions to television journalism and had conducted numerous high-profile interviews.

2016: Han Kang's novel *The Vegetarian*, translated by Deborah Smith, won the Man Booker International Prize, bringing international recognition to Korean literature.

2022: Élisabeth Borne, the French Minister of Labour, was appointed as the new Prime Minister of France by President Emmanuel Macron, succeeding Jean Castex.

528: Empress Dowager Hu, the regent of Northern Wei, executed her disgruntled lovers but ultimately met her demise, along with the nominal Emperor, Yuan Zhao, when they drowned in the Yellow River.

1838: An anti-abolitionist mob attacked and burned down Pennsylvania Hall in Philadelphia, a symbol of free speech, during the Anti-Slavery Convention of American Women.

1863: Rosalía de Castro published *Cantares Gallegos*, the first book in the Galician language, which played a significant role in the cultural revitalization of Galicia.

1984: The Museum of Modern Art opened the exhibition An International Survey of Recent Painting and Sculpture,"which showcased the work of 165 artists but only included 13 women. This gender disparity led to the formation of the Guerrilla Girls, an activist group advocating for gender and racial equality in art.

2010: Edurne Pasaban reached the summit of Shisha Pangma, becoming the first woman to climb all 14 eight-thousanders successfully, the world's highest mountains.

2011: Queen Elizabeth II embarked on her first state visit to the Republic of Ireland, which would be the first visit by a reigning British monarch since Irish independence in 1921.

2014: Marcia Kadish and Tanya McCloskey became the first legally married same-sex partners in the United States after marrying in Massachusetts.

2017: Chelsea Manning, a former United States Army soldier, was released from prison after serving seven years for leaking classified documents. President Barack Obama commuted her sentence.

2018: Gina Haspel was confirmed as the first female director of the Central Intelligence Agency (CIA) by the U.S. Senate.

2019: The U.S. House of Representatives approved the Equality Act, a significant piece of legislation aimed at preventing discrimination based on sexual orientation and gender identity.

2021: Iracı́ Hassler became the first Communist mayor of Santiago, Chile.

2021: The Supreme Court of Samoa cleared the way for Naomi Mata'afa to form a new government and become Samoa's first female Prime Minister, resolving a political deadlock.

May 17

1943: Marianne Joachim, a Jewish German resistance activist, organized an arson attack against the Soviet Paradise exhibition in Berlin during the Nazi era. The show aimed to depict a negative image of life in the "Jewish Bolshevist Soviet Union."

1952: Ann Davison became the first woman to sail across the Atlantic Ocean single-handedly.

1953: Jacqueline Cochran became the first woman to break the sound barrier by flying the Canadian-built *F-86 Sabrejet*.

May 18

1958: Maria Teresa de Filippis debuted at the World Championship Grands Prix, becoming the first woman to race in Formula One. She drove a *Maserati 250F*.

1988: Patricia Bath, an African-American scientist, was granted a U.S. patent for her invention of a laser device to remove cataracts. She became the first Black woman to receive a medical device patent.

1991: Helen Sharman became the first Briton in space when she launched into space with two cosmonauts in a Soyuz spacecraft.

2009: Hosne Ara Begum became the first woman in Bangladesh's history to be appointed as the chief officer of a police division in the capital city of Dhaka.

2013: Zahra Shahid Hussain, a senior vice-president of Imran Khan's Pakistan Tehreek-e-Insaf Party, was shot and killed by a gunman outside her residence in Karachi.

2013: Emmelie de Forest from Denmark won the 2013 Eurovision Song Contest with her song *Only Teardrops*.

2019: Former Argentine President Cristina Fernández de Kirchner declared her candidacy for Vice President in the 2019 Argentine general election, running alongside former Chief of Staff Alberto Fernández as her presidential running mate.

2021: Gladys Mae West, an American mathematician, received the Webby Lifetime Achievement Award for her work in developing satellite geodesy models.

2021: The French Rugby Federation announced that trans women players would be allowed to participate in the country's top-level women's rugby union, overturning World Rugby's guidance against this.

May 19

1914: Lydia Zvereva, a Russian pilot, became the first woman to execute a loop in a *Morane-Saulnier* monoplane successfully. She performed this aerobatic maneuver over the hippodrome in Riga, Latvia. She was also the first Russian woman (and 8th globally) to get a pilot license on August 10, 1911.

1955: Jean Sinclair, Ruth Foley, Elizabeth McLaren, Tertia Pybus, Jean Bosazza, and Helen Newton-Thompson, six middle-class white women, founded the Women's Defence of the Constitution League, also known as the Black Sashes. This nonviolent organization aimed to oppose apartheid in South Africa.

1962: Marilyn Monroe famously sang *Happy Birthday, Mr. President* to John F. Kennedy at Madison Square Garden in New York City. The performance took place during a celebration of President Kennedy's birthday.

1965: Patricia R. Harris became the first African-American woman to be appointed ambassador. She was appointed as the ambassador to Luxembourg.

1972: Sandy Eisenberg Sasso was ordained as a rabbi by the Reconstructionist Rabbinical College in Philadelphia, making her the first woman to be ordained a rabbi in Reconstructionist Judaism.

2012: Nishat Majumder became the first Bangladeshi woman to climb Mount Everest successfully.

2013: Samina Baig became the first Pakistani woman to reach the summit of Mount Everest at age 21. On the same day, Tashi and Nungshi Malik, twin sisters from India, also reached the summit, symbolizing peace by placing the Indian and Pakistani flags together. Additionally, Raha Moharrak became the first Saudi woman to summit Mount Everest on the same day.

2013: Taylor Swift won eight awards at the Billboard Music Awards, including Top Album and Top Artist.

2016: Masha Gordon reached the summit of Mount Everest, becoming the fastest woman to complete the Explorers Grand Slam, the quickest woman to scale the seven summits, and the fastest woman to complete the Three Poles Challenge.

May 20

1913: The *De Vrouw* 1813–1913 exhibition was held in Amsterdam, Netherlands, commemorating the nation's liberation from French occupation in 1813. It was organized by Mia Boissevain and Rosa Manus, who aimed for the exhibition to advance the cause of Dutch women's suffrage. The event provided insights into the women's movement and the role of women in Dutch society, showcasing various forms of expression, including visual arts, literature, and drama. Moreover, a conference hall hosted weekly lectures on feminist subjects. It lasted until October 10.

1919: The Chamber of Deputies in France approved a bill to grant universal suffrage to women with a vote of 377 in favor and 97 against. However, the bill did not pass the Senate, delaying women's voting rights in France until 1944.

1932: Amelia Earhart embarked on her historic solo nonstop flight across the Atlantic Ocean as the first female pilot to attempt such a feat. She took off from Newfoundland and landed in Ireland the following day.

1936: The first issue of *Mujeres Libres* (*Free Women*) was published. It was a Spanish anarchist feminist magazine created by a group of the same name. The publication aimed to end the

> "triple enslavement of women to ignorance, to capital, and to men."

The group later played a significant role in the Spanish Revolution that erupted in the same year.

1978: Mavis Hutchinson, aged 53, became the first woman to run across the United States. Her journey lasted 69 days.

1983: Françoise Barré-Sinoussi and her team of researchers from the Pasteur Institute in Paris published an article titled "Isolation of a T-lymphotropic retrovirus from a patient at risk for acquired immune deficiency syndrome (AIDS)" in the journal *Science*. This discovery played a crucial role in identifying the human immunodeficiency virus (HIV), the cause of AIDS.

1993: Rosemarie Köhn became the first woman to be appointed as a bishop in the Church of Norway.

2013: The General Assembly of the Church of Scotland voted to approve the eligibility of openly gay women and men to serve as ministers.

2016: The Centers for Disease Control and Prevention (CDC) reported that at least 270 pregnant women in the United States had been infected with the Zika virus, highlighting the health risks associated with the virus during pregnancy.

2016: Tsai Ing-wen was inaugurated as the first female President of Taiwan.

May 21

1881: Clara Barton and Adolphus Solomons founded the American National Red Cross, a humanitarian organization that provides emergency assistance, disaster relief, and support to those in need.

1892: Ida Wells-Barnett's editorial in Free Speech, in which she wrote that white women willingly engage in sexual relations with Black men, triggered a wave of hatred and anger among white men in the South. Such a notion clashed with the myth of innocent white womanhood and an animal-like brutal Black sexuality, which were at the foundation of lynching attacks. Wells-Barnett was an anti-lynching activist and a militant journalist born to an enslaved couple in Mississippi.

1932: Amelia Earhart completed her solo flight across the Atlantic Ocean by landing in a field at Culmore, Northern Ireland - a woman's first solo flight across the Atlantic.

1941: In Norway, an actors' strike against the Nazi occupation began after six actors refused to work on the radio when ordered to do so by the Nazi authorities. These actors, including Tore Segelcke, Lillemor von Hanno, Gerda Ring, and Elisabeth Gording, had signed a secret pledge to strike if any artist was fired for political reasons. As a result of their actions, their work permits were revoked, and the strike spread, leading to the shutdown of theaters in the capital and other cities.

1960: Leontyne Price, an African American soprano, became the first African American to sing the lead role at Teatro Alla Scala in Milan, Italy. She performed the role of *Aida*, a renowned opera by Giuseppe Verdi.

1965: Mary Kenneth Keller, an American Catholic nun, became the first person in the United States to receive a Ph.D. in computer science. Her doctoral dissertation, *Inductive Inference on Computer Generated Patterns*, focused on machine learning and pattern recognition.

1971: President Richard Nixon presented Barbara McClintock with The President's National Medal of Science for her groundbreaking work in plant genetics. McClintock's research significantly contributed to our understanding of genetic transposition and the role of transposable elements in gene regulation.

1988: Margaret Thatcher, the former Prime Minister of the United Kingdom, delivered her controversial "Sermon on the Mound" during the Church of Scotland General Assembly. In her speech, Thatcher discussed her views on the role of Christianity in society and the importance of individual responsibility and self-reliance.

2011: Manal al-Sharif was arrested for driving a car during a Saudi women's rights campaign. The event was filmed by another activist, Wajeha al-Huwaider, and uploaded to social media. Al-Sharif was charged with "inciting women to drive" and "rallying public opinion."

May 22

1712: Catherine of Bologna (Caterina de' Vigri), an Italian writer, teacher, mystic, artist, and member of the Poor Clares order, was canonized by Pope Clement XI. She is considered the patron saint of artists and is also venerated as a protector against temptations by the believers.

1972: In Derry, Northern Ireland, over 400 women attacked the offices of Sinn Féin, a political party associated with the Irish Republican Army (IRA). This incident followed the shooting of a young British soldier by the IRA, and the women's actions were a response to the violence and unrest in the region.

1994: Pope John Paul II issued the Apostolic Letter *Ordinatio sacerdotalis* from the Vatican, reaffirming the Catholic Church's position on the reservation of priestly ordination for men only. The letter emphasized that the Church does not have the authority to ordain women as priests.

1995: Astronomers Amanda S. Bosh and Andrew S. Rivkin discovered two new moons of Saturn in photographs taken by the Hubble Space Telescope. These findings expanded our understanding of Saturn's moon system and added to our knowledge of the outer solar system.

2012: Commander Sarah West, a senior Royal Navy officer, became the first woman to command a major British warship in the Royal Navy's 500-year history.

2014: Archaeologists led by Ulrike Beck of the German Archaeological Institute published an article describing the discovery of woven wool trousers in China's Tarim Basin. These trousers, dating back between 3,300 and 3,000 years ago, are the oldest known examples of this type of clothing. The finding provided insights into ancient textile production and the cultural practices of the people in the region during that time.

May 23

1067: Eudokia Makrembolitissa became the Byzantine Empress regnant (or regent) after the death of her husband, Constantine X Doukas.

1430: Joan of Arc, a French military leader and national heroine, was captured by troops from the Burgundian faction during the Siege of Compiègne.

1796: An advertisement was placed in a newspaper seeking the return of Ona "Oney" Judge, an enslaved Black woman who had escaped from the household of President George Washington two days earlier.

1906: Dora Montefiore, a socialist suffragette, protested for women's right to vote by refusing to pay her taxes and barricading her home in Hammersmith, London. This act of civil disobedience, known as the "Hammersmith Siege," aimed to draw attention to the demand for women's suffrage and their desire to have a say in the laws they obey and the taxes they pay.

1942: Ziba Pasha qizi Ganiyeva, an Azeri sniper who volunteered to join the Red Army after the German invasion, became a Soviet hero after the battle for Bolshoe Vragovo village in Maryovsky District. She was injured during a covert action and suffered blood poisoning. During the war, she participated in missions with Heroes of the Soviet Union, Natalya Kovshova and Mariya Polivanova.

1984: The Bangles, an American pop rock all-women band, released their debut studio album *All Over the Place*.

1984: Bachendri Pal, an Indian mountaineer, became the first Indian woman to reach the summit of Mount Everest.

1988: A group of lesbians wearing T-shirts saying "Stop the Clause" stormed the BBC News studio when the Six O'Clock News was broadcast live to protest the Clause 28 law, which was set to come into force the next day. The law banned any "promotion of homosexuality."

2011: Lady Gaga's *Born This Way* album was released worldwide. The album achieved platinum certification in numerous countries and further solidified Lady Gaga's status as a prominent pop artist.

2014: Former Prime Minister of Thailand Yingluck Shinawatra was detained by General Prayuth Chan-Ocha, the Royal Thai Army chief and leader of the coup that took place the day before. This event marked a significant development in Thailand's political landscape and led to political uncertainty.

May 24

1883: The Brooklyn Bridge, an iconic landmark connecting Manhattan to Brooklyn in New York, opened to the public. Emily Warren Roebling played a significant role in the bridge's completion, taking over as the project's chief engineer after her husband, Washington Roebling, fell ill.

1899: Jadwiga Olszewska, a pioneering Polish woman in medicine, received her medical license to practice in the Austrian-Hungarian Empire. She focused on providing medical care to the poor, primarily the Muslim community, in Tuzla (now Bosnia and Herzegovina).

1919: Women's suffrage was granted in Sweden, allowing women to vote in elections. Women's suffrage was implemented for the first time in the 1921 election.

1930: Aviator Amy Johnson landed in Darwin, Northern Territory, completing her solo flight from England to Australia as the first woman ever.

1947: Yamakawa Kikue became the first head of the newly established Women's and Minors' Bureau under the Ministry of Labor, where she served until 1951.

1948: Agnes Arber, a renowned botanist, became the first woman to receive the Gold Medal of the Linnean Society of London to recognize her contributions to botanical science.

1988: Section 28 was passed into law in the United Kingdom under the Conservative government of Margaret Thatcher. The amendment to the Local Government Act of 1988 restricted the "promotion of homosexuality" and teaching about homosexuality in maintained schools.

1990: Judi Bari, a revolutionary construction worker and environmentalist, was injured when a bomb exploded in her car, also injuring her colleague Darryl Cherney.

2011: Oprah Winfrey, a prominent U.S. television personality, recorded the final episode of *The Oprah Winfrey Show*, ending the long-running talk show.

2015: A group of female activists successfully crossed the Demilitarized Zone (DMZ) separating North and South Korea by bus despite being denied permission to walk.

2019: After Taiwan legalized same-sex marriage, becoming the first nation in Asia to officially recognize and grant marriage rights to same-sex couples. The new law also provided limited joint custody rights (later broaden).

2019: Theresa May, the Prime Minister of the United Kingdom, announced her resignation as the leader of the Conservative Party, effective June 7. She would continue to serve as Prime Minister until a successor was elected.

2021: Fiame Naomi Mata'afa, a High Chiefess (*matai*), became the first woman to serve as the Prime Minister of Samoa.

2021: Dame Cindy Kiro was announced as the next Governor-General of New Zealand, becoming the first Māori woman, the third person of Māori descent, and the fourth woman to hold the office.

May 25

1384: Juana, the wife of Arnaldo Sarrovira, a citizen of Barcelona, received a license to practice medicine, making her one of the early recorded women in history to be granted permission to practice medicine.

1537: Margaret Cheyne (later Margaret Bulmer) was burned at the stake for high treason during Henry VIII's reign following the Pilgrimage of Grace and Bigod's Rebellion. She was arrested in April and imprisoned in the Tower of London before the trial and execution.

1555: Jeanne and her husband, Antoine de Bourbon, became the joined rulers of the Kingdom of Navarre and were crowned on August 18.

1611: Nur Jahan, a powerful and influential woman, married Emperor Jahangir, becoming Empress and co-ruler of the Mughal Empire in India. She played a significant role in the administration of the empire.

1861: Emma Edmonds, using the alias Frank Thompson, became a male nurse in the Second Regiment Michigan Volunteer Infantry of the Union Army during the American Civil War. She later published a best-selling book titled *Nurse and Spy*, recounting her experiences as a nurse and spy on missions into Confederate territory.

2014: Catherine Corless, an amateur Irish historian, brought attention to the deaths of almost 800 children at the Bon Secours home for young single mothers in Tuam, Galway, Ireland.

2014: Dalia Grybauskaitė won re-election as the President of Lithuania in the second round of the presidential elections. She became the first female President of Lithuania when she was initially elected in 2009.

2018: In Ireland, a referendum was held to repeal the Eighth Amendment of the Irish Constitution, severely restricting access to abortion in the country. The referendum resulted in the repeal of the amendment and paved the way for the passage of legislation allowing for broader access to abortion services in Ireland. The Thirty-sixth Amendment of the Constitution of Ireland replaced the Eighth Amendment.

May 26

1303: Elizabeth Richeza, at 14, married King Wenceslaus II of Bohemia. The wedding occurred at Prague Cathedral in Bohemia (now in the Czech Republic), and Elizabeth was crowned as the Queen Consort of Bohemia.

1824: The first recorded factory strike in U.S. history occurred at the Slater Mill in Pawtucket. Around 102 women and girls working at the mill went on strike in response to increased working hours and reduced pay for power-loom weavers. The strike lasted for a week and resulted in negotiations between the workers and mill owners, leading to a compromise.

1849: Djoumbé Fatima (Djoumbé Soudi, or Queen Jumbe-Souli) was crowned in a ceremony arranged by the French, hoping to gain more power in the region, although she already ruled as the Sultana of Mohéli (Mwali) from 1842, since the death of her father. She was able to resist the French efforts to make Mwali a colony.

1936: MacNolia Cox, a 13-year-old from Akron, and Elizabeth Kenny, a 15-year-old from Plainfield, New Jersey, became the first African-American children to compete as finalists in the National Spelling Bee.

2007: Hung Wan-ting, a second lieutenant with Taiwan's Chinese Military Academy, became the first Taiwanese and Asian woman to graduate from the U.S. Military Academy at West Point. She was among a group of international students from 27 countries.

2016: Chinese state media Xinhua News Agency criticized Taiwan President Tsai Ing-wen, making derogatory remarks about her being politically extreme and highlighting her unmarried and childless status to discredit her emotional balance.

2020: Costa Rica became the first country in Central America to legalize same-sex marriage.

May 27

1857: The Female Medical Education Society was reorganized as the New England Female Medical College, which later merged with Boston University to become the co-educational Boston University School of Medicine in 1874.

1892: A white mob attacked and destroyed the office of Ida B. Wells' newspaper, *The Free Speech and Headlight,* in Memphis, Tennessee, in response to Wells' investigative work on lynching. Wells, who was visiting Philadelphia then, was threatened with violence if she returned to the city.

1935: Women in New York City, organized as the City Action Committee Against the High Cost of Living, picketed butcher shops to demand a reduction in the price of meat. This action was part of their efforts to address the rising cost of living.

1976: Janet Guthrie, an accomplished aerospace engineer and physicist, became the first woman to qualify for a NASCAR race. She secured the 27th starting position in the World 600 at the Charlotte Motor Speedway and finished 15th in the race.

1981: Thanks to the initiative by Martha Ackelsberg, Sue Elwell, Judith Plaskow, Myra Rosenhaus, and T. Drora Setel, the first retreat of *B'not Esh* (the Daughters of Fire) Jewish Feminist Spirituality Collective took place to explore Jewish feminist spirituality, becoming a regular annual conference and inspiring many Jewish feminist projects, seminars, books, and other programs.

2010: The American Academy of Pediatrics rescinded a controversial policy statement suggesting that doctors in some communities should be able to substitute demands for female genital cutting with a harmless clitoral "pricking" procedure. The AAP clarified its opposition to all forms of female genital cutting.

2022: Sheikha Asma Al Thani became the first Qatari woman to reach the summit of Mount Everest. She carried a football for the FIFA World Cup Qatar as part of her climb.

May 28

1677: The Treaty Between Virginia And The Indians 1677 (or Treaty of Middle Plantation) was signed between the British Crown and representatives from various Virginia Native American tribes. Cockacoaeske, called Queen of the Pamunkey, was the first signatory, reflecting her strong negotiating position and ability to claim other tributary groups under her leadership. Among the first four signatories was also the Queen of the Weyanokes.

1876: The U.K. Medical Act of 1876 repealed the previous Medical Act in the United Kingdom, allowing medical authorities to license all qualified applicants regardless of gender. Before this act, women practiced as unlicensed physicians. However, the law did not guarantee the acceptance of women in medical schools. It left the decision to medical schools, and many continued to exclude women from their programs.

1913: More than two hundred women from the Bantu Women's League (BWL), led by Charlotte Maxeke and Cecilia Makiwane, marched from Waaihoek to the city hall to submit a petition with over 5,000 signatures against the passes laws requiring women of color to carry identifications in South Africa. The next day, hundreds of women marched into town and publicly destroyed their passes by tearing and burning them. Approximately 80 women were arrested over the two days. Despite pressure from the women, the Union of South Africa's government refused to remove the laws.

1914: Selma Lagerlöf, a Swedish author, became the first woman to join the Swedish Academy. She was also the first woman to receive the Nobel Prize in Literature, awarded to her in 1909.

1915: The International Congress of Women took place in The Hague as a significant peace initiative during World War I. The congress brought together women from various countries to discuss peace efforts and advocate for international cooperation.

2012: Laura Jane Grace, the lead singer of the punk rock band Against Me!, performed in public for the first time after publicly coming out as transgender. Her performance raised the visibility of transgender individuals in the music industry.

May 29

1800: The last examinations, which started on the 24th, for Maria Dalle Donne to obtain qualifications to teach Medicine took place in Bologna, gathering crowds. The 22-year-old woman, who received her Doctor of Philosophy and Medicine degree just half a year before, astonished all with her knowledge of *Anatomia, Physiologia*, and *Universa Medicina*. The event was so popular that it was described in the *Gazzetta di Bologna* in detail. She was enrolled at the Accademia dei Benedettini of the Institute of Sciences. After some discussions and disagreements over her position, she officially received her qualification on June 15, 1801.

1851: Sojourner Truth, an American abolitionist, and women's rights activist, delivered her famous speech titled "Ain't I a Woman?" at the Women's Rights Convention in Akron, Ohio. Her powerful address challenged gender and racial inequalities, advocating for women's rights and equality.

1943: The iconic illustration *Rosie the Riveter* by Norman Rockwell appeared on the cover of the *Saturday Evening Post*. This image symbolized the contribution of women to the American war effort during World War II and became an iconic representation of female empowerment and strength.

1977: Janet Guthrie, an American race car driver, became the first woman to compete in the Indianapolis 500, one of the most prestigious automobile races in the world. She finished in 29th place, breaking gender barriers in the sport.

1984: Tina Turner released her fifth solo album, *Private Dancer*, which achieved tremendous success worldwide. The album sold millions of copies, earned multi-platinum certifications, and marked a significant comeback in Tina Turner's career, solidifying her status as a music legend.

2002: Tina Sjögren from Sweden accomplished the Three Poles Challenge, becoming the first woman to complete this feat. She reached the North Pole, adding to her previous achievements of summiting Mount Everest in 1999 and skiing unsupported to the South Pole from 2001 to 2002.

2011: Malta held a referendum in which 53% of voters supported the introduction of divorce in the country. As a result, a law allowing divorce under specific conditions was enacted later in the year, marking a meaningful change in Malta's legislation regarding marital dissolution.

2014: *Zanan-e Emrooz* (*Today's Women*), an Iranian monthly magazine owned by Shahla Sherkat, started its publication. It was a re-launching of the *Zanan* (*Women*) Magazine, which began in 1992 and was banned in 2008 for "endangering the spiritual, mental and intellectual health of its readers, and threatening psychological security of the society."

2015: *Bonhishikha* - Unlearn Gender, a Bangladeshi organization dedicated to challenging gender stereotypes and roles, presented the play *It's a SHE Thing* for the first time. Inspired by Eve Ensler's *The Vagina Monologues* and based on real-life accounts gathered from women and girls across Dhaka, it represented various age groups and backgrounds.

2020: Taiwan decriminalized adultery through a landmark ruling. Previously, marital infidelity could be punished with up to a year of imprisonment. This ruling signaled a shift in societal attitudes and a recognition of personal freedom and autonomy in marital relationships.

May 30

1842: Queen Victoria of the United Kingdom survived an assassination attempt while traveling down Constitution Hill in London with Prince Albert. An unemployed Irishman, John Francis, attempted to take her life but was quickly apprehended. Queen Victoria emerged unharmed from the incident.

1899: Pearl Hart, a female outlaw known as "The Bandit Queen," successfully robbed a stagecoach in Arizona. This audacious act made her one of the few women to engage in criminal activities during the Old West era.

2002: Koneru Humpy, a chess player from India, achieved the title of Grandmaster (GM) at 15 years, one month, and 27 days. She became the youngest woman to attain this prestigious title, surpassing the previous record held by Judit Polgár by three months.

2005: Farkhondeh Sadegh, a graphic designer, and Laleh Keshavarz, a dentist, became the first Muslim women to climb Mount Everest, together with 38 other climbers, including Christine Joyce Feld Boskoff from the United States and Mona Mulepati from Nepal, who became the first non-Sherpa woman from Nepal to reach the summit.

2021: Paretta Autosport, led by team owner Beth Paretta, competed for the first time as a majority-women team in the history of the Indianapolis 500 races. The team featured driver Simona de Silvestro.

May 31

693: Wak Chanil Ajaw assumed regency and governed the Mayan city-state of Naranjo in present-day Guatemala when her son, K'ak' Tiliw Chan Chaak, became the new ruler at the age of 5.

1783: Élisabeth Vigée Le Brun, an acclaimed portraitist and the official painter of Marie Antoinette, along with Adélaïde Labille-Guiard, were accepted as members of the *Académie royale de peinture et de sculpture* (Royal Academy of Painting and Sculpture) in France. They were among the few women who gained full membership in the Academy from 1648 to 1793.

1864: Mary Jane Montgomery, an innovative inventor, received a patent for her improved locomotive wheels. *Scientific American* called her as "the only professional woman inventor."

2007: The Barbadian singer Rihanna released her breakthrough album *Good Girl Gone Bad*.

2011: Despite assurances from British Deputy Prime Minister Nick Clegg that the U.K. government would cease deporting individuals facing persecution based on their sexual orientation, Betty Tibikawa, a 22-year-old Ugandan woman who had been assaulted due to her sexual orientation, was denied asylum by British authorities. This incident raised concerns about the treatment of LGBTQ+ individuals seeking refuge.

2015: Harriette Thompson, aged 92 years and 65 days, became the oldest woman to complete a marathon. She accomplished this feat by finishing the Suja Rock 'n' Roll Marathon in San Diego, California.

2021: Sarab Abu-Rabia-Queder, an Israeli-Arab sociologist, anthropologist, and feminist activist specializing in gender studies, was promoted to Associate Professor at the Ben-Gurion University of the Negev. She was the first Bedouin woman in Israel to receive a doctorate in 2006.

June 01

1310: Marguerite Porete, a mystic and author of *The Mirror of Simple Souls*, was burned at the stake after refusing to recant her ideas and withdraw her book. She was declared a relapsed heretic.

1660: Mary Dyer was hanged for defying a law that banned Quakers from the Massachusetts Bay Colony.

1670: Jane, Lady Mico, included clauses in her will intended to relieve slavery. The funds set aside eventually accrued interest and were used in the 19th century to build schools and establish Mico University College in Jamaica, contributing to education and the fight against slavery.

1730: Enslaved woman Sally Basset was put on trial for murder in Bermuda, and despite protests and petitions, she was convicted and burned at the stake.

1843: Isabella Baumfree, who had been enslaved, changed her name to Sojourner Truth and embarked on a career as an anti-slavery activist. She became a prominent advocate for the abolition of slavery and women's rights, impacting the struggle for equality.

1914: Annie Besant founded the *New India* newspaper in Madras (now Chennai) to advocate for Indian independence from British colonial rule.

1943: *Die Naturwissenschaften* published an article by Berta Karlik, *"Eine neue natürliche α-Strahlung"* ("An Alpha-Radiation Ascribed to Element 85"), in which she shared her discovery that the element with the atomic number 85, Astatine, was a product of natural decay. Astatine's primary use is in radiotherapy to kill cancer cells. Due to this discovery, Karlik was awarded the Haitinger Prize for Chemistry from the Austrian Academy of Sciences in 1947. A year later, she published another article, *"Das Element 85 in den natürlichen Zerfallsreihen"* ("Element 85 in the Natural Disintegration Series"), in the *Zeitschrift für Physik* journal, further sharing her research findings.

1963: Josephine Okwuekeleke Tolefe became Nigeria's first woman to become an Army Captain.

1972: The first edition of *Spare Rib*, a feminist magazine, was published in the United Kingdom. The magazine provided a platform for women's voices and was founded by a collective that included Rosie Boycott, Marsha Rowe, Sue O'Sullivan, and Amanda Sebestyen.

1982: *All the Women Are White, All the Blacks Are Men, But Some of Us Are Brave*, a landmark feminist anthology in Black Women's Studies, was published. It was co-edited by Akasha Gloria Hull, Patricia Bell-Scott, and Barbara Smith.

1993: Connie Chung became the second woman to co-anchor the evening news, following in the footsteps of Barbara Walters, who had become the first in 1976.

1999: Jennifer Lopez released her debut album, *On the 6*, which showcased her talent in R&B and Latin music. The album began her successful music career and solidified her status as a versatile artist.

2018: Helen G. James, who had been discharged from the U.S. Air Force in the 1950s due to her LGBTQ+ identity during the "Lavender Scare" era, sued the Air Force for discrimination. She won her case, leading to an upgrade of her discharge to honorable and gaining full veterans benefits.

2021: Chilean President Sebastián Piñera announced his government's support for a bill legalizing same-sex marriage in Chile, signaling progress in recognizing LGBTQ+ rights and equality in the country.

June 02

1786: The Tignon law was enacted by Spanish Governor Esteban Rodríguez Miró in Louisiana, which forced Black women to wear Tignon headscarves. The law aimed to restrict and control the appearance of Black women.

1852: The first Pennsylvania Woman's Rights Convention occurred in West Chester, Pennsylvania. The convention addressed various women's rights issues, including legal rights, suffrage, equal pay, and access to education. It played a significant role in advocating for gender equality and raising awareness of women's rights in Pennsylvania.

1863: Harriet Tubman, a prominent abolitionist, and conductor of the Underground Railroad, led a military operation during the American Civil War known as the Combahee River raid. Tubman and 150 Black Union soldiers ventured into Maryland, freeing approximately 750 enslaved people and causing damage to the properties of wealthy secessionist landowners.

1924: The California Supreme Court ruled unanimously in favor of Alice Piper, a Paiute (Nüümü) girl, who sued after being denied entry to a newly built school due to her Native American heritage. This landmark ruling acknowledged the importance of equal access to education regardless of race and set a precedent for future antidiscrimination efforts.

1930: Sarah Dickson became the first woman ordained Presbyterian elder in the United States.

1953: The coronation of Queen Elizabeth II at Westminster Abbey became the first British coronation to be televised.

1975: In Lyon, France, a hundred sex workers occupied the church of Saint Nizier, protesting against their convictions for soliciting. Although they were evicted after a week, the occupation led to a legal judgment that nullified their impending prison sentences, setting a precedent for the rights and visibility of sex workers.

2010: Chemical biologist Carolyn Bertozzi became the first woman and one of the youngest scientists (at 43) to receive the Lemelson-MIT Prize, recognizing her significant contributions to the chemical biology field.

2012: Feng Jianmei, a resident of Zhenping County, Shaanxi, China, underwent a forced abortion seven months into her second pregnancy due to the enforcement of China's one-child policy. The incident sparked outrage and raised concerns about human rights violations and reproductive freedom.

2014: The U.N. Development Programme's N-Peace Awards recognized activists in various categories, including "Untold stories" - Bimala Kadayat (Nepal), Hasina Jalal (Afghanistan), Mi Kun Chan Non (Myanmar), Mona Parkash (Pakistan), Syarifah Aliyyah Shihab (Indonesia); "Breaking Stereotypes" - Rabiah Jamil Beg (Pakistan), "campaigning for action - Miriam Coronel Ferrer (Philippines), and "Peace Generation" - Wai Wai Nu (Myanmar) for their engagement in promoting equality, access, community, and empowerment of women.

2018: Following the death of Eyvi Ágreda, a 22-year-old woman fatally burned by her stalker, *NiUnaMenos* protesters were teargassed by the police as they gathered outside the Palace of Justice in Lima. They demanded justice in cases of femicide and an end to impunity for perpetrators of violence against women.

2021: Nicaraguan opposition figure Cristiana Chamorro Barrios was placed under house arrest in Managua on accusations of money laundering. This move was widely criticized as an attempt to stifle political opposition and undermine democratic processes in Nicaragua.

June 03

1900: The International Ladies' Garment Workers' Union (ILGWU) was founded in New York City. It was one of the first U.S. unions primarily composed of female members. The ILGWU played a crucial role in advocating for better working conditions, fair wages, and protective legislation for female workers in the garment industry.

1904: Susan B. Anthony, a prominent suffragist and women's rights advocate, officially opened the Second Conference of the International Woman Suffrage Alliance in Berlin.

1949: Georgia Neese Clark Gray became the first female Treasurer of the United States.

1968: Valerie Solanas, a radical feminist, shot artist Andy Warhol at his New York City studio, The Factory. Warhol survived the attack after undergoing a lengthy operation.

1972: Sally Priesand was ordained as a rabbi by the Hebrew Union College-Jewish Institute of Religion, becoming the first woman in America to be ordained as a rabbi by a rabbinical seminary. Following Regina Jonas, she was the second woman to be formally ordained as a rabbi in Jewish history.

1991: Volcanologist Katia Krafft, her husband, Maurice Krafft, and thirty-five others died during the eruption of Mount Unzen in Japan. The eruption produced fast -flowing pyroclastic flows, resulting in their deaths.

2013: Chelsea Manning, a former United States Army private, stood trial at Fort Meade, Maryland, for leaking classified material to WikiLeaks. The trial garnered significant attention and raised debates about whistleblowing, government transparency, and national security.

2016: A U.S. federal judge ruled against a women's soccer strike despite an expired agreement with a no-strike clause. The dispute was over pay inequality, with female players earning less despite their team's success and higher revenue.

June 04

1784: Madame Elizabeth Thible became the first woman to ride as a passenger in a hot-air balloon.

1913: Emily Davison, a suffragette, suffered fatal injuries during the Epsom Derby in England. In a deliberate protest, she stepped onto the racetrack and ran in front of Anmer, the racehorse owned by King George V. Despite efforts to avoid the collision, Davison was trampled by the horse, sustaining severe injuries and died four days later.

1919: The U.S. Congress approved the 19th Amendment to the United States Constitution, which guarantees women suffrage (the right to vote). The Amendment was then sent to the U.S. states for ratification, leading to its eventual adoption.

1950: *Gerwis* (*Gerakan Wanita Indonesia Sadar*, Movement of Conscious Indonesian Women) was founded in Semarang, Central Java. It later changed its name to *Gerwani*

(*Gerakan Wanita Indonesia*, Indonesian Women's Movement). It was founded by six women's organizations' representatives who shared a common experience fighting for the Indonesian National Revolution against the Dutch and the Japanese. The founding conference was chaired by activists such as Tris Metty, Umi Sardjono, S. K. Trimurti, and Sri Koesnapsijah.

1973: Yad Vashem, the World Holocaust Remembrance Center, recognized Jeannette Brousse-Maurier, a member of the French resistance, as Righteous Among the Nations. She was honored for her courageous efforts in providing safe passes and false documents to Jews during World War II, risking her own life to save others.

2011: Elaine Frances Sturtevant, an American artist, received the Golden Lion for lifetime achievement at the 54th Venice Biennale.

2013: The Marriage (Same-Sex Couples) Bill received approval from members of the House of Lords in the United Kingdom. This legislation granted equal marriage rights to LGBTQ+ couples in the U.K.

2014: Eimear McBride won the Baileys Women's Prize for Fiction with her novel *A Girl Is a Half-formed Thing*. Her work triumphed over other notable contenders, including Donna Tartt's acclaimed novel *The Goldfinch*.

June 05

830: Theodora was crowned the Byzantine Empress consort of Theophilos. Twelve years later, she became queen regnant, ruling in her own right.

1575: Diana Scultori, an Italian engraver, received a Papal Privilege to produce and sell her engravings and prints, protecting her work by imposing heavy fines on unauthorized publishers or vendors.

1834: Sol Hachuel, a Moroccan Jewish girl, was publicly executed at 17. Despite pressure from the Moroccan Sultan, Abd al -Rahman, she refused to convert to Islam. Even though she had never converted, Sol was charged with apostasy from Islam, and the accusation was based on a rumor.

1851: Harriet Beecher Stowe's antislavery novel, *Uncle Tom's Cabin*, was first published in serial form in The National Era. This influential work shed light on the harsh realities of slavery and became a significant catalyst in the abolitionist movement.

1899: Helena Donhaiser became the first Polish woman to complete high school with the final *Matura* exam, with the same curriculum as male students.

1912: Tsuruko Haraguchi received a Ph.D. in psychology from Columbia University, becoming the first Japanese woman to achieve this.

1915: Denmark amended its constitution to grant women's suffrage, allowing women to vote in national elections.

1949: Orapin Chaiyakan was elected the first Thai female member of Thailand's Parliament.

1972: The United States announced that Reserve Officers' Training Corps (ROTC) programs in high schools would be open to girls, expanding opportunities for girls to receive military training and education.

1977: The National Council of Women of Kenya, led by Wangarĩ Muta Maathai, initiated the Green Belt Movement. They marched from downtown Nairobi to Kamukunji Park and planted seven trees in honor of historical community leaders—this movement aimed to promote environmental conservation, sustainable development, and women's empowerment.

2002: Biochemist Peggy Whitson became the first resident scientist at the International Space Station (ISS). During her six-month mission, she contributed to installing the station's Mobile Base System, performed a spacewalk, and conducted numerous human life science and microgravity science experiments.

2007: Nigerian author Chimamanda Ngozi Adichie won the Orange Prize (now the Women's Prize for Fiction) for her second novel, *Half of a Yellow Sun*. Adichie's work has received critical acclaim, and she was later crowned the *Winner of Winners* in 2021, recognizing her contribution to the Women's Prize for Fiction over 25 years.

2012: The Diamond Jubilee celebrations for Queen Elizabeth II took place in Great Britain on the 60th anniversary of her accession to the throne, commemorating her reign and contributions to the country.

June 06

913: After the death of Emperor Alexander III, his 8-year-old nephew, Constantine VII Porphyrogennetos, succeeded him as the emperor of the Byzantine Empire. He was guided by a regency council led by Empress Zoë Karbonopsina.

1770: A revolt occurred on the slave ship *The Unity*, led by two women from Dahomey (present-day Benin). These women, known for their skills as warriors, played a significant role in the uprising.

1785: María de Guzmán, at 17, earned her doctoral degree at the University of Alcalá, specializing in the Faculty of Human Arts and Letters. She held the titles of Honorary Professor in Conciliatory and Examining Philosophy. She was the first woman in Spain to become a Doctor of Philosophy

1920: The International Woman Suffrage Alliance Congress began in Geneva, Switzerland.

1942: Adeline Gray made the first parachute jump in the United States using a nylon parachute.

1960: Barbra Streisand, an 18-year-old from Brooklyn, started her professional singing career by winning $50 in a talent contest at The Lion, a nightclub in Greenwich Village, marking the beginning of Streisand's successful career as a singer and actress.

1971: *Stern* magazine featured 28 German actresses and journalists on its cover, declaring, "We Had an Abortion!" (*Wir haben abgetrieben!*). This act sparked a powerful campaign against the restrictive abortion ban. Journalist Alice Schwarzer led this protest, inspired by a similar movement in France.

1998: An American romantic comedic-drama television series, *Sex and the City*, aired for the first time on HBO. The series has won several accolades, including Emmy, Golden Globe, and Screen Actors Guild Awards. It was also criticized for its portrayal of female characters and is seen as an example of the post-feminist tendencies of the time.

2005: Stephanie Yarber, who received an ovarian transplant from her twin sister, gave birth to a healthy baby girl. This event was considered encouraging news for women struggling with fertility issues, highlighting the potential of transplant procedures.

2009: Alysa Stanton became the world's first Black female rabbi after being ordained at the Hebrew Union College-Jewish Institute of Religion.

June 07

1557: Mary I of England, also known as Bloody Mary, joined her husband, Philip II of Spain, in his war against France, demonstrating her involvement in military affairs during her reign as queen.

1886: Winifred Edgerton Merrill became the first woman at Columbia University and the first woman in the United States to receive a Ph.D. in mathematics. She completed her thesis after just two-and-a-half years of studies.

1920: The Women's International Zionist Organization (WIZO; *Vitzo*) was established in London by Rebecca Sieff, Vera Weizmann, Edith Eder, Romana Goodman, and Henrietta Irwell to provide community services for the residents of Mandate Palestine.

1953: Mary Church Terrell, an African-American civil rights activist, successfully fought to end segregation in eating places in the District of Columbia, United States.

1965: In the landmark case of *Griswold v. Connecticut*, the U.S. Supreme Court ruled that access to birth control was a fundamental human right.

1968: In Dagenham, United Kingdom, 850 women machinists at the Ford factory went on strike to demand equal pay. They contested the classification of their work as unskilled, leading to lower wages than their male colleagues.

1971: Carole King, an American singer, songwriter, and musician, released her iconic album *Tapestry*. The album was a critical and commercial success, earning King four Grammy Awards in 1972.

2016: African-American Black Lives Matter activist Jasmine Abdullah was sentenced to prison in California under felony lynching. Although the term "lynching" typically refers to extrajudicial killings of African Americans, in California law, it was defined as attempting to remove someone from police custody. After public outcry, the term was removed from the law in 2016, while the rest remained intact.

2019: The 2019 FIFA Women's World Cup began in France, with the host nation defeating South Korea 4-0 in the opening match.

June 08

1929: Margaret Bondfield was appointed Minister of Labour in the United Kingdom, becoming the first woman to hold a Cabinet position.

1937: A law was passed in Nazi Germany stating that only men could fill university posts, which was part of the policy of removing women from higher-education positions, judiciary (from the roles of judge and prosecutor), and medical practice - the Association of Medical Women was dissolved. Women could only keep their positions or complete their doctoral studies in exceptional situations.

1949: During the Second Red Scare in the United States, a Federal Bureau of Investigation (FBI) report named notable figures such as Helen Keller and Dorothy Parker as members of the Communist Party, reflecting the heightened anti-communist sentiments and investigations during that period.

1961: Gwendolyn Greene and Joan Mulholland were among a group of Freedom Riders who were arrested in Jackson, Mississippi. The Freedom Riders were activists who fought against the non-enforcement of the ban on segregation in public transportation in the Southern United States.

2006: Alison Bechdel, author of the comic strip *Dykes to Watch Out For*, published a graphic memoir *Fun House*.

2012: Emma Martin, a writer from New Zealand, won the £5,000 Commonwealth Short Story Prize for her story *Two Girls in a Boat* in The Commonwealth Writers Prizes.

2019: Plant breeders Viru and Girija Viraraghavan named a new rose variety, *E. K. Janaki Ammal*, in honor of an Indian botanist who significantly contributed to plant breeding, cytogenetics, and phytogeography. The botanist co-authored the *Chromosome Atlas of Cultivated Plants* (1945) with C.D. Darlington and obtained her Ph.D. from the University of Michigan as an Oriental Barbour Fellow in 1931.

2021: In Ghana, a court denied bail to 21 LGBTQ+ rights activists arrested during an assembly. The group, consisting of 16 women and five men, faced prosecution under the country's laws against homosexuality. Engaging in homosexual acts could lead to imprisonment for up to three years. Local LGBTQ+ organizations contended that the activists had gathered to discuss the human rights of gay people in Ghana, which they argued should not be considered illegal.

June 09

1909: Alice Huyler Ramsey, a 22-year-old, embarked on a cross-country automobile trip, becoming the first woman to drive across the United States. She drove a *Maxwell 30* and covered 3,800 miles from Manhattan to San Francisco over 59 days.

1910: Lucrezia Bori, a talented opera singer, made her debut with the Metropolitan Opera in a remarkable way. She stepped in to replace an ill singer in the role of Manon in Puccini's *Manon Lescaut* during the Met's first visit to Paris.

1914: Bertha Ryland, a militant suffragette, resorted to vandalism to draw attention to the women's suffrage cause when she slashed a painting at the Birmingham Art Gallery.

1919: The Philippine Women's University was founded in Manila, providing women in the Philippines with access to higher education opportunities.

1944: Johanna Kirchner, a German socialist and member of the anti-fascist resistance was killed by the Nazis. After going underground following Hitler's rise to power, she sought refuge in France. However, she was arrested by the collaborationist Vichy regime and handed over to the Gestapo. Kirchner was initially sentenced to 10 years of hard labor but later faced a retrial, which led to her being sentenced to death for "Marxist high-treason propaganda."

1949: Georgia Neese Clark made history as she became the first woman to hold the position of Treasurer of the United States.

1963: Fannie Lou Hamer, a prominent activist of the Student Nonviolent Coordinating Committee, endured a brutal beating by the police in Winona, Mississippi. Alongside her fellow activists, she was unjustly jailed after their bus made a stop in the town.

1976: Susie Orbach and Luise Eichenbaum established the Women's Therapy Centre in London and later expanded their efforts by founding the Women's Therapy Centre Institute in New York in 1981. These organizations provided essential spaces for women to seek therapy and support, addressing their unique psychological and emotional challenges.

1994: The Belém do Pará Convention, also known as the Inter-American Convention on Violence Against Women, was adopted in Belém do Pará, Brazil, by the Inter-American Commission of Women (CIM), part of the Organization of American States (OAS). This treaty was the first in the world to legally prohibit all forms of violence against women, especially sexual violence. The Follow-Up Mechanism (MESECVI) agency was established to ensure compliance with the Convention on October 26, 2004.

2006: Habiba Sarabi, Afghanistan's former women's minister, was appointed by President Karzai to govern the province of Bamiyan. She became one of the few women to hold a high-ranking government position in the country.

2011: In Saudi Arabia, five women were arrested for practicing driving, an act prohibited for women in the country at the time.

2015: U.S. Army Brig. Gen. Giselle Wilz assumed the 21st Commander and Senior Military Representative role at NATO Headquarters in Sarajevo as the first-ever female Commander in the history of NATO Headquarters in Sarajevo.

June 10

1692: The Salem witch trials, a dark chapter in colonial Massachusetts, began with the hanging of Bridget Bishop. Accused of witchcraft, Bishop became the first victim of the trials, starting the tragic period of persecution and hysteria.

1861: Dorothea Dix was appointed the Superintendent of Female Nurses for the Union Army by the United States War Department. This significant appointment made Dix the first woman to hold a military job.

1907: In Tokyo, the first edition of *Tianyi* (*Natural Justice*), a Chinese anarchist feminist magazine, was published in exile. Founded by He-Yin Zhen, a prominent Women's Rights Recovery Association member, the magazine advocated for resistance against various forms of oppression. It rejected women's subservience to men, concubinage, and second-wife status. It also offered support to members facing abuse or dominance. Through its radical stance, Tianyi aimed to address the systemic issues of inequality and the concentration of power in the hands of the ruling class.

1963: President John F. Kennedy signed the Equal Pay Act. This landmark legislation aimed to prohibit sex-based wage discrimination by employers engaged in commerce or producing goods for commerce.

1996: Elouise P. Cobell, Mildred Cleghorn, and other Native American plaintiffs filed a class-action lawsuit against the U.S. federal government. The lawsuit accused the government of mismanaging Indian trust assets intended for individual Native American trust beneficiaries, both present and past.

2019: The Vatican released a teaching instruction titled *Male and Female He Created Them*, which expressed opposition about the theory of gender and questioned the binary classification of sexes. This document sparked controversy and received criticism from LGBTQ+ groups for its stance on gender identity.

June 11

1824: Maria Szymanowska, a Polish composer and one of the first professional virtuoso pianists of the 19th century performed a concert at the Hanover Square, with members of the royal family present, during her West European tour.

1893: Princess Teri'inavaharoa was crowned the Queen of the Kingdom of Huahine and Mai'ao, using the regal name Tehaapapa III. She was the last Queen of Huahine from 1893 to 1895, when the French abolished the monarchy.

1913: Women in Illinois celebrated the passage of a state Woman Suffrage Bill, granting them the right to vote in presidential elections.

1941: Louise Boyd led a geophysical expedition along the west coast of Greenland and down the coast of Baffin Island and Labrador.

1963: Vivian Malone, one of the two black students attempting to enroll at the University of Alabama, faced Governor George Wallace's refusal to accept a U.S. District Court order. With the presence of federalized National Guard troops, Malone successfully registered at the university later that day.

1966: The movie *Kinokawa* (*River Ki*), based on the book by Sawako Ariyoshi, was released in Japan. The novel focuses on three generations of women representing modern Japanese history. Ariyoshi was a prolific Japanese novelist, widely recognized as one of the country's foremost female writers. Her literary works centered on the portrayal of significant societal issues, such as the challenges faced by older people, the consequences of social and political transformations on Japanese domestic life and values, and the environmental ramifications of pollution, with a particular focus on women's roles and experiences.

1987: Diane Abbott became the first Black woman elected to the House of Commons in the United Kingdom.

1998: Landscape architect Kathryn Gustafson won the inaugural Jane Drew Prize for her collaborative architectural work.

2019: Botswana decriminalized homosexuality.

2021: Marcia Chatelain received the Pulitzer Prize for History for her book, *Franchise: The Golden Arches in Black America.*

2022: Jeanine Áñez, the former President of Bolivia, was sentenced to ten years in prison for breach of duty and resolutions contrary to the Constitution and laws of Bolivia during the 2019 Bolivian political crisis.

June 12

918: Æthelflæd, while fighting the Vikings, died in Tamworth. She was laid to rest beside her husband Æthelred at St. Oswald's Priory in Gloucester. Her daughter Ælfwynn succeeded her as the ruler of Mercia.

1552: After many years of disputes and familial conflict, an agreement was signed between two powerful sisters, Doña Gracia Mendes Nasi and Brianda, which the Venetian Senate later endorsed. One hundred thousand gold ducats were deposited in the Zecca for Gracia's niece, Gracia Junior. In exchange, Brianda received a dowry of 18,123.5 Italian gold *écus* and accrued interest for her daughter's education during her minority. She agreed to drop all claims against her sister, João Miques, and their representatives in Lyons, Paris, Venice, and Florence. She also acknowledged Gracia and her daughter's freedom to choose their residence.

1754: Dorothea Erxleben obtained her Doctor of Medicine degree as the first woman in Germany. She practiced medicine in her hometown of Quedlinburg. There was no other female doctor in Germany for another 150 years.

1821: Ranavalona (Ranavalo-Manjaka I) was crowned as the first female sovereign of the Kingdom of Imerina (Madagascar) since its establishment in 1540.

1912: The organization Big Sisters was established eight years after the creation of Big Brothers.

1942: Anne Frank began writing in her new diary on her 13th birthday.

1963: The film *Cleopatra,* starring Elizabeth Taylor, premiered in U.S. theaters as one of the most expensive films made at the time.

1967: In a unanimous 9-0 decision, the U.S. Supreme Court ruled in favor of Mildred and Richard Loving, overturning their criminal convictions and invalidating Virginia's anti-miscegenation law.

1990: Mariah Carey released her debut studio album and became the first artist to have her first five singles reach number one on the Billboard Hot 100 chart, from *Vision of Love* to *Emotions.*

2005: On the day before Iran's presidential election, women called for a demonstration before Tehran University, demanding changes to the "discriminatory laws." A year later, women again tried to gather at the Hafte Tir Square to demand change and were met with violence from the security forces. Many women were beaten, and seventy were arrested. The events prompted the One Million Signatures campaign (*see:* August 28).

2009: Fatima Zahra Mansouri, a 33-year-old lawyer, was elected as the first female mayor of Marrakech, one of Morocco's largest cities.

2009: Cleaning workers at the School of Oriental and African Studies in London, employed by subcontractor ISS, were subjected to an unexpected "staff meeting" orchestrated by immigration officers. Several workers, including a pregnant employee, were detained. The incident was believed to respond to the workers' organizing efforts for better pay and conditions.

2019: The Supreme Court of Ecuador legalized same-sex marriage.

2020: The U.S. Department of Health and Human Services removed protections that previously safeguarded transgender individuals and women seeking abortions under the Affordable Care Act ("Obamacare").

2022: Linn Grant, a Swedish golfer, became the first female winner on the PGA European Tour after her victory in the Scandinavian Mixed tournament, co-sanctioned with the Ladies European Tour in 2020.

June 13

1541: Jeanne d'Albret, at age twelve, was forced into marriage with William "the Rich," Duke of Jülich-Cleves-Berg, the brother of Anne of Cleves, the fourth wife of Henry VIII of England. Despite coercion, she continued to object and had to be physically escorted to the altar. Before the wedding, Jeanne signed two documents. Her household officers also signed, stating,

> "I, Jeanne de Navarre, persisting in the protestations I have already made, do hereby again affirm and protest by these present, that the marriage which it is desired to contract between the duke of Cleves and myself, is against my will; that I have never consented to it, nor will consent..."

The marriage was annulled four years later.

1655: Adriana Nooseman-van de Bergh became the first actress in Amsterdam theater.

1782: Anna Göldi, a Swiss maid, was executed by decapitation for alleged witchcraft. She worked for the Tschudi family and was accused of supernatural acts like placing needles in her employer's daughter's food. After her arrest, she confessed under torture but later recanted. Though officially charged with "poisoning" rather than witchcraft, her case stirred outrage across Switzerland and the Holy Roman Empire. In 2008, the Canton of Glarus posthumously exonerated her, acknowledging the injustice she suffered.

1971: Geraldine Brodrick of Canberra, Australia, gave birth to nonuplets, with two babies stillborn. The remaining seven infants, weighing between one and two pounds, survived for a few days.

1978: Gayle Rubin and others founded Samois, the first exclusively lesbian BDSM group in the U.S. The name was inspired by the fictional estate in Anne-Marie's *Story of O*. Samois originated from a women's discussion group within the Society of Janus called Cardea.

2013: Alicia Garza posted the phrase "Black lives matter" on Facebook, sparking a widespread movement in the United States and globally.

2016: A 22-year-old Dutch woman who had reported rape in Qatar was released after nearly three months of detention. The court ruling resulted in a one-year suspended prison sentence, but the punishment given to the accused man was unclear.

2022: Masih Alinejad, an Iranian-American journalist, author, and women's rights activist, received the American Jewish Committee's Moral Courage Award for fearlessly supporting the oppressed Iranian people against their government. In 2014, Alinejad launched "My Stealthy Freedom" on Facebook, inviting Iranian women to post hijab-free photos. She served as a presenter and producer at VOA Persian Service, a Radio Farda correspondent, a regular Manoto television contributor, and a contributing editor for *IranWire*.

June 14

1907: Norwegian women were granted the right to vote in parliamentary elections due to the efforts of The National Association for Women's Suffrage.

1913: The funeral procession for Emily Davison, an English suffragette who died after being trampled by a horse during a protest at the Epsom Derby, took place. Thousands of suffragettes marched to St George's Church, where Miss Davison was laid to rest.

1926: Carrie Chapman Catt, a prominent suffragette, appeared on the cover of *TIME* magazine and was interviewed about her fight for women's suffrage.

1939: Ethel Waters became the first African American, male or female, to star in her own television show, The Ethel Waters Show, which was broadcast on NBC.

1991: Approximately half a million women in Switzerland participated in a nationwide women's strike, demanding legal enforcement of gender equality. The demand was incorporated into the federal constitution on June 14, 1981. Women went on strike again on the same date in 2011 and 2019, calling for better recognition and compensation for care work, ending sexual harassment, and action against wage inequality.

2023: At the annual meeting of the International Society for Stem Cell Research, developmental biologist Magdalena Żernicka-Goetz announced a significant development. Researchers from the United States and the United Kingdom successfully created synthetic human embryo-like structures using stem cells. Żernicka-Goetz highlighted the potential of these findings to enhance our understanding of miscarriages and their underlying causes.

June 15

1686: The Maison Royale de Saint-Louis, a boarding school for girls, was founded in Saint-Cyr (now part of Saint-Cyr-l'École, Yvelines), France, by Louis XIV at the request of his second wife, Françoise d'Aubigné, Marquise de Maintenon, who aimed to provide education to girls from poor noble families. The Maison Royale de Saint-Louis admitted girls aged 7 to 12 whose fathers served the state and faced difficulties like illness, death, or financial hardship. Admission was decided by the king, with input from genealogy experts to ensure at least four generations of noble heritage on the father's side. The school housed up to 250 students, cared for by female educators, domestic helpers, priests, and staff. Students aged 7 to 20 wore uniforms with colored ribbons to indicate their class, and each class (age group) had its own room.

1921: Bessie Coleman obtained a pilot's license from the *Fédération Aéronautique Internationale*, becoming the first woman of color in the U.S. to become an aviator.

1942: Luise Brunner became employed as a guard in the Ravensbrück concentration camp for women. In October 1942, she was temporarily transferred to the Auschwitz Nazi Camp. In January 1944, she was awarded *Kriegsverdienstkreuz II. Klasse* for her "constant commitment" and later moved back to Ravensbrück, where she became *Oberaufseherin* (senior inspector, the highest position a woman could have). After the war, she was sentenced to three years and released after two.

1985: The Third World Conference on Women took place (until June 26) in Nairobi, Kenya, assessing progress and setbacks in achieving goals set by the World Plan of Action. Notably, it introduced discussions on lesbian rights at a U.N. official meeting and spotlighted the issue of violence against women. The Conference recommended ongoing evaluation of women's achievements and challenges through 2000.

2005: Hanadi Zakaria al-Hindi completed her final exams at the Middle East Academy for Commercial Aviation in Amman, Jordan, becoming the first Saudi woman to become a pilot. She received certification to fly within Saudi Arabia in 2014.

2019: Zuzana Čaputová was inaugurated as Slovakia's first elected female President.

2020: The United States Supreme Court ruled in the *Bostock v. Clayton County, Georgia* case, stating that the Civil Rights Act of 1964 prohibits employment discrimination based on sexual orientation and gender identity.

2021: The Hungarian National Assembly passed a law prohibiting the "depiction or promotion of same-sex relationships and gender reassignment" to individuals under 18.

2022: Seraphine Warren commenced a 2,400-mile prayer walk from Sweetwater, Arizona, on the Navajo Nation, to Washington, D.C., arriving in October. The journey aimed to raise awareness of the high number of missing and murdered Indigenous people, particularly women, in honor of her aunt Ella Mae Begay, a Dineh (Navajo) elder who went missing precisely one year prior.

June 16

1654: Christina abdicated the Swedish throne, passing it to her cousin Charles X Gustav. On the same day, she covertly converted to Catholicism after being the queen of a Protestant nation.

1901: Sultan Jahan succeeded her mother, *Nawab Begum* Sultan Shah Jahan, at her death, becoming *Nawab Begum* of Dar-ul-Iqbal-i-Bhopal (now Madhya Pradesh, India).

1915: Women's Institutes were established in Britain, a community-based organization for women that had also been created in other countries such as Canada, South Africa, and New Zealand.

1962: *The New Yorker* magazine published the first three chapters of Rachel Carson's upcoming book, *Silent Spring*, which received an unprecedented response and surpassed any previous article in the magazine's history. *Silent Spring*, credited with launching the environmental movement, was officially released in late September that year.

1963: Cosmonaut Valentina Tereshkova became the first woman in space, spending three days orbiting the Earth. She remains the only woman to have conducted a solo space mission.

2012: China successfully launched the *Shenzhou 9* spacecraft, which carried a crew of three, including China's first female astronaut, Liu Yang. The mission aimed to dock with the Tiangong-1 space station module.

2012: Aung San Suu Kyi, the Burmese politician, personally accepted the Nobel Peace Prize 21 years after being awarded the prize in absentia.

2017: The Ibn Rushd-Goethe Mosque was founded in Germany by Seyran Ateş, a Kurdish-German lawyer and Muslim feminist, to promote liberal Islamic practices. It bans face coverings, encourages mixed-gender prayer, and welcomes LGBTQ+ worshippers. Its name honors the legacies of Ibn Rushd and Johann Wolfgang von Goethe.

June 17

1873: Susan B. Anthony's trial began for illegally voting in Rochester on November 5, 1872. The U.S. district attorney argued that she was incompetent to stand as her witness because she was a woman.

1911: The Women's Coronation March took place, with 40,000 women marching in London to advocate for British women's suffrage. The march spanned from Thames Embankment to Albert Hall along the coronation procession route.

1912: Julia Clark, the second American woman to receive a pilot's license, died in a plane crash at an airshow in Springfield, Illinois. She crashed into a tall tree while flying in foggy conditions, becoming the third woman to die in a plane crash, following Deniz Moore and Suzanne Bernard.

1913: The College of the Holy Spirit Manila was established in Manila as an all-female school, a status it held until 2005.

1926: The Vice Squad of the NYPD raided Eve's Hangout, a gathering place for lesbians, Jewish migrants, and individuals from various backgrounds. The bar's owner, Eva Kotchever, was charged and found guilty of obscenity and disorderly conduct and deported to Europe.

1929: A 7.3-magnitude earthquake struck the South Island of New Zealand. Seismologist Inge Lehmann discovered anomalies in the recorded wave patterns from seismometers worldwide, leading to her groundbreaking revelation that the Earth's core is solid, contrary to previous beliefs.

1937: Austrian anti-fascist Katia Landau, who had joined the fight against nationalists in Spain, was arrested by the Soviet secret police alongside comrades. They endured torture and false accusations, but Landau and her fellow prisoners steadfastly refused to cooperate. She later went on a hunger strike and received support from other women inmates.

1971: A group of citizens calling themselves "the Battlers" (and who were called the "13 bloody housewives" by the local Council) organized the blueprint for the modern-day protest movement. They fought against constructing luxury houses over Kelly's Bush, the last remaining open space in the suburb of Sydney. After years of effort, the builders' trade union joined their protest and issued a "black ban," later known as the "green ban" – a form of strike action to preserve the environment.

2010: A major exhibition of surrealist painter Leonora Carrington's work, the first in the U.K. in twenty years, was held at Chichester's Pallant House Gallery in West Sussex.

2011: The U.N. Human Rights Council condemned discrimination against gays, lesbians, and transgender people for the first time.

2011: A few dozen Saudi women participated in civil disobedience by defying the driving ban in Riyadh, Jeddah, and Dammam, with no reported arrests this time, despite prior detentions.

2014: A letter signed by one thousand women of color commended President Obama and various organizations for their efforts to include young women and girls in programs similar to My Brother's Keeper, which focused on young men of color.

June 18

1858: Rani Lakshmibai, the brave Queen of Jhansi, fought in the historic battle near the Phool Bagh in Gwalior. She dressed as a cavalry leader and fought courageously but was eventually killed in a clash with the 8th (King's Royal Irish) Hussars.

1873: Susan B. Anthony was fined $100 for attempting to vote in the 1872 presidential election. Her actions were part of her ongoing activism in the suffrage movement.

1900: Empress Dowager Cixi of China ordered the *I-Ho-Chuan* (Boxers) to kill all foreigners during the Boxer Rebellion, a violent anti-foreign and anti-Christian uprising.

1928: Amelia Earhart, an American aviator, became the first woman to fly across the Atlantic Ocean. She landed in Burry Port, Wales, in a significant achievement in aviation history.

1943: Maria Kislyak, an 18-year-old Ukrainian anti-Nazi fighter, was executed alongside her friends Fedor Rudenko and Vasiliy Bugrimenko. Kislyak had lured two Nazi officers into the woods, where her friends killed them. She confessed to protecting innocent civilians when the Gestapo threatened reprisals.

1959: The film *The Nun's Story*, based on a best-selling novel, premiered. It starred Audrey Hepburn in the lead role and received critical acclaim and commercial success.

1972: The Japanese feminist group *Chūpiren* (an abbreviation for *Chūzetsu Kinshi Hō ni Hantai Shi Piru Kaikin o Yōkyū Suru Josei Kaihō Rengō*, Women's Liberation Federation for Opposing the Abortion Prohibition Law and Lifting the Pill Ban) was formed by Misako Enoki and others. They organized well-attended demonstrations for a series of campaigns addressing the concerns of women. *Chūpiren* was concerned with legal rights in divorce and marriage, access to birth control, abortion, and equal pay. Wearing pink hard hats to ensure maximal media attention, the demonstrators marched in white military-style uniforms. They held protest rallies and sit-ins and took part in publicity stunts, such as confronting unfaithful husbands in their offices. The male-dominated media covered Chūpiren but did not take them seriously, instead ridiculing the movement.

1983: Iranian teenager Mona Mahmudnizhad and nine other women from the Bahá'í Faith were hanged in Iran on charges including "misleading children and youth" and being a "Zionist." The Bahá'í World Centre location in Israel was used as a pretext for persecution.

1983: Sally K. Ride became the first American woman to travel to space when she was launched aboard the space shuttle *Challenger*.

2001: An Islamist lawyer attempted to legally divorce Nawal El Saadawi, an Egyptian feminist writer and anti-FGM activist, from her husband, citing the obscure 9th-century Sharia law principle of *Hisbah*, which is the right of any citizen to bring "violators of public mores" to court. The evidence presented was an interview in which it was claimed she had abandoned Islam.

June 19

1603: Merga Bien was arrested for witchcraft in Fulda, Germany, along with approximately 250 other people. They were later burned at the stake as victims of the witchcraft trials.

1915: In Iceland, a dependency of Denmark at the time, women's suffrage was granted to those over 40.

1937: The Women's Day Massacre occurred in Youngstown, Ohio. The wives of striking workers at Republic Steel organized a Women's Day event to support the men, but they were ordered to leave by the police captain. When the women refused, tear gas was fired at them, including women, children, and babies. The police then opened fire, resulting in numerous casualties and deaths.

1949: Sara Christian became the first woman to race in NASCAR at Charlotte Speedway. She qualified 13th in the #71 Ford, owned by her husband, Frank Christian.

1953: Ethel Rosenberg and her husband were executed in New York for conspiracy to commit treason. The Rosenberg Case was highly controversial and remains a subject of debate.

1963: Soviet cosmonaut Valentina Tereshkova, the first woman in space, successfully returned to Earth after spending nearly three days in space aboard the *Vostok 6* spacecraft.

1970: Diana Ross, following her departure from the Supremes, released a successful debut solo album. The album included the U.S. number-one hit *Ain't No Mountain High Enough* and the song *Reach Out and Touch (Somebody's Hand)*.

1975: The first World Conference on Women was held in Mexico City (to July 2). It was the first U.N. conference solely dedicated to women's issues. It reshaped perceptions, emphasizing women's active role in policymaking rather than passive aid recipients. This key event underpinned International Women's Year and led to the United Nations Decade for Women and subsequent conferences. Two essential outcomes were the World Plan of Action with specific women's advancement targets and the Declaration of Mexico on the Equality of Women and Their Contribution to Development and Peace, analyzing the impact of foreign policies on women. The Conference also led to the creation of the International Research and Training Institute for the Advancement of Women, monitoring progress, and the United Nations Development Fund for Women, supporting developmental programs. It empowered parallel Tribune meetings, catalyzing global women's group formation.

2020: Lawmakers in Tennessee passed stringent anti-abortion laws, making it one of the strictest states in the U.S. regarding abortion restrictions. The legislation banned abortions once a "fetal heartbeat" (electric proto-cardiac activity) was detected, typically around six weeks of pregnancy.

June 20

1837: Princess Alexandrina Victoria of Kent succeeded to the British throne, becoming Queen Victoria. She went on to reign for over 63 years, making her the longest-reigning monarch in British history until Queen Elizabeth II surpassed her.

1895: Caroline Willard Baldwin became the first woman to earn a Ph.D. in Science from an American university. She obtained her doctoral degree from Cornell University.

1901 (or 1903): Charlotte Maxeke, a South African religious leader, social activist, and political activist, became the first black woman to graduate with a university degree in South Africa. She obtained a B.Sc from Wilberforce University in Ohio, where she studied under the prominent Pan-Africanist W.E.B. Du Bois.

1908: Melitta Bentz was granted a patent by the *Kaiserliche Patentamt* (Imperial Patent Office) for her innovative coffee filter. Her easy-to-clean coffee filter revolutionized coffee brewing, producing a tastier cup of coffee and paving the way for modern coffee brewing methods.

1911: Actress Sarah Bernhardt broke tradition during her visit to the United States by becoming the first woman admitted to a reception at the all-male Players Club in New York.

1936: Marta Suchanek-Kłyszewska, the first female student at the *AGH* University of Science and Technology in Kraków, Poland, became the first woman in Poland to obtain a master's degree in mining engineering.

1960: Nan Winton became the first national female newsreader on BBC television.

June 21

1913: Tiny Broadwick, an American aerial stunt jumper and parachutist, became the first woman to parachute from an airplane intentionally. She performed this historic feat at an air show at the U.S. Army base in San Diego.

1946: The United Nations established the Commission on the Status of Women, the first intergovernmental body dedicated to promoting women's rights globally.

1956: Cecilia Payne-Gaposchkin, an astronomer, was appointed Professor of Astronomy at Harvard University. She became the first woman to achieve a full professorship at Harvard through regular faculty promotion.

1957: Ellen Fairclough was sworn in as Canada's first female Cabinet Minister, serving as the Minister of Citizenship and Immigration.

1960: American jazz singer Etta Jones recorded the album *Don't Go to Strangers*, which became a significant success. The album was later inducted into the Grammy Hall of Fame in 2008, showcasing Jones' talent and contributions to the jazz genre.

1997: The Women's National Basketball Association (WNBA) played its first game.

2021: Laurel Hubbard, a weightlifter from New Zealand, became the first transgender athlete to be selected to compete in the Olympic Games. The New Zealand Olympic Committee announced her selection to participate in the Tokyo Olympics as part of the women's weightlifting team.

June 22

1484: Anna Rügerin, a woman from Augsburg, printed the first known book produced by a female printer. The book was an edition of Eike of Repgow's compendium of customary law, the *Sachsenspiegel*.

1813: Laura Secord, a Canadian woman, embarked on a 30-kilometer trek on foot to warn Lieutenant James FitzGibbon about American plans for a surprise attack on Beaver Dams in Ontario during the War of 1812.

1897: The Diamond Jubilee of Queen Victoria was celebrated throughout the United Kingdom. The jubilee marked the 60th anniversary of Queen Victoria's reign and was commemorated with various festivities and events.

1917: Lucy Burns and Katherine Morey, National Woman's Party members, were arrested for "obstructing traffic" while picketing the White House. They were among the first suffragists to engage in such protests and faced legal consequences for their activism in the fight for women's right to vote.

1954: Sarah Mae Flemming, an African American woman, was mistreated and physically assaulted by a bus driver in South Carolina for sitting in a "white-only" section of the bus. This incident led to a legal case, *Flemming v. South Carolina Electric and Gas*, which played a role in challenging racial segregation on public transportation.

1970: Bernadette Devlin, an Irish socialist, republican, and Member of the British Parliament, lost her appeal against a six-month prison sentence for "incitement to riot." The verdict was imposed due to her involvement, in support of the residents, in the Battle of the Bogside during the Northern Ireland conflict.

1971: The Where We At Black Women Artists exhibit occurred at Acts of Art Gallery in New York's West Village. It featured the works of fourteen African-American artists, including Dindga McCannon, Kay Brown, Faith Ringgold, Carol Blank, Jerri Crooks, Charlotte Kâ (Richardson), and Gylbert Coker. The exhibition's success led to the formation of a collective called Where We At Black Women Artists, Inc. (WWA).

2006: A historical marker was unveiled to mark the 40th anniversary of the Gene Compton's Cafeteria Riot at the corner of Taylor and Turk in San Francisco. The riot in August 1966 in the Tenderloin district of San Francisco was a form of resistance against the police brutality and harmful treatment of local transwomen (some of them sex workers). It was reported that the customers resisted arrests by throwing various items, including sugar shakers, tables, and dinnerware, at the police and the windows, causing them to break. Some also used their purses and high heels as weapons against the officers.

June 23

778: Hygeburg, an Anglo-Saxon nun who lived in a monastery in Heidenheim (today Bavaria, Germany), listened and took notes of the story of her relative Willlibald's pilgrimage to the Holy Land. She later worked on this text, making it into a biography called *Hodoeporicon* ("relation of a voyage"), also known as *Vita Willibaldi*, (*Life of Willibald*). Hygeburg is considered the first Englishwoman to write a full-length literary work and the only woman author of a saint's life from the Carolingian period. Encouraged by Walpurga (the sister of Willibald and Wynnebald, responsible for the female section of the monastery, later a saint), Hygeburg later wrote a biography of Wynnebald (Willibald's brother and the founder of the monastery in Heidenheim, later made a saint), the *Vita Wynnebaldi*.

1848: Dorothea Dix, an American reformer and humanitarian, was granted the use of an alcove in the Capitol Library by Congress, allowing her to meet with members of Congress and advocate for the welfare and improved treatment of individuals with mental illnesses.

1888: Annie Besant, a social activist, published an article in her paper, *The Link*, exposing the poor working conditions in the match factory. The report highlighted long work hours, low pay, unsanitary eating conditions, and health complications caused by working with white phosphorus, leading to the Matchgirls' strike by women and teenage girls working at the London Bryant & May match factory.

1919: The Women's Engineering Society was founded in London to support the increasing number of women entering the engineering industry and to promote their professional advancement.

1931: Lili de Alvarez, a Spanish tennis player, introduced practical attire for women in athletic competition by wearing a hybrid style skirt-culotte garment designed by Elsa Schiaparelli at Wimbledon, challenging traditional clothing norms for female athletes.

1936: Maryse Hilsz, a French aviator known for high altitude and endurance flights, set a new women's altitude record of 14,309 m (46,946 ft).

1965: Hull House, established in 1889 by social reformers Jane Addams and Ellen Gates Starr in Chicago, was designated a U.S. National Historic Landmark. Hull House was the first settlement house in the United States and provided a range of services to the community, including legal aid, childcare, employment assistance, and skills training.

1972: U.S. President Nixon signed Title IX of the Education Amendments of 1972 into law. This legislation aimed to ensure equal access and opportunities for both female and male students in educational institutions, including prohibiting gender-based discrimination in educational programs and activities.

1996: Sheikh Hasina Wazed became the prime minister of Bangladesh, beginning her tenure as the country's leader. She became the longest-serving prime minister in the history of Bangladesh.

2011: Under Brazil's new same-sex union laws, dozens of gay and lesbian couples participated in mass gay weddings, attempting to set a world record for the biggest number of same-sex marriages conducted simultaneously.

June 24

1748: The *Pachter* riots broke out in Amsterdam, with Marretje Arents (known as *Mat van den Nieuwendijk* or *het limoenwijf*) as one of the leaders. She was sentenced to death for her involvement in the riots.

1912: Suffragists Emmeline Pankhurst and Emmeline Pethick-Lawrence were freed from prison.

1913: Danish Prime Minister Carl Theodor Zahle announced in the Danish Parliament (*Rigsdagen*) that he would support women's suffrage in Denmark, signaling his advocacy for granting women the right to vote.

1916: Mary Pickford, a prominent silent film actress, became the first female film star to sign a million-dollar contract, solidifying her status as a highly successful and influential figure in the film industry.

1958: Nina Simone, an American singer, songwriter, and pianist, released her debut jazz album titled *Little Girl Blue*. The album showcased Simone's remarkable talent and marked the beginning of her influential career in the music industry.

1972: Yvonne Brathwaite Burke became the first African-American chair of a Democratic convention.

1990: Kathleen Margaret Brown and Irene Templeton were ordained priests in St Anne's Cathedral in Belfast, becoming the first female Anglican priests in the United Kingdom.

2003: Beyoncé, an American singer, released her first solo album, *Dangerously in Love*. The album succeeded, debuting at the top of the Billboard 200 and solidifying Beyoncé's status as a successful solo artist.

2011: The New York Senate voted to legalize same-sex marriage in New York, making it the largest state to approve such legislation since California reversed its legalization in 2008.

2019: The *Soyuz MS-11* spacecraft safely returned to Earth, landing in Kazakhstan. American astronaut Anne McClain, Canadian astronaut David Saint-Jacques, and Russian cosmonaut Oleg Kononenko completed their 204-day mission aboard the International Space Station, setting a record for the longest continuous spaceflight by a Canadian astronaut.

2022: The United States Supreme Court overturned the landmark cases *Roe v. Wade* and *Planned Parenthood v. Casey*, effectively ending the federal protection of the right to abortion and returning regulation to the states. This decision had significant implications for reproductive rights in the United States, with several states subsequently enacting or reinstating laws restricting abortion access.

June 25

1682: Ivan V and Peter I were jointly crowned as Tsars of Russia after a compromise between their mothers, Natalya Naryshkina and Maria Miloslavskaya. However, their older sister, Sophia Alekseyevna, assumed actual power for the following seven years.

1678: Elena Cornaro Piscopia became the first woman to earn a Doctor of Philosophy degree (Ph.D.) from the University of Padua in the Republic of Venice.

1740: Maria Theresa of Austria was crowned Queen Regnant of Hungary in Bratislava, solidifying her position as a powerful monarch in the region.

1876: A battalion of the 7th Cavalry, led by George Armstrong Custer, was defeated by a large force of Lakota, Dakota, Northern Cheyenne, and Arapaho warriors in what became known as the Battle of the Little Bighorn. Notable women warriors who fought in the battle included Pretty Nose, One-Who-Walks-With-The-Stars, Minnie Hollow Wood, Lakota Moving Robe Woman, and Cheyenne Buffalo Calf Road Woman.

1903: Marie Skłodowska-Curie successfully defended her doctoral thesis on radioactive substances at the Université de la Sorbonne in Paris, becoming the first woman in France to receive a doctoral degree.

1910: The United States Congress passed the Mann Act, also known as the "White

Slave Traffic Act," which aimed to combat human trafficking. The legislation prohibited the transportation of women across state lines for "immoral purposes."

1947: The *Diary of a Young Girl* by Anne Frank was published for the first time in Amsterdam, providing a poignant and widely read account of her experiences during the Shoah (Holocaust).

1957: Elizabeth Lee Hazen and Rachel Fuller Brown developed and patented the first antifungal antibiotic, *nystatin*, and the process for its production. Nystatin has since been instrumental in treating various fungal infections.

1993: Tansu Çiller became Turkey's first female Prime Minister. She was the first elected Muslim woman prime minister in Europe.

2019: Ibaraki Prefecture in Japan announced a new policy to issue partnership certificates for lesbian, gay, and transgender couples, making it the first prefecture in Japan to take this step toward recognizing and supporting LGBTQ+ relationships.

2021: Gibraltar held a referendum in which 62% of voters favored the legalization of abortion, resulting in the proposed Amendment to the criminal law bill, allowing pregnancies to be terminated within the first 12 weeks by a registered physician, with exceptions for later-stage abortions under specific circumstances.

2022: Fuschia Anne Ravena of the Philippines was crowned Miss International Queen, the world's largest beauty pageant for transgender women, held in Pattaya, Thailand.

June 26

1952: Women from various organizations, including the African National Congress Women's League, Congress of Democrats, and South African Indian Congress, played a significant role in acts of defiance against unjust apartheid laws in South Africa. Their efforts aimed to challenge laws such as the Group Areas Act, Bantu Authorities Act, Suppression of Communism Act, and Separate Representation of Voters.

1967: Mariam Aloma Mukhtar became the first woman from Northern Nigeria to be called to the bar.

1976: Elena Quinteros, a teacher and anarchist activist, was arrested and taken to the infamous torture center "300 Carlos" during the civic-military dictatorship of Uruguay (1973-1985). Quinteros tried to escape by jumping into the Venezuelan Embassy, but the Uruguayan forces broke international law by storming it and forcibly capturing her. She was never seen again.

1985: Coretta Scott King, along with her daughter Bernice and son Martin Luther King III, was arrested during an anti-apartheid protest at the Embassy of South Africa in Washington, D.C.

1993: Following the success of a Dyke March the evening before an LGBTQ+ March on Washington in April 1993, the New York Lesbian Avengers organized the first of what would become an annual unpermitted Dyke March in New York City.

1997: J.K. Rowling published the first book in her Harry Potter series, *Harry Potter and the Philosopher's Stone,* in the United Kingdom.

2009: Giorgia Boscolo became the first woman to pass the rigorous test to become a trainee gondolier in Venice, breaking the nine-century-long tradition of male monopoly on the canals of Venice.

2012: The members of the Spice Girls reunited to launch Viva Forever!, a West End musical based on their hit songs. The event brought nostalgia to fans and celebrated the impact of the popular girl group.

2015: The U.S. Supreme Court ruled, in a 5–4 decision, that same-sex couples have a constitutional right to marriage under the 14th Amendment of the United States Constitution. This landmark ruling legalized same-sex marriage across the United States.

2018: Alexandria Ocasio-Cortez won the Democratic Party's primary election for New York's 14th congressional district, defeating a 10-term incumbent, Joe Crowley. Her victory marked a significant moment in U.S. politics, as Ocasio-Cortez became a prominent advocate for progressive policies.

June 27

1833: Prudence Crandall, a white woman, was arrested for operating an academy for Black women in Canterbury, Connecticut.

1918: Marie Equi, an American physician, suffragist, activist, and pacifist, was arrested for giving an anti-war speech in Portland, Oregon.

1936: The Soviet Union reversed the 1920 Bolshevik decree that protected women's health and granted reproductive rights, including the legalization of abortion. The new law severely restricted access to abortion, criminalizing both doctors and women seeking the procedure. This ban remained in effect until Joseph Stalin died in 1953.

1969: Canada abolished criminal penalties for homosexuality and abortion (with specific conditions) by passing the C-150 bill in the House of Commons and the Canadian Senate.

2012: Queen Elizabeth II of Britain and Martin McGuinness, a former IRA commander and *Sinn Féin* deputy First Minister of Northern Ireland, shook hands at a historic meeting in Belfast.

2021: Saudi Arabia released two women's rights activists, Samar Badawi and Nassima al-Sadah after they completed their sentences. Both women were detained in July 2018, along with several other activists.

June 28

1762: Russian Tsarina Catherine II, also known as Catherine the Great, seized power and declared herself the sovereign ruler of Russia. Her reign marked a period of significant political and cultural changes in the country.

1778: Mary Hays McCauley, known as "Molly Pitcher," fired a cannon during the Battle of Monmouth in New Jersey during the American Revolutionary War. Her actions and bravery on the battlefield earned her the nickname and later a soldier's pension from the U.S. government.

1819: María Antonia Santos Plata was executed by a firing squad for her role in organizing and leading rebel guerrillas against the invading Spanish troops during the Reconquista of the New Granada (present-day Colombia).

1841: Italian ballerina Carlotta Grisi starred in the ballet *Giselle,* which premiered at the Salle Le Peletier in Paris, France. Grisi's performance in this ballet became one of her most notable and influential roles in dance.

1884: The Norwegian Association for Women's Rights was founded.

1969: The Stonewall riots began in New York City. It was a pivotal moment in the LGBTQ+ rights movement. The protests and resistance that emerged in response to a police raid on the Stonewall Inn bar ignited a wave of activism and led to the establishment of the modern Gay Rights Movement.

2007: The Egyptian Health Ministry issued a decree stating that it was "prohibited for any doctors, nurses, or any other person to carry out any cut of, flattening or modification of any natural part of the female reproductive system, either in government hospitals, nongovernment hospitals or any other places." The decision came after the public outcry when a 12-year-old girl, Badour Shaker, died earlier that month while undergoing the procedure in an illegal clinic. Nawal El Saadawi wrote:

> "Bedour, did you have to die for some light to shine in the dark minds? Did you have to pay with your dear life a price ... for doctors and clerics to learn that the right religion doesn't cut children's organs?"

2011: Myanmar (formerly known as Burma) deported and blacklisted actress Michelle Yeoh, who was planning to portray Opposition Leader Aung San Suu Kyi in an upcoming movie.

2023: The European Union ratified the Council of Europe Convention on preventing and combating violence against women and domestic violence (CETS No. 210), commonly called the Istanbul Convention.

June 29

1785: Letitia Ann Sage became the first English woman to take to the skies in a hot air balloon.

1916: Women gun workers at the Dion munitions factory in France went on strike in protest against increased workloads and reduced piece-rate pay during World War I. Despite initial dismissive attitudes from their foreman, the women persisted in their strike for 11 days, and a government arbitration panel ruled partially in favor of the workers.

1961: Djamila Boupacha, a former Algerian National Liberation Front militant, was sentenced to death for allegedly attempting to bomb a cafe in Algiers. Her confession, which was purportedly obtained through torture and rape, and the trial affected French public opinion about the methods used by the French army in Algeria after publicity by Simone de Beauvoir and her counsel, Gisèle Halimi. The women exposed the fact that many women faced torture, accompanied by the systematic use of rape to terrorize and shame the Algerian community during the conflict. Boupacha was given amnesty under the Evian Accords and was later freed on April 21, 1962.

1974: Isabel Perón was sworn in as the first female President of Argentina, succeeding her husband, Juan Perón, who passed away two days later.

1980: Vigdís Finnbogadóttir was elected as the President of Iceland, becoming the world's first democratically elected female President.

1995: English yachtswoman Lisa Clayton completed her 10-month solo circumnavigation, starting from the Northern Hemisphere.

2017: Ana Brnabić became the first woman and openly gay person to serve as the Prime Minister of Serbia.

2019: Carola Rackete, the captain of a migrant rescue ship, was arrested in Italy for docking without authorization.

June 30

1870: Ada Kepley became the first American female law college graduate, earning her degree from the Old University of Chicago, later known as Northwestern University.

1892: The Woman's Building, designed and built for the World's Columbian Exposition held in Chicago in 1893 under the patronage of the Board of Lady Managers, was completed. Fourteen women architects submitted designs for the project. The Board chose Sophia Hayden's three-story Italian Renaissance-style design with Corinthian columns. Alice Rideout sculpted the exterior and pediment, while Enid Yandell crafted the roof garden's caryatid. Candace Wheeler oversaw interior decorations. Prominent contributors to the Woman's Building included artists such as Mary Fairchild MacMonnies Low, Mary Cassatt, Lucia Fairchild Fuller, Dora Wheeler Keith,

Amanda Brewster Sewell, Rosina Emmet Sherwood, and Lydia Field Emmet, known for their murals. Ellen Mary Rope created a bas-relief, and Elisabeth Parsons, Edith Blake Brown, and Ethel Isadore Brown designed stained glass windows. The Woman's Building featured exhibitions by women from various fields, and its library displayed at least 8,000 books representing 24 different nations, all of which were written by women.

1919: Marie Equi, a physician and activist, was arrested for protesting at a War Preparedness parade. Charged with sedition under the Espionage Act, she was sentenced to three years at San Quentin Prison in California. Her sentence was later reduced, and she was released early for good behavior after serving ten months.

1981: A court in West Germany sentenced to life imprisonment Hermine Braunsteiner Ryan on three counts: the murder of 80 people, abetting the murder of 102 children, and collaborating in the murder of 1,000 people. Braunsteiner was an Austrian SS helper and camp guard at Ravensbrück and Majdanek. She was the first Nazi war criminal extradited from the United States to face trial in West Germany. Braunsteiner earned the grim nickname "Stomping Mare" for her reported ruthless acts. For a few decades, she lived freely in the U.S. before Simon Wiesenthal, with the help of survivors, was able to find her.

1992: Former Prime Minister Margaret Thatcher was granted a life peerage and joined the House of Lords as Baroness Thatcher of Kesteven, allowing her to continue her involvement in politics from the House of Lords.

2015: Misty Danielle Copeland became the first African American woman to be promoted to principal dancer in the 75-year history of the American Ballet Theatre.

2019: Princess Haya bint Hussein of Jordan fled to London with her two children, seeking asylum, due to fear for her life. She escaped her husband, Sheikh Mohammed bin Rashid Al Maktoum, the Vice President and Prime Minister of the UAE and the Ruler of Dubai. A high-profile court battle over custody and non-repatriation of the children was expected.

2021: The trial of Yemeni actress and model Intisar al-Hammadi began in Sanaa. She was accused of "indecent acts" for posting photos of herself without a headscarf on social media.

2021: U.S. Secretary of State Antony Blinken announced that the U.S. passport would include an option for a third gender, allowing applicants to indicate their gender without providing medical proof.

2022: Ketanji Onyika Brown Jackson was sworn into office as the United States Supreme Court Justice, becoming the first African American woman and former federal public defender to serve on the Supreme Court.

JULY

July 01

1891: Tui Manu'a Matelita became the *Tui Manu'a* (paramount chief or queen) of Manu'a, a group of islands in the eastern part of the Samoan Islands (present-day American Samoa).

1912: Harriet Quimby, a pioneering American woman with a pilot's license, lost her life at 37 in a plane accident. She and her passenger, William A.P. Willard, were ejected from their seats when their airplane unexpectedly pitched forward.

1921: The *Sejm* (Polish parliament) passed a law to address gender inequalities for married women. This law gave women more rights: control over their property (except dowry), the ability to be legal witnesses, custody of children if the husband was unable, and the freedom to live apart from their husbands. It also removed the need for a wife to obey her husband and seek his permission for legal actions.

1929: Nurkhon Yuldashkhojayeva was killed by her brother in an honor killing at 16. She was one of the first Uzbek women actors and dancers, symbolizing women's liberation from feudal traditions. A year earlier, she ran away from home to join the theater troupe in Samarkand. During a March 8 show, Yuldashkhojayeva and another dancer publicly removed their face veils to celebrate International Women's Day. Her attitude enraged religious traditionalists. Her brother confessed he was compelled to murder by his father, a local official, and a *mullah*. Thousands came for her funeral, where women threw off their face veils in front of her coffin.

1933: Ethel Waters made history as the first African-American to host her radio show on NBC.

1966: Teruko "Terry" Ishizaka, along with her husband Kimishige Ishizaka, described their discovery of the antibody class Immunoglobulin E (IgE) in an article, "Physico-Chemical Properties of Human Reaginic Antibody: IV. Presence of a Unique Immunoglobulin as a Carrier of Reaginic Activity," published in the *Journal of Immunology*. This work was seen as a breakthrough in allergy understanding.

1970: *It Ain't Me Babe Comix*, a one-shot underground comic book, which was the first comic book produced entirely by women. The artists involved in the project included Trina Robbins, Barbara "Willy" Mendes, Nancy Kalish, Carole Kalish, Lisa Lyons, Meredith Kurtzman, and Michele Brand, with editing by Trina Robbins and Barbara "Willy" Mendes.

1972: The first Gay pride march in England took place, providing a platform for the LGBTQ+ community to advocate for their rights and visibility.

1972: The feminist magazine *Ms.*, founded by Gloria Steinem, published its first regular issue with Wonder Woman on the cover, combining elements of popular culture with feminist perspectives.

1984: Woman suffrage was passed in Liechtenstein, making it the last European country to approve the right of women to vote and stand for election.

2005: Pamela Taylor, co-chair of the New York-based Progressive Muslim Union, became the first woman to lead Friday prayers in a Canadian mosque, challenging traditional gender roles and advocating for inclusivity in religious practices.

2007: Drew Gilpin Faust became the 28th president of Harvard University, making history as the first woman to hold that position since the university's establishment in 1636.

2009: President Obama signed a bill granting the Congressional Gold Medal to the Women Airforce Service Pilots (WASP) who volunteered for non-combat duty during World War II as test pilots and trainers. The WASP played a crucial role by freeing up their male counterparts to serve in combat.

2014: After winning a legal case against her employer for harassment related to pregnancy and maternity, Sayaka Osakabe formed a support group called *Matahara Net* (the name comes from the English "maternity and harassment," which has now become a legal term). The group focuses on harassment before pregnancy (during infertility treatment), harassment against those returning to work after giving birth, and those raising children or caring for their parents (men may also be targeted in this regard).

2016: Marcia McNutt, an American geophysicist, became the 22nd president of the National Academy of Sciences (NAS) of the United States, making her the first woman ever to hold that position.

July 02

1644: Jane Ingilby, known as "Trooper Jane," is said to have held Oliver Cromwell prisoner after the Battle of Marston Moor during the English Civil War. Protecting her brother William, who fought on the side of the Royalists, she claimed she needed her guns to protect her virtue.

1888: The London matchgirls, approximately 200 workers, primarily teenage girls, went on strike. The strike was sparked by the dismissal of three of their colleagues from the Bryant and May match factory. Journalist Annie Besant's article, published on June 23, exposed the poor working conditions. On July 27, the workers formed a union.

1919: Iowa ratified the Nineteenth Amendment to the United States Constitution, granting women the right to vote.

1928: The Representation of the People (Equal Franchise) Act 1928 was passed in the United Kingdom Parliament. This act expanded suffrage by granting women electoral equality with men.

1937: Amelia Earhart and navigator Fred Noonan disappeared while departing from New Guinea during Earhart's attempt to become the first woman to circumnavigate the globe by air.

1951: Rachel Louise Carson's book *The Sea Around Us* was published, becoming a bestseller and remaining on *The New York Times* Best Seller list for 86 weeks. The book explored the wonders and mysteries of the ocean.

1986: Carmen Gloria Quintana and Rodrigo Rojas were burnt alive during a street demonstration against the dictatorship of General Augusto Pinochet in Chile, highlighting the brutality and repression of the regime.

2010: UN Women, the United Nations body for gender equality and women's empowerment was established to promote gender equity and empower women globally. UN Women advocates for women's and girls' rights and addresses various issues, including combating violence against women and supporting LGBTIQ+ rights. The former President of Chile, Michelle Bachelet, was appointed as the first head of UN Women.

2021: Former Minister for Infrastructure and Tourism 'Akosita Lavulavu and her husband were sentenced to six years in prison by a court in Tonga. The Supreme Court found them guilty of obtaining money by false pretenses.

July 03

1860: Princess Maevarua Pōmare became the Queen of Bora Bora, reigning as Teri'i-Maeva-rua II until she died in 1873. Her kingdom included the islands of Bora Bora, Tupai, Maupiti, Maupihaa, Motu One, and Manuae.

1930: The First Eastern Women's Congress occurred in Damascus, Syria. It was arranged by the General Union of Syrian Women under the leadership of Nour Hamada, with participants from the Arab World and Eastern Asia. The Congress provided a platform for women to discuss and advocate for women's rights and gender equality in the Eastern region.

1950: The Hazel Scott Show premiered on the DuMont Television Network. It was the first television program hosted by an African-American woman. Hazel Scott, a singer, appeared live on DuMont stations three times a week.

1972: Indira Gandhi, the Prime Minister of India, signed the Simla Agreement with Zulfikar Ali Bhutto, the President of Pakistan. The agreement aimed to resolve disputes peacefully, release prisoners of war, and withdraw military forces to their sides of a 460-mile-long border.

2001: Roni Zuckerman became the first female jet fighter pilot for the Israeli Air Force when she received her wings.

2005: Spain's national law legalizing same-sex marriage took effect, making Spain the third country in the world to legalize same-sex marriage.

2014: Caitlin Moran published *How to Build a Girl*, a semi-autobiographical coming-of-age novel that garnered critical acclaim for exploring identity, sexuality, and feminism.

July 04

414: Emperor Theodosius II of the Eastern Roman Empire, at the age of 13, passed power to his elder sister Aelia Pulcheria. She assumed the role of regent and declared herself the empress (*Augusta*) of the Eastern Roman Empire.

1643: Queen Henrietta Maria of England led the battle to take Burton-Upon-Trent during the English Civil War on behalf of her husband, King Charles I. She actively participated in the military campaign.

1876: Suffragists crashed the Centennial Celebration in Independence Hall to present the Vice President with the Declaration of the Rights of Women authored by Matilda Joselyn Gage.

1880: Mary H. Myers became the first woman to ascend and pilot her balloon. She had a successful career as an aviation star, undertaking daring balloon flights and executing precise landings.

1903: Dorothy Levitt, known as "Dashing Dot," became the first English woman racing driver to compete in a motorcar race. She pioneered female motoring and taught Queen Alexandra and the Royal Princesses driving lessons.

1916: Mabel Vernon interrupted President Woodrow Wilson's speech, challenging him on his opposition to the national enfranchisement of women. Wilson dismissed her bold question, and when she repeated it later, she was ordered to leave the meeting by the police.

1972: The legal age of adulthood for women in Spain was reduced to 21 after being maintained at 23 for 83 years.

1988: Kylie Minogue released her first studio album, *Kylie*. The album began her successful music career and established her as a pop icon.

2006: Helene Hayman, Baroness Hayman, became the first person to hold the newly formed position of Lord Speaker in the Parliament of the United Kingdom. As the presiding officer and highest authority of the House of Lords, she played a significant role in the parliamentary proceedings.

2021: Marine Le Pen was re-elected without opposition by the National Rally party, strengthening her candidacy for the 2022 French presidential election and positioning her as a key contender in the upcoming election.

July 05

1659: Five women, Gironima Spana, Giovanna De Grandis, Maria Spinola, Graziosa Farina, and Laura Crispoldi, were executed by hanging in Rome. They were convicted of murder for distributing the *Aqua Tofana* poison, primarily sold to women seeking to eliminate their husbands. The executions took place in the public square at the Campo de' Fiori.

1888: Around 1,400 women and girls employed at the Bryant & May Match factory in east London went on strike in solidarity with workers who had been sacked on June 23. The strike highlighted the poor working conditions and helped draw attention to labor rights issues.

1946: Micheline Bernardini, a French dancer and model, famously modeled the first modern bikini at a swimming pool in Paris.

1965: Greek-American soprano Maria Callas made her final opera stage appearance, portraying the title role in Giacomo Puccini's *Tosca* at Convent Garden in London, England.

1972: Lobsang Dolma Khangkar joined and was appointed chief physician at Men-Tsee-Khang, the Tibetan Institute of Medicine and Astrology in Dharamsala. She was named "Doctor of the Dalai Lama" for her contributions to Tibetan medicine.

2011: Christine Lagarde officially began her tenure as the Managing Director of the International Monetary Fund (IMF). A French lawyer and politician, Lagarde became the first woman to hold this position.

2021: Anti-LGBTQ+ right-wing groups stormed and ransacked the offices of an LGBT+ organization in Tbilisi, Georgia, before the city's pride march.

2022: Maryna Viazovska, a Ukrainian mathematician, was awarded the Fields Medal for her work on the E8 lattice and its applications in packing problems and Fourier analysis. She became the second woman, following Maryam Mirzakhani, and the first Ukrainian to receive this prestigious honor in mathematics.

July 06

1320: Charles I of Hungary married Princess Elizabeth of Poland, strengthening the alliance between Hungary and Poland. The marriage was approved by Pope John XXII and aimed to foster diplomatic ties between the two countries.

1819: A French aeronaut, Sophie Blanchard, tragically died in the Tivoli Gardens in Paris. During a balloon flight, her hydrogen-filled balloon caught fire, causing her to become entangled in the surrounding net.

1944: Catherine Dior was arrested by the Gestapo for her involvement in the resistance F2 group. She was sent to the all-women Nazi camp Ravensbrück and Torgau's military prison, where she was part of the "Anton Kommando" to produce explosives in a disused potassium mine. Later, she worked in Abberode, a Buchenwald satellite camp, and at an aviation factory in Leipzig-Markkleeberg. Dior was finally freed near Dresden and could return to Paris on May 28, 1945.

1957: American tennis player Althea Gibson became the first Black athlete to win the Wimbledon championships.

1960: Barbara Moore completed an impressive 3,207-mile walk from Los Angeles to New York.

1993: Aimee Carandang made history as Southeast Asia's first female commercial pilot. Hailing from the Philippines, she flew as a full-fledged captain on a Fokker 50 flight from Manila to Baguio.

2021: Inuk leader Mary Simon was appointed the 30th Governor General of Canada. She became the first Indigenous person to assume this role.

July 07

1456: Joan of Arc, who had been executed for heresy 25 years earlier, was retried and acquitted of her charges.

1851: Thereza Dillwyn Llewelyn, a 16-year-old aspiring astronomer and astrophotographer, proudly described in a letter that she laid the foundation stone of an observatory.

1917: The British Army Council established the British Women's Auxiliary Army Corps (WAAC), allowing women to serve alongside men in France during World War I.

1976: The first class of women entered the U.S. Military Academy at West Point.

1981: Sandra Day O'Connor was nominated by President Ronald Reagan as the first woman Supreme Court Justice in the United States.

1996: The Spice Girls, a famous British girl group consisting of Victoria Adams, Melanie Brown, Melanie Chisholm, Michelle Stephenson (briefly), Geri Halliwell, and Emma Bunton, released their debut single *Wannabe*, which became a global hit.

2016: Germany passed a new law redefining rape, acknowledging that sexual activity without explicit consent constitutes rape. The legislation also addressed groping, deportation of convicted migrants for sex offenses, and simplified prosecution for group assaults.

2019: Gisela Carrasco Miró published an article titled "Encountering the colonial: religion in feminism and the coloniality of secularism" in the journal *Feminist Theory*, exploring the debate on Islamic and Western feminism from a decolonial perspective.

2019: The United States won the 2019 Women's World Cup in a final match against the Netherlands with a score of 2-0. Megan Rapinoe and Rose Lavelle scored the goals that secured the victory.

2021: Gulalai Ismail, an advocate for Pakistani women's rights who had to flee the country due to false accusations, was awarded the Geneva Summit International Women's Rights Award during the 13th annual Geneva Summit for Human Rights and Democracy.

July 08

1824: Queen Kamāmalu of Hawaii passed away from measles while visiting the United Kingdom with her husband. Her husband also died a few days later, highlighting the devastating impact of diseases introduced to indigenous populations by European explorers and travelers.

1868: Maerehia became the Queen of Huahine and Maia'o and took the reign name of Teha'apapa II.

1933: Amelia Earhart set a new airplane speed record by crossing the United States in 17 hours and 7 minutes, arriving in Newark at 9:19 p.m.

1948: The United States Air Force accepted its first female recruits into the Women in the Air Force (WAF) program.

1982: Aracy de Carvalho, a Brazilian, was honored by Yad Vashem with the Righteous Among the Nations award for helping Jews escape the Holocaust during World War II.

2019: Pope Francis appointed female members to the Congregation for Institutes of Consecrated Life and Societies of Apostolic Life - a historic first in the Vatican's history.

2020: The United States Supreme Court, in a 7-2 decision in the case of *Little Sisters of the Poor Saints Peter and Paul Home v. Pennsylvania*, upheld regulations that allowed employers with religious or moral objections to opt out of providing contraception-coverage mandated by the Affordable Care Act.

2022: The Constitutional Court of Slovenia ruled in a 6-3 decision that bans on same-sex couples marrying and adopting children were unconstitutional. The Parliament was given six months to amend the necessary laws to reflect this ruling.

July 09

1610: Lady Arbella Stuart was imprisoned for marrying William Seymour, 2nd Duke of Somerset, without royal permission. This marriage threatened the English throne, as Arbella Stuart had a claim to the crown.

1762: Catherine II, also known as Catherine the Great, ascended to the throne of Russia after orchestrating the overthrow of her husband, Tsar Peter III. Catherine II became one of Russian history's most influential and longest-reigning female rulers.

1848: Abolitionists Jane Hunt, Elizabeth Cady Stanton, Lucretia Mott, Martha Wright, and Mary Ann McClintock met in Hunt's home, where they decided to organize the Seneca Falls Women's Rights Convention. This Convention, held in Seneca Falls, New York, became a significant event in the women's suffrage movement and is often regarded as the birthplace of the women's rights movement in the United States.

1868: The 14th Amendment to the U.S. Constitution was ratified, which included the word "male" in the section on voting rights, explicitly denying women the right to vote.

1898: The *Nationale Tentoonstelling van Vrouwenarbeid* (National Exhibition of Women's Work) occurred in The Hague, Netherlands, promoting women's labor conditions and advocating for women's participation in professional fields during the first-wave feminism movement in the Netherlands.

1917: The anarchists Emma Goldman and Alexander Berkman were sentenced to serve two years in prison, to pay fines of $10,000 each, and to be subsequently deported to Russia for violating conscription law during World War I. The pair had previously formed a No-Conscription League and agitated against the war.

1959: The first class of twelve female gardaí began training to join An Garda Síochána, the national police service of Ireland.

2005: Queen Elizabeth II unveiled the Memorial to the Women of World War II in London, the first national Memorial in Britain dedicated to honoring the contributions of the nearly seven million service and civilian women during the war.

2016: The Gambia and Tanzania outlawed child marriages. The Tanzanian High Court ruled to protect girls from the adverse consequences of early marriage, and Gambian President Yahya Jammeh announced a ban on child and forced marriages.

July 10

1040: According to legend, Lady Godiva rode naked on horseback through Coventry to protest against high taxes imposed by her husband, the Earl of Mercia.

1553: Lady Jane Grey, also known as the "Nine-Day Queen," ascended to the throne of England following the death of King Edward VI. Her reign was short-lived as Mary I overthrew her and eventually executed her.

1669: Naturalist and illustrator Maria Sibylla Merian and her daughter sailed to Suriname in South America to study and document the region's insects and other species. Her illustrations and scientific observations contributed significantly to the field of entomology.

1952: The Republican Party in the United States decided to support an Equal Rights Amendment (ERA) as part of its party platform. However, the party later reversed its position and actively campaigned against the ERA and women's rights.

1971: Gloria Steinem, a prominent feminist and co-founder of the National Women's Political Caucus (NWPC), delivered a powerful speech titled "Address to the Women of America" during the founding of the NWPC in Washington, D.C. Her speech played a pivotal role in advancing the ideas and goals of the American Women's Movement.

2019: The 27th annual ESPY Awards occurred in Los Angeles, California. The United States women's national soccer team was honored with the Outstanding Team Award for victory in the 2019 FIFA Women's World Cup. Alex Morgan, a team member, received the Best Female Athlete Award.

2020: Dame Vera Lynn, known as the "Forces' Sweetheart" for her iconic performances during World War II, was honored with a military funeral in East Sussex, England, on the 80th anniversary of the Battle of Britain. Lynn's music and support for the troops made her a beloved figure during the war.

July 11

937: Conrad I, at 12, became the king of Burgundy. However, his widowed mother, Queen Bertha, effectively ruled over unified Burgundy and moved its capital to Arles.

1656: Ann Austin and Mary Fisher, the first Quakers to arrive in America, landed in Boston. However, they were arrested and imprisoned by the Puritan colonial government. After five years of captivity, they were deported back to Barbados.

1919: The International Federation of University Women was established in London to promote women's access to higher education on a global scale.

1960: Harper Lee's novel *To Kill a Mockingbird* was first published in the United States. The book, exploring themes of racial injustice and the loss of innocence, became a classic of American literature.

1979: The European Parliament held its inaugural session following the direct elections of its members. During this session, Simone Veil from France was chosen as the first President of the European Parliament.

2013: The television series *Orange Is the New Black*, created by Jenji Kohan, premiered on Netflix. The comedy-drama series, based on Piper Kerman's memoir, revolves around the experiences of a woman in a women's federal prison.

July 12

1624: A renowned Italian artist, Sofonisba Anguissola, at the age of 92, received a visit from a young artist named Anthony van Dyck. Van Dyck recorded sketches during his visit and later painted her portrait.

He claimed that his conversation with Anguissola taught him more about the "true principles" of painting than anything else.

1912: The silent film *Les Amours de la reine Élisabeth,* featuring the renowned stage actress Sarah Bernhardt, premiered in the United States under *Queen Elizabeth,* with English title cards.

1919: Suffrage was granted to married women whose husbands were ratepayers and women over 30 who paid an annual rent of £10 or more on the Isle of Jersey.

1937: Tsuneko Gauntlett, a Japanese temperance, suffrage, and peace activist, presided at the Fourth Pan-Pacific Women's Association Congress in Vancouver, Canada. Women from such places as New Zealand, Australia, Hawaii, China, the West Dutch Indies, Canada, the United States, Korea, and Java participated in the sessions, whose general topic was "Practical Ways and Means of Promoting Peace," with the additional subject discussed, like the issues of arms trafficking, labor and living standards, socialized health programs, education, and changing social relationships.

1976: Barbara Jordan became the first African-American to deliver a keynote address at a major political convention - at the Democratic National Convention.

1984: Geraldine Ferraro, a vocal advocate of women's rights in Congress, was chosen as the first woman to run for Vice President of the United States on the Democratic Party ticket alongside Walter Mondale.

2001: The first installment of Hiromu Arakawa's *Fullmetal Alchemist* (*Hagane no Renkinjutsushi*) was published in the monthly manga magazine *Monthly Shōnen Gangan.* The series gained widespread popularity and has since become a beloved franchise.

2013: Malala Yousafzai, a Pakistani education activist and Nobel laureate, addressed the United Nations and called for worldwide access to education. Her powerful speech drew attention to the importance of education in empowering individuals and promoting peace.

2014: Rokudenashiko (Megumi Igarashi) was arrested for "distributing obscene material," becoming the first Japanese woman to face such charges. She spent a week in a Tokyo women's prison, and her arrest gained international attention, leading to over 21,000 people signing an online petition demanding her release. She was released on July 18 after a successful appeal. A few months before, the artist launched the Man-Boat project, abbreviated "manko boat." She created a kayak attachment modeled after her vulva. In March 2014, she sailed it down Tokyo's Tama River, calling it the Ta-manko River. That same month, she shared the 3-D vulva scan with her supporters to inspire creative genitalia artwork with this data.

2022: Ada Limón was named the 24th U.S. Poet Laureate by the Librarian of Congress, Carla Hayden. Limón, who is of Mexican ancestry, became the first woman of Mexican heritage to be appointed as the U.S. Poet Laureate.

July 13

923: When Duke Raoul (Rudolf) of Burgundy was elected to become the King of France (West Francia), his wife, Emma of the Robertian family, became the queen and administrator of the Duchy of Burgundy. Emma played a significant role in military and political affairs, mediating Raoul and her brother, Hugh the Great. She exerted authority, captured the Avallon fortress in 931, and besieged Château-Thierry in 933.

1793: Marie-Anne Charlotte de Corday d'Armont assassinated Jean-Paul Marat, a prominent member of the radical Jacobin faction during the French Revolution. Corday, who opposed the violence of the Reign of Terror, wrote an address explaining her motives for the assassination. She was swiftly tried and executed by guillotine on July 17, wearing the red overblouse reserved for condemned traitors who had assassinated representatives of the people.

1915: Zofia Baltarowicz-Dzielińska signed up for a course with the sculptor Zygmunt Kurczyński. Later, she sought admission to Kraków's *Akademia Sztuk Pięknych* (Academy of Fine Arts) despite its historical ban on women. Her talent earned praise from art professors, leading the rector to offer her a trial. In late October 1917, the Senate officially welcomed Zofia, though only as an auditor, denying her an official certificate. Thus, she became the academy's first female student, paving the way for future generations of women. The academy formally admitted women over a year later, in December 1918.

1948: Japan enacted the Eugenics Protection Act, legalizing abortion and contraception. The law, however, primarily aimed to promote forced sterilizations of disabled individuals to prevent the birth of what was considered "poor-quality" children. Over the following decades, approximately 17,000 people, primarily women and girls, were forcibly sterilized, and an additional 8,000 were sterilized under pressure or coercion. The law also led to nearly 60,000 abortions based on alleged "hereditary illnesses." It was only repealed in 1996.

1965: France passed a law granting women the right to independently manage their property and assets, including the ability to open bank accounts in their names and engage in professional activities without their husbands' permission.

1979: The Women's History Summer Institute held at Sarah Lawrence College led to the establishment of Women's History Month, a time dedicated to recognizing and celebrating the contributions and achievements of women throughout history.

2016: Theresa May succeeded David Cameron and became the Prime Minister of the United Kingdom, serving as the country's second female prime minister.

2016: Carla Hayden was confirmed as the 14th Librarian of Congress, making history as the first woman and African-American to hold this position and lead the Library of Congress.

July 14

664: Queen Seaxburh became the regent of Kent in modern-day Britain. She ruled in place of the young Ecgberht until he came of age following the death of King Eorcenberht due to the plague.

1885: Sarah Elisabeth Jacobs received a patent for her invention, a folding cabinet bed designed for small apartments. She is believed to be the first African-American woman to receive a United States patent.

1914: Dorothy de la Hey established Queen Mary's College in Madras, India, becoming the third women's college in the country and focusing on education.

1917: Sixteen National Women's Party members were arrested for picketing the White House and demanding universal women's suffrage. They were charged with obstructing traffic.

1957: Rawya Ateya assumed her position in Egypt's National Assembly, becoming the first female parliamentarian in the entire Arab world.

1960: Jane Goodall arrived at the Gombe Stream Reserve in present-day Tanzania to begin her groundbreaking study of chimpanzees in the wild.

1980: The Second World Conference on Women was held in Copenhagen, Denmark, to assess progress towards the 1975 World Plan of Action goals. The Convention on the Elimination of All Forms of Discrimination Against Women was formally signed during the opening ceremony. Despite challenges and political complexities, the conference led to a revised World Programme of Action and plans for a follow-up conference at the decade's end, furthering the cause of gender equality.

2008: Rhonda "Randi" Weingarten became the American Federation of Teachers President. She used to preside over the United Federation of Teachers and was the first openly gay person to preside over a national American labor union.

2011: After Daphni Leef learned she could not afford a flat, she pitched a tent in central Tel Aviv. Within 24 hours, dozens joined her, sparking a nationwide protest against high housing prices, living costs, and social inequality.

2014: The Church of England voted to allow women to become bishops.

2015: Harper Lee's second novel, *Go Set a Watchman*, was released for sale in 70 countries. The book was a sequel to her famous work, *To Kill a Mockingbird*.

2016: Elizabeth Truss was appointed Secretary of State for Justice and became the first-ever female Lord Chancellor of the United Kingdom.

July 15

1907: Qiu Jin, a Chinese revolutionary, feminist writer, and poet, was publicly beheaded for her involvement in the Anqing Uprising, a plot to overthrow the Qing Dynasty.

1939: Clara Adams became the first woman to complete a round-world flight as a passenger, contributing to the popularization of air travel. The journey lasted sixteen days and nineteen hours, covered 24,609 miles, and cost $1,935.

1941: Jeanne Mandello, an avant-garde female artist and pioneer in modern photography, arrived in Uruguay after escaping Nazi Germany. She was a notable photographer who left a significant impact on the field.

1951: Darina Bancikova became Slovakia's first ordained woman in the Evangelical Church of the Augsburg Confession (ECAC), a Lutheran World Federation member church.

1997: Missy Elliott released her first solo album, *Supa Dupa Fly*, which included popular tracks like *The Rain (Supa Dupa Fly)*, *Sock It 2 Me*, *Hit Em wit da Hee*, and *Beep Me 911*. The album debuted at number three on the U.S. Billboard 200 and topped the U.S. Top R&B/Hip-Hop Albums chart.

2012: Nkosazana Dlamini-Zuma of South Africa became the first African woman elected as the Chairperson of the African Union Commission, defeating incumbent Jean Ping of Gabon.

2012: Cat Cora was inducted into the American Academy of Chefs (AAC) Hall of Fame, receiving recognition as the 2012 Celebrated Chef. She became the first woman to receive this honor from the American Culinary Federation.

2015: Tashi and Nungshi Malik became the first twins and siblings, as well as the first South Asians, to complete the Explorers Grand Slam. This achievement involves reaching the North Pole and the South Pole and climbing the Seven Summits, which include Mount Everest, Aconcagua, Denali, Kilimanjaro, Elbrus, Vinson, and either Puncak Jaya or Kosciuszko.

2016: Louise Hearman was awarded the 2016 Archibald Prize for her portrait of Australian comedian, satirist, and actor Barry Humphries. The Archibald Prize is a prestigious art award in Australia.

2021: The European Commission launched legal challenges against Hungary and parts of Poland due to their anti-LGBT+ laws. The Commission emphasized that Europe would not tolerate stigmatizing any aspect of society.

July 16

1546: Anne Askew, an English writer, poet, and Protestant preacher opposing the idea of transubstantiation, was burned at the stake as a heretic. Even though she endured months of torture in the Tower of London, she refused to denounce her beliefs or to inform on other like-minded women.

1840: Catherine Brewer became the first woman to earn a bachelor's degree in the United States, graduating from Wesleyan College in Macon, Georgia.

1880: Emily Stowe became the first woman to practice medicine in Canada.

1881: Ida Lewis received the rare Gold Lifesaving Medal from the United States government, becoming the first woman to be honored with this distinction. She received the award for her heroic rescue of two soldiers who had fallen through the ice while attempting to return to Fort Adams on foot.

2004: Martha Stewart was sentenced to five months in prison, followed by five months of home confinement, for lying to federal investigators. The case garnered significant media attention due to Stewart's prominence as a businesswoman and television personality.

2009: Judy Chu became the first Chinese-American woman elected to Congress.

2010: The Vatican formalized rules in response to abuse by priests, including declaring the ordination of women as a "grave crime." This decision sparked outrage and further discussions and debates on gender equality within the Catholic Church.

2017: Jodie Whittaker was announced as the thirteenth incarnation of The Doctor in the long-running science fiction television series, *Doctor Who*, the first woman in that role.

2019: Ursula von der Leyen, hailing from Germany, was elected as the President of the European Commission by the European Parliament. When she assumed office in December, she became the first woman to hold this position in the history of the European Union, succeeding Jean-Claude Juncker.

2020: Rose Christiane Raponda became Gabon's first female Prime Minister, assuming the leadership role in her country.

July 17

1341: Anna Anachoutlou (the Trapezuntine emperor Alexios II Megas Komnenos's eldest daughter) escaped from a convent, captured Trebizond without a fight, and was crowned empress. She faced opposition from nobles who preferred a male ruler. She was deposed and strangled to death on September 3, 1342.

1397: Queen Margaret I of Denmark organized the Kalmar Union, a personal union that united the three kingdoms of Denmark, Sweden, and Norway (including other territories) under a single monarch. The union aimed to counter the influence of the Hanseatic League and lasted for nearly two hundred years.

1837: Sarah Moore Grimké wrote a pamphlet titled *Letters on the Equality of the Sexes and the Condition of Woman* in response to a pastoral letter from the General Association of Congregational Ministers of Massachusetts. Grimké's work advocated for gender equality and challenged prevailing societal norms.

1912: Mary Leigh threw a hatchet wrapped with a text declaring the extinction of the Liberal Party into the carriage of H.H. Asquith, narrowly missing him but cutting Irish Nationalist MP John Redmond on the ear. Redmond's opposition to women's suffrage made him a target for suffragette protests.

1951: The *Knesset* (Israeli Parliament) passed the Women's Equal Rights Law, aimed at gender equality, inspired by the Declaration of Independence, which promised equal social and political rights for all, regardless of religion, race, gender, or marital status.

1958: The second SAFFA (*Schweizerische Ausstellung für Frauenarbeit* - Swiss Exhibition for Women's Work) opened in Zürich (the first one was held in 1928). It was organized and designed exclusively by women, including ETH Zurich alumnae Berta Rahm and Claire Rufer-Eckmann, with Annemarie Hubacher-Constam as the chief organizer, who led the exhibition with the theme "The Life Journey of Women: Family, Career, and Nation." SAFFA empowered women in education, work, and leisure, promoting a three -phase model: pre-marital employment, motherhood, and return to work. They aimed to foster family harmony and raise awareness of women's societal contributions, combatting discrimination. Exhibition profits supported women's solidarity initiatives.

1959: Mary Leakey, an archaeologist and paleoanthropologist, discovered an ancient hominid skull in the Olduvai Gorge in Tanganyika (now Tanzania). This skull belonged to a species later identified as a significant ancestor of early humans and was dated to approximately 1.8 million years BCE.

1962: Jerrie Cobb and Janey Hart testified before the Special Subcommittee on the Selection of Astronauts about the Mercury 13 program, a private initiative by William Randolph Lovelace to train women for space exploration. Thirteen women underwent rigorous physiological screening tests similar to those undertaken by NASA's male astronauts in Project Mercury, but the program was ultimately canceled.

1971: 38 Women from the left-wing *Tupamaros* guerrilla group escaped from the Cabildo women's prison in Uruguay. They used a tunnel linked to the sewers.

1972: Joanne Pierce Misko and Susan Roley Malone became the first women to train as FBI agents in Quantico, Virginia.

1980: Marjorie Matthews was elected as the first woman bishop in the United Methodist Church, breaking new ground for women in religious leadership roles.

1987: The inaugural Johanna Löwenherz Prize, named after a prominent figure in the German socialist women's movement, was awarded to Simone Veil, a French lawyer and politician known for advocating women's rights and her role in legalizing abortion in France.

2009: Major Jennifer Grieves became the first female helicopter aircraft commander in the history of the presidential Marine One fleet, which transports the President of the United States.

2012: Marissa Mayer, who had previously held executive positions at Google, was appointed as the CEO of Yahoo! Inc., becoming one of the most prominent women leaders in the tech industry.

2012: Sunita Williams of the United States, Yuri Malenchenko of Russia, and Aki Hoshide of Japan arrived at the International Space Station for a three-month visit. Williams, an astronaut, conducted scientific experiments and performed spacewalks during her stay.

2019: Ursula von der Leyen, elected President of the European Commission, resigned from her position as the Federal Minister of Defence of Germany. Annegret Kramp-Karrenbauer, the leader of the ruling CDU, was appointed as her successor by Chancellor Angela Merkel.

2020: Tlaleng Mofokeng of South Africa was appointed as the United Nations Special Rapporteur on the Right to Health by the United Nations Human Rights Council. She became the first woman and first African to hold this position.

July 18

707: Emperor Monmu of Japan passed away after a ten-year reign, and his aunt, Empress Genmei, succeeded him. Genmei became the 43rd empress of Japan and was the sister of former empress Jitō and the niece and wife of the late Emperor Tenmu.

1912: Four suffragettes, namely Mary Leigh, Gladys Evans, Lizzie Baker (also known as Jennie Baines), and Mabel Capper, attempted to set fire to the Theatre Royal in Dublin during a lunchtime meeting that was to be addressed by Prime Minister H.H. Asquith. They placed a canister of gunpowder near the stage and threw petrol and lit matches into the projection booth, which contained highly flammable film reels. After being arrested and tried, Mary Leigh and Gladys Evans were sentenced to five years of penal servitude, Jennie Baines received seven months of hard labor, and the charges against Mabel Capper were dropped.

1913: Jovanka Bončić, a Serbian/Yugoslav architect, graduated with two degrees – in architecture and engineering, as the first woman in the history of Germany after graduating from Darmstadt University.

1919: *Zaban-e Zanan* (*Women's Voice*), a radical women's periodical, was published for the first time in Isfahan, Iran. It was edited by the activist Sediqeh Dowlatabadi, who wanted to challenge the "backwardness and feeble-mindedness" surrounding women's rights and explicitly advocating for the 'Unveiling' of women in Iran. The magazine was forced to close on January 1, 1921, due to its anti-British stance. It was later re-established in Teheran.

1976: Nadia Comăneci, at 14, became the first gymnast in the history of the Olympic Games to score a perfect ten. She achieved this seven times during the Montreal Games.

1989: Rebecca Schaeffer, an actress known for her role in the T.V. series *My Sister Sam*, was murdered by an obsessed fan, prompting stricter stalking laws in California and bringing attention to the issue of celebrity privacy and security.

July 19

1848: The Women's Rights Convention commenced in Seneca Falls, New York. The convention was a significant event in the women's suffrage movement and featured notable speakers and organizers such as Elizabeth Cady Stanton, Lucretia Mott, Mary M'Clintock, Martha Coffin Wright, and Jane Hunt. The discussions at the convention addressed women's rights and the abolition of slavery.

1883: Thousands of telegraphers working for Western Union across the United States walked out on strike demanding equal pay for equal work for men and women, along with other demands, like a pay increase and an eight-hour day. The strikers lacked support from other labor groups and were forced to return to work defeated. Some refused on principle.

1963: The SNCC and NAACP organized a protest march in Americus, Georgia. Young women were arrested during the protest for attempting to buy tickets at the segregated theater. A group of African-American girls, some as young as twelve, were arrested and imprisoned without charges for 45 days in deplorable conditions in the Lee County Public Works building in Leesburg, Georgia. It became known as the Leesburg Stockade incident, with the young prisoners called the Stolen Girls.

1979: Maria de Lourdes Pintasilgo, a chemical engineer, became Portugal's first female Prime Minister.

1983: The second *Encuentro* was held in Lima as part of a series of *Encuentros Feministas Latinoamericanas y del Caribe* (Latin

American and Caribbean Feminist *Encuentros*) conferences, which started in 1981 for women in Latin America and the Caribbean aiming to create transnational networks and address women's issues. These conferences sparked discussions on the nature of feminism, inclusivity, and its role within existing systems. They led to initiatives recognizing diverse groups of women and continue to shape regional policies for women's rights.

1984: Lynn Rippelmeyer became the first woman to captain a *Boeing 747* aircraft across the Atlantic.

1984: The Dunnes Stores anti-apartheid strike began in Dublin, Ireland. Shop worker Mary Manning refused to check out a customer's South African fruit, as members of her union, Idatu, had voted not to handle South African goods. Manning was then suspended, and she and 11 of her colleagues went on strike in protest. The stoppage lasted for three years, ending when the Irish government introduced a ban on South African products.

1985: Christa McAuliffe, a teacher from New Hampshire, was selected as the first participant in the Teacher in Space Project. She was chosen to ride aboard the Space Shuttle *Challenger* to bring the space exploration experience to the classroom. Tragically, the *Challenger* exploded shortly after liftoff in January 1986, resulting in the loss of McAuliffe's life and the rest of the crew.

2012: The Reverend Ellinah Ntombi Wamukoya was elected as the bishop of Swaziland, becoming the first woman to hold the position of bishop in any of the twelve Anglican Provinces in Africa.

July 20

1396: Queen Margaret I of Denmark, Norway, and Sweden announced the Treaty of Kalmar, which proposed the personal union of the three kingdoms. The treaty aimed to unite Denmark, Norway (including its territories of Iceland, Greenland, the Faroe Islands, Shetland, and Orkney), and Sweden (including Finland and Åland) under a single monarch.

1947: *Begum*, a Bengali-language women's magazine, debuted with a cover featuring women's rights activist Begum Rokeya. Although initiated by a progressive male journalist, it boasted a talented team of women writers and contributors, including Nurjahan Begum, Razia Khatum, Shamsunnahar Mahmud, Selina Panni, Begum Sufia Kamal, Protibha Ganguly, and Selina Hossain.

1969: JoAnn Morgan made history as the only woman in the launch firing room when *Apollo 11* landed on the Moon.

1989: Aung San Suu Kyi, a pro-democracy activist in Myanmar (formerly Burma), was placed under house arrest by the military junta ruling the country. Suu Kyi's dedication to democratic principles and refusal to leave Myanmar despite political persecution garnered international attention and support.

2005: The Civil Marriage Act was passed in Canada, legalizing same-sex marriage. Canada became one of the first countries to recognize and provide equal marriage rights to same-sex couples.

2009: Amy Wambach, a U.S. women's national soccer team member, scored her hundredth goal in an international soccer match. Wambach's achievement solidified her position as one of women's soccer's most successful and prolific goal-scorers.

2012: The custody of three members of the protest group Pussy Riot, known for their anti-Putin demonstrations, was extended for another six months before their trial began. The case attracted international attention and sparked debates about freedom of expression and human rights in Russia.

July 21

1896: As a result of Josephine St. Pierre Ruffin's efforts, the Colored Women's League (est. June 1892 with Helen Appo Cook as the President) merged with the National Federation of Afro-American Women to form the National League of Colored Women (from 1904, the National Association of Colored Women's Clubs) in Washington D.C., with Mary Church Terrell elected as its first president.

1904: Harriet Brooks, in a letter to *Nature*, described her observation of the recoil of atomic nuclei as nuclear particles were emitted during radioactive decay.

1913: British suffragette Nellie Hall threw a brick through the window of Prime Minister H.H. Asquith's automobile during his visit to Birmingham. This act was part of the suffragette movement's militant tactics to draw attention to their demand for women's right to vote.

1919: Women in Azerbaijan were granted the right to vote, becoming one of the first Muslim-majority countries to give suffrage to women.

1923: On the 75th anniversary of the first women's rights convention held in Seneca Falls, New York, the National Woman's Party launched its Equal Rights Amendment campaign.

1942: The Women's Auxiliary Army Corps (WAAC) class began at Fort Des Moines, USA. It was the beginning of the training program for women joining the U.S. Army during World War II.

1945: Laundry workers in Ireland, part of the Irish Women's Workers Union, went on strike demanding a second week of holidays for all Irish workers. After 14 weeks, they successfully won their demand, improving holiday rights for workers in the country.

1960: Sirimavo Bandaranaike won Sri Lanka's election, becoming the world's first woman head of state to hold the position without inheriting it through birth or marriage. She served as the Prime Minister of Sri Lanka.

1972: Women shoemakers in Fakenham, England, who had occupied their factory protesting redundancy, launched a workers' cooperative in a new plant. The cooperative, known as Fakenham Enterprises Ltd., aimed to keep their jobs but closed five years later.

1979: Maria de Lourdes Pintasilgo assumed the position of Prime Minister of Portugal, becoming the country's first female Prime Minister.

1980: Dame Mary Eugenia Charles, the first female lawyer in Dominica, became Dominica's first female Prime Minister. She served until 1995, becoming the world's longest-continuously serving female prime minister.

2022: Italian astronaut Samantha Cristoforetti completed her first spacewalk, spending 7 hours and 5 minutes outside the International Space Station.

2022: Droupadi Murmu was elected as the President of India, becoming the first woman from a scheduled tribe to hold the position.

July 22

1274: After her father's death, Joan became the Countess of Champagne and Queen of Navarre at the age of one. Due to her age, her mother, Blanche, was her guardian and regent in Navarre. After she married the future Philip IV of France at eleven, she became the queen consort of France in 1285.

1612: In England, four women and one man were hanged during the Northamptonshire witch trials. These trials were part of the larger witch hunts phenomenon and trials that occurred across Europe and

North America during the Early Modern period.

1893: Katharine Lee Bates wrote the poem *America the Beautiful* while on a trip to Pike's Peak in Colorado. The poem became one of the most beloved patriotic songs in the United States.

1933: Caterina Jarboro, an African-American opera singer, performed the role of Aida at the New York Hippodrome. She became the first Black female opera singer to perform in the United States.

1939: Jane Bolin, who became the first African American woman to be admitted to the New York State Bar in 1932, was appointed as a judge of the Domestic Relations Court (later called Family Court). She served on the bench until her retirement and made significant contributions to the legal field.

2016: American hurdler Kendra Harrison set a new world record in the women's 100-meter hurdles during the London Anniversary Games at the Olympic Stadium, completing the race in 12.20 seconds.

2016: A three-judge panel issued a verdict for a Peruvian man, sentencing him to a one-year suspended prison term and directing his release from incarceration. In July 2015, he was captured on video attacking his girlfriend, lawyer Cindy Arlette Contreras Bautista, in a hotel in Ayacucho, dragging her by the hair. The attack resulted in damage to one of her legs, necessitating the use of a cane. Following the decision, a protest *#NiUnaMenos* (Spanish: Not one less) was organized to express outrage following his release from jail.

July 23

1396: Queen Margaret of Denmark, Norway, and Sweden made her great-nephew and adopted son Eric of Pomerania a joint ruler of Sweden, adding to his current role as joint ruler of Norway. Queen Margaret retained de facto power in the realm.

1436: Margery Kempe, an English Christian mystic, hired a priest to write down the story of her life she dictated to him, as she was illiterate. The work became known as *The Book of Margery Kempe* and is considered one of the first autobiographies in the English language. The work combined her life tribulations, religious visions, and spiritual experiences. She described her visit to the famous female mystic Julian of Norwich.

1727: Seventeen Ursuline Sisters from France arrived in New Orleans, Louisiana, in the territory of New France. They established an orphanage, eventually becoming the predecessor of Catholic Charities and the Ursuline Academy, the oldest Catholic school in the United States.

1944: Madeleine Riffaud, a French poet, journalist, and member of the French Resistance during World War II, gained fame for killing a German officer on a bridge over the River Seine in broad daylight. She was captured, beaten, and deported to a concentration camp despite attempting to shoot herself to avoid torture. Riffaud was later released in a prisoner swap and participated in the armed uprising in August.

1961: Grace Bumbry, an American opera singer, became the first Black singer to perform at the Bayreuth Festival in Germany. Her outstanding performance earned her 42 curtain calls.

1986: Wanda Rutkiewicz, a Polish mountain climber and computer engineer, became the first woman to reach the summit of K2, the second-highest mountain in the world. She had previously climbed Mount Everest in 1978, becoming the third woman and the first European woman to do so.

1992: Naamah Kelman-Ezrachi became the first woman in Israel to be ordained as a rabbi when she received her rabbinic ordination from Rabbi Alfred Gottschalk, the President of the Hebrew University of Jerusalem.

1996: Fiona Apple released her debut album, *Tidal*. The album received critical acclaim and launched Apple's successful music career, earning her a dedicated fanbase.

1999: The Space Shuttle *Columbia* launched on the STS-93 mission, with Eileen Collins as the first woman to command a space shuttle.

2001: Megawati Sukarnoputri became the 5th President of Indonesia and the first woman to serve in that office. She ran for re-election in the 2004 and 2009 presidential elections but was defeated by Susilo Bambang Yudhoyono both times.

2020: The Second Space Operations Squadron (SOPS) at Schriever Space Force Base in Colorado became the first all-women crew gained satellite control authority of its newest GPS III fleet satellite (SVN-76).

2021: The Court of Appeal of Samoa declared Naomi Mata'afa as the nation's new prime minister, ending a months-long political crisis.

July 24

1567: Mary, Queen of Scots, was forced to abdicate her throne, and her one-year-old son, James VI, became the new ruler.

1671: Articles of Agreement were signed between the Plymouth leaders and Indian leaders, among whom was Awashonks, a *saunkskwa*, a female *sachem* (chief) of the Sakonnet tribe in Rhode Island. Awashonks became a *saunkskwa* not by inheritance but through the quality of her leadership. During her tenure, she was challenged by both rivals within the Sakonnet and English colonists.

1868: Marie Goegg, a Swiss feminist and suffragist, founded the *Association Internationale des Femmes* (International Association of Women) in Geneva, Switzerland. It was the first continental feminist association dedicated to women's rights and peace.

1961: Kredelle Petway, along with her brother, father, and another man, was arrested at Jackson Airport in Mississippi. Petway had traveled from Tallahassee, Florida, to participate in a freedom ride from Montgomery to Jackson as part of the Civil Rights Movement.

1962: Beatrice Hicks, the first president of the Society of Women Engineers, patented her invention of a gas density sensor designed to protect electronic and aerospace equipment.

1969: Soon after the Stonewall Rebellion, the New York Gay Liberation Front held its first public meeting. The GLF emerged as a unique LGBT+ organization that advocated for complete sexual liberation and overthrowing societal norms rather than focusing solely on gay civil rights and assimilation.

1987: Hulda Crooks, at 91, climbed Mount Fuji in Japan, becoming the oldest person to reach the summit of the country's highest peak.

2021: Laurel Hubbard, a transgender woman who met all the requirements set by the International Olympic Committee (IOC) and the International Weightlifting Federation (IWF), participated in the weightlifting competition at the Tokyo Olympics. She competed in the women's 87 kilogram category, making history as the first openly transgender woman to compete in the Olympic Games. Hubbard, at the age of 43, also became the oldest weightlifter to qualify for the games.

July 25

1110: Matilda, the 8-year-old daughter of King Henry I of England, married Henry V and was crowned Queen of the Romans in Mainz, Germany. Matilda's education and upbringing were entrusted to Bruno, the archbishop of Trier, who taught her about German culture, manners, and governance.

1912: Marie-Adélaïde, Grand Duchess of Luxembourg, ascended to the throne following her father's death, becoming the first female monarch since Duchess Maria Theresa.

1924: Urani Rumbo founded *Përmirësimi* (Improvement), a feminist organization in Albania. The organization focused on organizing educational courses for women from various social backgrounds to empower and uplift them.

1978: Louise Brown, the world's first baby conceived through in vitro fertilization (IVF), was born in Oldham, Greater Manchester, U.K. Her birth revolutionized the field of reproductive medicine and provided hope for persons struggling with infertility.

1984: Svetlana Savitskaya, a cosmonaut aboard the *Salyut 7* space station, became the first woman to perform a spacewalk. She spent 3 hours and 35 minutes outside, cutting and welding metals in space.

2007: Pratibha Patil was sworn in as India's first female President, becoming the first woman to hold the highest office in India since its independence sixty years earlier.

2011: Thirty-four women workers, employed as promoters for Angkor beer by Cambrew (a company partially owned by Carlsberg), went on strike demanding payment for unpaid overtime. They also staged demonstrations in front of the company's headquarters, drawing attention to labor rights and fair treatment in the workplace.

July 26

1745: The first recorded women's cricket match occurred near Guildford, England.

1918: Emmy Noether's groundbreaking paper, known as Noether's theorem, was presented in Göttingen, Germany. The theorem led to the deduction of conservation laws for symmetries in angular momentum, linear momentum, and energy, making significant contributions to theoretical physics.

1937: Gerda Taro, a pioneering photojournalist and anti-fascist activist, died in an accident while covering the Republican retreat during the Battle of Brunete in the Spanish Civil War. Taro, born Gerda Pohorylle, was of German and Polish Jewish descent and changed her name to Gerda Taro to conceal her origins and enhance her commercial success in the field.

1952: Maria Eva Duarte de Peron, popularly known as "Evita," the first lady of Argentina, passed away from cancer. Her death prompted a national mourning period in Argentina, bringing all activities to a halt as the country grieved the loss of its beloved first lady.

1961: Anne X. Alpern became the first woman to serve on the Pennsylvania Supreme Court.

2005: Eileen M. Collins, the first woman to pilot and command a NASA space shuttle, commanded the Discovery on NASA's first shuttle mission following the tragic *Columbia* accident in 2003.

2016: Hillary Clinton was formally nominated for President by the Democratic Party, becoming the first woman ever nominated by a major US political party for the presidency.

2021: Linda Sinrod entered the Guinness World Records as the oldest female hockey player. At 80 years and 305 days, she played a full match in the Capitals Women's Hockey League (CWHL), showcasing her passion for the sport.

2021: Mary Simon became the 30th governor-general of Canada, making history as the first Indigenous person to hold the office.

2021: Hidilyn Diaz, a Filipino weightlifter, won the Women's 55 kg event at the Tokyo Olympics, securing the Philippines' first-ever Olympic gold medal and bringing immense pride to her country.

July 27

1377: Maria of Sicily, a fourteen-year-old, succeeded her father, Frederick the Simple, as the ruler of Sicily.

1912: Elise Sem made history as Norway's first female barrister.

1913: Rosalie M. Ladova, a Chicago physician, challenged societal norms by discarding the required "bathing skirt" for female swimmers, opting for a more comfortable and practical swimwear. Despite gaining international attention, Ladova was arrested by the police and charged with obscenity. Her actions sparked a conversation about women's swimwear and contributed to accepting more practical bathing costumes in the United States.

1982: Indian Prime Minister Indira Gandhi visited the United States for the first time in nearly 11 years.

1983: Madonna, the iconic pop artist, released her self-titled debut studio album, launching her successful and influential music career.

2009: Nina V. Fedoroff and Rita R. Colwell received the President's National Medals of Science for their significant contributions to plant molecular biology and marine microbial ecology, respectively.

2012: Sarah Attar, a middle-distance runner, and Wojdan Shahrkhani, a judo fighter, became the first Saudi women to compete in the Olympic Games. It was a historic moment as the London Olympic Games became the first edition where both male and female athletes represented every participating nation.

2021: Simone Biles, an accomplished American gymnast and four-time Olympic gold medalist, withdrew from the women's team final at the Tokyo Games, prioritizing her mental health and well-being.

2021: Flora Duffy, a triathlete from Bermuda, won the Women's event, securing Bermuda's first Olympic gold medal. Polina Guryeva, a weightlifter from Turkmenistan, claimed second place in the Women's 59 kg event, earning Turkmenistan its first Olympic medal.

July 28

1458: Charlotte, at 14 and already a widow, succeeded to the throne of Cyprus upon the death of her father, John II of Cyprus. She was crowned on October 7 in St. Sophia Cathedral.

1866: Vinnie Ream, at 18, became the first and youngest female artist to receive a commission from the United States government. She was commissioned to create a statue of Abraham Lincoln.

1869: The Daughters of St. Crispin, the first national women's labor organization in the United States, held its founding convention in Lynn, Massachusetts. It was a union of female shoe workers advocating for better working conditions and rights.

1925: Microbiologist and physician Gladys Dick, known for her co-discovery of the microbe that causes scarlet fever, co-patented the Dick Test, used to determine an individual's susceptibility to the disease.

2012: Chinese swimmer Ye Shiwen set a new world record in the women's 400-meter individual medley at the 2012 Summer Olympics in London.

2013: Tatyana McFadden became the first athlete to win six gold medals at championships during the 2013 IPC Athletics World Championships in Lyon. She claimed gold in every event from 100 meters to 5,000 meters. The same year, McFadden also won the Boston, Chicago, London, and New York marathons, which made her the first person – non-disabled or otherwise – to win the four major marathons in the same year. She also set a new course record for the Chicago Marathon (1 hour, 42 minutes, 35 seconds).

2018: Wendy Tuck, an Australian sailor, became the first woman skipper to win the Clipper Round the World Yacht Race, a challenging and prestigious sailing event.

2019: Niramon Ounprom, known as Sineenat Bilaskalayani, was granted the title of Royal Noble Consort by Crown Prince Vajiralongkorn of Thailand when he ascended to the throne as King Rama X. She became the first woman in nearly a century to hold the position of royal concubine to the King of Thailand.

2021: Lawmakers in Ghana proposed a bill to criminalize displays of same-sex affection and the promotion of LGBTQ+ rights, with potential penalties of up to ten years in prison.

2021: Belarusian opposition leader Sviatlana Tsikhanouskaya met with U.S. President Joe Biden at the White House. President Biden expressed his support for the Belarusian opposition activists in pursuing democracy and universal human rights. Tsikhanouskaya thanked Biden and expressed hope for a successful future for Belarus.

July 29

1862: Belle Boyd, known for her espionage activities during the American Civil War, was captured by Union officials for spying on behalf of the Confederacy. Despite being arrested multiple times, she managed to evade long-term incarceration.

1895: Representatives from 42 Black women's clubs across 14 states gathered at Berkeley Hall in Boston, USA, for the First National Conference of Colored Women of America, led by Josephine Ruffin. During the conference, prominent figures such as Ella L. Smith, Anna J. Cooper, Victoria Earle Matthews, Agnes Jones Adams, T. Thomas Fortune, Henry B. Blackwell, William Lloyd Garrison, Helen Appo Cook, Alexander Crummell, Anna Sprague, Ida B. Wells, and Eliza Ann Gardner delivered speeches on various topics, including education, organization, literature collection, social purity, political equality, and the ideal national union. The event also featured discussions on justice, temperance, and the importance of industrial training. Additionally, artists Alice T. Miller, Moses Hamilton Hodges, and Arianna Sparrow contributed with recitals and poetry readings. During the conference, the National Federation of Afro-American Women (NFAAW) was organized. Margaret Murray Washington served as President, with Florida Ruffin Ridley as Corresponding Secretary, L. C. Carter as Recording Secretary, and Libby B. Anthony as Treasurer. Vice Presidents included Mary Dickerson, Helen Crum, and Ella Mahammitt. The organization designated The Woman's Era as its official news outlet. In 1896, the NFAAW organized another conference and merged with other groups to form the National Association of Colored Women.

1938: The musical drama film *Little Miss Broadway* starring Shirley Temple and Edna May Oliver was released on this day. The film showcased Temple's talent and charm as a child actress.

1974: The Philadelphia Eleven, consisting of Merrill Bittner, Alla Bozarth-Campbell, Alison Cheek, Emily Hewitt, Carter Heyward, Suzanne Hiatt, Marie Moorefield, Jeannette Piccard, Betty Schiess, Katrina Swanson, and Nancy Wittig, were ordained as the first women Episcopal priests.

1976: Tina Anselmi became the first woman to serve as a government minister in Italy when she was appointed Minister of Labor by Prime Minister Giulio Andreotti.

1996: Four female anti-war activists in Liverpool were cleared of all charges related to damaging a Hawk fighter jet meant for sale to the Indonesian government. They were acquitted based on their aim to prevent the genocidal occupation of East Timor, the jet's intended use.

2021: Alessandra Perilli, a shooter from San Marino, won third place in the Women's Trap event at the Tokyo Olympics, securing San Marino its first Olympic medal, which was notable as San Marino, one of the smallest nations in terms of population, became the least populous country to win an Olympic medal.

July 30

1860: The official coronation of Teri'i-maeva-rua II as the Queen of Bora Bora took place.

1883: Ranavalona III ascended to the throne as the sovereign of the Kingdom of Madagascar. Her reign was marked by her resistance against the colonial attacks and influence of the French government in Madagascar.

1896: A strike started in the Imperialist Tobacco Factory in Krakow. Of the one thousand workers, nine hundred were women and girls demanding assurance of job stability from the perspective of new machines being introduced. After negotiations and appropriate guarantees, the women returned to work. It was the first workers' strike in the region of Galicia. The women workers created a union in the factory in 1907.

1942: The U.S. government established the Navy WAVES (Women Accepted for Voluntary Emergency Service) program. WAVES allowed women to serve in the U.S. Navy during World War II in non-combat roles, a significant development in expanding women's roles in the military.

1966: Catherine Conroy and Betty Friedan co-founded the National Organization for Women (NOW) in the United States. NOW became a prominent feminist organization advocating for women's rights and gender equality.

1977: Susanne Albrecht, Brigitte Mohnhaupt, and Christian Klar, members of the left-wing German terrorist group Red Army Faction, assassinated Jürgen Ponto, chairman of Dresdner Bank, in Oberursel, West Germany. This act was part of the Red Army Faction's campaign against what they perceived as capitalist and imperialist institutions.

1981: Hunger demonstrations erupted in Łódź, Poland, with an estimated 50,000 participants, primarily women and children. The protests were a response to food ration shortages experienced during Communist rule and symbolized the frustrations and hardships faced by the population.

2012: During the Summer Olympics, Rūta Meilutytė, a 15-year-old swimmer from Lithuania, won her country's first-ever Olympic gold medal in the pool. Additionally, Dana Vollmer of the United States set a new world record in the 100-meter butterfly event.

July 31

1913: Alys McKey Bryant became the first woman to fly an airplane in Canada.

1913: A motorcade of sixty automobiles traveled from Hyattsville, Maryland, to the United States Capitol to present petitions containing 200,000 signatures to the U.S. Senate. These petitions advocated for a constitutional amendment granting women the right to vote.

1928: Halina Konopacka of Poland set a world record in women's discus throw, hurling the discus 39.62 meters to win the first gold medal in women's Olympic athletics at the Amsterdam Games.

1938: Ruth Ella Moore published an article, "Discussion - The Immunology of Dental Caries," in *The Dentoscope*. Moore was a bacteriologist and microbiologist who became the first African-American woman awarded a Ph.D. in natural science in 1933.

1948: Elizabeth Bentley, a former Communist Party member turned informant, appeared before the House Un-American Activities Committee (HUAC) in the United States to testify about Communist espionage activities.

2007: Jane E. Salmon received the Carol-Nachman Prize for Research in Rheumatology for her innovative work on the pathogenesis of organ damage in systemic lupus erythematosus and other immune system disorders.

2011: Jennifer Pharr Davis set an unofficial record for the fastest assisted hike of the entire Appalachian Trail, completing the trail from Mount Katahdin in Maine to Springer Mountain in Georgia in 46 days, 11 hours, and 20 minutes.

2012: Three members of the Russian feminist punk rock band Pussy Riot went on trial in Moscow for holding an unsanctioned performance at Moscow's Christ the Savior Cathedral. The performance called for the ouster of Vladimir Putin, sparking international attention and discussions on freedom of expression.

2012: The United States women's gymnastics team, known as the Fierce Five, consisting of Aly Raisman, Gabby Douglas, Jordyn Wieber, McKayla Maroney, and Kyla Ross, won the Olympic gold medal in the artistic team final at the Summer Olympics. This victory marked the second women's team gold medal for the United States, and the first at an Olympics held outside the USA.

2016: Yuriko Koike, a member of the Liberal Democratic Party (LDP), was elected as the first female governor of Tokyo prefecture in Japan.

2022: The England women's football team defeated Germany 2-1 in the UEFA Women's Euro 2022 final, securing their first major football championship.

AUGUST

August 01

607: Empress Suiko of Japan appointed Ono no Imoko as the official envoy to the Sui Court in China. His mission was to pay tribute to Emperor Yángdi and deliver a letter from prince-regent Shōtoku, representing a crucial diplomatic exchange between Japan and China.

1786: a German astronomer, Caroline Herschel, identified a comet and became the first woman to discover one. She alerted other astronomers about her discovery, allowing them to study its path.

1911: Harriet Quimby earned her Aero Club of America aviator's certificate, becoming the first woman in the United States to do so.

1960: Frances O. Kelsey began her work for the U.S. Food and Drug Administration (FDA). Her meticulous scrutiny and refusal to approve the drug *thalidomide*, which had harmful effects on fetuses, prevented a potential health crisis and raised awareness about drug testing and safety regulations.

1979: Maria de Lourdes Pintasilgo became the first and, to date, the only woman to serve as the Prime Minister of Portugal.

2001: Rita Levi-Montalcini, a Jewish-Italian neurobiologist and a co-recipient of the 1986 Nobel Prize in Physiology or Medicine for discovering nerve growth factor (NGF) with Stanley Cohen was appointed as Senator for Life by the President of Italy, Carlo Azeglio Ciampi, at 92. She served in the Senate for 11 years.

2005: Suzanne Al-Houby, a Palestinian mountain climber, scaled Mount Elbrus in Europe, becoming the first Arab woman to achieve this feat. She had previously conquered prominent peaks, including Kilimanjaro, Mont Blanc, and Everest Base Camp.

2011: U.S. Representative Gabrielle Giffords returned to Congress to cast a debt ceiling vote after surviving a gunshot wound in an assassination attempt.

2020: Booker Prize-nominated author Tsitsi Dangarembga and twelve others detained for participating in anti-government protests in Zimbabwe were released and scheduled to appear for trials later.

2021: New Zealand Prime Minister Jacinda Ardern formally apologized to the Pacific Islander community for the Dawn Raids, a series of discriminatory police actions in the 1970s. She announced measures to address the historical injustice and support the affected community.

2021: American shot putter Raven Saunders made a symbolic gesture by raising and crossing her arms in the shape of an X during the Women's shot put medal ceremony at the Tokyo Olympics, expressing support for oppressed individuals. The International Olympic Committee launched an investigation into the incident, as podium demonstrations were prohibited.

2022: U.S. House Speaker Nancy Pelosi visited Taiwan, becoming the most senior U.S. official to visit the self-governing island since 1997. Her visit took place despite threats from China.

2022: In Kansas, voters rejected an amendment to the state constitution that aimed to allow state lawmakers to impose anti-abortion restrictions. This referendum marked a significant moment in the aftermath of the Supreme Court's decision to overturn *Roe v. Wade*.

August 02

1316: Matilda of Hainaut became the sole ruler of the Principality of Achaea after her husband, Prince Louis of Burgundy, died of poisoning shortly after securing his position during the Battle of Mandolada.

1343: Jeanne de Clisson, following the execution of her husband, became a pirate seeking revenge. She sold her estates and assembled a force to attack French ships and ports.

1942: Edith Stein, also known by her religious name, Saint Teresia Benedicta a Cruce, was captured by the Nazi SS, together with other 243 baptized Jews residing in the Netherlands. She was a German Jewish philosopher who converted to Catholicism and devoted herself to life as a Discalced Carmelite nun. She was canonized as a martyr and saint within the Catholic Church, and she is one of the six patron saints of Europe.

1946: Hattie Elizabeth Alexander and Grace Leidy published "Influence of Streptomycin on Type b *Haemophilus influenzae*" in *Science*. The article described the development of effective remedies for *Haemophilus influenzae* infections.

1948: Fanny Blankers-Koen, representing the Netherlands, won her fourth gold medal at the London Olympic Games. She became the first woman to achieve four Olympic gold medals in a single Olympics. Queen Juliana of the Netherlands honored her with a knighthood in the Order of Orange Nassau.

2013: Renée Richards was among the first inductees into the National Gay and Lesbian Sports Hall of Fame, recognizing her contributions as a transgender tennis player.

2019: Saudi Arabia implemented several changes aimed at enhancing women's rights. These changes included granting women the freedom to travel without requiring permission from a male guardian and expanding their marriage and custodial rights through royal decrees.

2019: Romanian Prime Minister Viorica Dăncilă fired Minister of Education Ecaterina Andronescu due to controversial remarks she made during a television interview regarding the murder of a 15-year-old girl named Alexandra Măceșanu. Andronescu's comment sparked widespread criticism, and a 65-year-old man later confessed to the murder of Alexandra Măceșanu and another missing teenage girl.

2021: Belarusian sprinter Krystsina Tsimanouskaya sought refuge in the Polish embassy in Tokyo after refusing to board a flight back to Belarus at Haneda Airport. She requested Japanese police protection, fearing repercussions from the Belarusian authorities.

August 03

435: Aelia Pulcheria convinced her brother, Theodosius II, to exile Nestorius, the archbishop of Constantinople, to a monastery in the Libyan desert. This action was taken due to theological disputes and Nestorius' views being deemed heretical.

1529: The Peace of the Ladies, or Treaty of Cambrai, was negotiated by Louise of Savoy and Margaret of Austria. The treaty was signed between the Holy Roman Empire and France to end hostilities between the two powers.

1929: Los Angeles children's summer camp run by socialists was raided by members of the American Legion, and six primarily young women and one man were arrested. 19-year-old communist Yetta Stromberg was arrested, later convicted, and jailed with five other women for having a red flag. California was one of 24 states which banned red or black socialist or anarchist flags. Stromberg later took her case to the Supreme Court, and in 1931, the Court overturned the bans as violating the First Amendment right to free speech.

1944: Ruth Gruber played a significant role in finding a haven in the United States for 1,000 Holocaust refugees, which was made possible by a temporary relaxation of America's restrictive immigration policy during World War II.

1948: Vicki Draves, an Asian American diver, became the first Asian American to win an Olympic gold medal in the 3-meter springboard event. She later won another gold medal on August 6 in the 10-meter platform, becoming the first American woman to win two gold medals in diving at the same Olympics.

2009: British adventurer Sarah Outen became the youngest person and the first woman to row alone across the Indian Ocean. She embarked on her journey from Fremantle, Australia, in April and arrived at the island of Mauritius after rowing for 124 days, 14 hours, and 9 minutes.

2011: Heather Purser, a member of the Suquamish tribe in Seattle, Washington, initiated and advocated for same-sex marriages within her tribe. As a result of her efforts, the Suquamish tribe voted to accept same-sex marriages, becoming the second Native American tribe to do so.

2022: American basketball player Brittney Griner was sentenced to nine years in prison by a Russian court after being found guilty of smuggling cannabis-infused vape cartridges into Russia.

August 04

1683: Turhan, the Valide Sultan of the Ottoman Empire and mother of Sultan Mehmed IV, passed away at 56. Her death marked the end of the "Sultanate of Women" era in Ottoman history. After the overthrow of Mehmed IV four years later, the role of the mother of the Ottoman Sultan became diminished, signifying a shift from the influential position previously held by women in power.

1928: Miriam O'Brien achieved the first ascent of the traverse from the Aiguilles du Diable to Mont Blanc du Tacul in the Alps.

1944: Acting on a tip from an informer, the Nazi Gestapo captured Anne Frank, a 15-year-old Jewish diarist, and her family. They were found hiding in a sealed-off area of an Amsterdam warehouse. Anne Frank's diary, which she wrote during their period in hiding, has since become one of the most well-known accounts of the Holocaust (Shoah).

1990: The term "Two-Spirit," referring to Indigenous people who embody diverse sexualities, genders, gender roles, or gender expressions, was adopted at the 3rd Annual Gathering of Native American Gays and Lesbians near Beausejour, Manitoba, Canada. Myra Laramee, a First Nations Cree teacher, counselor, administrator, mentor, and elder, introduced the term during a sharing circle at the gathering, and the Indigenous LGBTQ+ community quickly embraced it.

2022: U.S. Attorney General Merrick Garland announced charges against four police officers involved in the 2020 raid that resulted in the death of Breonna Taylor. The charges were brought forth for violations of Breonna Taylor's rights.

August 05

81 BCE: Ptolemy IX elevated his daughter, Berenice III, to co-regent. Berenice III, previously the wife and co-regent of Ptolemy X, became the sole ruler upon her father's death in December of the same year. She was then reintegrated into the dynastic cult as *Thea Philopator* ("Father-loving Goddess"), emphasizing the inheritance of power from her father.

1888: Bertha Benz embarked on the first long-distance automobile trip, driving from Mannheim to Pforzheim and back. This historic journey, undertaken by Benz, the wife of automobile inventor Karl Benz, demonstrated the feasibility and potential of the automobile as a mode of transportation.

1939: During the right-wing regime of General Francisco Franco in Spain, 56 people, including 13 women and girls who were members of the Unified Socialist Youth (JSU), were executed en masse. This event, became known as the execution of the "13 Roses."

1943: The United States Women Airforce Service Pilots (WASPs) were established by merging the Women's Auxiliary Ferrying Squadron (WAFS) and Women Airforce Service Pilots (WFTD). The WASPs played a crucial role during World War II by ferrying aircraft, conducting test flights, and performing other non-combat flight duties, freeing male pilots up for combat roles.

1975: Drummer Sandy West and guitarist Joan Jett formed the rock band The Runaways. They were later joined by singer Cherie Currie, lead guitarist Lita Ford, and bassist Jackie Fox. The Runaways gained recognition as one of the first all-female rock bands.

1993: After decades of denials, the Japanese government has acknowledged its historical involvement in forcing women to work in military brothels from 1932 to 1945. Up to 200,000 women and young girls, mainly from Korea and China but also from Japan, the Philippines, and some European settlers in Dutch Indonesia, were either abducted or deceived into working in over 100 brothels.

2010: Elena Kagan was confirmed by the U.S. Senate as a Supreme Court Justice, becoming the fourth woman to serve on the United States Supreme Court.

2011: Yulia Tymoshenko, the former Prime Minister of Ukraine and leader of the largest opposition party, was arrested in Kyiv.

2011: Yingluck Shinawatra was officially elected as the Prime Minister of Thailand by the parliament. She became Thailand's first female Prime Minister and served in that role until 2014.

2020: Belarusian opposition activist Olga Kovalkova sought refuge in Poland after being released from prison. She fled from the authorities, who had warned her of potential further arrests if she remained in Belarus.

August 06

1774: Ann Lee and the Shakers religious group immigrated to America and settled in New York. The Shakers, officially known as the United Society of Believers in Christ's Second Appearing, were known for their communal living, celibacy, and belief in gender equality.

1926: American swimmer Gertrude Ederle became the first woman to swim across the English Channel. She broke the previous men's record by over two hours, accomplishing the feat in 14 hours and 34 minutes.

1965: The Voting Rights Act was signed into law in the United States. It aimed to overcome discriminatory voting practices that disenfranchised African Americans, particularly in the Southern states. It prohibited literacy tests and other methods to prevent African Americans from exercising their right to vote. The act also extended suffrage to African-American women, ensuring, in theory, equal voting rights for all.

1986: Alice Auma, an Acholi spirit medium from Uganda, claimed to have been directed by the spirit of a deceased army officer named Lakwena to form the Holy Spirit Movement (HSM). The movement had religious and political elements and aimed to bring about social and political change in Uganda.

1991: Takako Doi, chair of the Social Democratic Party, became Japan's first female speaker of the House of Representatives.

2009: The South East Asia Court of Women on HIV and Human Trafficking met in Nusa Dua, Bali, Indonesia, organized by the United Nations Development Programme (UNDP) and regional bodies. The event acted as a symbolic court with a panel of six legal and human rights experts. They listened to 22 Southeast Asian women sharing their stories of trafficking, violence, and exploitation. The event also included data presentations and analyses on the dignity and human rights violations faced by Southeast Asian women. The attendees included political leaders, organizations, and individuals dedicated to empowering women and reducing trafficking and HIV risks in the region. Key discussions covered topics like the human rights of vulnerable communities, the public health impact of anti-trafficking laws, and community responses.

2019: The Israeli lawyer and human rights defender Gabriela "Gaby" Lasky received a Human Rights Award in memory of the Swedish lawyer Anna Dahlbäck. The Fund argued their choice:

> "The Israeli lawyer Gaby Lasky has for years fought for the basic values of democracy. Her ambition is to strengthen human rights and the rule of law in the conflict between Israel and Palestine. In her profession she takes on controversial cases, defends both Palestinian and Israeli clients and litigates with great juridical skill. Her efforts to back up Israel's movement to bring a more peaceful society into being have caused her harassments and threats. In accordance with the regulations of Anna Dahlbäck's Memorial Fund Gaby Lasky has shown strong engagement and courage to stand up for equality and justice."

2021: The Moldovan parliament elected Natalia Gavrilița as the new Prime Minister of Moldova. Gavrilița became the first woman to hold the position in Moldova's history, leading the government and addressing the country's challenges.

August 07

1909: Alice Huyler Ramsey and three friends became the first women to complete a transcontinental automobile trip. They traveled from New York to San Francisco, covering approximately 3,800 miles over 59 days. Their journey played a significant role in challenging gender stereotypes and promoting women's independence and capabilities.

1948: Alice Coachman became the first African-American woman to win an Olympic gold medal. She achieved this feat in the high jump competition at the 1948 London Olympics.

1980: Anna Walentynowicz, a Polish free trade union activist and co-founder of Solidarity, the first non-communist trade union in the Eastern Bloc, was fired from her job at the Lenin Shipyard in Gdańsk which triggered mass strikes at the shipyard, quickly turning into a wave of strikes across Poland. Walentynowicz became disillusioned with the communist system and engaged in social justice activism, speaking loudly against the mistreatment of workers and corruption. She was targeted by the secret police and harassed before being fired. Thanks to women protesters like Walentynowicz and Alina Pienkowska, a simple strike for better pay turned into a political movement.

1985: Chiaki Mukai (with Takao Doi and Mamoru Mohri) was chosen as Japan's first astronaut. Mukai later became the first Japanese woman to travel to space, demonstrating a significant achievement for Japanese space exploration and women in the field. She became the first Japanese citizen to have two spaceflights and the first Asian woman in space.

1987: Lynne Cox, an American long-distance open-water swimmer, became the first to swim between the United States and the Soviet Union in the Bering Strait. The challenging swim covered approximately 2.7 miles (4.3 kilometers) in frigid waters. Cox's achievement showcased her exceptional endurance and determination.

1993: Ada Deer, a Menominee activist, made history by being sworn in as the head of the Bureau of Indian Affairs (BIA). She became the first woman to hold this position, leading efforts to address critical issues affecting Native American communities in the United States.

2017: The all-women crew of eXXpedition embarked on their eighth sailing project around Britain. The eXXpedition, initiated in 2014 by Emily Penn and Lucy Gilliam, aimed to raise awareness about plastic pollution in the Earth's oceans.

August 08

1969: President Richard Nixon issued Executive Order 11478, which mandated federal departments and agencies to establish and maintain affirmative action programs for equal employment opportunities for civilian employees and applicants.

1972: Admiral Elmo Zumwalt, the Chief of Naval Operations, issued an order that significantly changed the United States Navy. The ruling allowed women to serve aboard ships, pursue careers as aviators, and attend the U.S. Naval Academy. Before this, women's roles in the Navy were limited to operating within the states. Admiral Zumwalt emphasized the importance of providing equal opportunities for women and recognized the progress achieved by society in breaking down barriers.

2007: Barbara Morgan, an educator, became the first educator astronaut to reach space. She flew on the U.S. Space Shuttle *Endeavour* to the International Space Station as part of NASA's efforts to involve teachers in space exploration and inspire students.

2010: Elena Kagan was sworn in as the fourth woman to serve as a United States Supreme Court Justice.

2012: Sarah Attar became the first woman from Saudi Arabia to compete in track and field at the Olympic Games. She participated in the 800-meter heat.

2016: Blackpink, a South Korean girl group, released their debut single album titled *Square One*. Blackpink quickly gained international recognition and popularity, becoming one of the leading K-pop groups known for their energetic performances and catchy music.

August 09

1956: The Women's March to Pretoria took place in South Africa, with an estimated 20,000 women participating. The march was led by Helen Joseph, Rahima Moosa, Lilian Ngoyi, and Sophie Williams-De Bruyn to protest the discriminatory pass laws imposed on Black women. The marchers delivered a petition with around 100,000 signatures to Prime Minister J.G. Strijdom, demanding the abolition of pass laws. During the march, the women chanted slogans expressing their defiance and determination for change.

1979: Women workers from the Y.H. wig -making company in Seoul, South Korea, occupied the headquarters of the opposition New Democratic Party. They were protesting against the closure of their employer and had previously gone on strike. However, their attempts to escalate the protest by occupying the party headquarters were met with violence. The military dictatorship sent 2,000 riot police to evict the 187 women, resulting in clashes that led to the death of one woman, Kim Kyung Sook. Despite the unsuccessful occupation, the violent repression of the workers fueled widespread anger and played a significant role in sparking further uprisings later that year.

1995: Roberta Cooper Ramo became the first woman to serve as the president of the American Bar Association (ABA). Ramo was a prominent attorney and advocate for legal reform.

2011: Penny Wong, the first openly gay member of the Australian Cabinet, announced that her partner would be having a baby. Wong's announcement contributed to the visibility and acceptance of LGBTQ+ individuals in political and public spheres.

August 10

1387: Margaret I ascended to the throne as Queen of Denmark, and in the following years, she became the Queen of Norway (February 1388) and Sweden (a year later). Margaret I held significant power and was recognized as one of European history's early influential female rulers.

1792: Claire Lacombe, an actress and revolutionary, played a prominent role in the storming of the Tuileries Palace in Paris during the Insurrection of August 10, 1792. Despite being shot, Lacombe continued fighting and later co-founded the Society of Revolutionary Republican Women, which advocated for women's rights during the French Revolution.

1890: Fay Fuller, a journalist and schoolteacher, became the first recorded woman to reach the summit of Mount Rainier in Washington State, USA. She described the experience as a profound and indescribable moment of natural beauty and wonder.

1970: The proposed Equal Rights Amendment (ERA) to the United States Constitution received strong endorsement from the House of Representatives, with a vote of 350 to 15. The ERA aimed to guarantee equal rights under the law regardless of sex and had been consistently introduced since 1923. Although it was also approved in the Senate, the final version that both houses could agree on was not submitted for ratification by the states before the conclusion of the 91st United States Congress session.

1993: Ruth Bader Ginsburg was sworn in as the second female Justice of the U.S. Supreme Court. Ginsburg, known for her dedication to gender equality and women's rights, served on the Supreme Court until she died in 2020.

2012: Mariam Aloma Mukhtar became the first female Chief Justice of Nigeria.

August 11

1834: The Ursuline Convent riots occurred when a Protestant mob set fire to a convent of Ursuline nuns near Boston. The attack was fueled by anti-Catholic sentiments prevalent at the time.

1876: The British Parliament passed a bill allowing women to qualify for medicine.

1942: Actress Hedy Lamarr and composer George Antheil were awarded a frequency-hopping spread spectrum communication system patent. Their invention laid the foundation for modern wireless technologies, including wireless telephones, two-way radio communications, and Wi-Fi.

1984: During the U.K. miners' strike, around 25,000 women marched in London to protest against pit closures. Women were crucial in supporting the strike, with miners' wives and other women forming support groups nationwide. Women Against Pit Closures, a national organization, was also created during this time.

2012: Nicola Adams of Great Britain made history at the Summer Olympics by becoming the first female boxer to win an Olympic gold medal. She achieved this feat in the flyweight category by defeating China's Ren Cancan.

2020: Belarusian opposition leader Sviatlana Tsikhanouskaya fled to Lithuania to reunite with her family. Tsikhanouskaya had been hiding since the contested presidential election in Belarus, where she alleged electoral fraud by President Alexander Lukashenko. The Lithuanian Foreign Minister confirmed her escape to Lithuania.

August 12

1248: Queen Margaret of Provence and her sister, Beatrice of Provence, joined King Louis IX in leaving Paris to participate in the Seventh Crusade.

1911: A strike of working women and girls began in south London, quickly spreading into a mass walkout. This strike symbolized the growing labor activism and demands for better working conditions and rights for women.

1972: Wendy Rue founded the National Association for Female Executives (NAFE), one of the most prominent businesswomen's organizations in the United States. NAFE aimed to support and advocate for the advancement of women in executive and leadership roles.

2009: President Barack Obama awarded Janet D. Rowley the Presidential Medal of Freedom. Rowley, an American geneticist and pioneer in cancer research, made significant contributions to understanding genetic abnormalities and their connection to various forms of cancer.

2009: Lubna al-Hussein, a Sudanese woman, faced the threat of forty lashes for wearing trousers in public. Additionally, she was barred from leaving the country for a planned visit to Lebanon, where she was scheduled to address women's issues on a televised talk show.

2017: Heather Heyer, a 32-year-old antiracist activist, was killed in a white supremacist terrorist attack in Charlottesville, Virginia. Heyer participated in a counterprotest against the Unite the Right rally organized by neo-Nazis, Ku Klux Klan members, and other white nationalists. She was struck and killed by a car deliberately driven into the crowd by a 20-year-old white supremacist.

August 13

1918: Opha May Johnson became the first woman to enlist in the United States Marine Corps.

1934: Nina Kamneva, a Soviet athlete and engineer, broke the women's world record for free fall after jumping from 2,750 meters and only opening the parachute at 250 meters up. She was in free fall for 58 seconds.

1938: Orleana Hawks Puckett, a pioneering midwife in Virginia, assisted in her last delivery. Puckett played a vital role in providing healthcare and support to women in the rural mountains of Patrick and Carroll County, contributing to the well-being of her community.

2012: Thousands of Tunisians, primarily women, took to the streets of Tunis to protest against the Islamist-led government's attempts to diminish women's rights.

2012: Helen Gurley Brown, an influential American publisher and editor, passed away at 90 in New York City. Brown served as the editor-in-chief of Cosmopolitan magazine and played a significant role in promoting female empowerment and discussing sexual liberation during the 1960s and beyond.

2014: Maryam Mirzakhani, an Iranian mathematician, was awarded the Fields Medal, the most prestigious award in mathematics. Mirzakhani was honored for her groundbreaking contributions to dynamics and geometry, becoming the first woman and Iranian to be recognized with the Fields Medal.

2016: *#NiUnaMenos* (Spanish: Not one less) march, organized by a Peruvian group against femicides and violence against women, took place in Lima.

2020: Belarusian women formed human chains as a protest against the crackdown on demonstrations following the disputed presidential election in Belarus.

2022: Women's rights activists in Kabul marched toward the education ministry to demand broader rights under the Taliban regime. However, the Taliban violently dispersed the demonstration, chasing and beating women while firing gunshots into the air.

August 14

1859: Harriet E. Wilson copyrighted her first novel, *Our Nig, or Sketches from the Life of a Free Black*, making it the first African-American novel published in the United States. The book, which explores themes of race, slavery, and identity, was an essential work in African-American literature.

1933: The radio show *Ma Perkins*, starring Virginia Payne, debuted on station WLW in Cincinnati. The show gained popularity and became available nationwide on the NBC Red Network. It aired on weekdays from 1933 to 1960 and was one of the longest-running radio soap operas, capturing listeners' attention nationwide.

1942: Mariya Semyonovna Polivanova (19) and Natalya Kovshova (21), both Soviet snipers who worked as a team, got surrounded by German Wehrmacht soldiers while fighting near Novgorod. They had only two hand grenades left, which they detonated, killing themselves and the approaching soldiers.

1944: Irma Bandiera, a 29-year-old Italian resistance partisan known as 'Mimma,' was brutally murdered by the Nazis. Despite enduring torture and blindness for seven days, she refused to disclose the names of her comrades. Her bravery and sacrifice serve as a poignant reminder of the courage exhibited by resistance fighters during World War II.

1947: U.S. Military Commission Court at Dachau found Ilse Koch guilty and sentenced to life imprisonment. She was a German war criminal who committed heinous atrocities during her husband Karl-Otto Koch's command at Buchenwald. Despite holding no official Nazi role, Koch became infamous during the war. She earned the moniker "The Witch of Buchenwald" (*Die Hexe von Buchenwald*) from inmates due to suspected cruelty and inappropriate behavior toward prisoners. Koch was also dubbed "The Beast of Buchenwald," the "Queen of Buchenwald," the "Red Witch of Buchenwald," "Butcher Widow," and "The Bitch of Buchenwald." Koch took her life at Aichach women's prison on September 1, 1967, at 60.

1970: Angela Davis, an influential civil rights activist and academic, was added to the FBI's Most Wanted list by J. Edgar Hoover. Davis was targeted for her political activism and involvement in the Black Panther Party and Communist Party USA, becoming a symbol of the government's efforts to suppress dissent during the era.

1986: Rear Admiral Grace Murray Hopper, a pioneering computer scientist and inventor of the computer language COBOL, retired from active duty in the U.S. Navy.

2011: Asmaa Mahfouz, an Egyptian activist, was charged with inciting violence, raising concerns about human rights violations. Mahfouz played a prominent role in the Egyptian Revolution and was known for her activism through social media platforms, calling for political change and advocating for human rights.

2015: Mathematicians Jennifer McLoud-Mann and her colleagues at the University of Washington Bothell discovered a new type of pentagon tiling, demonstrating the first instance of "tiling the plane" with a single polygon since 1985. Their discovery had implications for mathematics and geometry, contributing to further understanding of tessellations and patterns.

2019: Stéphanie Frappart, a French referee, became the first woman to officiate a UEFA Super Cup game during the match between Liverpool and Chelsea in Istanbul, Turkey.

2021: BBC journalist Sarah Rainsford was permanently expelled from Russia after authorities ordered her to leave. The expulsion was a response to two reporters from the Russian state-run news channel Russia-24 being denied visas in the United Kingdom.

August 15

1185: Queen Tamar of Georgia consecrated the cave city of Vardzia, an impressive monastic complex carved into the rock. The city served as a center of culture, religion, and learning during Queen Tamar's reign, and it remains an important historical and architectural site in Georgia.

1686: Christina, the former monarch of Sweden, responded to the revocation of the Edict of Nantes in France by declaring her protection for Jews within Sweden, showcasing her support for religious tolerance and her willingness to offer refuge to those facing persecution.

1851: Angélique Brûlon became the first woman to receive the recognition of *Chevalier* (Knight) of the French Legion of Honour. Napoleon III bestowed this honor upon her, although her initial request filed in 1804 had been unsuccessful.

1970: Patricia Palinkas became the first woman to play professionally in an American football game. She played for the Orlando Panthers in the Atlantic Coast Football League.

1973: Margaret Sloan, the chair of the National Black Feminist Organization (NBFO), officially announced the organization's formation and invited Black women to join.

1977: Reba McEntire, a talented country music artist, released her self-titled debut album under Mercury Records, indicating the beginning of a successful recording career for McEntire, who would become one of the most renowned and influential country singers in history.

1981: The Eternal Word Television Network (EWTN), founded by Mother Angelica, made its cable television debut. EWTN was dedicated to spreading the Roman Catholic faith and has grown to become the world's most prominent religious cable network, reaching viewers in numerous countries.

2006: Te Arikinui Dame Te Atairangikaahu, the Māori Queen of New Zealand, passed away at 75. She held the title for 40 years, making her the longest-reigning monarch in the history of the *Kingitanga* movement, which seeks to unify Māori tribes. Her funeral drew immense attendance, reflecting the respect and admiration she garnered during her reign.

2014: Nadia Murad Basee Taha, a Yazidi woman, was captured by ISIS in Iraq and subjected to enslavement, torture, and sexual violence. She eventually escaped and became an advocate for human trafficking awareness and refugee rights. In 2018, Murad and Denis Mukwege were awarded the

Nobel Peace Prize for their efforts to combat sexual violence in conflict zones.

2015: Jen Welter became the first woman to coach in the National Football League (NFL) as a coaching intern for the Arizona Cardinals. Additionally, Sarah Thomas became the first full-time female on-field official in NFL history, working as a line judge in the Chiefs-Cardinals preseason game.

2019: Ilhan Omar and Rashida Tlaib, American Muslim congresswomen, were denied entry into Israel for their scheduled visit due to their support for the Boycott, Divestment, and Sanctions (BDS) movement. The decision was supported by former U.S. President Donald Trump and sparked widespread debate and controversy regarding freedom of speech and political activism.

August 16

1816: Juana Azurduy de Padilla was formally granted the title of Lieutenant Colonel for her military achievements in the fight against the Spanish.

1858: Queen Victoria of Britain telegraphed U.S. President James Buchanan for the first time using the transatlantic telegraph cable. This historic communication marked a significant advancement in international telegraphy and facilitated quicker and more direct contact between the two countries.

1977: Judge Alfred M. Ascione of New York ruled in favor of Renee Richards in her lawsuit against the United States Tennis Association (U.S.T.A.). The ruling allowed Richards, a transgender woman, to compete in the U.S. Open.

1979: Pasqualina Chianese gave birth to octuplets in Naples, Italy, with two infants surviving, the first confirmed occurrence where octuplets lived long enough to be taken home. Unfortunately, six children passed away within two weeks of their birth.

1980: The demands of shipyard employees were addressed by the Lenin Shipyard in Gdańsk, Poland, leading to the conclusion of a three-day strike. As Lech Wałęsa, the leader of the strike, prepared to celebrate the achievement, Alina Pienkowska voiced concerns on behalf of workers across the rest of Poland who had also participated in similar strikes. Her message had a significant impact, rallying workers to continue their efforts.

2002: The Africa Women's Peace Train departed from Kampala, Uganda, bound for Johannesburg, South Africa. The train journey aimed to raise awareness about the impact of civil wars, corruption, and genocide in various African countries. Women from across Africa participated in this initiative to promote peace, justice, and sustainable development in the region.

2021: The Supreme Court of Uganda unanimously struck down a 2014 law that outlawed the distribution of pornography and wearing of "indecent" clothes as unconstitutional. Women's rights groups had campaigned against this law, arguing that it unfairly targeted and discriminated against women.

August 17

1987: Steffi Graf reached the number-one ranking in the Women's Tennis Association (W.T.A.), representing the beginning of her dominance in women's tennis. She spent a total of 377 weeks at the top of the rankings, including a consecutive streak of 186 weeks (tied with Serena Williams), the longest of any female player.

1996: Ruth Sando Fahnbulleh Perry was elected as the leader of Liberia, becoming the first woman to serve as a head of state in Africa.

2008: Jamaican women excelled in the Athletics 100m event at the Summer Olympics. Shelly-Ann Fraser won the gold medal, while Sherone Simpson and Kerron Stewart took silver, both finishing with an equal time of 10.98 seconds.

2008: Constantina Diță-Tomescu of Romania set a record by winning the Women's Marathon at the Olympic Games with a time of 2:26:44. At 38 years old, she became the oldest woman to achieve such a victory in the marathon event, highlighting her endurance and athletic achievements.

2012: Three members of the Russian punk band Pussy Riot were sentenced to two years in jail for their protest performance in a Moscow cathedral. Their imprisonment sparked international attention and raised debates about freedom of expression and human rights in Russia.

2012: Jennifer Doudna and Emmanuelle Charpentier published a groundbreaking paper titled "A programmable dual RNA-guided DNA endonuclease in adaptive bacterial immunity" in *Science*. Their research introduced the CRISPR-Cas9 genome editing technology, revolutionizing genetic engineering and leading to future advancements. Both women were later jointly awarded the Nobel Prize in Chemistry for their contributions to genome editing.

2017: Pauline Hanson, the leader of Australia's anti-immigrant One Nation party, sparked controversy when she wore a burqa into the Australian parliament. Her action received widespread criticism and ignited debates about religious freedom, cultural sensitivity, and the role of political leaders in promoting inclusivity.

August 18

1882: The Parliament of the United Kingdom passed The Married Women's Property Act, which granted married women the right to own and control property in their own name.

1920: The 19th Amendment to the U.S. Constitution was ratified, guaranteeing women the right to vote. This achievement in women's suffrage ended the exclusion of women from participating in the democratic process based on sex.

1941: Ruby Payne-Scott joined the Radiophysics Laboratory of the Australian government's Commonwealth Scientific and Industrial Research Organisation (CSIRO). During World War II, she worked on top-secret projects involving radar technology and became an expert in aircraft detection using Plan Position Indicator (PPI) displays. Her contributions were vital to Australia's efforts in radar research and development.

2015: The U.S. Food and Drug Administration (FDA) approved the use of *Flibanserin*, marketed as Addyi, as a treatment for Hypoactive Sexual Desire Disorder (HSDD) in women. It was an important development in addressing a specific sexual dysfunction in women and provided a pharmaceutical option for those experiencing HSDD.

2015: Raffi Freedman-Gurspan, a Honduran-American advocate and public policy specialist on matters concerning human rights, gender, and LGBTQ+ people, was hired by President Barack Obama as Outreach and Recruitment Director in the Presidential Personnel Office at the White House, becoming the first openly transgender person to work as a White House staffer. Freedman-Gurspan identifies as Lenca (indigenous people of western Honduras and eastern El Salvador) and Jewish.

2021: Zara Rutherford started a solo circumnavigation in a microlight aircraft, setting multiple records. She became the youngest female pilot to fly solo around the world, the first woman to circumnavigate the globe in a microlight aircraft, and the first Belgian to circumnavigate the world solo in a single-engine plane. Zara Rutherford's journey aimed to raise awareness about the gender gap in STEM fields, particularly aviation, and inspire more women and girls to pursue careers in science, technology, engineering, and mathematics.

August 19

1560: Mary, Queen of Scots, was denied passage through England upon her return from France. Instead, she was forced to arrive at Leith, Scotland.

1612: The Samlesbury Witches trial occurred in Lancashire, England. Three women from the village of Samlesbury were accused of practicing witchcraft, and their trial became one of the most famous witch trials in British history.

1895: The first issue of *Hanımlara Mahsus Gazete* (Ottoman Turkish: *Newspaper for Ladies*) was published. Its editorial board included Makbule Leman, Nigar Osman Hanım, Fatma Şadiye, Mustafa Asım, Faik Ali, Talat Ali and Gülistan İsmet. The magazine featured significant contributions from sisters Fatma Aliye and Emine Semiye. Fatma Aliye authored an editorial column throughout its existence. The publication covered various topics: education, family, household management, child-rearing, hygiene, health, beauty, embroidery, leisure, fashion, and women's rights. It also serialized literary works by women writers like Emine Semiye, Fatma Fahrünissa, Fatma Aliye, and Halide Edip.

1923: Ada Blackjack, an Iñupiat woman, was rescued as the sole survivor of an ill-fated expedition to claim Wrangel Island for Canada. The expedition, organized by Vilhjalmur Stefansson, ended in disaster, and Ada Blackjack's survival against the odds made headlines.

1958: Clara Luper and the NAACP Youth Council conducted a successful sit-in at drug store lunch counters in Oklahoma City, signifying a pivotal moment in the civil rights movement, as it was one of the largest and most successful sit-ins at the time and contributed to the desegregation efforts in Oklahoma City.

1987: The Most Noble Order of the Garter, founded by Edward III of England in 1348, was opened to women. This historic decision allowed women to become members of the order, which is the most senior order of knighthood in the British honors system.

2008: Lady Gaga released her debut studio album, *The Fame*, which propelled her to international stardom. The album featured chart-topping hits such as "Poker Face," "LoveGame," "Paparazzi," and "Just Dance."

2012: Japan won the 2012 Women's Baseball World Cup, securing its third consecutive title in the tournament, demonstrating Japan's dominance in women's baseball.

2019: Evelyn Hernández, a woman from El Salvador, was found not guilty of murder after her newborn child was discovered deceased in a toilet. The verdict was seen as a step in the right direction for women's rights in El Salvador, where extremely strict anti-abortion laws exist.

2022: Canadian Prime Minister Justin Trudeau nominated Judge Michelle O'Bonsawin to the Supreme Court of Canada. If appointed, O'Bonsawin, an Abenaki member, would become the first Indigenous Canadian to sit on the country's highest court.

August 20

1612: Nine individuals, primarily women, were found guilty of witchcraft and hanged at Gallows Hill in Lancaster. This event was part of the Pendle witch trials, a series of trials and executions in Lancashire, England, during which twelve people were charged with murder by witchcraft.

1922: The first Women's World Games occurred at Pershing Stadium in Paris. This multi-sport event was organized for female athletes and aimed to promote women's participation in sports.

2018: Greta Thunberg, a 15-year-old autistic school student, began a solo school strike demanding government action on climate change. It was the start of Thunberg's effective activism and her efforts to raise awareness about the urgency of addressing climate change.

2018: Camila Cabello won the Artist of the Year award, and her song *Havana* won Video of the Year at the MTV Video Music Awards, which took place at Radio City Music Hall.

2020: Kamala Harris accepted her nomination for vice president of the United States, becoming the first woman of color on a major-party ticket in the country's history.

August 21

1131: After the death of Baldwin II, his daughter Melisande became a co-ruler with husband Fulk of the Kingdom of Jerusalem. After Fulk died in 1143, Melisande ruled as queen regnant and a regent for her son Baldwin III.

1811: Barbara Zdunk, a Polish woman accused of arson and witchcraft, was executed by burning at the stake on a hill outside Rößel, East Prussia (now Reszel, Poland). This event is often considered one of the last alleged witches executed in Europe, despite witchcraft not being a crime in Prussia then.

1981: After a seven-month occupation of the Lee Jeans factory in Greenock, Scotland, 140 mostly women workers returned to work. They had successfully fought against the plant's closure and won their jobs back through occupation and activism.

1987: The film *Dirty Dancing*, directed by Emile Ardolino and starring Patrick Swayze and Jennifer Grey, opened in the United States. The movie became an iconic romantic drama known for its memorable soundtrack and dance sequences.

2013: In the case of United States v Bradley Manning, Chelsea Manning (formerly known as Bradley Manning), a United States Army private, was sentenced to 35 years in jail for disclosing classified material to WikiLeaks.

2014: Marina Silva, an internationally recognized environmental campaigner, assumed the role of the presidential candidate for the Brazilian Socialist Party. She became the candidate following the death of Eduardo Campos in a plane crash on August 13, 2014. Silva's candidacy brought attention to environmental issues and alternative political platforms in Brazil.

2015: First Lt. Shaye Haver, an Apache helicopter pilot, and Capt. Kristen Griest, a military police platoon leader, became the first women to complete the U.S. Army's Ranger School at Fort Benning.

2018: Liu Xiang, a Chinese swimmer, broke the world record in the women's 50-meter backstroke event, winning the gold medal at the Asian Games. She set a new record of 26.98 seconds.

August 22

1943: Tatiana Markus, also known as Tatiana Markusidze, was arrested by the Gestapo for her undercover intelligence-gathering activities and involvement in killing dozens of high-ranking Nazi officers. Despite being tortured for several months, she did not betray anyone and remained steadfast in her resistance against the Nazis.

1950: Althea Gibson, an African-American tennis player, was accepted by the United States Lawn Tennis Association (USLTA) into their annual championship at Forest Hills, New York, as the first African-American player to compete in a U.S. national tennis competition.

1964: Civil rights activist Fannie Lou Hamer delivered a powerful speech at the U.S. Democratic National Convention, highlighting her efforts to register to vote in Mississippi. Hamer's presence as an official delegate and her impassioned speech received a standing ovation, making her the first African-American to take a rightful seat at a national party convention since the Reconstruction period after the Civil War. She was also the first woman from Mississippi to accomplish this feat.

2012: Lucy-Anne Holmes started the campaign No More Page 3 to convince the owners and editors of *The Sun* to cease publishing images of topless glamour models on Page 3, which it had done since 1970, as an outdated, sexist tradition that demeaned girls and women. The campaign collected over 240,000 signatures on an online petition and gained support from over 140 MPs, several trade unions, over 30 universities, and many charities and advocacy groups. *The Sun* ceased publishing topless Page 3 images in its Republic of Ireland edition in 2013, its U.K. editions in 2015, and its Page3.com website in 2017. *The Daily Star* also ceased publishing images of topless glamour models in 2019.

2022: In a historic moment, Black women athletes Konnor McClain, Shilese Jones, and Jordan Chiles swept the All-Around podium at the U.S. Gymnastics Championships.

August 23

1200: Lilavati of Polonnaruwa, the fourth woman in Sri Lankan history to rule as sovereign in her own right, was removed from the throne by Sahassamalla, a prince of the Okkaka people, after three years of rule. She would return to the rule twice for short periods.

1856: Eunice Newton Foote, an American scientist, submitted her paper titled "Circumstances Affecting the Heat of the Sun's Rays" to the American Association for the Advancement of Science. Her article was published in the *American Journal of Science and Arts*, making her the first woman scientist to have her work published in a scientific journal in physics. In her paper, Foote discussed the warming effect of certain gases when exposed to sunlight and anticipated that increasing carbon dioxide (CO2) levels could impact atmospheric temperature and climate. Her findings preceded the later discoveries by John Tyndall regarding the greenhouse effect and infrared radiation.

1902: Fanny Farmer, a pioneering American culinary expert, opened the School of Cookery in Boston, Massachusetts. The school played a significant role in professionalizing culinary education and promoting standardized measurements in cooking, with Fanny Farmer becoming widely known for her cookbook and contributions to culinary techniques.

1944: Madeleine Riffaud, along with three other fighters and a train driver, successfully captured a Nazi supply train carrying 80 soldiers. Their tactic involved using grenades, explosives, and fireworks to create the illusion of a more significant and better-armed force. This act of resistance during World War II demonstrated the bravery and resourcefulness of the resistance fighters against the occupying Nazi forces.

1976: Jayaben Desai led picketing outside Grunwick Film Processing Laboratories in London, starting of a prominent strike by a predominantly Asian female workforce. The strike lasted for nearly two years until July 14, 1978, and became an iconic symbol of resistance and empowerment in the 1970s.

1989: Victoria Brucker became the first girl to play in a Little League World Series game in San Pedro, California.

2018: First Lieutenant Misa Matsushima became the first female fighter pilot in Japanese Defense Forces.

2022: Two individuals were found guilty of conspiring to obtain a weapon of mass destruction for a foiled plot to kidnap Michigan Governor Gretchen Whitmer. The trial brought attention to the issue of domestic extremism and highlighted the importance of law enforcement efforts to counter such threats and protect public officials.

August 24

1936: At the outset of the Spanish Civil War, Dolores Ibárruri, known as La Pasionaria, delivered her iconic speech "*¡No Pasarán!*" ("They shall not pass!") in Madrid. Her inspirational words became a rallying cry against fascism and represented the resistance against the Nationalist forces led by General Francisco Franco.

1950: Edith Sampson made history as the first Black U.S. delegate to the United Nations. She was a lawyer and social worker who played a crucial role in advancing civil rights and international diplomacy.

1996: The small Jewish community in Cairo, Egypt, staged a "revolt." For the first time in the community's more than a thousand years history, women had a seat on the local board of directors, with Esther Weinstein (at 86) elected the president. Behind the changes was Carmen Weinstein (Esther's daughter), who wanted the board to represent the actual demography of the community, where older women were in the majority, and to create a more democratic management style. In addition to Esther and Carmen, three more women were members of the new nine-person board.

2007: Janelle Monáe, a talented singer-songwriter and actress, released her first public album, *Metropolis: The Chase Suite*. The album was the initial installment of Monáe's innovative seven-part conceptual series inspired by Fritz Lang's science fiction film *Metropolis* from 1927. Monáe's unique musical style and storytelling approach garnered critical acclaim and established her as an influential artist.

2012: Vice Admiral Michelle Janine Howard made history as the first African-American woman to attain the rank of three-star admiral in the U.S. armed forces. She was appointed as the deputy commander of U.S. Fleet Forces Command.

2021: Jocelyn Bell Burnell, an astrophysicist, was awarded the prestigious Copley Medal by the Royal Society for her groundbreaking work on the discovery of pulsars. This astronomical discovery was one of the most significant advancements of the 20th century. Burnell became only the second woman to receive the Copley Medal since Dorothy Crowfoot Hodgkin in 1976, highlighting her tremendous contributions to science.

2021: Lieutenant Governor Kathy Hochul was sworn in as the governor of New York after Andrew Cuomo's resignation took effect. She became the first woman to hold the position of governor in the state's history.

August 25

1746: Following an attack by Native Americans on two white families, Lucy Terry, an African American woman, composed a ballad poem called *Bars Fight*. This work is considered the oldest known piece of literature by an African American and reflects Terry's experiences and perspectives during that time.

1804: Alicia Thornton made history as the first female jockey in England while participating in a race at Knavesmire in Yorkshire.

1920: Ethelda Bleibtrey became the first U.S. female Olympic champion. She won three gold medals in swimming at the Antwerp Olympics, making her a trailblazer for American female athletes on the international stage.

1945: Shigeri Yamataka, Fusae Ichikawa, Tsuneko Akamatsu, and Natsu Kawasaki founded the Women's Committee on Postwar Policy (*Sengo Taisaku Fujin Iinkai*) in Japan. The organization held its first meeting on September 11, 1945, with over 70 women in attendance. Their main priorities included welcoming returning soldiers, improving food production, increasing household savings, advocating suffrage for women over 20, enabling women over 25 to run for office, reforming local and central governments, and allowing women to hold civil service jobs.

1975: Vera Brown Starr made history as the first woman elected as chair of the Yavapai-Apache Nation.

1998: Lauryn Hill, a talented singer, songwriter, and rapper, released her debut solo album titled *The Miseducation of Lauryn Hill*. The album debuted at number one on the Billboard 200 chart and sold over 422,000 copies in its first week. This achievement broke the record for first-week sales by a female artist.

2017: President Donald Trump issued a memorandum that halted funding for sex reassignment (gender-affirming) procedures in the military and barred transgender individuals from serving openly. This policy sparked controversy and led to a federal lawsuit by LGBTQ+ rights organizations, challenging the policy's constitutionality.

August 26

1474: Catherine Cornaro became the queen regnant of Cyprus after her son's death, for whom she was a regent. She was forced to abdicate on March 14, 1489, and sell the country's administration to the Republic of Venice.

1920: The 19th Amendment to the U.S. Constitution was ratified, granting women the right to vote.

1928: The first SAFFA - *Schweizerische Ausstellung für Frauenarbeit* (Swiss Exhibition for Women's Work) opened in Bern. Coordinated by the *Bund Schweizerischer Frauenvereine* (BFS), Swiss Catholic Women's League (SKF), and 28 other Swiss women's associations, with Louise (Lux) Guyer, the first Swiss women architect, as the chief organizer, this effort highlighted the postwar challenges faced by working women.

1935: Felicitas Provencio, a 100-year-old midwife, was arrested for practicing midwifery without a license when she attempted to register a recent birth in South El Paso. Provencio proudly claimed to have been practicing midwifery for over sixty years without any fatalities at the births she attended.

1970: A nationwide Women's Strike for Equality commemorated the fiftieth anniversary of American women gaining the right to vote. The strike served as a platform for women to advocate for gender equality and draw attention to ongoing challenges women face in various spheres of life.

1971: The first Women's Equality Day was established by Presidential Proclamation, initiated by Representative Bella Abzug. This day, celebrated annually on August 26, serves as a reminder of the ongoing fight for gender equality and the accomplishments of women throughout history.

1988: Daw Aung San Suu Kyi, a prominent Myanmar politician and activist, addressed a rally of 500,000 peaceful demonstrators in Rangoon, Myanmar. This event began her political and activist career, as she advocated for a democratic multi-party system in Myanmar.

2012: Besse Cooper, recognized as the world's oldest living human at the time, celebrated her 116th birthday. She became one of only eight people in recorded history to reach this age indisputably. Cooper passed away on December 4, 2012.

2012: Lydia Ko, a 15-year-old amateur golfer from New Zealand, won the Canadian Women's Open, becoming the youngest-ever winner on the LPGA Tour. She also became the first amateur to achieve this feat since JoAnne Carner in 1969, showcasing her exceptional talent in golf.

2021: Italian nun Alessandra Smerilli was appointed by Pope Francis as the first female Secretary of the Dicastery for Promoting Integral Human Development.

August 27

1927: Five Canadian women, Henrietta Muir Edwards, Nellie McClung, Louise McKinney, Emily Murphy, and Irene Parlby, petitioned the Supreme Court of Canada in the *Persons Case*. This landmark case was part of a more significant movement for political equality and aimed to challenge the notion that women were not considered "persons" under the Canadian Constitution.

1968: Farrokhroo Parsa, an Iranian physician, educator, and outspoken supporter of women's rights, became Minister of Education in the cabinet of the Amir-Abbas Hoveyda as the first woman in the history of a cabinet position.

1974: Joan Little, a Black woman, killed a white corrections officer in self-defense at the Beaufort County jail in North Carolina. The guard had threatened her with an ice pick and forced her to perform a sex act. Little's case gained significant attention and support from civil rights activists, feminists, and anti-death penalty activists, including Rosa Parks and Angela Davis. She became the first woman to successfully use resisting sexual assault as a defense against using deadly force.

1996: Anne Beaumanoir was recognized as one of the Righteous Among the Nations by the Yad Vashem Institute. This honor was bestowed upon her for her courageous actions in saving the lives of two Jewish teenagers during World War II.

2020: Kurdish human rights lawyer Ebru Timtik died in a hospital after being on a hunger strike for 238 days to protest her imprisonment. She had been found guilty of being a member of the outlawed Revolutionary People's Liberation Party/Front. Timtik's hunger strike drew international attention to her case and the human rights issues faced by Kurds in Turkey.

August 28

632: Fāṭima al-Zahrā, the daughter of the Islamic prophet Muhammad and his wife Khadija, passed away. Her death, occurring just six months after her father's death, remains controversial. In Sunni Islam, it is generally believed that Fāṭima died from grief. On the other hand, Shia Islam believes that Fāṭima's death resulted from injuries sustained during a raid on her house ordered by Abu Bakr to subdue Ali.

1384: Dolcich, the wife of Maymo Gallipapa from Leyda, received a royal license to practice medicine, demonstrating a recognition of a Jewish woman's right to engage in the medical profession during that time.

1857: The Matrimonial Causes Act was enacted in the United Kingdom, making divorce legal without requiring parliamentary approval. This act introduced more accessible avenues for divorce and gave individuals greater control over their marital relationships.

1917: Ten Suffragettes were arrested while picketing the White House in their ongoing campaign for women's right to vote.

1942: Zofia Kossak-Szczucka, a Polish writer and leader of the underground organization Front for the Rebirth of Poland, published her protest against the mass murder of Jews in German-occupied Poland. Her work, "*Protest!*," highlighted the atrocities committed against Jews and aimed to raise awareness of the ongoing Holocaust.

2006: Iranian women's rights activists (Noushin Ahmadi Khorasani and Parvin Ardalan) launched the One Million Signatures for the Repeal of Discriminatory Laws (Persian: *Yek Milyun Emzā barā-ye Laghv-e Qavānin-e Tab'iz Āmiz*) campaign to collect one million signatures in support of legal reform and to promote collaboration for social change, identify women's needs and priorities, amplify their voices, increase knowledge, encourage democratic action, ensure equitable contributions, harness unity, and celebrate diversity. At its core, the campaign strived for equal rights in marriage and inheritance, the end of polygamy, and harsher penalties for honor killings and various forms of violence. Many women gathering the signatures were arrested and jailed. Both leaders - Noushin Ahmadi Khorasani and Parvin Ardalan, were arrested and sentenced to three years in prison for "threatening the national security."

2011: The 2011 MTV Video Music Awards concluded in Los Angeles, with Katy Perry winning the Video of the Year award for her song *Firework*.

2015: Julie Schumacher became the first female winner of the Thurber Prize for American Humor for her epistolary novel *Dear Committee Members*. All three finalists for that year's award were women, reflecting the talent and contributions of women writers in humor.

2019: Climate change activist Greta Thunberg arrived in New York after completing an emissions-free voyage across the Atlantic Ocean. Thunberg's journey by sailboat highlighted the need for urgent action on climate change and inspired a global movement of youth activism.

2020: The Brazilian Ministry of Health announced expansions to the country's abortion laws regarding cases of pregnancy resulting from rape. These expansions included requiring victims to provide detailed accounts to doctors and file reports with the police. The victims would also be warned about the possibility of prosecution for fraud in case of false or unverified claims. In response, Chamber of Deputies minority leader Jandira Feghali filed a bill to block the decree, arguing that it constituted psychological violence against women.

August 29

112: After the death of Marciana, the sister of Roman Emperor Trajan, Salonia Matidia, Trajan's niece, was granted the title of *Augusta*.

1911: Hilda Hewlett became the U.K.'s first woman (10th globally) to earn a pilot's license (Certificate No. 122 from the Royal Aero Club). In 1910, she co-founded the U.K.'s first flying school with Gustav Blondeau, her French flight instructor. Two years later, they ventured into successful aircraft manufacturing, producing over 800 aircraft and employing up to 700 people.

1929: Aviator Anne Morrow Lindbergh made her first solo flight.

1979: LGBTQ+ activists occupied the Swedish National Board of Health and Welfare to protest the classification of homosexuality as a mental illness. This direct action was part of their ongoing campaign to challenge societal discrimination and promote LGBTQ+ rights. Their efforts led to the removal of homosexuality as a mental illness designation in October of that year.

1995: Faith Evans, an American R&B singer, songwriter, and actress, published her first album, Faith, which became a success based on the singles *You Used to Love Me* and *Soon as I Get Home*. The album became platinum, with 1.5 million copies sold.

1997: Workers at the Lusty Lady Club in San Francisco voted to join the Exotic Dancers Union, part of the Service Employees International Union (SEIU). This move allowed the workers to organize and advocate for their rights, leading to improvements such as guaranteed work shifts, pay increases, removal of one-way mirrors, and protection from arbitrary discipline and firing. They later transitioned the club into a workers' cooperative with elected management.

2005: Rihanna, a Barbadian singer, released her first studio album, *Music of the Sun*. The album began her successful music career and showcased her pop and R&B artist talent.

2016: Anita Włodarczyk of Poland broke her own world record in the hammer throw, setting a new mark of 82.98 meters at the Kamila Skolimowska Memorial in Warsaw.

2019: The Cherokee Council approved the appointment of Kimberly Teehee as the Cherokee Nation's first-ever delegate to the United States House of Representatives. This historic appointment was based on the Treaty of Hopewell of 1785 and the Treaty of New Echota of 1835, which granted the Cherokee Nation the right to have a delegate in Congress. However, formal seating in Congress was still pending at the time.

August 30

30 BCE: Cleopatra, the Queen of Egypt, committed suicide by poisoning herself. Facing capture and humiliation by the Romans led by Octavian (later known as Emperor Augustus), Cleopatra chose to end her life rather than be subjected to their control.

526: Amalasuintha became the Queen of the Ostrogothic Kingdom, first as a regent of her son and, after his death, as the queen regnant until being murdered on April 30, 534.

1918: Fanni Kaplan, a Russian revolutionary, shot and seriously injured Vladimir Lenin, the leader of the Bolshevik Party and the future leader of the Soviet Union. The assassination attempt on Lenin prompted the Bolsheviks to respond with intense political repression, known as the Red Terror.

1966: Constance Baker Motley became the first African-American woman appointed to the federal judiciary. She served as a United States district judge in the Southern District of New York. Motley was a prominent civil rights activist and played a crucial role in advancing civil rights and promoting equality under the law.

1984: Judith A. Resnick became the second American woman and the fourth woman to travel into space. She was part of the crew on the Space Shuttle Discovery's maiden flight. Resnick lost her life in the Space Shuttle Challenger disaster in 1986.

2008: John McCain, the Republican nominee for the U.S. presidential election, chose Alaska Governor Sarah Palin as his vice-presidential running mate.

2019: Madeleine Westerhout, Director of Oval Office Operations at the White House, resigned after disclosing confidential information about the Trump family and White House affairs to journalists during a private dinner. Westerhout's actions violated the trust and confidentiality expected in her role.

2021: Avani Lekhara, an Indian Paralympic athlete and rifle shooter, became the first Indian woman to win a gold medal in the Summer Paralympics.

August 31

1869: Irish scientist Mary Ward was tragically killed by an experimental steam car built by her cousins. The accident resulted in her becoming one of the first recorded car accident victims.

1888: Mary Ann Nichols was murdered. She was the first confirmed victim of the infamous serial killer Jack the Ripper. The brutal and unsolved killings in the Whitechapel district of London during the late

19th century captured international attention and continue to be a subject of fascination and speculation.

1920: Marie Ruoff Byrum, an American citizen, became the first woman to vote under the 19th Amendment to the United States Constitution. She cast her vote in a special election in Hannibal, Missouri, to fill an alderman's seat, exercising her newly acquired right to participate in the democratic process.

1925: Anthropologist Margaret Mead arrived in Samoa for the first time, beginning her fieldwork that would later contribute to her influential book, *Coming of Age in Samoa*. Her observations and research in Samoan society challenged prevailing notions about adolescence and sexuality, emphasizing cultural variability and the influence of the social environment.

1944: Maria Dimadi, a Greek interpreter and anti-Nazi resistance activist, was executed by Greek collaborationist Security Battalions members. Dimadi had been working as a spy within the German garrison headquarters, providing valuable information to the resistance movement before being captured and killed.

1962: Fannie Lou Hamer, a prominent leader in the American civil rights movement, attempted to register to vote in Indianola, Mississippi. Her courageous efforts to exercise her right to vote despite facing discrimination and intimidation highlighted the ongoing struggle for voting rights and racial equality.

1967: Haydée Tamara Bunke Bider, known as Tania, was killed in an ambush by Bolivian Army members trained by the CIA. Bunke Bider, an Argentine revolutionary and guerilla fighter, was associated with the Marxist revolutionary Che Guevara and actively participated in armed struggle movements.

1970: *TIME* magazine published a cover story titled "The Politics of Sex," focusing on Kate Millett's book *Sexual Politics*. The article examined Millett's theories and analyzed the feminist movement and its political implications. The cover featured a portrait of Millett painted by artist Alice Neel.

1997: Diana, Princess of Wales, died in a car crash in a road tunnel in Paris. Her untimely death deeply impacted people worldwide, and she was mourned as a beloved public figure known for her charitable work and humanitarian efforts.

2016: Dilma Rousseff, the President of Brazil, was impeached and removed from office. The impeachment process stemmed from allegations of fiscal mismanagement, which resulted in widespread political controversy and ultimately led to Rousseff's removal from the presidency.

SEPTEMBER

September 01

1173: During the siege of Ancona by Emperor Frederick Barbarossa's forces, Stamira, a widow, sacrificed herself to raise the siege and protect the city.

1773: Phillis Wheatley, an enslaved African woman, had her book *Poems on Various Subjects, Religious and Moral* published in London. This publication made her the first African-American woman to have her poetry published.

1907: The first issue of the National Federation of Women Workers' newspaper, *Woman Worker*, was published. Initially a monthly publication, it quickly gained popularity and transitioned into a weekly one with a circulation of approximately 20,000.

1911: The first issue of *Bluestocking* (*Seitō*), Japan's first all-women literary magazine, was published by five women. The magazine is credited with sparking the feminist movement in Japan.

1913: Lucy Maud Montgomery, famous for creating the character Anne Shirley, published her novel *The Golden Road*. This book was inspired by childhood stories shared by her great aunt, Mary Lawson, to whom Montgomery dedicated the book.

1916: Annie Besant founded the India Home Rule League, an organization that advocated for self-government and independence for India.

1947: Kathleen Booth, along with her husband, Andrew Donald Booth, published the first assembly code in their work *Coding for ARC*. This code represented machine code instructions using a language, laying the foundation for computer programming languages.

1953: In the landmark case *Sarah Keys v. Carolina Coach Company*, Sarah Keys, a member of the Women's Army Corps (WAC), became the first African-American to challenge the "separate but equal" rule in bus segregation.

1963: June Almeida, a Scottish virologist and a pioneer in virus imaging, identification, and diagnosis, published an article (together with two colleagues, Bernhard Cinader and Allan Howatson) in the *Journal of Experimental Medicine*, "The Structure of Antigen-Antibody Complexes," in which she used a technique she pioneered in immune electron microscopy (IEM), to better visualize viruses by using antibodies to aggregate them. In 1966, she discovered a group of "previously uncharacterized human respiratory viruses," later called coronaviruses.

1979: The Sri Lanka Army Women's Corps was formed, providing opportunities for women to serve in the military. Female soldiers received equal pay to their male counterparts and primarily served in nursing, communications, and clerical roles.

2009: Charlotte Bunch, the founder and executive director of The Center for Women's Global Leadership (CWGL), transitioned to her new role as founding director and senior scholar. Radhika Balakrishnan succeeded her as the executive director, and in 2015, she transitioned to the position of Faculty Director while CWGL welcomed Krishanti Dharmaraj as the new executive director.

2015: Pope Francis released a letter granting priests the ability to give absolution to women who had received an abortion, emphasizing compassion and forgiveness.

2022: The High Court of Malaysia found Rosmah Mansor, the wife of former Prime Minister Najib Razak, guilty of corruption.

September 02

44 BCE: Queen Cleopatra VII of Egypt appointed her son Ptolemy XV Caesarion, fathered by Julius Caesar, as co-ruler.

1561: Mary, Queen of Scots, entered Edinburgh, marking a significant moment in her reign.

1910: Alice Stebbins Wells became the first U.S.-born female police officer to receive a regular appointment based on a civil service examination. She was appointed to the Los Angeles Police Department, paving the way for more women to join law enforcement agencies.

1944: Anne Frank, the Holocaust diarist, was sent to the Nazi Auschwitz concentration camp in occupied Poland during World War II.

1976: The first issue of *Lilith Magazine*, the first Jewish feminist publication, appeared. The name was inspired by the reimagining of the demoness by Judith Plaskow in her classic essay, "The Coming of Lilith," and reiterated in an article, "The Lilith Question," by Aviva Cantor Zuckoff, published in the opening issue.

1977: Renée Richards, a 43-year-old transwoman, lost to Virginia Wade at the U.S. Open. Richards had fought for over a year for the right to compete in the event and became one of the first professional athletes to openly identify as transgender, subsequently becoming a spokesperson for transgender individuals in sports.

2013: Diana Nyad completed a historic swim from Cuba to Florida, becoming the first person to achieve this feat without using a shark cage.

2014: The FBI announced its investigation into a significant iCloud leak that exposed nude photos of several celebrities, including Jennifer Lawrence, Kate Upton, and Ariana Grande.

2015: Sheila North Wilson became the first woman to be voted as the Manitoba Keewatinowi Okimakanak (MKO) Grand Chief by First Nations leaders.

2021: Sarah Joanne Storey, a Paralympic athlete, secured her 17th Paralympic gold medal in the women's road race C4-5 event, making her Great Britain's most successful Paralympic athlete.

2022: Liz Truss was elected as the Leader of the Conservative Party and was set to succeed Boris Johnson as the Prime Minister of the United Kingdom on September 6.

September 03

1981: The Convention on the Elimination of all Forms of Discrimination Against Women (CEDAW), an international treaty aimed at promoting gender equality and eliminating discrimination against women, was instituted by the United Nations General Assembly. One hundred eighty-nine states have since ratified it.

2003: Margaret Hamilton, the team leader who developed the flight software for NASA's *Apollo* missions, received a NASA Exceptional Space Act Award for her significant scientific and technical contributions.

2007: Moira Cameron, a 42-year-old Scottish woman, became the first female "Beefeater" or Yeoman Warder, taking up her post as a guardian of Britain's Tower of

London. She successfully secured the position after surpassing five male candidates.

2015: A plaque was unveiled in Loštice, Czechia, honoring Fanny Neuda, the author of the first Jewish prayer book known to have been written by a woman for women. Neuda's work, titled *Stunden der Andacht: Ein Gebetund Erbauungsbuch für Israels Frauen und Jungfrauen zur öffentlichen und häuslichen Andacht* (*Hours of Devotion: Book of Prayer and Edification for Jewish Wives and Young Women*), gained popularity for its collection of prayers.

2019: Asma Mohamed Abdalla became Sudan's Foreign Minister, making history as the first woman to hold this position.

2020: MacKenzie Scott, a philanthropist and the former wife of Amazon CEO Jeff Bezos, became the world's richest woman with a net worth of $68 billion.

2022: Serena Williams, a 23-time Grand Slam tennis champion, played her final match at the U.S. Open, representing the end of an illustrious career in professional tennis.

September 04

1893: English author Beatrix Potter wrote the beloved children's story *The Tale of Peter Rabbit*, which would become a classic in children's literature.

1911: Harriet Quimby, an American aviator, won her first air race and received a prize of $1,500 at the Richmond County Fair in New York.

1936: British-Kenyan aviator Beryl Markham embarked on a solo flight across the Atlantic Ocean, taking off from Abingdon in England. She crash-landed on Cape Breton Island, Nova Scotia, Canada, becoming the first woman to make the east-west trip successfully.

1987: Roopkuvarba Kanwar, a young Rajput widow, was burned alive in Deorala village, Sikar district, Rajasthan, India, in the forbidden practice of *Sati*, where widows were immolated on their deceased husband's pyre. Her death led to public outrage and created the Sati (Prevention) Act of 1987, which originated in Rajasthan and later became a national law in 1988 through The Commission of Sati (Prevention) Act. This law aims to deter sati and prohibit any glorification of this act.

1995: The Fourth World Conference on Women was held in Beijing, China. Sponsored by the United Nations, the conference brought together women from 185 countries to discuss issues of gender equality, development, and peace. During this event, governments from around the world collaborated to create the Beijing Platform for Action, a comprehensive plan for global legal equality, and the Beijing Declaration of Indigenous Women. Gertrude Mongella of Tanzania was the secretary-general of the conference.

2008: The film *The Hurt Locker*, directed by Kathryn Bigelow, premiered at the Venice Film Festival. Kathryn Bigelow would make history by becoming the first woman to win an Academy Award for Best Director for the same film.

2012: Pauline Marois became the first female premier of Quebec, Canada, as the Parti Québécois won a minority government, defeating the Liberal Party of Quebec.

2016: Pope Francis canonized Mother Teresa, the Albanian-Indian nun mostly known for her charitable work among the poor and sick, in a ceremony held at the Vatican. The canonization was met with criticism and accounts of mishandling of funds and problematic behavior toward the voiceless and suffering.

2021: Italian athlete Ambra Sabatini set a new world record for the women's 100-meter T63 event, achieving a time of 14.11 seconds.

September 05

1782: Bartolina Sisa Vargas, an Aymaran woman and indigenous heroine, was executed after leading several revolts against Spanish rule in Charcas (present-day Peru, Bolivia, Argentina, and Chile). Her bravery and resistance have made her a symbol of indigenous rights, and since 1983, her death has been commemorated as the International Day of Indigenous Women.

1859: Harriet E. Wilson published *Our Nig, or Sketches from the Life of a Free Black*, considered the first novel published by an African American in the United States. The book depicted the struggles of a mixed-race woman in the North and addressed themes of racial discrimination and identity.

1902: Anna J. Cooper, a prominent African-American scholar, delivered a speech titled "The Ethics of the Negro Question" at the Friends' General Conference in Asbury Park, NJ. She emphasized the importance of education and equality for African Americans and challenged the notion of a nation's greatness based solely on material possessions.

1910: Marie Skłodowska-Curie, the renowned scientist, announced her discovery of a process to isolate pure radium from radium chloride. This breakthrough allowed for the large-scale production of radium, a rare and valuable element.

1911: Cora Wilson Stewart initiated the Moonlight Schools, the first adult literacy program in the United States. These night classes, held in Rowan County, Kentucky, enabled men and women to learn to read and write, with the scheduling based on the moon's brightness for safe travel.

1912: The reported attack on Ellen Gric, a white woman in Forsyth County, Georgia, by two Black men led to violent attacks against African-American residents and the arrest of Black men suspected of the crime.

1979: Ann Meyers became the first woman to sign an NBA contract.

1979: Lolita Lebron, who had led the 1954 attack on the U.S. Congress by members of the pro-independence Nationalist Party of Puerto Rico, was granted clemency after serving a lengthy prison sentence.

1981: The Greenham Common Women's Peace Camp was established in the U.K. as a protest against nuclear weapon storage, with women activists advocating for peace and disarmament.

1981: The Shocking Pink Collective was formed, publishing issues addressing topics important to young women, including contraception, abortion, sexuality, lesbianism, violence against women, and women's culture. The group comprised Jo Brew, Louise Carolin, Ilona, Rebecca Oliver, and Angie Brew.

2017: Brenda Marjorie Hale, Baroness Hale of Richmond, became the first woman to serve as President of the Supreme Court of the United Kingdom.

2019: Rosa Elena Bonilla, the former First Lady of Honduras, was sentenced to 58 years in prison for misusing public funds to purchase jewelry, highlighting issues of corruption and misuse of power.

September 06

1722: Wälättä Giyorgis, later known as Empress Mentewab, married Ethiopia's Emperor Bakaffa after nursing him back to health. Following Bakaffa's death in 1730, Mentewab became the regent for their son, Iyasu II, and rose to power as a regent.

1870: Louisa Ann Swain of Laramie, Wyoming, became the first woman in the United States to cast a legal vote.

1891: The Committee on Abuses, formed by Elizabeth Morgan, published its findings in a report titled *The New Slavery: Investigation Into the Sweating System*, which pointed out the harsh working conditions faced by women and children who labored ten to fourteen hours daily. It highlighted the overcrowded tenements and meager wages of sweatshop workers. Morgan wrote in a persuasive tone backed by evidence and statistics to sway officials into taking action. The Chicago Trade and Labor Assembly also printed and distributed 10,000 copies of *The New Slavery*. The report carried weight, leading to Morgan's impactful testimony on April 5, 1892, against sweatshop practices before a United States Congressional committee. Her efforts, fueled by the report, testimonies, and advocacy, successfully influenced legislators to bolster labor laws, press officials for stricter enforcement, and mobilize the middle class against the exploitative sweating system.

1927: American mathematician Anna Pell-Wheeler became the first woman to present a lecture at the American Mathematical Society Colloquium.

2011: English musician PJ Harvey received her second Mercury Prize, an esteemed award recognizing the best album from the United Kingdom and Ireland. Her album *Let England Shake* was honored with this prestigious accolade.

2018: The Supreme Court of India decriminalized consensual same-sex relationships among adults in private, making homosexuality legal in the country.

2018: Dame Susan Jocelyn Bell Burnell, a renowned astrophysicist, was awarded the Special Breakthrough Prize in Fundamental Physics for her contributions to the discovery of pulsars. She used the prize money to establish a fund to support female, minority, and refugee students pursuing physics research.

2019: Architect Dana Cuff received recognition from Architectural Record for her design research aimed at making housing more accessible. Additionally, the journal honored Toshiko Mori, Sharon Johnston, Claire Weisz, and Mabel O. Wilson with the annual Women in Architecture Awards in various categories.

2021: Maria Kalesnikava, an opposition activist in Belarus, was found guilty of "trying to seize power and extremism" and received an 11-year sentence.

2022: Liz Truss succeeded Boris Johnson to become the Prime Minister of the United Kingdom.

2022: Fatima Payman, the first hijab-wearing Australian Muslim Senator, delivered her First Speech in Parliament, sharing her family's migrant story from Afghanistan and beginning with an Islamic greeting in Farsi.

September 07

1838: Grace Darling, along with her father, successfully rescued 13 survivors from the shipwreck of the Forfarshire near the Farne Islands, demonstrating extraordinary bravery and heroism.

1888: Edith Eleanor McLean became the first baby to be placed in an incubator at the State Emigrant Hospital on Ward's Island, New York, exhibiting a significant development in neonatal care.

1921: The first Miss America Pageant was held in Atlantic City, New Jersey, beginning a long-standing tradition in American beauty pageants.

1942: Mildred Fish-Harnack, an American writer and activist, was arrested in Lithuania along with her husband for their involvement in the German resistance to Nazism. They led a group of anti-fascist activists called the Red Orchestra. Despite initially receiving a prison sentence, Adolf Hitler intervened and ordered her execution. She became the only American woman executed on Hitler's direct orders.

1953: Sükhbaataryn Yanjmaa became the Chairwoman of the Presidium of the State Great Khural of Mongolia. She is considered the second woman in history to be a non-hereditary head of state after Khertek

Anchimaa-Toka of Tannu Tuva and the first in a sovereign country.

2008: Serena Williams won her third U.S. Open title by defeating Jelena Janković, reclaiming the World Number 1 ranking after a five-year gap.

2009: Sudanese activist Lubna al-Hussein was found guilty of breaching Sudanese criminal law by wearing trousers, which led to her trial and international attention. Although she was initially sentenced to flogging, due to global concern, she was fined instead. However, she chose to serve a month in jail rather than pay the fine as a form of protest against the law.

2021: The Mexican Supreme Court unanimously declared the criminalization of abortion unconstitutional, paving the way for the potential legalization of abortion in Mexico.

September 08

1429: Joan of Arc, the French military leader and national heroine, led an unsuccessful attack on Paris during the Hundred Years' War and was wounded.

1488: Anne of Brittany began her rule as the Duchess of Brittany. She later became the Queen of France on two occasions (1491 -1498 and 1499-1514). Anne also held the titles of Queen of Naples (1501-1504) and Duchess of Milan (1499-1512) during the Italian Wars.

1916: Augusta and Adeline Van Buren, two pioneering women, arrived in Los Angeles, completing a 60-day, 5,500-mile cross -country motorcycle trip. Their journey aimed to demonstrate that women could serve as military dispatch riders and contribute to advancing women's rights.

1944: Lela Carayannis, a Greek grandmother and leader of the resistance and intelligence organization known as *Bouboulina*, was shot along with 71 of her followers and co-workers by a Nazi execution squad. The event, known as the Chaidari Massacre, took place in what is now the Diomideios Garden.

1986: The first episode of the *Oprah Winfrey Show*, hosted by Oprah Winfrey herself, was broadcast nationwide. The show became America's number-one day-time talk show, making Oprah Winfrey a highly influential figure in the media industry.

1997: A popular American legal comedy-drama television series, *Ally McBeal*, aired for the first time on Fox channel. Although it received critical acclaim in its early seasons, winning the Golden Globe and Emmy Awards, it was also criticized for its portrayal of professional women, being seen as an example of post-feminist pop-culture production.

2021: The Mexican Supreme Court of Justice of the Nation, in a unanimous vote, declared the criminalization of abortion to be unconstitutional.

2022: Buckingham Palace announced Queen Elizabeth II's passing at 96 at Balmoral Castle in Scotland. She was succeeded as the monarch by her son, Charles III, becoming the new King of the United Kingdom.

2023: Spanish women footballers (soccer players) went on strike demanding a higher minimum salary, which was less than 1/10th of the men's pay. They also required continuing the contract during maternity leave and accessing the same medical professionals as men.

September 09

1543: Mary Stuart, commonly known as Mary, Queen of Scots, was crowned Queen of Scots at nine months in Stirling, Scotland.

1910: Alice B. Toklas moved in with Gertrude Stein. It was the beginning of their famous partnership and their home in Paris becoming a renowned artistic and literary salon that would play a significant role in the cultural scene for nearly three decades.

1912: Lillian Gish and Dorothy Gish, iconic sisters in the film industry, made their joint screen debut in the short film *An Unseen Enemy*. It was the beginning of their successful collaboration with filmmaker D. W. Griffith and their illustrious careers in the silent film era.

1916: Emily Griffith's Opportunity School opened its doors, recognized as the world's first school dedicated to providing primary adult education and training in marketable skills. The school aimed to empower adults through education and help them acquire practical skills for employment.

1947: Argentina's Congress approved women's suffrage, granting women the right to vote.

2012: Shannon Eastin made history as the first female National Football League (NFL) referee. She debuted in the Rams-Lions game, breaking barriers and paving the way for more women in officiating roles in professional sports.

2015: Queen Elizabeth II surpassed Queen Victoria's record to become the longest-reigning monarch in the history of the United Kingdom.

2021: Sarah Peluse, a researcher from the Institute for Advanced Study and Princeton University, was awarded the 2022 Maryam Mirzakhani New Frontiers Prize. She received this prestigious prize for her contributions to arithmetic combinatorics and analytic number theory, particularly in the study of polynomial patterns in dense sets.

September 10

1321: Francesca, the wife of Matteo de Romana of Salerno, received a license to practice medicine and surgery after examination by royal physicians and surgeons on behalf of Charles, the King of Naples. However, her practice was restricted to treating female patients due to reasons of "morals and decency."

1380: Bellayne, a Jewish woman and widow of Samuel Gallipapa, obtained a license to practice medicine in Zaragoza, Spain.

1623: Murat IV ascended the Ottoman Empire's throne at 11, following the deposition of his uncle Mustafa I. As a minor, his mother, Kösem Sultan, served as regent, overseeing the empire's affairs until 1632.

1898: Empress Elisabeth of Austria, also known as Empress Sisi, was assassinated in Geneva, Switzerland, by Italian anarchist Luigi Lucheni as an act of propaganda.

1918: A band of revolutionaries led by Marusya Nikiforova attacked the Russian army headquarters of Orichiv, where they executed officers and took all the weapons, which were transferred to the anarchist Revolutionary Insurgent Army of Ukraine.

1919: The New Hampshire Senate ratified the 19th Amendment to the United States Constitution, granting women the right to vote.

1942: The Women's Auxiliary Ferrying Squadron (WAFS) began operations in the United States. This squadron consisted of women pilots who ferried military aircraft during World War II, contributing to the war effort.

1962: In Mississippi, white supremacists attempted to assassinate civil rights activist Fannie Lou Hamer. She was staying with her friend Mary Tucker when racists drove by and fired 16 shots at her, all of which missed. Hamer, previously known as Fannie Lou Townsend, was working to register to vote but had been denied due to a racist Jim Crow registration test to prevent Black people and Native Americans from voting.

2013: Julia Michelle Serano, an American writer, musician, spoken-word performer, transgender and bisexual activist, and biologist, published her second book, *Excluded: Making Feminist and Queer Movements*

More Inclusive. Her first book, *Whipping Girl: A Transsexual Woman on Sexism and the Scapegoating of Femininity*, was published in 2007.

2013: Miley Cyrus set a new record for the highest number of views within 24 hours with her music video for *Wrecking Ball*.

2017: Artist Marta Minujin initiated the redistribution of a hundred thousand books worldwide from her art installation called the Parthenon of Banned Books. The structure aimed to commemorate books burned by the Nazis in Kassel, Germany, and promote freedom of expression.

2019: Sahar Khodayari, an Iranian woman and fan of Esteghlal FC, died after self-immolation. She had previously attempted to enter a match at the male-only Azadi Stadium disguised as a man, highlighting the ban on women attending such events in Iran.

2020: Catherine Dulac was awarded the 2021 Breakthrough Prize in Life Sciences for her research on the neural circuits underlying parenting behavior. Additionally, Nina Holden, Urmila Mahadev, and Lisa Piccirillo were recognized with the 2021 Maryam Mirzakhani New Frontiers Prize for their significant contributions to random geometry, quantum computation verification, and knot theory, respectively.

2021: A forum promoting LGBTQ+ rights was held in Kigali, Rwanda, focusing on addressing minority rights and advocating for greater equality and inclusivity.

September 11

1743: Russian noble Natalia Lopukhina was publicly flogged in Saint Petersburg as part of the Lopukhina Affair incident orchestrated by France and the Duchy of Holstein.

1906: Stefania Tatarówna became the first woman to complete a Ph.D. at the Jagiellonian University in Kraków, Austrian Empire (today Poland) in the Philosophy Department.

1942: Enid Blyton published *Five on a Treasure Island*, the first book in her popular Famous Five children's series. It marked the beginning of a highly successful book series with over 100 million copies sold worldwide.

1951: Florence Chadwick, an American long-distance swimmer, became the first woman to swim the English Channel from England to France, setting a new record. Despite challenging conditions, including solid headwinds and dense fog, Chadwick persevered and completed the swim in 16 hours and 22 minutes.

1969: Svetlana Gerasimenko, while working at the Alma-Ata Astrophysical Institute near Almaty, the then-capital city of the Kazakh Soviet Socialist Republic, photographed the comet 32P/Comas Solà using a 50-cm Maksutov telescope. After analyzing the photographs with Klim Ivanovych Churyumov, they realized the object could not be Comas Solà, but rather a new, unknown cometary object, now known as comet 67P/Churyumov–Gerasimenko.

1973: Hanna Holborn Gray was named provost of Yale University, becoming the first woman to hold this position in the university's history. She later served as Yale's acting president from 1977 to 1978, making her the first woman president of a major university.

1990: Myrna Mack Chang, a Chinese-Mayan anthropologist, was stabbed to death by members of the Guatemalan military due to her criticism of the Guatemalan government's treatment of the indigenous Maya and human rights abuses.

2002: Iranian security forces arrested Shiva Nazar Ahari for the first time at just 18. She has been since jailed multiple times for her human rights activism. Ahari was one of the founding members of the Committee of Human Rights Reporters (CHRR) and, along with Akram Eqbali, Hanieh

Ne'mati, and Maryam Araei, co-founded the Society of Tara Women (STW) to protect women's rights legally and peacefully. All four have faced continuous harassment from security forces.

2003: Anna Lindh, a Swedish Social Democratic politician and lawyer, died due to an assault. Lindh was known for her dedication to fostering international cooperation, promoting solidarity, and advocating for environmental causes. She was considered a potential successor to Göran Persson as the leader of the Social Democratic party.

September 12

1919: The Women's Peace Society was established in the United States after several members resigned from the Women's International League for Peace and Freedom. The resignations were due to a lack of unity within the overall membership and executive committee.

1992: Mae C. Jemison, a scientist, became the first African-American woman to go to space as the Science Mission Specialist on the Space Shuttle *Endeavour*. She spent over 190 hours in space, orbiting the Earth 127 times before returning on September 20.

1995: Bella Abzug, a prominent American lawyer, feminist, and politician, addressed the Fourth World Conference on Women in Beijing. She was known for advocating women's rights and played a significant role in advancing the feminist movement.

2013: The governing body of the Church in Wales approved the ordination of women as bishops.

2019: Wai Quayle became *Te Pihopa o Te Upoko o Te Ika*, making her the first female Māori bishop in the Anglican Church and the first New Zealand-born woman to become a bishop in the Anglican Communion.

2021: The Taliban education minister announced a series of restrictions on education for women and girls in Afghanistan. These restrictions included gender-segregated classrooms and requiring women and girls to wear hijabs. These measures were met with international concern and condemnation.

September 13

1745: Maria Theresa ascended to the throne as Holy Roman Empress and ruled until 1780. She was the only female ruler of the Habsburg dominions and implemented numerous reforms during her reign.

1933: Elizabeth McCombs became the first female Member of Parliament in New Zealand. She was elected to the House of Representatives and significantly contributed to social reform and women's rights.

1948: Margaret Chase Smith was elected as a United States senator, becoming the first woman to serve in both the U.S. House of Representatives and the U.S. Senate. She was essential in advancing women's rights and served in the Senate for over 24 years.

1994: President Bill Clinton signed the Violence Against Women Act (VAWA) as part of the Violent Crime Control and Law Enforcement Act. VAWA provided funding for programs to support victims of domestic violence, sexual assault, and other gender-related violence.

2016: The U.S. military agreed to cover the expenses for gender-affirming surgery for Chelsea Manning, a transgender former Army intelligence analyst. Manning was imprisoned at Fort Leavenworth and gained attention for disclosing classified documents to WikiLeaks.

2022: Mary Peltola was sworn in as the first Alaska Native and woman elected to the House for Alaska. This historic moment marked the first time in over 230 years that a Native American, an Alaska Native, and a

Native Hawaiian served as members of the House of Representatives. At that time, six Indigenous Americans were acting as representatives in the House.

September 14

326: Helena, the mother of Constantine I, discovered the True Cross and the Holy Sepulchre in Jerusalem during her pilgrimage. She also founded the *Panagia Ekatontapiliani* church on Patmos Island.

1131: Melisende became the ruler of Jerusalem following her father, Baldwin II. She jointly reigned with her husband, Fulk, as the King and Queen of Jerusalem. Their coronation at the Church of the Holy Sepulchre was celebrated with festive ceremonies.

1210: Maria of Montferrat married John of Brienne, a French nobleman, at 18. They were crowned the King and Queen of Jerusalem on October 3 and received a significant dowry from King Philip II and Pope Innocent III.

1791: Olympe de Gouges, a French activist, feminist, and playwright, wrote *The Declaration of the Rights of Woman and of the Female Citizen* in response to the 1789 *Declaration of the Rights of Man and of the Citizen*. It was published the next day.

1964: Five women, including Helen Keller, Lena Edwards, Lynn Fontainne, Helen Taussig, and Leontyne Price, received the U.S. Presidential Medal of Freedom.

1969: Male voters of the Swiss Canton Schaffhausen rejected female suffrage.

1975: Māori leader Whina Cooper led a march of 5,000 people supporting Māori land claims in New Zealand—the protest aimed to oppose the erosion of Māori rights and land by the actions of Europeans.

1994: Natalie Portman began her acting career at twelve when she starred in the film *Léon: The Professional*.

2012: Kate, Duchess of Cambridge (now Princess of Wales), and her husband initiated legal action following the publication of topless pictures of her taken during a holiday in France by the magazine *Closer*.

2020: A scientific team led by Jane Greaves announced the detection of phosphine in the atmosphere of Venus, raising the possibility of microbial life on the planet. Phosphine is considered a potential biosignature associated with biological processes on Earth.

September 15

921: Ludmila, the Duchess of Bohemia and Bořivoj I's widow, was murdered by her daughter-in-law Drahomíra in Tetín (modern Czech Republic). Ludmila was later canonized and became the Orthodox and Catholic Church patron saint.

1716: Maria, an enslaved woman from Curaçao, organized and led a slave rebellion at the St. Maria plantation, where she was held captive against the Dutch West India Company. Maria was executed by burning on November 9.

1762: Empress Go-Sakuramachi succeeded to the throne of Japan following the death of her brother, Emperor Momozono. She reigned for eight years before abdicating on January 9, 1771.

1942: The Women's Flying Training Detachment (WFTD) was established in the United States.

1963: Four girls (Addie Mae Collins, Cynthia Wesley, Carole Robertson, and Carol Denise McNair) were killed in the bombing of an African-American church in Birmingham, Alabama, USA.

1970: Phyllis F. Shantz became the first female member of the Secret Service Auxiliary to guard the U.S. president and his family.

1976: Ntozake Shange's play *For Colored Girls Who Have Considered Suicide/When* *the Rainbow Is Enuf* opened on Broadway at the Booth Theatre in Manhattan, New York, and ran for 742 performances.

1995: The Beijing Declaration was adopted by the U.N. at the end of the Fourth World Conference on Women. It agreed to establish principles for achieving gender equality.

2000: Karla Jessen Williamson, a Kalaaleq (the largest group of the Greenlandic Inuit), became the executive director of the Arctic Institute of North America (AINA), the first woman and first Inuk (a member of a group of culturally similar Indigenous peoples inhabiting the Arctic and subarctic regions of Greenland, Labrador, Quebec, Nunavut, the Northwest Territories, and Alaska) to hold the position.

2011: Australia introduced an option to select "indeterminate" as a gender choice in addition to the traditional male and female options in its passport system.

2014: Ewa Kopacz became Poland's second female prime minister.

2020: A whistleblower from a Georgia Immigration and Customs Enforcement facility reported a concerning pattern of hysterectomies and alleged medical neglect to the Department of Homeland Security.

2021: Simone Biles and three other U.S. gymnasts testified before Congress about the long-term sexual abuse of women in USA Gymnastics by team doctor Larry Nassar and the lack of investigation by the FBI after the abuse was initially reported in 2015.

2022: UNICEF appointed Ugandan climate activist Vanessa Nakate as Goodwill Ambassador, recognizing her outstanding global advocacy for climate justice.

September 16

1847: Elizabeth Caroline Newcom joined the military during the Mexican-American War disguised as a man and became the first female soldier to cross the Santa Fe Trail. She served for ten months until her true gender was discovered, and she was discharged. After suing Congress, she received payment for her service.

1913: Thousands of women in the Netherlands demonstrated for female suffrage.

1923: Japanese anarchist and feminist activist Itō Noe and her husband and his 6-year-old nephew were brutally killed during the so-called Amakasu Incident by the military police led by Lieutenant Amakasu Masahiko. During the chaotic aftermath of the catastrophic Great Kantō earthquake two weeks earlier, Japanese authorities killed many dissidents and ethnic Koreans in what became known as the Kantō Massacre. The brutal execution without a trial sparked widespread anger and patriotic fervor in support of the soldiers.

1991: Mary Ellen Avery received the President's National Medal of Science for her contributions to premature infant care.

1996: *Judge Judy* aired, and Judith Sheindlin became one of the most recognizable women on U.S. television.

2003: A House of Commons motion in Canada, presented by the Canadian Alliance, reiterating the heterosexual definition of marriage, was narrowly defeated. This motion was a precursor to the government's plan to introduce a bill to extend the federal marriage law to include same-sex couples.

2006: Elizabeth Blackburn, Carol Greider, and Jack Szostak were awarded the 2006 Albert Lasker Award for Basic Medical Research for their work on telomeres and telomerase. They discovered the enzyme telomerase, which replenishes the ends of chromosomes and guards cells against chromosome loss.

2020: Barbados' Prime Minister, Mia Mottley, announced that the country would become a republic the following year, replacing Queen Elizabeth II as the head of state with a Barbadian.

2022: Mahsa Amini, a 22-year-old Kurdish woman, died after falling into a coma following her detention by Iran's "morality police" for violating the country's strict hijab rules. Her death sparked protests by Iranian women and supportive men, with many women removing their hijabs and cutting their hair as a sign of defiance.

September 17

1224: To express gratitude for her support, the new Emperor Lizong made Empress Dowager Yang a co-regent during the Southern Song Dynasty rule. They ruled jointly until she died in 1233.

1382: Mary of Anjou was crowned "King" of Hungary seven days after Louis the Great's death. Her mother, Elizabeth of Bosnia, assumed regency.

1849: Harriet Tubman and her brothers, Ben and Henry, escaped from slavery in Maryland. After the escape, Ben and Henry decided to return, which also made Tubman return. But shortly after, she ran once more and traveled to Philadelphia.

1968: Diahann Carroll starred in the title role in the television series *Julia,* becoming the first African-American actress to star in her own television series where she did not play a domestic worker.

1983: Vanessa Williams became the first Black Miss America, winning the title in the Miss America pageant.

1991: Hole, the American alternative rock band formed by frontwoman Courtney Love, released their debut album, *Pretty on the Inside.*

2009: JoAnne Stubbe received the National Medal of Science for her contributions to understanding the mechanism of enzymes involved in DNA replication and repair.

September 18

1889: Jane Addams and Ellen Gates Starr co-founded Hull House, a settlement house in Chicago, Illinois. Hull House aimed to serve recently arrived European immigrants and provided education and guidance to help women from lower socioeconomic backgrounds find new societal roles.

1919: Women in the Netherlands were granted the right to vote, following the earlier grant of the right to stand in elections in 1917.

1937: Zora Neale Hurston published the novel *Their Eyes Were Watching God,* which has since become a classic of the Harlem Renaissance.

1948: Margaret Chase Smith of Maine became the first woman elected to the United States Senate without completing another senator's term.

1967: *Love Is a Many Splendored Thing* debuted on U.S. daytime television as the first soap opera to address an interracial relationship. The show faced controversy and was eventually discontinued due to demands from CBS censors.

2008: Hou Yifan, a Chinese chess prodigy, became the youngest girl to qualify for the highest title in chess, Grandmaster, at 14 years, six months, and 16 days.

2010: Iranian human rights activist Shiva Nazar Ahari was convicted of various charges, including gathering and plotting to commit crimes against the Iranian state.

2012: Mats Brännström and his team performed the world's first mother-to-daughter uterus transplantation in Sweden, a groundbreaking medical procedure.

2013: The French parliament passed a law prohibiting beauty pageants for children to address concerns about the excessive sexualization of young girls and promote their well-being.

September 19

1893: New Zealand became the first country to recognize women's right to vote. The Electoral Bill was passed after a successful campaign by women such as Kate Sheppard, Amey Daldy, Ada Wells, Meri Te Tai Mangakahia, Harriet Russell Morison, and organizations like the Women's Christian Temperance Union led by Anne Ward.

1896: Rose O'Neill, an American artist, published a four-panel comic strip in an issue of *Truth* magazine, making her the first American woman to publish a comic strip.

1969: After the University of California enforced a no-hiring Communists policy, the Board of Regents fired Angela Davis due to her Communist Party ties, following Governor Ronald Reagan's advice. However, Judge Jerry Pacht later ruled they couldn't fire her solely for her Communist Party affiliation, so she resumed her position.

1978: Cathy Davis became the first female boxer to receive the New York State Athletic Commission's boxing license.

2009: Singer Vera Lynn, at 92, set a record as the oldest artist to have a number-one album in the U.K.

2022: Irish judge Síofra O'Leary was elected as the new president of the European Court of Human Rights, making her the first woman to hold that position.

September 20

1058: Agnes de Poitou, Empress of the Holy Roman Empire, met with King Andrew I of Hungary to discuss the border zone in Burgenland (now Austria).

1675: During the Polish–Ottoman war, the Ottoman army laid siege to the Trembowla castle with a defense under the command of Captain Jan Samuel Chrzanowski. It is said that even though he was losing all hope in the face of dwindling food supplies, his wife, Anna Dorota Chrzanowska, threatened self-harm if her husband surrendered. This determination strengthened his resolve and inspired the castle's defenders. Chrzanowska also urged the garrison to attack the Ottoman positions (with some stories even suggesting she led them), leading to significant enemy losses. After almost a month, the Turks left, as King Jan III Sobieski was amassing his forces near Lviv, ready to intervene if needed. The couple was rewarded later with nobility titles.

1763: María Josefa Gabriela Cariño de Silang, a Filipino military leader of the Ilocano independence movement from Spain, was executed by hanging along with her troops in Vigan's central plaza by the Spanish.

1952: Martha Chase and Alfred Hershey published a report confirming that DNA holds hereditary data, contributing to our understanding of genetics.

1954: The first Moomins comic strip, created by Finnish writer and illustrator Tove Jansson, was published in *The Evening News*, a London newspaper.

1973: Billie Jean King defeated Bobby Riggs in the famous "Battle of the Sexes" tennis match at the Houston Astrodome, challenging gender stereotypes in sports.

1987: Alfre Woodard won an Emmy award for "Outstanding Guest Performance" in the T.V. drama L.A. Law during the 39th Emmy Awards.

2006: Anousheh Ansari, an Iranian-born American, became the first Muslim woman, the first Iranian, and the first private female space tourist traveling to space.

2011: The United States military ended its "Don't ask, don't tell" policy, allowing gay men and women to serve openly for the first time in the military.

2018: After the Israeli organization *Kolech* – The Religious Women's Forum filed a class action against the religious radio station *Kol B'Ramah* alleging the exclusion of women from its broadcasts in the first years of its activity, District Court in Jerusalem ruled that the station must pay one million NIS to a class action fund for the benefit of empowering traditional, religious and ultra-Orthodox women, and another 300,000 NIS for compensation for *Kolech*'s legal expenses. The organization fights for women's rights in Israel as part of the religious Jewish community.

2020: Mya-Rose Craig ("Birdgirl") and Greenpeace organized the most northerly protest against climate change, standing atop floating ice in the Arctic.

September 21

1832: Maria W. Stewart, an American educator, journalist, abolitionist, and prominent speaker known for her significant roles in the anti-slavery and women's rights movements in the United States, delivered a speech at Franklin Hall, Boston, to the New England Anti-Slavery Society. It was the first time an American woman of any race made a speech to a mixed audience – men and women, Black and white. In it, she demanded equal rights for African-American women and criticized the discriminatory social norms:

> "And such is the powerful force of prejudice. Let our girls possess whatever amiable qualities of soul they may; let their characters be fair and spotless as innocence itself' let their natural taste and ingenuity be what they may; it is impossible for scarce an individual of them to rise above the condition of servants."

1898: Empress Dowager Cixi seized power through a coup d'état in China, effectively ending the Hundred Days Reform, which aimed at modernizing various aspects of Chinese society.

1944: A Filipina spy, Josefina Guerrero, prepared a map that helped American soldiers crush Japanese defenses in Manila Harbor during World War II.

1955: The first founding meeting of The Daughters of Bilitis, the first lesbian civil and political rights organization in the United States, occurred in San Francisco. Founding members included Rose Bamberger, Rosemary Sliepen, Del Martin, Phyllis Lyon, Marcia Foster, June, Noni Frey, and Mary.

1981: Sandra Day O'Connor was unanimously approved by the U.S. Senate as the first female Supreme Court justice.

1981: Belize, formerly known as British Honduras, gained independence with Dame Minita Gordon serving as Governor-General.

1982: Janet Jackson released her debut solo album, *Janet Jackson*.

2009: Lisa Cummins became the first Irish person and the twentieth overall to complete a two-way swimming crossing of the English Channel.

2009: Singer Jade Ewen was confirmed as the new member of the girl band Sugababes, replacing the only original member, Keisha Buchanan.

2022: The New York Attorney General, Letitia James, filed a civil lawsuit in state court against Donald Trump, his three children, and The Trump Organization's affiliated companies. The lawsuit alleged fraudulent conduct, accusing Donald Trump of intentionally inflating his net worth for personal gain.

September 22

1139: Empress Matilda landed in England to claim the throne. Despite being named heir by her father, Henry Longshanks, she was usurped by her cousin Stephen. Matilda was never crowned Queen and later became known as the "Lady of the English."

1656: In Patuxent County, Maryland, an all-female jury of seven married and four single women heard the case of Judith Catchpole, who was accused of witchcraft and infanticide. Catchpole was acquitted.

1941: The first solo show for American sculptor Louise Nevelson was held at the prestigious Nierendorf Gallery in New York City.

2006: Aviation Cadet Saira Amin became the first female aviation cadet to win the Sword of Honour at The Pakistan Air Force Academy.

2010: Switzerland's parliament appointed women to the majority of cabinet posts in the country's seven-member executive branch for the first time, giving women the majority in the cabinet.

2011: Former television journalist Shelly Yachimovich was elected the head of the Israeli Labor Party.

2022: Professor Anna Grassellino was awarded the 2023 New Horizons in Physics Prize by the Breakthrough Prize Foundation for her discovery of major performance enhancements to niobium superconducting radio-frequency cavities, with applications ranging from accelerator physics to quantum devices.

September 23

1884: Judy W. Reed received a U.S. patent for the "Dough Kneader and Roller," possibly becoming the first African American woman to receive a U.S. patent officially.

1963: Georgette Ciselet became the first woman to serve on the Belgian Council of State.

1978: Debbie Harry, along with her group Blondie, released their third album, *Parallel Lines*, which achieved international success.

1988: The French government announced that *mifepristone* (RU486), commonly known as "the abortion pill," would be made available publicly through hospitals and clinics under medical supervision. It would take another 12 years for the FDA to approve the drug in the United States.

2013: After rowing solo for 150 days and covering 3,750 miles, Sarah Outen became the first woman to row solo from Japan to Alaska. She also became the first woman to complete a mid-Pacific row from West to East.

2021: Same-sex marriage was legalized in Sonora, Mexico, granting marriage equality to same-sex couples.

September 24

1230: Sancha of León briefly ruled as Queen of León in her own right, reigning alongside her younger sister, Dulce, until December 11, when the throne passed to Ferdinand. It was a result of an agreement negotiated by Berengaria (Queen of Castile and Ferdinand's mother) and Theresa (Sancha's and Dulce's mother), known as the "Pact of the Mothers."

1326: Isabella of France and her supporters, including Roger Mortimer, landed in Suffolk, England, to depose King Edward II and place Prince Edward as the new ruler.

1921: The first official women's football/soccer game occurred in Australia between North Brisbane and South Brisbane. The match attracted a crowd of ten thousand fans, highlighting the growing popularity of women's football.

1948: Mildred Gillars, known as "Axis Sally," pleaded not guilty to eight treason charges. She was an American broadcaster employed by the Third Reich in Nazi Germany during World War II to spread Axis propaganda. Gillars was the first woman to be convicted of treason against the United States.

1967: Dian Fossey, an American primatologist and conservationist, founded the Karisoke Research Center in Rwanda. This remote rainforest camp became her base for studying mountain gorilla groups, and Fossey became known locally as "The woman who lives alone on the mountain."

1988: Barbara C. Harris of Massachusetts was elected as the first woman Episcopal bishop, making history in the Episcopal Church.

1988: Christa Luding-Rothenburger, an East German cyclist, won the silver medal at the Seoul Olympics in cycling. She became the first athlete to win medals at both the Summer and Winter Games in the same year. Luding-Rothenburger had previously won a gold medal in speed skating at the 1988 Winter Olympics in Calgary.

2015: Gaia Vince became the first female outright winner of Britain's Royal Society Winton Prize for Science Books. She won the prestigious award for her book *Adventures in the Anthropocene: A Journey to the Heart of the Planet We Made*.

2021: Katalin Karikó, along with Drew Weissman, received the 2021 Lasker Award, one of America's top biomedical research prizes. They were honored for their discovery of a new therapeutic technology based on modifying messenger RNA (mRNA), which played a crucial role in the development of highly effective COVID-19 vaccines.

2021: Huawei executive Meng Wanzhou reached a deferred prosecution agreement after pleading not guilty to multiple fraud charges. As a result, her extradition case was dropped, and she was released after nearly three years under house arrest in Vancouver, Canada, reportedly traveling to Shenzhen, China.

September 25

1951: The Māori Women's Welfare League was established on the first day of a conference. Eighty-seven delegates from 187 branches, comprising 2503 women, gathered at Ngāti Poneke Young Māori Club. These groups emerged from the Department of Māori Affairs' efforts in the late 1940s, particularly under Controller of Māori Welfare Te Rangiātaahua Royal. Dame Whina Cooper was elected president of the national executive. It was the first time Māori women appointed their representatives on a state level.

1957: The Little Rock Nine, a group of nine African American students, including Elizabeth Eckford, entered Central High School in Little Rock, Arkansas, under heavily armed guard to desegregate the school. This event marked a significant moment in the civil rights movement, as the students faced violent threats and resistance from racist mobs.

1981: Sandra Day O'Connor was sworn in as the first female justice of the United States Supreme Court.

1982: The first group of women firefighters was sworn into the New York City Fire Department (FDNY). Their hiring came after a contentious lawsuit, and they faced hostility and harassment as they entered a traditionally male-dominated profession.

2005: Sex workers in Kyonggi province, South Korea, organized themselves into the Democratic Coalition of Sex Workers and reached the first collective bargaining agreement with brothel owners in the country's history, an important step towards improving the rights and working conditions of sex workers in the region.

2006: Safia Amajan, an Afghan women's rights activist, educator, politician, and vocal critic of the Taliban's suppression of women, was assassinated by two Taliban men on a motorcycle in Kandahar.

2017: First Lt. Marina A. Hierl became the first woman to complete the rigorous Infantry Officer Course in the United States Marine Corps.

2022: Cubans voted on legalizing same-sex marriage and same-sex adoption.

September 26

1910: After the death of Pang Nanggroe, his wife and fellow guerilla soldier, Cut Nyak Meutia, became the new commander, with only 45 men and 13 guns left to fight the Dutch colonizers in Aceh (western Indonesia). She fought to the end, wielding a *rencong* (a type of sword). She was killed when the Dutch troops shot her in the head and chest. She was declared a National Hero of Indonesia in 1964.

1933: The Roman Catholic Church officially recognized St. Zita as the patron saint of maids and domestic servants. St. Zita, who lived in the 13th century, became known for her devotion to serving others.

1973: Captain Lorraine Potter, an American Baptist minister, became the first woman to serve as a United States Air Force chaplain.

1975: Waunetta McClellan Dominic, an Odawa rights activist, delivered a speech at the U.S. Congress, advocating for the United States government to honor its treaty obligations to Native Americans. Her activism aimed to raise awareness and promote justice for Indigenous communities.

2002: Three female officers were appointed as fighter pilots in the South Korean Air Force, becoming the first women in history to hold such positions.

2018: An all-women-staffed engine company served in the New York City Fire Department (FDNY) for the first time in its 153-year history.

2019: The *Soyuz-MS* spacecraft successfully docked with the International Space Station, bringing astronauts Jessica Meir, Oleg Skripochka, and Hazza Al Mansouri on board. Hazza Al Mansouri became the first astronaut from the United Arab Emirates to travel to space.

2021: Adrienne Warren won a Tony Award for Best Performance by a Leading Actress for portraying Tina Turner in the Broadway musical *Tina: The Tina Turner Musical.*

2021: Khalida Jarrar, a member of the Palestinian Legislative Council, was released from Israeli prison after nearly two years in detention. Jarrar had been charged for her affiliation with the Popular Front for the Liberation of Palestine.

2021: Citizens in Switzerland voted on the legalization of same-sex marriage. The proposal aimed to extend the legal recognition of same-sex partnerships and garnered substantial support.

2021: San Marino held a referendum on the legalization of abortion to determine whether the procedure should be permitted up to 12 weeks of pregnancy or in cases where the mother's or fetus's health was at risk.

2022: Lizzo played various collectible flutes at the Library of Congress's Great Hall, including former President James Madison's crystal flute. She later performed with the crystal flute in front of a large audience at Capitol One Arena, showcasing her musical talent and the historical significance of the instrument.

2022: Cuba voted to legalize same-sex marriage.

September 27

1692: The trial for sorcery of Anne Palles of Denmark began, during which she confessed to dedicating her body and soul to Satan. On November 2, she was found guilty and sentenced to death.

1916: Zewditu was crowned Empress of Ethiopia following a palace coup. Zewditu's official title was "Queen of Kings" (*Negiste Negest*), a modification of the traditional title "King of Kings" (*Nəgusä Nägäst*). As Menelik II's daughter, Zewditu represented the final link in the direct male lineage of the Solomonic dynasty.

1919: Emma Goldman, an anarchist and activist, was released from a two-year prison term only to be immediately reimprisoned. Her incarceration was linked to her radical political beliefs and activities.

1933: Lotfia Elnadi became the first Egyptian woman and woman from the Arab world and Africa to earn a pilot's license.

1962: Rachel Carson's book *Silent Spring* was published. The book exposed the environmental damage caused by the widespread use of pesticides, particularly DDT, and played a crucial role in raising awareness about the need for environmental protection.

1970: Pope Paul VI named Saint Teresa of Ávila the first female Doctor of the Church. This recognition highlighted the significant contributions of Saint Teresa to Christian theology and spirituality.

1988: Aung San Suu Kyi and other activists formed The National League for Democracy in Myanmar (formerly Burma) to oppose the military dictatorship. Aung San Suu Kyi became a prominent figure in the fight for democracy and human rights in Myanmar.

2014: Amy Hughes, from the U.K., ran 53 marathons in 53 days, thus setting the record for the most marathons run on consecutive days by any person, male or female.

2019: The brother of Pakistani social media star Qandeel Baloch was sentenced to life in prison for her honor killing, while six others were acquitted. Qandeel Baloch's murder drew international attention and sparked conversations about women's rights and honor-based violence.

2021: Three regions in Poland repealed their status as "LGBT-free zones" following pressure from the European Commission and activists. The declaration of being "free of LGBTQ+ ideology" was imposed in 2019, reflecting a right-wing push of the ruling powers against the progressive changes, including LGBTQ+ rights.

September 28

1865: Elizabeth Anderson became the first licensed female physician in Britain. Elizabeth Blackwell, the first practicing woman physician in the United States, inspired her to study medicine.

1923: About 100 leaders formed the Tokyo Federation of Women's Organizations (*Tokyo Rengo Funjinkai*), divided into five sections: society, employment, labor, education, and government. The government section focused on women's rights and state representation. In November 1924, the government section led by Kubushiro Ochimi convened a meeting to advance women's rights, which led to the creation of the League for Women's Suffrage (*Fujin Sanseiken Kakutoku Kisei Domei*), intending to improve Japanese women's status and promote equal rights.

1942: Zofia Kossak-Szczucka and Wanda Krahelska-Filipowicz founded the Provisional Committee to Aid Jews (later *Żegota*), an underground organization. Irena Sandler joined the group as a welfare coordinator. She organized a network of homes and temporary shelters where Jews escaping the Warsaw Ghetto could hide. She focused on helping to smuggle Jewish children to hide them with Polish-Catholic families, religious orphanages, convents, and other charity facilities and homes. With volunteers, Irena Sandler saved the lives of more than two thousand Jewish children, carefully documenting their identities for future reunions with their families.

1970: The Canadian Royal Commission on the Status of Women concluded its examination of women's status and proposed measures for the federal government to promote gender equality across all facets of Canadian society. Prime Minister Lester B. Pearson initiated it on February 16, 1967. Public sessions were held the following year to gather input from the public, which the Commission considered as it formulated its recommendations. Florence Bird (a journalist and broadcaster) chaired the Commission. Other commissioners included Elsie MacGill (a feminist and the first female aeronautical engineer), Lola M. Lange (a rural feminist with a background in farming and community activism), Jeanne Lapointe (a literature professor), Doris Ogilvie (a juvenile court judge), Jacques Henripin (a professor of demography), and John Peters Humphrey (a law professor).

1985: Dorothy "Cherry" Groce, an immigrant from Jamaica, was wrongfully shot by the Metropolitan police in Brixton, London, leading to widespread riots.

2011: Japan requested South Korea to halt plans for constructing a monument dedicated to Korean World War II "comfort women" near the Japanese embassy in Seoul. The issue of comfort women remains a sensitive and contentious topic between Japan and South Korea, relating to the history of women forced into sexual slavery by the Japanese military during World War II.

2019: Annemiek van Vleuten won the women's road race at the 2019 UCI Road World Championships. Her victory came through a solo attack covering a distance of 105 kilometers (65 miles), finishing with a comfortable lead ahead of the second-placed rider, Anna van der Breggen.

2022: Italian astronaut Samantha Cristoforetti assumed command of ISS *Expedition 68.*

2022: Virgin Atlantic Airlines announced that their employees would no longer have to choose gendered uniform options. The airline emphasized the importance of individuality and allowed employees to select the clothing that best represented their gender identity or expression, irrespective of gender norms.

September 29

1314: As part of an exchange for captured English nobles, Edward II agreed to release Elizabeth de Burgh, the wife of Robert the Bruce, along with his sister Mary Bruce and his daughter Marjorie Bruce. This exchange took place during the time of the Scottish Wars of Independence.

1833: Isabella II, at the age of three, became the Queen of Spain, with her mother, Maria Christina of the Two Sicilies, serving as regent. Her uncle, Don Carlos, challenged Isabella's claim to the throne, which led to the First Carlist War in Spain.

1923: The First American Track and Field championships for women took place.

1949: Iva Toguri D'Aquino, also known as "Tokyo Rose," was convicted in the United States for broadcasting on behalf of Japan during World War II.

1988: Stacy Allison became the first American woman to reach Mount Everest's summit, the world's highest peak.

1988: Florence Griffith Joyner, or Flo-Jo, broke the 200m world and Olympic record (21.34 seconds) during the Seoul Olympic Games.

2002: Judit Polgár, a renowned chess player, defeated Garry Kasparov during the Russia vs. the Rest of the World Match. This victory marked the first time in chess history that a female player had beaten the world's number one player in competitive play.

2007: Fay Ajzenberg-Selove, an American nuclear physicist, received the National Medal of Science for her experimental work in nuclear spectroscopy of light elements and her contributions to understanding light atomic nuclei.

2020: The World Health Organization announced its intention to launch an investigation into allegations of sexual exploitation and abuse committed by its officials during their mission to control the Kivu Ebola outbreak in the Équateur Province of the Democratic Republic of the Congo.

2021: Nepal's Central Bureau of Statistics added an option for a third gender to its census forms for the first time, acknowledging and recognizing the existence of non-binary and gender-diverse individuals.

2021: Najla Bouden Romdhane was appointed the first female prime minister in Tunisia and the Arab world.

September 30

1860: After serving as a regent of her nine-year-old daughter Shah Jahan Begum since 1844, Sikandar Begum was recognized as the *Nawab of Bhopal* (Muslim ruler of Bhopal, now part of Madhya Pradesh, India). She ruled until October 30, 1868.

1888: Elizabeth Stride and Catherine Eddowes were killed on this day. They were the third and fourth victims of the infamous unidentified serial killer, Jack the Ripper, who terrorized the Whitechapel district of London.

1918: President Woodrow Wilson delivered a speech in Congress advocating for the passage of the "Susan B. Anthony Amendment," which aimed to secure nationwide woman suffrage and grant women the right to vote in the United States.

1937: Hedy Lamarr, an Austrian actress of Jewish descent, arrived in New York City to escape her possessive husband, Friedrich Mandl. Mandl was engaged in arms deals with the Nazis, and Lamarr pursued a successful career in Hollywood and in science.

1993: President Bill Clinton presented the President's National Medals of Science to Salome G. Waelsch for her contributions to developmental genetics and Vera C. Rubin for her pioneering research programs in observational cosmology.

2016: The 2016 FIFA U-17 Women's World Cup, the first-ever FIFA women's football tournament in the Middle East, commenced in Jordan.

2017: Thousands of protesters marched through Dublin, Ireland, demanding a change in the country's abortion laws. Anti-abortion activists also staged counter-demonstrations, and a pro-choice rally took place outside the Irish embassy in London.

2019: Moroccan journalist Hajar Raissouni and her husband Rifaat al-Amin were sentenced to one year in jail by a Rabat court. The charges against them included premarital sex and unlawful abortion. Raissouni's lawyer argued that the evidence was fabricated to suppress criticism of the government, and the verdicts received criticism from international observers, including Amnesty International.

OCTOBER

October 01

686: Empress Jitō ascended to the throne of Japan following the death of Emperor Tenmu. She ruled until 697.

1553: Mary Tudor I, also known as "Bloody Mary," was crowned Queen of England, France and Ireland, Defender of the Faith, and of the Church of England and also of Ireland in Earth Supreme Head.

1846: Ndaté Yalla Mbodj was crowned the *Lingeer* (Queen) of Waalo in Nder, the capital of Waalo (one of the four Jolof kingdoms in present-day Senegal). She succeeded her elder sister Ndjeumbeut Mbodj and ruled as *Lingeer* from 1846 to 1855 when Waalo fell to the French.

1847: Maria Mitchell, the first woman astronomer in the United States, discovered a comet called C/1847 T1.

1878: A labor uprising broke out on the island now known as St. Croix. The Danish occupying government had passed the Labor Act of 1849, which replaced chattel slavery with a wage slavery arrangement. Three women leaders, known as the "Queens of the Fireburn." ("Queen Mary" Thomas, "Queen Agnes" Salomon, and "Queen Mathilda" McBean), played a significant role in organizing the laborers' community.

1887: Ida Gray passed the entrance examinations for the University of Michigan School of Dentistry and graduated in June 1890, becoming the first African-American woman dentist in the United States.

1888: Franciszka Arnsztajnowa, a Polish-Jewish poet, playwright, and translator, debuted with a poem *Na okręcie* (*On Board a Ship*) in the newspaper *Kuryer Codzienny*. Much of her creative work occurred within the Young Poland period (1890-1918), stylistically incorporating the twilight of neo-romanticism.

1914: Amalia Celia Figueredo became the first Argentinian woman to gain a pilot license. On January 21, 1970, she was honored with the *Precursora de la Aeronáutica Argentina* title.

1919: The Women's Royal Naval Service was dissolved, but it would later be reinstated in 1939 with the onset of World War II.

1931: Clara Campoamor persuaded the Constituent Cortes to include women's suffrage in Spain's new constitution.

1968: Probable date of when the first issue of *No More Fun and Games, A Journal of Female Liberation*, was published. It was created by Cell 16, a progressive feminist organization active in the United States from 1968 to 1973, known for its program of celibacy, separation from men, and self-defense training (specifically karate) in Boston. Contributors included Roxanne Dunbar, Dana Densmore, Betsy Warrior, Jayne West, Abby Rockefeller, Marilyn Terry, Lisa Leghorn, Ellen O'Donnell, Donna Allen, Hilary Langhorst, Patricia Murphy Robinson, Jeanne Lafferty, Gail Murray, Stella Kingsbury, Mary Ann Weathers, Indra Allen, Eleni Porphyry, Jessie Bernard, Robin Morgan, and others.

1972: Six women (Lynn Blackstone, Jane Muhrcke, Liz Franceschini, Pat Barrett, Nina Kuscsik, and Cathy Miller) participated in the 1972 New York City Marathon, sitting at the start line to protest separate start times for men and women. Nina Kuscsik became the first official female New York City Marathon winner.

1983: Anita Cornwell published her first book, *Black Lesbian in White America*, a collection of essays and an interview with activist Audre Lorde. It's celebrated as the first-ever anthology of essays by a Black lesbian. The book's preface, by fellow African-American lesbian writer Becky Birtha, highlights Cornwell's sharp analysis of challenges faced by lesbians—racial, sexual, and gender-based, addressing the task of overcoming internalized homophobia and sexism.

1989: Denmark introduced the world's first legal same-sex registered partnerships.

2017: The Yayoi Kusama Museum opened in Tokyo, dedicated to showcasing the works of the renowned avant-garde artist Yayoi Kusama.

2019: In leaked audio, Facebook C.E.O. Mark Zuckerberg threatened to sue Senator Elizabeth Warren if she were elected president and attempted to "break up" large tech companies.

2019: Kristalina Georgieva replaced Christine Lagarde as the Managing Director of the International Monetary Fund.

2020: Belgium's court of appeal officially recognized the genealogical D.N.A. test confirming Delphine Boël as the daughter of King Albert II. As a result, she was granted the title of Princess of Belgium with the predicate "Her Royal Highness." Previously, Boël had been acknowledged as Albert's illegitimate daughter and held the honorary title of *Jonkvrouw*, the lowest rank within the Belgian nobility.

October 02

1614: Louis XIII, at 23, was granted full power as the King of France, ending his mother's regency. However, Queen Regent Marie retained her position as the leader of the *Conseil du Roi* and continued to exert control over the French government.

1718: Lady Mary Wortley Montagu returned to London after spending two years in Ottoman Istanbul with her husband. She wrote about her experiences as a woman in Ottoman Istanbul in a collection of letters called the *Turkish Embassy Letters*. These letters are considered the first secular female description of the life and customs of the "Muslim Orient," with a focus on the lives of Muslim women.

1925: Josephine Baker, an American entertainer, performed for the first time in *La Revue Nègre* at the Théâtre des Champs-Élysées in Paris.

2018: Donna Strickland, a Canadian physicist, was awarded the Nobel Prize in Physics for her groundbreaking work with pulsed lasers and pulse amplification.

2021: Sister Pietra Luana (Etra) Modica, a Scalabrinian Catholic nun, became the Secretary General of the Pontifical Urbaniana University. It was the first time in the university's history since its founding in 1627 that a woman had been appointed to this position.

2022: Yalemzerf Yehualaw of Ethiopia, born in 1999, became the youngest woman to win the London Marathon.

October 03

1688: Paduka Seri Baginda Sultan Zainatuddin Kamalat Syah became the seventeenth ruler of Aceh Darussalam (modern-day Indonesia) and the fourth and last ruling queen (*sultanah*) in succession. She ruled until 1699.

1903: Dorothy Levitt became the first British woman to participate in a speed competition at the Southport Speed Trials in the U.K. She won the class for cars priced between £400 and £550 in her four-seater *Gladiator*, covering the flying kilometer in one minute and forty-five seconds.

1904: Mary McLeod Bethune opened her first school for African-American students in Daytona Beach, Florida. This school later grew into what is now known as Bethune-Cookman University.

1970: Pope Paul VI named Saint Catherine of Siena the second female Doctor of the Church, recognizing her significant contributions to Catholic theology and spirituality.

1991: Nadine Gordimer, a South African writer, was announced as the Nobel Prize in Literature winner. She was recognized for her exceptional literary works that highlighted the effects of apartheid in South Africa.

1992: Irish singer-songwriter Sinéad O'Connor sparked controversy during her U.S. television program Saturday Night Live performance. She protested against Catholic Church child sexual abuse by ripping up a photograph of Pope John Paul II.

2011: Helle Thorning-Schmidt presented her new coalition government, becoming Denmark's 41st Prime Minister and the country's first female Prime Minister.

2016: The *Czarny Poniedziałek* (Black Monday) protest strike took place in Poland, with people wearing all black as a sign of solidarity against the government's near-total ban on abortion.

2017: The U.S. House of Representatives approved a bill known as the Pain-Capable Unborn Child Protection Act, which aimed to make abortions performed after 20 weeks of pregnancy illegal, except in cases where the mother's life was at risk or in situations of rape or incest.

October 04

1893: Emma Goldman, a Jewish anarchist immigrant, began her trial in New York City. The charges were related to a speech she delivered on August 21 during a protest of unemployed workers in Union Square. Goldman was found guilty of incitement to riot and sentenced to a year in Blackwell's Island Penitentiary.

1913: Annie Oakley, the famous sharpshooter, performed her last public shooting display in Marion, Illinois, ending her prominent career with Buffalo Bill's Wild West Show, which had faced financial difficulties earlier that year.

1920: Sophie Mannerheim founded The Mannerheim League for Child Welfare, a Finnish non-governmental organization dedicated to the well-being and rights of children.

1976: Barbara Walters became the first woman co-anchor of the evening news in the United States, joining ABC News.

1993: Ruth Bader Ginsburg joined the U.S. Supreme Court as its second woman Justice, significantly contributing to constitutional law and women's rights during her tenure.

2004: The Nobel Prize in Physiology or Medicine was awarded jointly to Linda B. Buck and Richard Axel for their discoveries of odorant receptors and the organization of the olfactory system.

2010: Ellen Johnson Sirleaf, the first female President of Liberia, signed into law the Freedom of Information Bill, promoting transparency and accountability in West Africa.

2012: The Moroccan port of Smir blocked the entry of a ship operated by Women on Waves. This Dutch non-profit organization provided abortions and medical services to women in countries with restrictive abortion laws. The ship's presence was part of the efforts of abortion rights activists.

2022: The Slovenian National Assembly passed legislation codifying the legalization of same-sex marriage and adoption for same-sex couples.

October 05

1789: Women marched on Versailles during the French Revolution to protest high bread prices. They demanded to meet with King Louis XVI to request bread and progress on a revised constitution. A delegation of women met with the king, who agreed to their demands, while others occupied the national assembly.

1853: The Fourth National Women's Rights Convention began in Cleveland, Ohio, providing a platform for women's rights and equality discussions.

1892: Victoria Earle Matthews and Maritcha Remond Lyons organized a testimonial dinner in New York's Lyric Hall for Ida B. Wells, spurring the founding of the Woman's Loyal Union of New York and Brooklyn, which supported Ida B. Wells's anti-lynching crusade and fought racial discrimination.

1944: Women in France gained suffrage, granting them the right to vote.

1984: Kathryn D. Sullivan and Sally K. Ride participated in the same space mission, making it the first American spaceflight to include two women as crew members.

2009: Elizabeth Blackburn, Carol Greider, and Jack Szostak were awarded the Nobel Prize in Physiology or Medicine for their discoveries related to telomeres and telomerase.

2015: Tu Youyou received the Nobel Prize in Physiology or Medicine for her discoveries in developing a novel therapy against malaria, making her the first Chinese woman to win the Nobel Prize.

2017: The Trump administration, through the Department of Justice, overturned an Obama-era policy that aimed to protect transgender employees against discrimination using Title VII of the Civil Rights Act.

2019: A renowned gymnast, Simone Biles, landed a triple-twisting double backflip in a tucked position during the World Artistic Gymnastics Championships. The skill was named "Biles 2" and was assigned a high-difficulty value.

2022: The Nobel Prize in Chemistry was awarded to Carolyn Ruth Bertozzi, jointly with Morten P. Meldal and Karl Barry Sharpless, for their click and bioorthogonal chemistry work.

2022: Nicole Aunapu Mann became the first Native American woman in space as part of SpaceX's four-person crew to the International Space Station, representing NASA.

October 06

1868: During the Battle of Aizu in Japan, Nakano Takeko, along with her mother and sister, led the *Jōshitai*, or "Girls' Army," against the imperial forces. Takeko fought with a *naginata* (polearm weapon) and displayed exceptional courage and skill. She lost her life in the battle on October 16.

1919: Brena Vineyard Runyon established The First Women's Bank of Tennessee in Clarksville, Tennessee. It was the first bank in the United States to be run entirely by women, including managers, directors, and staff.

1978: The U.S. Congress passed a bill prohibiting cross-examining a victim's prior sexual history in rape trials. This change aimed to protect victims from having their personal history scrutinized in court while the criminal and sexual history of the accused remained off-limits.

1991: Sònia Rescalvo Zafra and Doris Romero, both trans women, were brutally attacked by a group of neo-Nazis in Barcelona, Spain. Doris survived by chance, but Sònia did not. The press dead-named her when describing the event. Police treated the attack as a hate crime, even though Spanish criminal law did not distinguish between crimes motivated by prejudice and others. This case changed the way hate crimes and discrimination were prosecuted in Barcelona, which ultimately led to the creation of a specialized prosecutor's office.

1992: Rigoberta Menchú Tum was awarded the Nobel Peace Prize for her work in social justice and ethnocultural reconciliation, particularly her advocacy for the rights of indigenous peoples.

2003: Aviel Barclay became the first Torah *soferet* (female scribe), contributing to the traditionally male-dominated field of Jewish scribal arts.

2008: Françoise Barré-Sinoussi and Luc Montagnier were recognized for their groundbreaking discovery of the human immunodeficiency virus (HIV), responsible for AIDS.

2020: Andrea M. Ghez was awarded the Nobel Prize in Physics for discovering a supermassive black hole at the center of our galaxy.

2021: Frances Haugen, a former Facebook employee, testified before U.S. lawmakers, highlighting the harmful effects of the company's platforms on children, societal divisions, and democratic processes.

2022: Annie Ernaux was announced as the Nobel Prize in Literature recipient for her courageous and insightful exploration of personal memory, societal constraints, and estrangement.

October 07

1889: Barnard College, the first women's college in New York to offer rigorous coursework equivalent to male liberal arts colleges, opened. Its establishment was made possible through the efforts of activist Annie Nathan Meyer.

1919: American playwright Alice Gerstenberg debuted her satirical play *Fourteen* in San Francisco.

1944: The *Sonderkommando*, a group of 250 prisoners responsible for handling bodies after gassings, staged an uprising in the Auschwitz-Birkenau Nazi Camp. The explosives were stolen by a group of young Jewish women from the Union Werke armament factories: Ala Gertner, Regina Safirsztajn, Estera Wajsblum, and Roza Robota. The detonations partially destroyed Crematorium IV and killed 70 men among the Nazi SS and Kapos. All four women were hanged the following year (*see*: January 5) after months of torture in the infamous Bloc 11. Still, they refused to reveal the names of others who participated in the smuggling operation.

1954: Marian Anderson became the first African-American singer hired by the Metropolitan Opera Company in New York City.

1971: Mary Ellen Rudin published an article in *Fundamenta Mathematicae*, in which she constructed a large Dowker space, refuting a conjecture by Clifford Hugh Dowker and driving topological research for over two decades. Her example stimulated the search for smaller Dowker spaces.

2009: Yuki Kihara, a New Zealand and Pacific Islander artist, had her solo exhibition titled Shigeyuki Kihara: Living Photograph at the Metropolitan Museum of Art in New York. It was the first time a New Zealander and Pacific Islander had a solo show at the institution.

2009: President Obama awarded National Medals of Science, Technology, and Innovation to Esther Sans Takeuchi (Medicine) and Joanna S. Fowler (Chemistry).

2011: The Nobel Peace Prize was jointly awarded to three women: Tawakul Karman,

Ellen Johnson Sirleaf, and Leymah Gbowee. They were recognized for their nonviolent struggle for women's safety and rights in peace-building efforts in Yemen and Liberia.

2011: Alison Redford of the Progressive Conservatives became the first female Premier of the Canadian province of Alberta.

2012: Hildegard of Bingen was named a Doctor of the Church by Pope Benedict XVI to recognize her holiness of life and the originality of her teachings.

2012: The Cork women's Gaelic football team, known as the Rebelettes, won the All-Ireland Senior Ladies Football Championship with a scoreline of 0-16 to 0-7 against Kerry at Croke Park.

2020: Jennifer Doudna and Emmanuelle Marie Charpentier were jointly awarded the Nobel Prize in Chemistry for the development of CRISPR-Cas9, a method for genome editing with wide-ranging applications in various fields of science and medicine.

October 08

1645: Jeanne Mance opened the first lay hospital in North America in Montreal, contributing to healthcare services in the region.

1895: Korean Empress Myeongseong was assassinated by Japanese infiltrators, leading to political tensions between Korea and Japan.

1951: Christine Jorgensen, in a letter to her friends, described her experiences after successfully undergoing the first of a series of gender-affirming surgeries,

> "I have changed a great deal. But it is the other changes that are so much more important. Remember the shy, miserable person who left America? Well, that person is no more and, as you can see, I'm in marvelous spirits."

1993: Toni Morrison became the first African American woman to win the Nobel Prize for Literature, recognizing her profound contributions to literature.

1998: Jennifer Doudna and her colleagues published a groundbreaking study in Nature, deciphering the molecular structure of RNA enzymes (ribozymes) and other functional RNAs. This research shed light on how these molecules can perform complex functions similar to proteins.

2004: Wangarĩ Muta Maathai, an environmental and political activist from Kenya, won the Nobel Peace Prize for her significant contributions to sustainable development, democracy, and peace. She became the first Black African woman to receive this prestigious honor.

2012: Isatou Ceesay from Gambia and Ndeye Dague Gueye Dieye from Senegal were honored with The International Alliance for Women Difference Maker Award. Isatou Ceesay was recognized for her environmental work and empowerment of women. At the same time, Ndeye Dague Gueye Dieye received the award for advocating for the rights and advancement of persons with disabilities.

2015: Inspired by a similar campaign in the U.K., Kristina Lunz started a campaign Stop Bild Sexism (German: *Schluss mit dem Bild-Sexismus*) opposing what its organizers described as the objectification of women in *Bild-Zeitung*, the most popular newspaper in Germany. The paper had been criticized by numerous sources over the years for its sexist representations of women. The campaign's first aim was to persuade the newspaper to stop publishing photographs of the "*Bild*-Girl," a topless model. It also demanded that the newspaper start reporting on women and women's issues as it writes about men.

2020: Louise Glück, an American poet, was awarded the Nobel Prize in Literature for her unmistakable poetic voice that captures the essence of individual existence with austere beauty, making it universally relatable.

2020: The F.B.I. announced the charging of 13 men from the militia group Wolverine Watchmen in a plot to kidnap Michigan Governor Gretchen Whitmer at her vacation home, highlighting the issue of U.S. domestic extremism.

2021: Maria Angelita Ressa, alongside Dmitry Muratov of the Russian Federation, became the first Filipino recipient of the Nobel Peace Prize. They were recognized for their efforts to safeguard freedom of expression, a crucial element for democracy and lasting peace.

October 09

1669: Frances Boothby's play *Marcelia: or the Treacherous Friend. A Tragicomedy. As it is Acted at the Theatre-Royal, by His Majesties Servants* was licensed to Roger L'Estrange. Frances Boothby was the first woman to have a play professionally produced in London.

1930: Laura Ingalls became the first woman to fly across the United States, completing a journey from Long Island to Glendale, California, with nine stops totaling 30 hours and 27 minutes.

1949: Margot Fonteyn, a renowned ballerina, made her debut in the United States, portraying the role of Princess Aurora in Sleeping Beauty at the Metropolitan Opera House in Manhattan, New York. Her performance received tremendous acclaim, with the audience giving her 48 curtain calls.

1992: The punk rock group Bikini Kill, formed in Olympia, Washington, in October 1990, released their debut album titled *Bikini Kill*. Their music and performances pioneered the riot grrrl movement, characterized by feminist lyrics and passionate energy.

2009: Annette Gordon-Reed received the Pulitzer Prize in History for her book *The Hemingses of Monticello: An American Family*. Her work delves into the history of the Hemings family, enslaved by Thomas Jefferson, shedding light on their complex relationships and contributions to American history.

2012: Malala Yousafzai, a 15-year-old Pakistani activist advocating for women's education rights, was shot by Taliban gunmen in the Swat Valley. Her courageous efforts and subsequent recovery brought international attention to the importance of education and the challenges faced by girls in certain regions.

2014: Estonia became the first former Soviet republic to legalize gay partnerships and grant equal rights to same-sex couples.

2020: 1500 police officers took part in an eviction of fifty-seven people from a squat in Berlin known as Liebig 34, at Liebigstraße 34 in Berlin's Friedrichshain-Kreuzberg district, which was occupied since 1990 and from the outset, expressly feminist, aiming to combat the typical patriarchal behavior within the activist counterculture. It featured a self-proclaimed "queer -anarcho-feminist collective," the L34-Bar, and the Daneben infoshop on the ground floor.

October 10

1866: Elizabeth Cady Stanton, a prominent suffragist and women's rights activist was the first female candidate for the United States Congress. Although she did not win the election, her candidacy marked a meaningful step toward women's political participation.

1903: The Women's Social and Political Union (WSPU) was founded in the United Kingdom to advocate for women's suffrage and political rights. Led by Emmeline Pankhurst and her daughters, the WSPU played a pivotal role in the suffrage movement in Britain.

1906: Mary Church Terrell published an article, "What It Means to Be Colored in the Capital of the United States", in the *Independent*.

1911: Božena Laglerová became the first Czech woman to earn a pilot license.

1912: Australia enacted the Maternity Allowance Act, which introduced a "baby bonus" of five pounds for each child born in the country. However, the benefit excluded indigenous mothers and non-citizens.

1945: At the 5th Pan-African Congress in Manchester, Amy Ashwood and Alma La Badie, the only two women presenters, addressed issues concerning Jamaican women.

1983: Barbara McClintock, an American scientist, was awarded the Nobel Prize in Physiology or Medicine for her groundbreaking work in genetics, particularly her discovery of mobile genetic elements and transposition.

2003: Shirin Ebadi, an Iranian human rights lawyer and activist, received the Nobel Peace Prize for promoting democracy and human rights, particularly advocating for the rights of women and children. She became the first Iranian and Muslim woman to receive the Nobel Peace Prize.

2012: One of the three members of the punk rock protest group Pussy Riot, imprisoned for staging a performance critical of the Russian government, was freed at an appeal hearing in Moscow, Russia.

2014: Malala Yousafzai, a Pakistani education activist who survived an assassination attempt by the Taliban, was awarded the Nobel Peace Prize for her advocacy for girls' education rights.

2017: Allegations of sexual assault and harassment against film producer Harvey Weinstein were reported in an article by Ronan Farrow in *The New Yorker*. The article detailed allegations from numerous women, including incidents of rape, and played a significant role in sparking the #MeToo movement.

2019: Olga Tokarczuk, a Polish writer, was awarded the Nobel Prize in Literature for her narrative imagination and her creative exploration of the boundaries of fiction.

2019: Women supporters were allowed to attend a men's football match in Iran for the first time in decades. The game between Iran and Cambodia resulted in Iran's 14-0 victory.

2020: Iga Świątek, a Polish tennis player, won the Women's Singles title at the French Open, defeating Sofia Kenin from the United States in the final. She became the first Polish player to win a Grand Slam singles title.

October 11

1865: The Morant Bay rebellion began in Jamaica, with hundreds of Black women and men participating. The uprising was a response to social and economic injustices faced by the local population, and it ultimately led to significant political and social changes in Jamaica.

1911: Annie Jump Cannon, an American astronomer, initiated the classification of stars at Harvard University. She developed the Harvard Classification Scheme, which categorized stars based on spectral characteristics. Cannon's work revolutionized the field of stellar classification and laid the foundation for our understanding of stellar evolution.

1963: The final report of the U.S. Presidential Commission on the Status of Women, titled *American Women*, was published. The report highlighted the pervasive sexual discrimination women face in various aspects of society and called for legal reforms to address gender inequality. It also urged the Supreme Court to clarify women's constitutional rights.

1984: Astronaut Kathryn D. Sullivan became the first American woman to perform a spacewalk during the Space Shuttle *Chal-*

lenger mission. She ventured outside the spacecraft to conduct experiments and test equipment.

1987: The Second National March on Washington for Lesbian and Gay Rights took place in Washington, D.C. Organizers chose seven main demands for the march:

> "the legal recognition of lesbian and gay relationships; the repeal of all laws that make sodomy between consenting adults a crime; a presidential order banning discrimination by the federal government; passage of the Congressional lesbian and gay civil rights bill; an end to discrimination against people with AIDS, AIDS related complex (A.R.C.), AIDS related conditions, HIV-positive status and those perceived to have AIDS; massive increases in funding for AIDS education, research, and patient care; money for AIDS, not for war; reproductive freedom, the right to control our own bodies, and an end to sexist oppression; an end to racism in this country and apartheid in South Africa."

1991: Professor Anita Hill testified before the U.S. Senate Judiciary Committee during the Supreme Court nomination hearings of Clarence Thomas. Hill accused Thomas of sexual harassment, sparking a national conversation about workplace harassment and gender dynamics.

2007: British author Doris Lessing was awarded the Nobel Prize in Literature. The Swedish Academy recognized her as an influential writer who explored the female experience and tackled social and political issues with skepticism, passion, and visionary power.

2012: The first International Day of the Girl Child was celebrated worldwide. The United Nations designated October 11 as a day to promote girls' rights, address their challenges, and promote gender equality in education, health, and other areas.

2012: The Marie Stopes organization opened the first private clinic in Northern Ireland to offer abortion services to women.

2022: The Federal State of Mexico legalized same-sex marriage, granting equal marriage rights to same-sex couples.

October 12

1799: Jeanne Geneviève Labrosse became the first woman to jump from a balloon with a parachute.

1850: The Women's Medical College of Pennsylvania opened its doors to students, becoming the first medical school exclusively for women. It was also the first accredited medical school worldwide to grant women the degree of Doctor of Medicine.

1874: The London School of Medicine for Women was established in London by Sophia Louisa Jex-Blake with the support of prominent medical professionals as lecturers. The school opened with fourteen students and played a crucial role in promoting medical education for women.

1883: Toshiko Kishida, one of the first Japanese feminists who wrote under the name Shōen, delivered the *Daughters in Boxes* speech, which addressed issues with Japan's family system and how it impacted young Japanese girls. It recognized that this system was deeply embedded in Japanese culture, often leaving parents unaware of its constraints on their daughters. Kishida acknowledged that well-intentioned upper and middle-class Japanese parents inadvertently restricted their daughters' freedom while trying to instill specific cultural values.

1890: The Uddevalla Suffrage Association was founded in Sweden, laying the foundation for the women's suffrage movement in the country. The association advocated for women's right to vote and contributed to the eventual achievement of suffrage in Sweden.

1915: British nurse Edith Cavell was executed by a German firing squad during World War I. Cavell had been helping Allied soldiers escape occupied Belgium.

1978: Chaka Khan, born Yvette Marie Stevens, released her solo debut album *Chaka*. The album featured the disco hit *I'm Every Woman* and marked the beginning of her successful solo career.

2012: The High Court of Botswana overturned a customary law prohibiting women from inheriting the family home.

2018: The Society for Advancement of Chicanos/Hispanics and Native Americans in Science (SACNAS) announced the winners of the SACNAS Distinguished Awards. Adriana Mejía, an evolutionary biologist and lepidopterist, and Ofelia Olivera, a pioneer in discovering anti-AIDS drugs-induced carcinogenesis, were recognized for their contributions in their respective fields.

2022: Nury Martinez, a councilwoman in Los Angeles, announced her resignation from the Los Angeles City Council following controversy over an audio recording containing racist and denigrating remarks. Martinez had previously stepped down from the council presidency amid increasing pressure related to the recording.

October 13

1908: Margaret Travers Symons made history by bursting into the U.K. Parliament and becoming the first woman to speak there.

1939: Evelyn "Pinky" Kilgore, an American pioneer aviator, became the first woman to receive a flight instructor's license from the Civil Aeronautics Authority.

1970: Political activist Angela Davis was arrested on charges of kidnapping, murder, and conspiracy. She had been listed on the FBI's Ten Most Wanted Fugitive List, and her arrest garnered significant attention. Davis's subsequent trial and acquittal became a highly publicized event and highlighted social justice and political activism issues.

1970: The Gay Liberation Front (G.L.F.) was founded in the United Kingdom. The G.L.F. played a vital role in advocating for LGBTQ+ rights and raising awareness about LGBTQ+ societal issues.

1986: Rita Levi-Montalcini, an Italian – Jewish neurologist, won the Nobel Prize in Physiology or Medicine for her groundbreaking work on nerve growth factor. Her discoveries contributed significantly to our understanding of how cells develop and function.

2001: Patricia A. Locke, also known as Tawacin WasteWin, received the Those Who Make a Difference award from the Indigenous Language Institute (I.L.I.). She was recognized for her efforts in preserving Native American languages, highlighting their cultural importance, and promoting their continued use.

2011: Jetsun Pema was crowned Bhutan's *Druk Gyaltsuen*, or Dragon Queen. She has advocated for environmental issues and was the patron of the Royal Society for Protection of Nature (R.S.P.N.) in Bhutan. Additionally, she works closely with organizations that support children with special needs, serving as the patron of the Ability Bhutan Society.

2017: Former U.S. First Lady Michelle Obama selected Amy Sherald to paint her official portrait for the Smithsonian's National Portrait Gallery. Sherald's portrait captured national attention and became an iconic representation of Michelle Obama's grace, strength, and influence.

October 14

1586: Mary, Queen of Scots, went on trial for conspiring against Queen Elizabeth I of England. The trial marked a significant moment in the conflict between the two queens and ultimately led to Mary's execution.

1911: Emma Albani, a renowned opera singer, gave her farewell performance at London's Albert Hall. She captivated audiences with her rendition of the emotional aria *Goodbye* by Paolo Tosti.

1977: Anita Bryant, an anti-gay crusader and singer, was "pied" in the face by gay rights activist Thom Higgins. Bryant had led the Save Our Children campaign, which aimed to overturn legal protections for the LGBTQ+ community in Dade County, Florida. The incident became a symbol of resistance against homophobia and bigotry.

1979: The first National March on Washington for Lesbian and Gay Rights took place, drawing thousands of participants advocating for LGBTQ+ rights. The march was led by the Salsa Soul Sisters (later known as the African Ancestral Lesbians United for Societal Change), the oldest African-American and Latina-American lesbian organization in the United States. The organization identified as lesbians, womanists, and women of color. Speakers included Charlotte Bunch, Flo Kennedy, Audre Lorde, Kate Millett, Eleanor Smeal, First P.F.L.A.G. President Adele Starr, and the activist and comic Robin Tyler emceed the program.

1991: Aung San Suu Kyi, the Burmese opposition leader and pro-democracy activist, was awarded the Nobel Peace Prize for her nonviolent struggle for democracy and human rights in Myanmar (formerly Burma).

2007: In response to violent attacks by residents of El Alto, Bolivia, on brothels and bars, the police closed all such establishments. Sex workers were forced to look for work on the streets and were met with harassment, which sparked protests and led to mass strikes (*see:* October 22).

2019: The International Federation for Human Rights (F.I.D.H.) elected Alice Mogwe, a Botswana human rights advocate and the founder of Ditshwanelo - The Botswana Centre for Human Rights (in 1993), as their new president during its 40th Congress in Taiwan. Mogwe was reelected in 2022.

2019: The Nobel Memorial Prize in Economic Sciences was jointly awarded to Esther Duflo, Abhijit Banerjee, and Michael Kremer for their experimental approach to alleviating global poverty. Their research and innovative methods have significantly contributed to the field of development economics.

October 15

1581: The *Ballet Comique de la Reine*, the first narrative ballet, premiered at the Louvre Palace in Paris. Devised by Louise of Lorraine, wife of Henry III of France, and choreographed by Balthasar de Beaujoyeulx, the ballet was performed as part of the wedding celebrations for Marguerite of Lorraine.

1793: Queen Marie Antoinette of France was tried and convicted of treason during the French Revolution. The trial marked a significant moment in the revolutionary period, leading to her subsequent execution.

1851: The Second National Woman's Rights Convention occurred at Brinley Hall in Worcester, Massachusetts. Presided over by Paulina Wright Davis and Lucretia Mott, the convention addressed various topics related to women's rights, including education, labor, and political equality.

1852: The seventh issue of *Die Deutsche Frauen-Zeitung* (*The German Woman's Journal*), a German-language newspaper founded in March by Mathilde Franziska Anneke in Milwaukee, Wisconsin, U.S.A., was published. It was a pioneering publication that concentrated on issues related to women's rights, making it one of the first feminist journals produced by a woman in the United States during the mid-19th century. It advocated for women's rights, education, suffrage, and societal participation. Although the newspaper had a relatively short lifespan of about two and a half years, it left a lasting impact on the early women's rights movement in the United States.

1885: Alpha Chi Omega, a national women's fraternity, was founded at DePauw University in Indiana. Seven women established it, including Anna Allen Smith, Olive Burnett Clark, and Bertha Deniston Cunningham.

1891: The first school for girls opened in Albania, with the Qiriazi siblings (Gjerasim, Sevasti, and Parashqevi) serving as teachers. Parashqevi, at only 11 years old, started teaching written Albanian at the school.

1917: Dutch dancer Mata Hari was executed by France on charges of espionage during World War I. Her case became widely known and controversial, often associated with intrigue and espionage.

1948: Frances L. Willoughby became the first female doctor in the U.S. Navy, breaking new ground for women in the military.

1951: Luis E. Miramontes, a Mexican chemist, synthesized *norethisterone*, a progestin used in the combined oral contraceptive pill. This breakthrough played a crucial role in the development of hormonal birth control.

2013: New Zealand author Eleanor Catton received the Man Booker Prize for her novel *The Luminaries*, earning recognition for her literary achievement.

2016: Law enforcement authorities in China arrested 75 individuals involved in an illegal service that facilitated the determination of fetal gender for selective abortion—this action aimed to address gender-based discrimination and illicit practices.

2019: Bernardine Evaristo, for her novel *Girl, Woman, Other*, and Margaret Atwood, for *The Testaments*, jointly won the Booker Prize. Evaristo became the first Black woman to win this prestigious literary award.

October 16

690: Empress Wu Zetian ascended to the throne of the Tang dynasty and declared herself ruler of the Chinese Empire. She became the only female emperor in Chinese history and held power for over 20 years.

1384: Jadwiga, a 10-year-old, was crowned King of Poland following the death of her father, King Louis, in 1382. Due to the laws of succession and her young age, she was crowned as "King" rather than "Queen." She ruled as the first female monarch of the Kingdom of Poland and is recognized for her contributions to education, culture, and social welfare.

1869: The College for Women, the precursor to Girton College, Cambridge, was founded in England. It was the country's first residential university-level women's college and significantly promoted women's education.

1893: Patty Hill and Mildred J. Hill, American sisters, obtained the copyright for their book *Song Stories for the Kindergarten*, which included the song *Good Morning to All*" This song later served as the basis for the popular tune *Happy Birthday to You* after a modification by Robert H. Coleman.

1916: Margaret Sanger, her sister Ethel Byrne, and Fania Mindell opened the first family planning clinic in the United States.

1967: Joan Baez and 38 other individuals were arrested in Oakland, California, for obstructing the entrance of the city's military induction center. This act of civil disobedience protested the Vietnam War.

1983: Cyndi Lauper's debut album, *She's So Unusual*, succeeded wildly. She became the first female artist to have four top-five hits from a debut album on the Billboard Hot 100.

2012: Hilary Mantel won the Man Booker Prize for her novel *Bring Up the Bodies*, becoming the first British author and woman to win the award twice.

2017: Maltese journalist and blogger Daphne Caruana Galizia, known for investigating corruption allegations involving Prime Minister Joseph Muscat, was killed by a car bomb near her home.

2022: Rebecka Fallenkvist, a member of the right-wing Swedish Democrats, was suspended for insulting comments about Anne Frank, the young Jewish diarist who perished in the Holocaust (Shoah).

October 17

1630: Empress Meishō of Japan was officially crowned in a coronation ceremony, signifying the formal ascension to the throne.

1968: The Feminists, previously known as the October 17th Movement, a radical feminist group, was founded in New York. Members included Ti-Grace Atkinson, Anne Koedt, Sheila Michaels, Barbara Mehrhof, Pamela Kearon, and Sheila Cronan. They believed women were oppressed by adopting patriarchal gender roles and advocated for complete autonomy from men. The group opposed the sexual revolution, initially promoting celibacy and later endorsing political lesbianism. They enforced separatism by limiting membership to women without male partners, ultimately disbanding in 1973. The Feminists played a crucial role in shaping cultural feminism, separatist feminism, and anti-pornography feminism within the radical feminist movement.

1980: Becoming Visible: The First Black Lesbian Conference was held at The Women's Building in San Francisco, California. Some activist speakers were involved in the African-American Lesbian Liberation Movement, like Andrea Ruth Canaan, Pat Norman, and Angela Davis.

1988: Chemists Gertrude Elion, George Hitchings, and Sir James Black were awarded the Nobel Prize in Physiology or Medicine for their discoveries of important principles for drug treatment. Elion's work focused on developing drugs to treat various diseases, including leukemia, herpes, and organ transplantation.

2015: During the mayoral race in Cologne, Germany, Henriette Reker, a candidate for mayor, was stabbed in the neck by a man who was angered by Germany's refugee policies. Reker and one of her aides were seriously injured, while three others sustained minor injuries.

2020: New Zealand Prime Minister Jacinda Ardern won a historic landslide victory, securing a second term in office. The Labour Party, led by Ardern, became the first party to win a majority under New Zealand's proportional system since its introduction in 1996.

2022: A prisoner exchange between Russia and Ukraine took place, resulting in the release of 108 Ukrainian women, including officers, sergeants, privates, and civilians. Many of these women had been captured during the Azovstal steelworks siege in Mariupol in May.

2022: Alexia Putellas, a Spanish footballer, retained her Women's Ballon d'Or title. She scored 18 goals for Barcelona, who won all 30 league games and the Spanish Cup and Super Cup. Barcelona also reached the Women's Champions League final.

October 18

1326: Isabella of France initiated the Siege of Bristol, capturing the city within eight days. Her husband, King Edward II, escaped to Wales during this time.

1737: Elizabeth Sexton led a riot in Macclesfield, U.K., involving hundreds of women silk button makers. They protested against Mr. Thornley, who was mechanizing the button-making process at his mill.

1775: African-American poet Phillis Wheatley was freed from slavery after gaining fame for her publication of *Poems on Various Subjects, Religious and Moral* in September 1773 in London. Her work brought recognition both in England and the American colonies.

1848: Elizabeth Gaskell published her debut novel, *Mary Barton: A Tale of Manchester Life*, anonymously in London.

1854: The Fifth National Woman's Rights Convention took place in Philadelphia. Ernestine L. Rose served as the president, with Lucretia Mott and Martha Wright as officers. Susan B. Anthony encouraged attendees to petition their state legislatures for law changes.

1911: Chinese feminist, nationalist, and revolutionary Wu Shuqing led a Women's Revolutionary Army into the Battle of Hankou against the forces of the Qing Dynasty, contributing to the dynasty's eventual fall.

1929: The Famous Five, including Emily Murphy, Nellie McClung, Henrietta Muir Edwards, Louise McKinney, and Irene Parlby, successfully fought for women to be legally recognized as "persons" under Canadian law in what is known as the Persons Case, though it did not include women of all races at the time.

1950: Conchita Cintrón, a Chile-born Peruvian *torera* (a female bullfighter), fought her last bullfight in Spain.

1992: Rwandan women's organization *Pro-Femmes Twese Hamwe* was established. It gained international recognition for its role in post-1994 genocide reconstruction. They initiated projects to boost the economy, promote peace, and create opportunities. Founded to combat gender discrimination, it has contributed to Rwanda's global leadership in women's representation. Beyond gender issues, it champions human rights and peace through mediation and reconciliation. *Pro-Femmes* received the 1996 UNESCO-Madanjeet Singh Prize and the 2003 Gruber Prize for Women's Rights.

1997: Liz Heaston became the first woman to play and score in a college football game, kicking two extra points in the Linfield vs. Willamette football game.

2006: Kit Deslauriers became the first person to ski down Mt. Everest, completing the challenge of skiing the Seven Summits, the tallest peaks on each continent.

2019: Christina Koch and Jessica Meir made history by completing the first spacewalk conducted by an all-women team. The spacewalk took over seven hours outside of the International Space Station (I.S.S.) and involved the replacement of a faulty battery unit.

October 19

1469: Ferdinand II of Aragon and Isabella I of Castile married leading to the unification of Aragon and Castile into the country of Spain.

1759: The Royal Brevet acknowledged the invention of the first life-size obstetrical mannequin for practicing mock births by Angélique du Coudray. This dummy, known as The Machine, helped in learning techniques for delivering breech babies and caring for newborns.

1847: Charlotte Brontë released her debut novel "Jane Eyre" in England under the pseudonym Currer Bell, which became a literary classic that explored themes of love, independence, and social class.

1919: Anna Howard Shaw became the first living woman awarded the Distinguished Service Medal.

1920: Sylvia Pankhurst was arrested and charged under Regulation 42 of the Defence of the Realm Act for editing and publishing two articles in the newspaper *The Workers' Dreadnought*, which were deemed attempts to cause sedition in the Navy.

2017: The New Zealand Labour Party formed a coalition government, with Jacinda Ardern becoming the country's leader at age 37, making her the youngest New Zealand leader in 161 years.

2022: The Congress of Tabasco in Mexico voted to legalize same-sex marriage.

October 20

1839: Margaret Fuller, an American journalist, editor, critic, translator, and women's rights advocate, agreed to become an editor of Ralph Waldo Emerson's transcendentalist journal *The Dial*.

1847: Elizabeth Blackwell's application to medical school was accepted, making her the first woman to receive a medical degree in the United States and the first woman on the U.K. Medical Register. Before this, she had been denied admission to 29 medical schools.

1905: The first open three-partitions Conference of Polish Women took place in Kraków, initiated by Maria Turzyma. The participants aimed to influence political parties to include *Emancypantki*'s ("Female Emancipator", Suffragists) demands in their programs. They were also working on cooperation between activists under the three divided regions of Poland (under Russian, Prussian, and Austrian rule) and on various social, cultural, and political issues related to women.

1917: Alice Paul, an American Quaker, suffragist, feminist, and women's rights activist, was jailed, along with other activists, under harsh conditions for their advocacy.

1919: Virginia Woolf's novel *Night and Day* was published by Duckworth Books.

1928: Virginia Woolf read a paper to the women-only Newnham Arts Society at Newnham College at the invitation of Pernel Strachey, the college principal. A few days later, she also spoke at Girton College. Both lectures became the basis for the book *A Room of One's Own*, published the following year.

1943: Irena Sendler, a Polish woman involved in the underground resistance against Nazi occupation, was arrested by Nazi soldiers for her efforts in saving the lives of approximately 2,500 Jewish children by hiding them with non-Jewish families.

2021: Sarah Park, a 14-year-old from Jacksonville, Florida, was named the winner of the 2021 3M Young Scientist Challenge by 3M and Discovery Education. She created an innovative project called Spark Care+, which personalized music therapy treatment for mental health improvement using artificial intelligence (AI), galvanic skin response (GSR), and photoplethysmography (PPG).

2022: Prime Minister Liz Truss announced her resignation, which would take effect once a replacement was appointed.

October 21

1854: Florence Nightingale and a group of thirty-eight nurses were sent to the Crimean War.

1910: Alice Guy, a pioneering female film producer, released her first production titled *The Solax Kid*, which was the beginning of her career in the film industry. She went on to produce over 300 films.

1928: Elinor Smith, an American aviatrix, became the first pilot (and likely the only one) to fly under four East River bridges in New York at the age of 17. She also set a light plane altitude record three months after her first solo flight at 15.

1941: The superheroine Wonder Woman, whose civilian name was Diana Prince, debuted in *All-Star Comics* and later became the star of her own comic book series. She has since become an iconic figure in the world of comics.

1943: Lucie Aubrac, a member of the French Resistance, and her resistance cell successfully freed Raymond Aubrac from Gestapo captivity during World War II.

1945: Women in France were granted the right to vote for the first time in the French Legislative Election.

1969: Zelda D'Aprano, an Australian feminist and women's rights activist chained herself to the Commonwealth Building in Melbourne doors to protest against the failure of the *Equal Pay Case* in the Arbitration Court.

1970: The first women's liberation demonstration took place in Tokyo, Japan, sparking a new wave of the feminist movement in the country. The protest demanded the legalization of the contraceptive pill and opposed any prohibition of abortion. The contraceptive pill was eventually legalized in 1999.

2010: Dakar, Senegal hosted the third African Feminist Forum, drawing over 180 activists from diverse African regions. Lasting four days, the event centered on communities, encompassing discussions on women's citizenship, state accountability, the market, the environment, and activists' roles. Notable sessions included in-depth analyses of countering religious fundamentalism, combatting gender inequality entrenched through culture, and a spirited debate among feminists holding or pursuing political positions. Complementing these discussions were practical workshops covering sustainable energy solutions and the effective use of technology in feminist activism.

2012: Kateri Tekakwitha, also known as Lily of the Mohawks, became the first Native American Catholic saint when Pope Benedict XVI canonized her at Saint Peter's Basilica. She was recognized for her devotion to Christianity and her indigenous heritage.

2021: The Benin National Assembly voted to legalize abortion within the first three months of pregnancy if it was likely to cause distress or harm to the woman or the unborn child's interest, making Benin one of the few African countries to authorize abortions.

2022: Taylor Swift became the first artist to occupy the entire Top 10 of the Billboard Hot 100 chart with songs from her album *Midnights*.

2022: Giorgia Meloni, the leader of the Brothers of Italy political party, was sworn in as the Prime Minister of Italy, becoming the country's first female prime minister.

October 22

612: Sak K'uk' became the Queen of the Maya state of Palenque in modern-day Mexico, succeeding her father, Aj Ne' Yohl Mat.

1692: Madeleine Jarret de Verchères, at the age of 14, led the defense of Fort Verchères against the Iroquois during the French colonization of Canada. The Canadian government designated her as a Person of National Historical Significance.

1824: Kittur Chennamma, an Indian queen of Kittur in present-day Karnataka, led an armed resistance against the British East India Company to maintain control over her dominion. She initially defeated the British forces in the early stages of the revolt.

1884: Letitia Alice Walkington became the first woman to graduate from the Royal University of Ireland.

1947: Ethel Stark became the first woman to conduct at Carnegie Hall, an iconic concert venue in New York City.

1966: The Supremes' album *A' Go-Go* reached No. 1 on the Billboard 200 chart in the United States. It was the first album by an all-female group to achieve this feat.

1972: Feminists in Vancouver, Canada, founded the Service, Office, and Retail Workers Union of Canada (SORWUC). The union aimed to represent workers in marginalized, low-paying, and predominantly female-dominated sectors that were not prioritized by larger business unions.

2007: In response to mob violence and police harassment (*see*: October 14), 35 thousand sex workers staged a mass strike across Bolivia, refusing to undergo mandated medical check-ups. Organized by the Association of Night Workers led by Lily Cortéz, some of the strikers occupied a medical center, others participated in a hunger strike, and some even sewed their lips together to raise awareness, drawing attention from international media outlets. They also threatened to organize a naked march and bury themselves alive. On October 29, the El Alto government agreed to work on legislation that would protect the rights of sex workers.

2012: Members of the Russian feminist punk rock group Pussy Riot, Maria Alyokhina and Nadezhda Tolokonnikova, were exiled to remote prison camps in Perm and Mordovia, locations associated with the Soviet-era gulag system. Their exact whereabouts were unknown even to their lawyers and family members. They had petitioned to be held in Moscow to be closer to their young children.

2019: The Northern Ireland (Executive Formation) Act 2019 came into effect due to the failure of the local government to reconvene on time. As a result, abortion was decriminalized in Northern Ireland, and same-sex marriage was set to commence in February 2020.

2020: The Constitutional Tribunal of Poland declared abortions in cases of fetal defects as unconstitutional, further restricting the country's already stringent abortion laws. This decision allowed terminations only in cases of rape, incest, or when the mother's life was endangered. In response, mass protests known as the Women's Strike or *Strajk Kobiet* erupted across the country. Prominent figures involved in the Women's Strike movement, such as Marta Lempart, Klementyna Suchanow, and Agnieszka Czerederecka, faced legal charges.

2022: Quinn Young, a 10-year-old girl from Inverness, Scotland, became one of the youngest individuals to conquer all 282 Munros, peaks over 3,000 feet (914 meters) in Scotland. She embarked on this challenge alongside her father, Ian, when she was four.

2022: Khadija Abdalla Bajaber won the 2022 Ursula K. Le Guin Prize for Fiction for her novel *The House of Rust*.

October 23

425: Valentinian III, at the age of six, became the emperor (*Augustus*) of the Western Roman Empire. His mother, Galla Placidia, acted as regent and held actual power during his reign.

1619: Empress Nur Jahan, the co-ruler of the Mughal Empire in India, known for her marksmanship, killed a man-eating tiger that was terrorizing locals near the Himalayan mountains.

1675: After the previous ruler, *Sulṭāna* Taj ul-Alam, died without children or close relatives, Sri Para Puteri ascended to the throne of Aceh (modern-day Sumatra, Indonesia) and took the name *Sulṭāna* Nurul Alam Naqiatuddin Syah.

1805: Madame Clicquot, whose husband passed away, took over his champagne business in France and became known as Veuve Clicquot, playing a significant role in expanding and popularizing the brand.

1850: The first National Women's Rights Convention commenced in Worcester, Massachusetts, United States—the convention aimed to secure political, legal, and social equality for women. Prominent women's rights and anti-slavery activists such as Frederick Douglass and Sojourner Truth were among the speakers.

1910: Blanche Stuart Scott became the first American woman pilot to make a public flight.

1913: The inaugural global convention of the Woman's Christian Temperance Union (W.C.T.U.) took place in Brooklyn, New

York, bringing delegates from 50 nations together.

1934: Jeanette Piccard, a female balloonist, set an altitude record by reaching a height of 10.9 miles (17.5 km) during a flight over Lake Erie. She controlled the balloon throughout the entire journey.

1947: Two married couples were jointly awarded Nobel Prizes. Gerty and Carl Cori received the Nobel Prize in Physiology or Medicine for their glycogen and sugar metabolism research. At the same time, Marie and Pierre Curie were awarded the Nobel Prize in Physics for their groundbreaking work on radiation.

1966: Elise Meitner received the Enrico Fermi Award, awarded jointly with Otto Hahn and Fritz Strassmann by the United States Atomic Energy Commission, for their discovery of nuclear fission.

1973: Rabbi Sally J. Priesand became the first woman and rabbi to bless the U.S. Congress.

1995: Christiane Nüsslein-Volhard, Edward B. Lewis, and Eric F. Wieschaus were awarded the Nobel Prize in Physiology or Medicine for their groundbreaking discoveries concerning the genetic control of early embryonic development.

October 24

1375: Margaret I of Denmark became the regent of Denmark following the death of her father, Valdemar IV.

1901: Annie Edson Taylor, a schoolteacher from Michigan, became the first person to go over Niagara Falls in a barrel successfully.

1929: Virginia Woolf's highly influential book, *A Room of One's Own*, was published. The book explores women's role in literature and calls for financial and intellectual independence for women writers.

1956: Reverend Margaret Towner became the first woman ordained minister in the Presbyterian Church.

1975: Icelandic women went on strike in what is known as the Women's Day Off or the Women's Strike, protesting gender inequality and demanding equal rights and representation.

2006: Taylor Swift released her self-titled debut album, *Taylor Swift*, which achieved significant success and spent 157 weeks on the U.S. Billboard 200 chart, making it the most prolonged stay by any release in the U.S. during that decade.

2009: Rosanna Al-Yami, a journalist from Saudi Arabia, received a sentence of sixty lashes and a two-year travel ban for her involvement in a controversial sex program in which a Saudi man discussed his extramarital sex life. The program's broadcast on the Lebanese satellite network L.B.C. caused a scandal in conservative Saudi Arabia when it was later aired.

October 25

1915: Lyda Conley became the first Native American woman to be admitted to practice law before the United States Supreme Court.

1918: Róża Rock became Kraków's Jewish Orphans House director. Thanks to her diligent activism to better the situation of poor orphans, she became known as the "Mother of Jewish Orphans." After her efforts, the building was renovated and modernized. When she died in 1926, her burial became a mass demonstration of gratitude from the residents, and the Orphanage was named after her.

1919: The Medical Women's International Association was founded at an international conference for female doctors in New York City. The association aims to promote women's professional and personal development in medicine.

1920: Lilly Reich, a German early Modern Movement designer of textiles, furniture, interiors, and exhibition spaces, became the first woman on the Deutsche Werkbund (an association of artists, architects, designers, and industrialists established in 1907) Board of Directors.

1967: The Abortion Act 1967 was passed by the British Parliament, legalizing abortions on specific grounds and regulating their provision by registered practitioners. The act also provided funding for abortions through the National Health Service (NHS) in the United Kingdom.

1974: Ruby Myers, also known as Sulochana, won the Dada Saheb Phalke Award, considered Indian cinema's most prestigious lifetime achievement award.

1997: The Million Woman March took place in Philadelphia, U.S.A. It was a protest march organized by Phile Chionesu to address the social and economic issues affecting African-American women.

2007: International Space Station commander Peggy Whitson greeted arriving STS-120 shuttle commander Pam Melroy in orbit, which was the first time two female spacecraft commanders concurrently led space shuttle and space station missions.

2017: Alicia Boler Davis was voted the 2018 Black Engineer of the Year by the Black Engineer of the Year Awards (BEYA) Selection Committee. She was recognized for her contributions as a leader in science, technology, engineering, and math (STEM) and advocacy for underrepresented minorities and women in STEM.

2021: Princess Mako of Akishino, a member of the Japanese imperial family, married commoner Kei Komuro, which resulted in her nullifying her imperial title under Japanese law and adopting the name Mako Komuro.

2022: The Congress of Guerrero in Mexico voted to legalize same-sex marriage, granting marriage equality to same-sex couples in the region.

October 26

1919: The vice squad raided the first birth control clinic opened by Margaret Sanger in New York City. The staff was arrested, and the stock of diaphragms and condoms was seized. At the time, the "Comstock Laws" banned contraceptives and the sharing of information about them.

1929: The Arab Women's Association of Palestine (A.W.A.; also known as the Arab Women's Association), a Palestinian women's organization, was founded by the Arab Women's Executive Committee (A.W.E.) in Jerusalem in the British mandate of Palestine.

1942: Annie G. Fox, the first lieutenant and head nurse in Pearl Harbor, became the first woman awarded the Purple Heart. The Purple Heart is a military decoration awarded to members of the armed forces wounded or killed in action.

1968: Drahşan Arda officiated her first match as FIFA's world's first female football/soccer referee.

1976: The Domestic Violence and Matrimonial Proceedings Act (U.K.) was enacted, allowing married women in the United Kingdom to obtain a court order against their violent husbands without going through divorce or separation proceedings.

2022: Leanne Fan was named America's Top Young Scientist in the 2022 3M Young Scientist Challenge. Her invention, Finsen Headphones, uses machine learning and blue light therapy to detect and treat mid-ear infections, potentially preventing up to 60% of hearing loss in children.

2022: The Congress of Tamaulipas, a Mexican state, approved legislation legalizing same-sex marriage, making Tamaulipas the last Mexican state to do so.

October 27

1893: In Toronto, Canada, 1,500 women founded the National Council of Women of Canada, with Lady Aberdeen elected its first president. The council aimed to unite women in Canada to speak on matters of public interest with a unified voice.

1960: Madalyn Murray O'Hair and her son William gained national attention for their protest against Bible reading in Baltimore public schools. They vowed to take the case to the Supreme Court, and in 1963, the United States Supreme Court ruled in their favor, declaring religious services in public schools unconstitutional.

1967: The Abortion Act of 1967 received royal assent from Queen Elizabeth II, for its enactment on April 27, 1968. This law replaced previous legislation from 1801, allowing for broader grounds for legal abortions in the United Kingdom. It permitted abortions if the mother's life or physical health was at risk if there was a risk of severe handicap in the child, or if there were significant risks to the mental health of the mother or her existing children. The Abortion Act also made abortions accessible through the national healthcare system without cost.

2009: The autonomous Aceh province in Indonesia announced a new law banning women from wearing tight trousers. The law also included provisions authorizing stoning to death for adulterers and whipping for homosexuals, which were scheduled for review.

2019: Sophie Wilmès became Belgium's first female Prime Minister, succeeding Charles Michel.

2020: A sacred yellow box tree, significant to the Djab Wurrung indigenous group of western Victoria, Australia, was cut down to make way for a new highway. During protests at the site, 50 people were arrested for violating social distancing laws.

October 28

1419: Joanna II was crowned the Queen of Sicily and Naples. She was the last of the Capetian House of Anjou.

1775: Harriett Abrams, a professional opera singer, made her début in the opera *May-Day, or The Little Gipsy* at the Theatre Royal, Drury Lane in London. The opera was specially written for her by librettist David Garrick and composer Thomas Arne.

1826: Clara Wieck, who would later become Clara Schumann, one of the most renowned pianists of the Romantic era, officially debuted at the Gewandhaus in Leipzig at the age of nine.

1886: The Statue of Liberty was dedicated in New York Harbor. Women were barred from the ceremony due to concerns about the crowd's roughness. However, a group of suffragists chartered a boat and circled the island, singing and advocating for women's rights.

1912: Léonie de Waha, a Belgian suffragist, played a significant role in co-founding the Union of Women of Wallonia.

1919: The First International Congress of Working Women (I.C.W.W.), organized by the Women's Trade Union League of America, began in Washington, U.S. The congress lasted until November 6 and involved over two hundred women. The I.C.W.W. created a document addressing various labor-related issues and presented it at the International Labor Conference.

1958: Mary Roebling became the first woman director of the American Stock Exchange.

2000: The Battered Immigrant Women Protection Act, introduced by Congresswoman Jan Schakowsky, became law in the United States.

2015: Bidhya Devi Bhandari of the Communist Party of Nepal Unified Marxist-Leninist was voted by Parliament members to become the President of Nepal. Bhandari had been an active campaigner for women's rights in Nepal, advocating for women's representation in parliament and leadership positions.

2020: A nationwide women's strike took place in Poland, with participants rallying under the slogan "I'm not going to work" (Polish: *Nie idę do roboty*). Many workplaces and offices showed solidarity by allowing employees to participate in the protest or dressing in all-black. The strikes were part of a larger movement advocating for pro-choice and women's rights in Poland.

2022: A man broke into the home of Nancy Pelosi, the Democratic House Speaker, in San Francisco and attacked her husband. The perpetrator demanded to see Nancy Pelosi, but she was not home during the incident.

October 29

1919: Women in New Zealand were granted the right to run for election to parliament. Although none were elected, Rosetta Baume, Aileen Cooke, and Ellen Melville were among the first female candidates.

1945: Anna Rosenberg became the first woman to receive the Medal of Freedom, the highest civilian award offered by the United States. During World War II, she served on the New York State War Council, and in 1944, she served as President Roosevelt's representative in Europe. A year later, she became an advisor to President Truman.

1966: The National Organization for Women (NOW) was founded in the United States. NOW is an advocacy group promoting women's rights and gender equality.

2015: Adele's music video for *Hello* surpassed Miley Cyrus's *Wrecking Ball* as the fastest video on Vevo to reach 100 million views. It also received certification as the official Vevo Record holder.

2015: Simone Biles, representing the United States, made history in artistic gymnastics by becoming the first female gymnast to win three successive all-around championships at Glasgow's 2015 World Artistic Gymnastics Championships. Biles is widely regarded as one of the greatest gymnasts of all time.

October 30

1503: Queen Isabella of Spain issued a decree banning violence against Native people in the Americas. This decree aimed to protect indigenous populations from mistreatment and promote humane treatment.

1793: After the overthrow of the monarchy during the French Revolution, the French National Convention assembly decided to create a new constitution that prohibited all "clubs and popular societies of women." Two weeks later, the Paris Commune also barred women from its sessions, limiting their political participation.

1868: Shahjahan Begum became the *Nawab Begum* of Bhopal, ruling over the Islamic principality of Bhopal in central India. However, she was recognized as the ruler of Bhopal in 1844 at the age of six, with her mother acting as regent during her minority.

1875: The Theosophical Society was established in New York by Helena Blavatsky and others. The society aimed to promote the study of comparative religion, philosophy, and science, and it played a significant role in developing spiritual and esoteric movements.

1944: Anne Frank and her sister Margot Frank were deported from Auschwitz to the Bergen-Belsen concentration camp during World War II.

1950: Blanca Canales and other leaders of the Puerto Rican Nationalists staged an armed uprising in the town of Jayuya, Puerto Rico, declaring Puerto Rico a Free Republic. The rebellion was met with military force from the U.S. military and the Puerto Rican National Guard, which suppressed the uprising.

1992: To honor Hattie Mae Cohens and Brian Mock (lesbian and gay man roommates who were killed when a Molotov cocktail was thrown into their apartment) and to "...transform the image of their deaths by learning to eat fire," the first fire-breathing event took place organized by the Lesbian Avengers. It was reported that they said, "The fire will not consume us. We take it and make it our own." The fire-eating events became common during Dyke Marches, organized by the Lesbian Avengers.

2012: Bridget Riley became the first woman artist to receive the Sikkens Prize, a prestigious Dutch art award that recognizes the use of color in visual arts. Riley is known for her abstract paintings that explore optical illusions and geometric patterns.

2017: The U.S. District Court for the District of Columbia blocked President Donald Trump's proposed ban on transgender individuals serving as recruits in the U.S. military. The court ruled that the ban was likely unconstitutional and issued an injunction to prevent its implementation.

2020: The military of Taiwan held its first mass weddings that included same-sex couples since Taiwan became the first Asian nation to legalize same-sex unions in 2019.

October 31

802: Byzantine Empress Irene was dethroned after a five-year reign and was subsequently exiled to the island of Lesbos.

1321: Edward II captured Leeds Castle in England after Margaret de Clare, wife of Bartholomew Badlesmere, refused Queen Isabella's entry in her husband's absence. The conflict resulted in the death of six individuals. Lady Badlesmere was imprisoned in the Tower of London, becoming the first woman held there. She was released on November 3, 1322.

1396: Richard II of England, aged 29, and Isabella of Valois, a six-year-old daughter of Charles VI of France, were married in Calais. This marriage temporarily brought peace between England and France.

1590: Scottish authorities claimed that approximately 200 witches gathered to prevent King James from reaching his future queen in Denmark. The witches were accused of engaging in various acts of sorcery and witchcraft to create a storm and delay James's journey. Dozens were arrested, and many confessed after severe torture.

1919: Louise Pearce and Wade Brown published an article, "Chemotherapy of Trypanosome and Spirochete Infections," in the *Journal of Experimental Medicine*. Their report presented findings from their studies on the causes and treatments of sleeping sickness caused by the parasite trypanosome.

1954: Anna Kéthly became the president of the short-lived revival of the Hungarian Social Democratic Party during the Hungarian Revolution. However, five days later, the Soviet Union invaded Hungary, and Kéthly had to flee.

1968: A group of socialist feminists, including Robin Morgan, Florika, Peggy Dobbins, Judy Duffett, Cynthia Funk, and Naomi Jaffe, former members of the New York Radical Women group, founded the Women's International Terrorist Conspiracy from Hell (W.I.T.C.H.). They opposed the idea of feminist women solely fighting "patriarchy" and instead advocated collaborating with various left-wing causes for broader social change in the United States.

1968: Soong Ching-ling became Head of State and Chairwoman of the People's Republic of China, becoming the world's first female acting co-head of state (Co-Chairperson). She later served as Honorary President for 12 days in 1981.

1984: Indian Prime Minister Indira Gandhi was assassinated by two Sikh security guards in retaliation for the Indian Army's raid on the Golden Temple, a Sikh holy site, earlier that year.

2000: The U.N. Security Council passed Resolution 1325 (S/RES/1325) on women, peace, and security. It recognizes the unique challenges women and girls face in armed conflicts, advocating for a gender perspective in all conflict phases, including their specific needs during conflict, repatriation, resettlement, rehabilitation, reintegration, and post-conflict reconstruction, promoting a fairer, more inclusive world.

2006: The court in Istanbul cleared Muazzez İlmiye Çığ and her publisher from the accusation that she "has insulted the people and provoked hatred and disrespect among people." The case was based on a book in which İlmiye Çığ, a renowned archaeologist and an expert on Sumerian civilization, shared that headscarves were first worn more than 5,000 years ago by Sumerian priestesses during sexual rituals.

2019: Kara Fan, who developed a nanoparticle liquid bandage as an alternative to antibiotics, won the U.S.'s Top Young Scientist title for her innovative invention.

2020: Annastacia Palaszczuk, the incumbent Premier, led the Labor Party to expand its majority in the Queensland state election in Australia. Palaszczuk became the first woman in Australian history to win three elections as Premier.

NOVEMBER

November 01

1112: Eight-year-old Hildegard von Bingen was given to Jutta von Sponheim at the monastery at Disibodenberg, forming the core of a growing community of women associated with the monastery.

1848: The New England Female Medical School, later known as the Boston University School of Medicine (BUSM), opened as the first medical school for women in the United States.

1929: Women in Nigeria organized nonviolent protests, later known as the "Women's War," which ultimately led to the recognition of women's rights.

1939: Dahlov Zorach Ipcar, the first woman and youngest artist, had her first solo exhibition titled Creative Growth at the Museum of Modern Art in New York City. The exhibition showcased her creative work from the age of three to twenty-two.

1944: Army flight nurse Lieutenant Aleda E. Lutz became the first U.S. woman to die in combat during World War II when her plane crashed near Saint-Chamond, Loire, France.

1948: Isabel Morgan published a paper challenging the prevailing scientific consensus that only live viruses could convey immunity to polio. Her work on the killed-virus polio vaccine was crucial to obtaining Jonas Salk's vaccine for general use in 1955.

1959: Miriam Makeba, a South African singer, songwriter, actress, and civil rights activist, made her American debut on *The Steve Allen Show* in Los Angeles. She performed in Xhosa, Zulu, and Yiddish, captivating a television audience of 60 million.

1961: The Women Strike for Peace movement saw 50,000 women marching in 60 cities across the United States to protest against nuclear weapons.

2012: In Pakistan's Azad Kashmir, parents killed their 15-year-old daughter in an "honor killing" by pouring acid on her after they saw her talking to a young man.

2012: Nine female political prisoners, including Iranian human rights lawyer Nasrin Sotoudeh, initiated a hunger strike to protest their conditions at Tehran's Evin prison.

2018: Meaza Ashenafi was appointed the President of the Federal Supreme Court of Ethiopia by the Federal Parliamentary Assembly, where she served until her resignation on January 17, 2023.

2019: Christine Lagarde became the President of the European Central Bank, making her the first woman to hold this position.

2021: Marina del Pilar Ávila Olmeda was sworn in as the Governor of Baja California, becoming the first woman to represent Baja California, Mexico.

2022: Tokyo officially began recognizing same-sex relationships, allowing LGBTQ+ partners to be treated as married couples for certain public services in areas such as housing, medicine, and welfare.

November 02

1867: The women's fashion magazine *Harper's Bazaar* was published for the first time, becoming an influential publication in the fashion industry.

1883: Emma Lazarus wrote *The New Colossus*, a poem that would later be inscribed on the pedestal of the Statue of Liberty in New York City, symbolizing the welcoming of immigrants to the United States.

1920: Women in the United States voted in a presidential election for the first time following the ratification of the 19th Amendment, which granted women the right to vote.

1929: The Ninety-Nines: International Organization of Women Pilots, also known as The 99s, was founded following the United States Women's Air Derby when a small group of female pilots agreed there was a need for an organization to support women in aviation. An invitation was sent to 117 licensed female pilots, and 99 responded by Christmas – hence the name. Amelia Earhart was elected as their first president in 1931.

1933: Eleanor Roosevelt, the First Lady of the United States, presided over the White House Conference on the Emergency Needs of Women, addressing the challenges and issues faced by women during the Great Depression.

1942: Odette Sansom, code-named Lise, an agent for the United Kingdom's Special Operations Executive (SOE), arrived in France to work as a courier in the Spindle network of the SOE during World War II.

1970: Actor and Vietnam War protester Jane Fonda was arrested at Cleveland airport after attending a Vietnam Veterans Against the War (VVAW) event in Canada. She was charged with drug smuggling, but the charges were later dismissed.

1979: Former Black Panther and Black Liberation Army member Assata Shakur escaped from prison in New Jersey with the assistance of three BLA members. In 1984, she was granted political asylum in Cuba.

1994: Princess Alice of Battenberg (Princess Andrew of Greece and Denmark) was posthumously recognized by Yad Vashem as Righteous Among the Nations for her efforts in sheltering Jews in Athens during the Holocaust.

2004: Cecilia Fire Thunder became the first woman elected as President of the Oglala Sioux Tribe of the Pine Ridge Reservation, contributing to the advancement of indigenous women in leadership positions.

2004: Sheikha Lubna al-Qasimi, a member of the Sharjah royal family, was appointed as the United Arab Emirates' first female government minister, breaking barriers for women's participation in government.

2017: Katrín Jakobsdóttir, the leader of Iceland's Left-Green Movement, was mandated to form a government after coalition negotiations with the Social Democratic Alliance, the Progressives, and the Pirates.

2020: News U.K. emerged victorious in the libel case brought by Johnny Depp against them over claims he had assaulted his ex-wife, Amber Heard. The High Court of Justice dismissed Depp's claims.

November 03

1322: Margaret de Clare, the widow of Baron Baldesmere, was released from the Tower of London after being imprisoned for over a year. She subsequently retired to the convent of the Minorite Sisters.

1324: Petronilla de Meath, the maidservant of Dame Alice Kyteler, was charged with being an accomplice in Kyteler's witchcraft accusations in Ireland. Petronilla was tortured, forced to confess, and ultimately burned at the stake - the first known case of death by fire for heresy in Ireland or Great Britain.

1793: Olympe de Gouges, a French playwright, journalist, and proto-feminist, was guillotined. She is known for writing the *Declaration of the Rights of Woman and the Female Citizen* in 1791.

1868: Charlotte Parkhurst, an early California settler and stagecoach driver, became the first woman to vote in a U.S. presidential election. She disguised herself as a man for most of her life.

1912: The Jewish League for Women's Suffrage was founded by Laura and Leonard Franklin in the United Kingdom. It was dedicated to advancing the political and religious rights of women. The league's membership included prominent figures such as Edith Ayrton, Inez Bensusan, Nina Salaman, Hugh Franklin, Alice Model, Romana Goodman, Lily Montagu, and Henrietta Franklin.

1914: Men in Nevada voted in favor of women's suffrage, granting women the right to vote in the state six years before the national suffrage movement succeeded. Anne Henrietta, a suffrage leader, and National Woman's Party president, played a significant role in this victory.

1948: Uemura Shōen became the first woman to receive Japan's prestigious Order of Culture, recognizing her contributions to the arts.

1970: Bella Abzug, a prominent feminist, anti-war advocate, and environmentalist, was elected to the U.S. Congress.

1992: Dianne Feinstein and Barbara Boxer were elected to the U.S. Senate, becoming the first Jewish women senators, the first female senators from California, and the first pair of women representing any state simultaneously.

1998: A museum dedicated to the art of Setsuko Migishi opened at the place of her birth in Ichinomiya City, Japan. Migishi, born in 1905, was a prominent Japanese yōga (Western-style) painter. She used vibrant colors and bold brushwork in her still -life and landscape compositions.

2015: Michelle J. Payne became the first and only female jockey to win the Melbourne Cup, a prestigious horse racing event in Australia.

2015: Sarah Dilys Outen completed a remarkable round-the-world journey using various modes of transportation, including a rowing boat, bicycle, and kayak. Her journey showcased her determination and resilience.

November 04

1429: Joan of Arc, a French military leader and saint, liberated Saint-Pierre-le-Moûtier during the Armagnac–Burgundian Civil War, which played a significant role in the Hundred Years' War.

1913: The East London Federation of Suffragettes (ELFS) held its first paramilitary assembly and gun drill in Victoria Park, London. The ELFS, led by Sylvia Pankhurst, fought for women's rights and working-class emancipation. They later inaugurated the People's Army, a community militia to resist police repression.

1919: Grace Campbell, the first woman to run for office in the state of New York, received 10% of the vote for State Assembly as a candidate of the Socialist Party. Campbell also played a role in founding the African Blood Brotherhood, which later merged with the Communist Party.

1924: Nellie Tayloe Ross became the first elected female governor in the United States when she won a special election in Wyoming.

1924: Cora Reynolds Anderson was inaugurated as the first woman and Native American to serve in the Michigan House of Representatives.

1947: Rosa Lee Ingram, an African-American sharecropper and widowed mother of 12 children, was struck with a gun by her neighbor for talking back to him and refusing his sexual harassment. Her sons came to her rescue, and the man was killed. Ingram and her four teenage sons were found guilty of murder and sentenced to death after a one-day trial with an all-white, all-male jury on January 26, 1948, leading to a national outcry and protests led by Sojourners for Truth and Justice.

1960: Jane Goodall, a renowned primatologist, observed chimpanzees creating tools, signifying the first documented observation of tool use in non-human animals.

1960: Mary Leakey, along with her husband Louis Leakey, discovered the first fragments of the *Homo habilis* jaw (OH 7) at Olduvai Gorge in Tanzania, contributing to our understanding of human evolution.

2011: Jill Evans, a Member of the European Parliament (MEP) from Wales, was fined £575 for refusing to pay the T.V. license fee, protesting against modifications made to the Welsh-language channel S4C.

2012: Fowsiyo Yussuf Haji Aadan became Somalia's first female Foreign Minister when Prime Minister Abdi Farah Shirdon appointed her.

2014: Elise Marie Stefanik, a U.S. Republican politician, became the youngest woman ever elected to Congress at 30.

2014: Mia Love, a Brooklyn-born daughter of Haitian immigrants and a convert to Mormonism, won the House of Representatives election in Utah's 4th congressional district, becoming the first Black female Republican to serve in Congress.

2021: Raffaella Petrini was appointed by Pope Francis as the new secretary general of the Pontifical Commission for Vatican City State, making her the highest-ranking woman in the Roman Curia and the first woman to hold the position.

November 05

1843: Carlota Lucumí, also known as La Negra Carlota, an enslaved African woman of Yoruba origin in Cuba, was among the leaders and organizers of the slave rebellion at the Triunvirato plantation in Matanzas. This rebellion occurred during the Year of the Lash, a period of intense repression against the enslaved people.

1872: Susan B. Anthony, a prominent American suffragist and women's rights activist, voted in the presidential election, challenging the legal restrictions on women's suffrage. She was later arrested, found guilty, and fined $100 for illegal voting. Anthony refused to pay the fine.

1891: Marie Skłodowska, later known as Marie Curie, enrolled as a poor immigrant at the Sorbonne in Paris. In 1906, she delivered her inaugural lecture at the Sorbonne, becoming the first female physics lecturer in the institution's history. Curie's groundbreaking work in radioactivity earned her two Nobel Prizes in physics and chemistry.

1930: Norma Shearer, an American actress, won the Academy Award for Best Actress for her role in the film *The Divorcee*. Shearer's win was notable as the first Academy Award received by a Jewish American woman.

1968: Shirley Chisholm, an American politician and educator, became the first African-American woman elected to the United States House of Representatives, representing the N.Y. District. While in office, she focused on issues of gender and racial equality and worked to expand the food stamp program.

2009: Mass arrests of the Mothers of Laleh Park, also known as the Mourning Mothers, took place in Tehran, Iran. The Mourning Mothers were a group of women who peacefully protested against human rights violations and demanded justice for their children imprisoned or killed during political unrest.

2015: Rona Ambrose assumed leadership of the Conservative Party of Canada following Stephen Harper's tenure as the party's leader.

2017: Shalane Flanagan, an American long-distance runner, became the first American woman since 1977 to win the

New York City Marathon, one of the world's most prestigious marathons.

November 06

1939: *Hedda Hopper's Hollywood* radio show premiered in the United States. Hosted by renowned gossip columnist Hedda Hopper, the show provided insight into the lives of Hollywood celebrities and became popular among listeners. The show continued until 1951, establishing Hopper as a prominent figure within the Hollywood elite.

1940: Agatha Christie's mystery novel *And Then There Were None* was released in book form in the United States. The novel, considered one of Christie's best-known works, tells the story of ten individuals lured to a remote island and mysteriously murdered one by one.

1947: *The Everglades: River of Grass*, a non-fiction book by Marjory Stoneman Douglas, was published. The book highlighted the ecological importance of the Everglades in Florida and advocated for its preservation. Douglas's work played a crucial role in raising awareness about environmental issues and ultimately led to the protection of the Everglades.

2012: Tammy Baldwin, a lesbian politician, became the first openly LGBTQ+ woman, and the first Wisconsin woman elected to the United States Senate.

2013: Lady Gaga's third studio album, *Artpop*, was released. The album showcased a fusion of electronic, dance-pop, and art-pop styles and featured hit singles such as *Applause* and *Do What U Want*.

2018: The United States witnessed a historic moment with a record-breaking 118 women securing congressional seats in the elections, including at least 95 new women joining Congress. Notable milestones were achieved, with Rashida Tlaib and Ilhan Omar becoming the first Muslim congresswomen and Sharice Davids and Deb Haaland becoming the first Native American congresswomen. Alexandria Ocasio-Cortez, a young American politician and activist, also became the youngest woman ever to serve in the United States Congress when she won the election for New York's 14th congressional district.

2018: Cori Bush became the first African -American woman from Missouri to serve in the U.S. House of Representatives.

November 07

656: Aisha, the widow of Muhammad and a prominent figure in Islamic history, led a rebellion against Ali, the fourth caliph of the Rashidun Caliphate, in what is known as the Battle of the Camel. The revolt occurred in Basra, resulting in Aisha's defeat and subsequent exile to Medina.

1376: Virdimura of Catania, a Jewish woman, obtained a royal medical license to practice medicine on the island of Sicily. She was the first woman physician to receive this designation and focused on treating poor and disabled patients, charging them lower fees than her male counterparts.

1893: Women in Colorado in the United States were granted the right to vote, becoming the second state to do so after Wyoming.

1911: Marie Curie was announced as the recipient of the Nobel Prize in Chemistry, making her the first person to receive a second Nobel Prize. She had previously won the Nobel Prize in Physics in 1903 with her husband, Pierre Curie. Curie is one of only two individuals, along with Linus Pauling, to have won Nobel Prizes in different categories.

1916: Jeannette Rankin became the first woman elected to the United States Congress. She represented the state of Montana and played a significant role in the women's suffrage movement.

1942: Rabbi Regina Jonas, the first woman ordained as a rabbi, was arrested by the Nazi Gestapo and deported to the Theresienstadt concentration camp. Despite her internment, she continued her work as a rabbi and helped establish a crisis intervention service to prevent suicide attempts in the camp.

1972: During the Presidential Election, Theodora "Tonie" Nathan, a Libertarian Party nominee for the Vice President, became the first woman to receive an electoral vote when the Republican elector Roger MacBride of Virginia chose to vote for Hospers and Nathan instead of Nixon and Agnew. Nathan was a founding member and former vice chair of the Libertarian Party, as well as a founding member and former President of the Association of Libertarian Feminists.

1978: Indira Gandhi was re-elected to the Indian Parliament. Gandhi served as the Prime Minister of India from 1966 to 1977 and again from 1980 until her assassination in 1984.

1990: Mary Robinson defeated Brian Lenihan in the presidential election and became the first female President of Ireland. She served as President from 1990 to 1997 and focused on human rights and social issues during her tenure.

2016: Regine Yau Wai-ching, a member of the Youngspiration party, was prevented from assuming her position in Hong Kong due to a ban imposed by China, which was the result of the contentious oath-taking controversy, which involved pro-independence activists and led to legal disputes.

November 08

1610: The Basque witch trials concluded after nearly two years. Of approximately 7,000 accused of witchcraft, only six were sentenced to execution by the Spanish Inquisition. Four women named María de Echachute, Graciana Xarra, Maria Baztan de Borda, and Maria de Arburu, along with two men, were burned at the stake in Logroño.

1837: Mary Lyon founded Mount Holyoke Female Seminary, which later became Mount Holyoke College. It was one of the first higher education institutions for women in the United States.

1910: Thanks to the efforts of Emma Smith DeVoe of Tacoma and May Arkwright Hutton of Spokane, Washington state's male electorate ratified Amendment 6 to the state constitution, granting women the right to vote.

1946: Viola Desmond, a Canadian civil and women's rights activist, challenged racial segregation at a cinema in New Glasgow. She refused to leave her seat designated for white patrons and was arrested. Desmond's case became an important symbol in Canada's struggle against racial discrimination.

2016: Hillary Clinton, the first woman ever to receive a major party's nomination for President, was defeated by Donald Trump, who was elected as the 45th President of the United States.

2017: Andrea Jenkins became the first openly transgender person of color elected to public office in the United States. She won a seat on the Minneapolis City Council.

2017: Danica Roem became the first openly transgender candidate elected to a state legislative body. She won a seat in the Virginia House of Delegates.

2022: A federal judge approved an order requiring Brown University to pay over $1 million to cover attorneys' fees and other expenses related to a legal case brought by several student-athletes. They challenged the university's plan to eliminate several women's varsity sports.

2022: In Massachusetts, Maura Healey, a Democrat, defeated Republican Geoff Diehl in the gubernatorial election, becoming the first elected female Governor of Massachusetts. Healey also became the first openly lesbian governor in U.S. history.

November 09

1957: The Pakistani government issued a six-month ban on the women's magazine *Mirror* – a result of the outspoken criticism by Zaib-un-Nissa Hamidullah, its founder, publisher, and editor. Although she was told the ban could be lifted once she apologized, instead, Hamidullah appealed to the Supreme Court of Pakistan – and won.

2005: Aretha Franklin, the renowned singer-songwriter and pianist, received the Presidential Medal of Freedom, the highest civilian award in the United States.

2007: Benazir Bhutto, the former Prime Minister of Pakistan, was put under house arrest shortly before a planned mass rally against the 2007 Pakistani state of emergency. Thousands of supporters of the Pakistan People's Party were also arrested. However, the situation was resolved when Bhutto was released from house arrest, ending the day-long stand-off with security forces.

2011: Taylor Swift won the Entertainer of the Year award at the American Country Music Association Awards, recognizing her contributions to the country music industry.

2014: Jennifer A. Doudna and Emmanuelle Charpentier received the 2015 Breakthrough Prizes in Life Sciences for their pioneering work on CRISPR-Cas9, a revolutionary gene-editing technology with vast implications for biology and medicine.

2017: *The New York Times* published a report detailing sexual misconduct allegations against comedian Louis C.K., as five women came forward with their accounts.

2018: Imelda Marcos, the former Philippine First Lady, and Ilocos Norte Representative, was found guilty of seven counts of graft. She was sentenced to at least six years and one-month imprisonment for each count. The charges were related to transferring funds to private foundations in Switzerland.

2019: Yayoi Kusama's Every Day I Pray For Love art exhibit opened at the David Zwirner Gallery in New York. The show featured the debut of her immersive installation, *Infinity Mirrored Room Dancing Lights That Flew Up To The Universe.*

2021: Julia Hawkins, a 105-year-old woman, set a world record as the first woman and American in her age group to run 100 meters at the Louisiana Senior Olympic Games.

November 10

1236: Razia Sultana, the daughter of Mamluk Sultan Shamsuddin Iltutmish, became the first female Muslim ruler of the Indian subcontinent. She deposed her half-brother, Ruknuddin Firuz, and took over as the *sultan* of the Delhi Sultanate.

1891: The Women's Christian Temperance Union held its first meeting in Boston, United States. The organization aimed to promote temperance, women's suffrage, and social reforms.

1903: Mary Anderson, an American inventor, was awarded a U.S. Patent for the windshield wiper, an automatic car window cleaning device controlled from inside the car. Despite her invention's practical value, she faced challenges selling her patent and did not profit from it.

1961: Estelle Griswold and C. Lee Buxton opened a clinic in New Haven, Connecticut, providing contraception in defiance of a state law prohibiting it. Their arrest and subsequent legal challenge led to the landmark Supreme Court case Griswold v. Connecticut in 1965, in which the court ruled that laws infringing upon marital privacy were unconstitutional.

1963: Maria Goeppert-Mayer, an American theoretical physicist, became the first woman from the United States and the second woman overall to be awarded the Nobel Prize in Physics. She received the award for her discoveries concerning nuclear shell structure.

1975: Patti Smith, an American musician and poet, released her debut album *Horses*, which became a significant part of the New York City punk rock movement and had a lasting impact on music.

1984: In Rugby, England, 1,000 people protested against the local council removing LGBTQ+ people from their equal opportunities policy—the demonstration aimed to advocate for inclusivity and equality.

2004: Canadian writer Alice Munro won the Giller Prize for her short story collection *Runaway*, her second Giller Prize, recognizing her outstanding contributions to Canadian literature.

2005: Ellen Johnson Sirleaf won the Liberian presidential run-off election, becoming Africa's first elected female head of state. She defeated George Weah and assumed the position of the President of Liberia.

November 11

1028: Zoë Porphyrogenita became the Empress of Byzantium by marrying Romanos III. She played a significant role in the Byzantine Empire as a ruler and influenced political affairs.

1572: Sophie Brahe, sister of astronomer Tycho Brahe, assisted him in astronomical observations. Together, they discovered the supernova known as SN 1572, an essential contribution to astronomy.

1865: Mary Edwards Walker, the first female Army surgeon, was awarded the Medal of Honor for her service during the Civil War. She remains the only woman to have ever received this prestigious honor.

1874: The Gamma Phi Beta sorority was founded at Syracuse University - the first women's Greek letter organization to be called a sorority.

1979: The Bethune Museum and Archives opened in Washington, D.C., as a center dedicated to African-American women's history. It pays tribute to Mary McLeod Bethune, an influential civil rights movement and education figure.

1993: The Vietnam Women's Memorial was dedicated in Washington, D.C. The memorial, conceived by former army combat nurse Diane Carlson Evans and sculpted by Glenna Goodacre, honors the 265,000 women who voluntarily served during the Vietnam War.

2011: The Voice of Libyan Women (VLW) organized the International Women's Conference in Libya, known as One Voice – the first in Libya.

2014: Eleven women died, and many others were in critical condition after undergoing sterilization surgery in Bilaspur, Chhattisgarh, as part of India's state-run mass sterilization campaign.

2015: Abby Stein, formerly a member of an ultra-Orthodox Jewish community known as Chasidic, publicly came out as a transgender woman. She became the first openly transgender woman from her community, sharing her journey and raising awareness about transgender issues.

November 12

1598: Louise (Bourgeois) Boursier became the first woman to obtain a diploma and license to practice midwifery legally. She also wrote a book on obstetrics and was appointed as the royal midwife by King Henry IV of France for his wife, Marie de' Medici.

1892: After the early death of Tamaeva IV, Heimataura succeeded as *Arii vahine no Rimatara* (Queen of Rimatara) as Tamaeva

V. She was the last independent monarch in the Austral Islands until she was forced to cede Rimatara to France in a declaration dated to June 6, 1901. The island was incorporated into the territory of French Oceania, today part of the overseas country of French Polynesia.

1912: Ruth Bancroft Law earned a pilot's license and specialized in death-defying stunts performed at night. Although she was rejected as an Army pilot in World War I, she made significant contributions to aviation.

1924: The Women's Electrical Association held its first meeting, advocating for the benefits of electricity in the home. The attendees included influential figures in engineering and women's organizations.

1941: Alma Heflin, the first American female test pilot for standard production aircraft, made her first test flight for the Piper Aircraft Corporation of Lock Haven, Pennsylvania.

1975: The Sex Discrimination Act was passed in the U.K., rendering certain types of sex discrimination and discrimination based on marriage unlawful. It also established a commission to eliminate such discrimination and promote gender equality.

1975: The Employment Protection Act was passed in the U.K., making statutory maternity pay a requirement for employers and protecting against dismissal on the grounds of pregnancy.

1977: The first Reclaim The Night march occurred in several cities in the U.K., including Leeds, York, Bristol, Manchester, Newcastle, Brighton, and London. Inspired by women-only Take Back The Night marches in West Germany, these marches aimed to raise awareness about sexual harassment and violence against women.

1997: Mary McAleese was elected as the eighth President of Ireland, succeeding Mary Robinson, which was the first time in the world that one woman succeeded another as an elected head of state.

2009: Flight Lieutenant Kirsty Moore became the first woman to join the elite Red Arrows, also known as the Royal Air Force Aerobatic Team.

2012: Gayatri Chakravorty Spivak, "a critical theorist and educator speaking for the humanities against intellectual colonialism in relation to the globalized world," became the Kyoto Prize Laureate in Arts and Philosophy. The Inamori Foundation expressed that

> "Professor Spivak has shifted a critical theory of 'deconstruction' into political and social dimensions, and applied a sharp scalpel to intellectual colonialism which is being reproduced in our heavily globalized modern world. She exemplifies what intellectuals today should be, through her theoretical work for the humanities based on comparative literature and her devotion to multifaceted educational activities."

2017: Hundreds of sexual abuse victims and their supporters marched in Hollywood, California, as part of the #MeToo movement, raising awareness about the prevalence of sexual harassment and assault.

2018: Alexandria Ocasio-Cortez, Ilhan Omar, Ayanna Pressley, and Rashida Tlaib, newly elected progressive members of the U.S. House of Representatives, participated in a live-streamed interview during a VoteRunLead event. Ocasio-Cortez called the group "Squad," and they have since become influential figures in U.S. politics.

2021: American singer Britney Spears was released from her 13-year conservatorship following a ruling by Judge Brenda J. Penny of the Los Angeles County Superior Court. The decision came after allegations of abuse and widespread public support for the end of her conservatorship.

November 13

1008: During the Kamo Special Festival, the famous court poet Fujiwara no Kinto gave the poet Murasaki Shikibu her name. It is believed that in that year, she likely started writing The Diary of Lady Murasaki.

1137: After the abdication of her father, Ramiro II, Petronilla became the Queen of Aragon at the age of one, with Ramon Berenger, to whom she was betrothed, de facto ruler.

1553: English Lady Jane Grey (the Nine Days' Queen) and Archbishop Thomas Cranmer were accused of high treason.

1889: Edward Charles Pickering made a presentation to the National Academy of Sciences in Philadelphia, which almost completely ignored the work and discoveries of Antonia Maury, crediting all the authorship to Pickering.

1909: Suffragette Theresa Garnett attacked then-Home Secretary Winston Churchill with a horsewhip in Bristol, protesting for women's rights. She was arrested for assault but was not charged as Churchill did not want to appear in court. However, she was jailed for one month for disturbing the peace and later joined other suffragettes on a hunger strike.

1912: Helen Gardner, a film actor and producer, launched her inaugural film Cleopatra under her production company, The Helen Gardner Picture Players, in Tappan, New York.

1913: British suffragist Emmeline Pankhurst gave her "Freedom or Death" speech in Hartford, Connecticut, advocating for women's rights and declaring their determination to fight for freedom.

1913: Regina Quintanilha received authorization from the President of the Supreme Court of Justice to become the first female lawyer in Portugal despite the law prohibiting women from practicing law.

1931: Hattie Caraway was appointed to the U.S. Senate, becoming the first woman to be elected to the Senate in her own right in 1932 and re-elected in 1938.

1974: A chemical technician and labor rights activist, Karen Silkwood, died under mysterious circumstances. Her death prompted investigations and lawsuits, and it was later depicted in the movie *Silkwood* (1984).

1982: Edna Moga Ramminger became the first female Lutheran pastor in Brazil.

1982: The Vietnam Veterans Memorial, designed by Maya Lin, was dedicated in the United States. Lin, an undergraduate student at the time, won the design competition out of over 1,400 submissions.

2000: Liv Arnesen and Ann Bancroft landed on Antarctica to begin their 94-day expedition to cross the continent's landmass and the Ross Ice Shelf.

2001: Shakira released her fifth studio album, *Laundry Service*, her first English-language album.

2005: Australian conductor Simone Young became the first woman to conduct the prestigious Vienna Philharmonic Orchestra.

2010: Aung San Suu Kyi, a pro-democracy leader in Myanmar, was released from house arrest after facing international pressure for her prolonged detention.

2013: The U.S. state of Hawaii legalized same-sex marriage.

2018: Michelle Obama published her memoir *Becoming*, which became a bestseller, selling 11.5 million copies within a year.

November 14

1643: Empress Meishō abdicated her position, clearing the way for Emperor Go-Kōmyō to ascend the throne of Japan.

1889: Nellie Bly (Elizabeth Cochrane) embarked on her journey around the world to surpass the fictional record set by Phileas Fogg in Jules Verne's *Around the World in Eighty Days*.

1903: The U.S. Women's Trade Union League was established to advocate for the rights and interests of women workers.

1917: The "Night of Terror" began at the Occoquan Workhouse in Virginia, where 33 suffragists imprisoned for picketing the White House were subjected to brutal torture and beatings by guards. The incarcerated women, many National Women's Party members, were fighting for women's voting rights.

1919: Zhao Wuzhen ("Miss Zhao") committed suicide inside her bridal sedan chair on the way to an arranged marriage. This event drew significant attention, prompting discussions within the New Culture Movement about women's liberation and the importance of love in marriage.

1946: Emily Greene Balch, co-founder of the Women's International League for Peace and Freedom, was awarded the Nobel Peace Prize for her peace advocacy and efforts toward disarmament.

1960: Ruby Bridges, an African-American child, became the first to integrate an all-white elementary school in the South when she enrolled at William Frantz School in New Orleans, Louisiana. Ruby was the only student in her classroom throughout the school year, taught by a single teacher.

2012: The death of Savita Halappanavar, a pregnant woman from septicemia, in an Irish hospital sparked international outrage, protests, and condemnation. The hospital had denied multiple requests for an abortion, citing Ireland's strict laws, which led to a debate on women's reproductive rights and healthcare in the country.

2014: Nicola Sturgeon became the Leader of the Scottish National Party, succeeding Alex Salmond. She became the first woman to hold this position in the party's history.

2019: Martha Yujra, a Bolivian politician and trade unionist, became the first indigenous member of the cabinet when she became the Minister of Cultures and Tourism in the Jeanine Áñez government.

November 15

1866: Cathay Williams enlisted in the United States Regular Army under the name "William Cathay," disguising herself as a man due to the prohibition against women serving in the military. She became the first documented Black woman to enlist and the only known woman to serve in the United States Army while posing as a man during the American Indian Wars.

1896: The National Council of Jewish Women held its first national convention, bringing together Jewish women's organizations across the United States to address social, educational, and philanthropic issues.

1913: *The Suffragist*, a weekly newspaper published by the Congressional Union for Woman Suffrage and started by Alice Paul and Rheta Childe Dorr, released its first issue. The newspaper played a significant role in advocating for women's suffrage and highlighting the movement's activities.

1983: The U.S. House of Representatives voted against reintroducing the Equal Rights Amendment (ERA), which had previously failed to be ratified by the required number of states. The ERA aimed to guarantee equal legal rights for all citizens regardless of gender.

2007: Ruth Wisse, a scholar of Yiddish literature and Jewish studies, was awarded the National Humanities Medal for her contributions to the field.

2009: Wu Chengzhen was appointed the principal abbess (*Fang Zhang*) of Wuhan's Changchun Temple, becoming the first woman to hold such a prominent position in Taoist clerical orthodoxy.

2020: Maia Sandu, a pro-European Union candidate, won the presidential election in Moldova, defeating the pro-Russian incumbent Igor Dodon. Sandu's victory marked a historic moment as she became the first female President of Moldova.

2021: The English translation of Olga Tokarczuk's novel *The Books of Jacob* (*Księgi Jakubowe*), considered her *magnum opus*, was published. Olga Tokarczuk was awarded the Nobel Prize in Literature in 2018 for her outstanding literary work.

November 16

1807: After her husband's death, Zheng Yi Sao inherited his informal command over the entire Pirate Confederation, which consisted of six fleets known by the color of their flags. Zheng Yi Sao's husband had commanded the Red Flag Fleet, the largest fleet in the confederation.

1928: Marguerite, also known as Radclyffe Hall, an English writer and poet, was deemed obscene by a British court for her novel *The Well of Loneliness*, a classic work centered around lesbian themes.

1988: Benazir Bhutto was elected as the Prime Minister of Pakistan after the first open election in over a decade. She became the first woman to hold the position in Pakistan.

1994: Bernette Johnson, an American lawyer, was sworn in as the Louisiana Supreme Court associate justice. She became the first African-American woman elected to the court.

2006: Ségolène Royal was nominated as the Socialist Party's candidate for the upcoming presidential election in France. She became the first female candidate from a major party in the country.

2018: Stacey Abrams, the Democratic candidate for Georgia governor, ended her campaign but did not concede the election to Brian Kemp. She planned to file a federal lawsuit against Georgia for alleged election mismanagement.

2022: Charlie Blackwell-Thompson, NASA's first female launch director, supervised her first mission, Artemis I. The mission took off from Kennedy Space Center and was an important step in NASA's Artemis program, aiming to return humans to the Moon.

November 17

1558: Queen Mary I of England passed away, and her half-sister Elizabeth I of England succeeded her.

1915: In Glasgow, thousands of housewives and workers marched on the sheriff's court to support 20,000 rent strikers. The strike eventually led to the implementation of rent controls across the United Kingdom.

1922: Shortly after Ivy Williams, Helena Normanton became the second woman to be called to the bar in England. She scored several achievements, such as obtaining a divorce for her client, leading the prosecution in a murder trial, conducting a trial in America, and appearing at the High Court and the Old Bailey.

1934: Ezlynn Deraniyagala obtained her law degree and was called to the bar, becoming the first female barrister in Sri Lanka. She later served as the long-time All -Ceylon Women's Conference president and the 5th President of the International Alliance of Women from 1958 to 1964.

1938: Mary Morris-Knibb testified on behalf of the Jamaica Progressive League, accusing the Child Welfare Association of discrimination against Black women who sought to participate in social work.

1976: Rosalyn S. Yalow, a Ph.D. in nuclear physics, became the first woman to receive the Albert Lasker Prize for her research. She was later awarded the Nobel Prize as well.

1980: The Women's Pentagon Action protest occurred under the declaration, "We women are gathering because life on the precipice is intolerable."

1982: Fifty sex workers, members of the English Collective of Prostitutes, occupied the Holy Cross Church in King's Cross, London, to protest against police harassment, violence, and racism, demand ending child separation, halt arrests of male relatives as "pimps" (mainly Black individuals), provide housing and support for those leaving the sex trade, and prioritize arrests of rapists and pimps. During the 12-day occupation, more sex workers joined. Camden Council promised to prevent illegal arrests but didn't follow through, spurring feminist sex workers organizing in England.

2010: Esther M. Conwell (Physics), Marye Anne Fox (Chemistry), Helen M. Free (Medicine), and Susan Lee Lindquist (Biological Sciences) received the National Medals of Science from President Obama.

2015: Dolores Huerta received the Order of the Aztec Eagle, the highest honor from the Mexican government to a foreign citizen, in recognition of her dedicated service to the Mexican community in the United States. Her efforts promoted equal pay, workplace dignity, and fair employment practices in Northern California, including Stockton, Salinas, and Delano.

November 18

1313: Queen Constance of Portugal, the mother of King Alfonso XI, passed away. The regency for young Alfonso was divided among his grandmother, Queen Dowager María de Molina, his uncle Peter of Castile, and his great-uncle John of Castile, with Queen María taking charge of educating the young king.

1861: Julia Ward Howe, an American author, poet, and women's rights activist, witnessed the defeat of Union troops by the Confederates, which inspired her to write the *Battle Hymn of the Republic*.

1869: Lucy Stone and others founded the American Woman Suffrage Association, focusing on amending state constitutions to work exclusively for women's suffrage.

1870: The "Edinburgh Seven" or *Septem contra Edinam*, consisting of Mary Anderson, Emily Bovell, Matilda Chaplin, Helen Evans, Sophia Jex-Blake, Edith Pechey, and Isabel Thorne, became the first group of matriculated undergraduate female students at any British university. They faced hostility, including an angry mob throwing mud and insults at them during an anatomy exam at Surgeons' Hall.

1872: Susan B. Anthony and fourteen other women were arrested for voting illegally in the United States presidential election as they advocated for women's suffrage.

1878: Soprano Marie Selika Williams became the first Black artist to perform at the White House. Frederick Douglass introduced her to President Rutherford B. Hayes and First Lady Lucy Webb Hayes.

1910: During the "Black Friday" protest, women advocating for voting rights in the United Kingdom, led by Emmeline Pankhurst, marched to the Palace of Westminster to challenge Parliament's rejection of a reform proposal. The protest turned violent when the women clashed with the London police, increasing support for women's suffrage.

1932: British aviator Amy Johnson completed a flight from England to South Africa in a record time of 4 days, 6 hours, and 55 minutes, surpassing the previous record set by her husband.

1938: The "Cherry Rebellion" occurred in Washington, DC, when 150 women, led by Eleanor "Cissy" Patterson, seized shovels from workers to save trees. They prepared for a stand-off against workers and bulldozers.

1940: Effat Tejaratchi, the first Iranian woman aviator, took her first solo flight, lasting 15 minutes. After World War II, the Iranian Royal Air Force hired her as a flight officer, and she served as the director of the Aero Club until shortly before the Islamic Revolution of 1979.

1977: Bella Abzug convened the National Women's Conference in Houston, the first federally funded conference of its kind.

2003: The Massachusetts Supreme Court ruled that the state's ban on same-sex marriage was unconstitutional, granting marriage rights to same-sex couples.

2004: Maria Victoria Torres became the first person in Chilean history to file for divorce, expressing her desire to recover her dignity and freedom.

2021: Gitanjali Rao was awarded as a Laureate of the Young Activists Summit at UN Geneva.

2022: Angela Álvarez won the Best New Artist award at the Latin Grammys at the age of 95.

2022: Elizabeth Holmes, the founder and CEO of Theranos, was sentenced to more than 11 years in prison on four counts of fraud and misleading investors about her company's technology.

November 19

1321: The trial of Fava, a Jewish surgeon from Paris, daughter of Astrugus, began. She was accused of touching her patient while treating a wound to his testicles. Fava denied the accusations, stating that her son had treated the patient.

1868: In Vineland, New Jersey, 172 women suffragists attempted to vote in the presidential election to test the 14th Amendment of the U.S. Constitution.

1919: Sylvia Beach, an American expatriate, founded the Shakespeare and Company bookstore in Paris, quickly becoming a popular gathering place for the literary community in the 1920s.

1933: Women in Spain won the right to vote during the Second Spanish Republic after the measure was adopted on October 1, 1931. Over seven million women cast their ballots, surpassing the number of men voting.

1966: The Women's Organization of Iran was established with the help of Princess Ashraf Pahlavi. It was a non-profit organization run mainly by volunteers, with local branches and centers for women nationwide, determined to enhance women's rights in Iran. The WOI had committees on health, literacy, education, law, social welfare, handicrafts, international affairs, provincial affairs, membership, and fundraising. Its Women's Centers provided literacy classes, vocational training, family-planning information, and legal advice. By 1975, the International Year of the Woman, the WOI had established 349 branches, 120 women's centers, a training center, and a center for research. It succeeded in making women's rights part of the national agenda but was dismantled with the Islamic Revolution in 1979.

2015: During the 16th Annual Latin Grammy Awards, *Hasta la Raíz*, a song by Mexican recording artist Natalia Lafourcade, won Song of the Year and Record of the Year.

2019: Silveria Jacobs was appointed as the new Prime Minister of Sint Maarten.

2021: While U.S. President Joe Biden underwent medical treatment, U.S. Vice President Kamala Harris briefly assumed presidential power, becoming the first female acting President of the United States.

2022: Salima Mukansanga of Rwanda became the first female African referee to officiate at the FIFA World Cup hosted in Qatar. Yoshimi Yamashita (Japan) and Stephanie Frappart (France) also joined Mukansanga as the first female referees at the men's World Cup.

November 20

1438: Maria Ormani degli Albizzi became a novice at San Gaggio, outside of Florence. She had access to a rich library and received an outstanding education. Maria became a scribe and a manuscript illustrator, with one of her most famous works being a self-portrait in a breviary. The self-portrait was signed and dated 1453, making it the earliest dated self-portrait by a woman artist in Italian Renaissance art.

1871: Victoria Woodhull, an activist for women's rights and labor reforms, delivered a famous "Steinway speech." In her speech, Woodhull advocated for women's sexual freedom and the right to control their own bodies.

1919: Lithuania implemented universal suffrage, granting all citizens over 21 the right to vote, as stated in its 1918 constitution.

1966: Lotte Lenya, an Austrian-American singer, and actress, portrayed the role of Fräulein Schneider in the original Broadway cast of the musical *Cabaret* for the first time. She remained in the cast for most of its three-year run and received a Tony Award nomination for Best Actress in a Musical in 1967.

1970: British feminists protested the objectification of women during the Miss World beauty pageant, using posters with the slogan

> "We're not beautiful, we're not ugly, we're angry!"

1999: Gwendolyn Ann Smith co-founded the Transgender Day of Remembrance, a day dedicated to memorializing people killed due to transphobia. It was created to honor the memory of transgender woman Rita Hester.

2014: Judith P. Klinman was awarded the President's National Medal of Science in Chemistry.

2014: Nicola Sturgeon was elected as Scotland's first female First Minister by the Scottish Parliament.

2017: Charlie Rose, host of *Charlie Rose* and anchor of CBS *This Morning*, was suspended and later fired following allegations of sexual harassment and obscene phone calls, which was part of the "Weinstein effect," a wave of revelations and consequences for individuals involved in sexual misconduct.

November 21

1249: Shajar al-Durr became the regent of Egypt after the death of her first husband (As-Salih Ayyub) during the Seventh Crusade against Egypt.

1922: Rebecca Latimer Felton of Georgia took the oath of office, becoming the first female United States Senator. Although her tenure lasted only one day, she paved the way for future women in the Senate.

1934: Ella Fitzgerald, known as the "Queen of Jazz," debuted at the Apollo Theater in Harlem. Originally planning to dance, she decided to sing after seeing the Edwards Sisters perform. This decision launched her career, and she became a legendary jazz vocalist.

1935: Rebekah Kohut was honored for fifty years of communal activism, recognizing her significant contributions to various social causes and community work.

2014: Edith M. Flanigen received the National Medal of Technology and Innovation from President Obama. She was recognized for her groundbreaking contributions to science.

2015: Anastasia Lin, Miss World Canada, spoke out against human rights abuses in China and was subsequently prevented from competing in the Miss World pageant held in China.

2015: British singer Adele released her highly anticipated album *25*, which became a massive success worldwide.

2020: Anika Chebrolu, a 14-year-old student, won the 3M Young Scientist Challenge for her innovative research on finding a molecule that can selectively bind to the spike protein of the SARS-CoV-2 virus, potentially aiding in the search for a cure for COVID-19.

2022: Olivia Pichardo, a first-year student from Queens, N.Y., became the first woman named to the Division I baseball team roster at Brown University.

2022: Amy Schneider won the *Jeopardy! Tournament of Champions* after achieving 40 consecutive wins during episodes aired earlier that year. Her impressive performance made her a celebrated contestant on the show.

November 22

1909: Clara Lemlich and other International Ladies Garment Workers Union members called for a general strike in New York's shirtwaist industry. Over 20,000 young immigrant women went on strike, demanding better working conditions and fair treatment. This strike became the largest strike by women in American history and played a significant role in the labor movement.

1980: Leeds Women Against Violence Against Women organized a demonstration in protest of police inaction regarding the Yorkshire Ripper murders and the proposed curfew for women. Around 500 protesters marched through Leeds, expressing their discontent and arguing that any curfew should not be imposed on women but on men, emphasizing the importance of addressing violence against women.

1990: Margaret Thatcher, the British Prime Minister, withdrew from the Conservative Party leadership election, indicating the end of her tenure as Prime Minister. Thatcher was a prominent figure in British politics and served as Prime Minister from 1979 to 1990, becoming the first woman to hold the position.

2005: Angela Merkel became Germany's first female Chancellor. She served as the Chancellor of Germany from 2005 to 2021, making her one of the longest-serving leaders in modern German history. Merkel played a crucial role in European and global politics during her tenure.

2007: Taslima Nasreen, a Bangladeshi feminist writer, faced violent protests by Muslims in Kolkata, India, leading to injuries to numerous people. The All-India Minority Forum demanded the revocation of Nasreen's Indian visa and her expulsion from the country due to her controversial remarks about the Prophet Muhammad and the Quran. Nasreen's writings have often sparked controversy and debate on religious and social issues.

2016: Margaret Hamilton, a computer scientist, received the Presidential Medal of Freedom from President Barack Obama. She was honored for her significant contributions to developing onboard flight software for NASA's *Apollo* Moon missions. Hamilton's work was crucial in ensuring the success and safety of the *Apollo* program.

November 23

1890: Princess Wilhelmina of the Netherlands was granted succession rights following her father's passing, King William III. Legislation was enacted to enable Princess Wilhelmina to assume the throne, as King William III did not have a male heir. She became Queen Wilhelmina and reigned as the queen regnant of the Netherlands from 1890 to 1948.

1920: Urani Rumbo, Hashibe Harshova, Naxhije Hoxha, and Xhemile Balili founded *Lidhja e Gruas* (League of Women), an influential feminist organization in Albania. The organization was crucial in promoting women's emancipation and advocating for gender equality in the country.

1936: The first issue of Life magazine was published, featuring a cover photo of the Fort Peck Dam's spillway taken by Margaret Bourke-White. Life magazine became one of the most popular and influential magazines in the United States, known for its photojournalism and coverage of significant events.

1944: The Lotta Svärd Movement, a Finnish women's voluntary auxiliary paramilitary organization, was disbanded under the terms of the armistice treaty during the Continuation War. The organization was established in 1918 and played an essential role in mobilizing women during the Second World War to support the war effort and perform crucial tasks while men were conscripted into the army.

2005: Ellen Johnson Sirleaf was elected as the President of Liberia, becoming the first woman to lead an African country. Sirleaf served as the President from 2006 to 2018 and played a significant role in stabilizing and rebuilding Liberia after years of civil war.

2014: Samantha Cristoforetti and two other astronauts launched from the Baikonur Cosmodrome in Kazakhstan in the Soyuz TMA-15M spacecraft. She spent 199 days at the International Space Station, setting a record for a woman's longest single mission duration.

2016: South Carolina Governor Nikki Haley was appointed by President-elect Donald Trump as the United States Ambassador to the United Nations. She was the ambassador from 2017 to 2018, representing the United States in international diplomacy at the U.N.

November 24

654: Emperor Kōtoku of Japan passed away, and his elder sister, Kōgyoku, ascended to the throne, taking on the name Saimei, and becoming the Empress of Japan.

1429: Joan of Arc, leading French forces, began the siege of La Charité during the Hundred Years' War. However, the siege proved unsuccessful and was abandoned about a month later.

1877: Anna Sewell's novel *Black Beauty* was published. The book, narrated by a horse, became a classic of children's literature and raised awareness about animal welfare.

1928: María Bernaldo de Quirós became the first Spanish woman to earn a pilot license.

1951: Audrey Hepburn, the renowned actress, starred as the lead character in the Broadway play *Gigi*, which opened that day. Hepburn's performance in the play helped further establish her career.

2014: Suzan Shown Harjo, a Cheyenne and Hodulgee Muscogee activist and advocate for Native American rights, received the Presidential Medal of Freedom from President Barack Obama. This prestigious award recognizes individuals who have contributed significantly to the United States.

2015: Vietnam's National Assembly unanimously passed a revised civil code recognizing and permitting gender affirming surgery. The new law was enacted in 2017, providing legal recognition and support for individuals undergoing gender transition in Vietnam.

2015: President Barack Obama awarded the Presidential Medal of Freedom to 17 individuals, including notable figures such as Barbra Streisand, Gloria Estefan, Barbara Mikulski, Katherine Johnson, Bonnie Carroll, and Shirley Chisholm. The Presidential Medal of Freedom is the highest civilian honor in the United States, acknowledging individuals who have made exceptional contributions to society.

November 25

1910: Hélène Dutrieu, a cycling world champion, stunt cyclist, motorcyclist, driver, automobile racer, wartime ambulance driver, and director of a military hospital, got her pilot license as the first woman in Belgium (and 4th globally). She achieved a lot of "firsts" in her flying and acrobatic career.

1913: In four hours, Raymonde de Laroche, a French aviator, flew solo for 325 kilometers (202 miles). Her remarkable feat earned her the 1913 Femina Cup.

1952: Agatha Christie's murder-mystery play *The Mousetrap* opened at the Ambassadors Theatre in London's West End after its premiere in Nottingham, U.K. The play became history's longest continuously-running play, captivating audiences for decades.

1960: The Mirabal Sisters - Patria Mercedes, Minerva, and Antonia María Teresa, were assassinated for their opposition to the US-backed Dominican dictatorship of Rafael Trujillo in the Dominican Republic. The sisters had formed the *Agrupación Política 14 de Junio* (June 14 Movement) to voice their dissent. In 1999, the United Nations designated November 25 as the International Day for the Elimination of Violence against Women in honor of the Mirabal Sisters.

2005: The Maputo Protocol, or the Protocol on Women's Rights in Africa, was enacted. It was adopted by the African Union in Maputo, Mozambique, in 2003. It guarantees extensive rights for women, including political participation, social and political equality with men, reproductive health autonomy, and an end to female genital mutilation.

2016: Researchers led by Jennifer Kan and her team created the first living cells capable of forming silicon-carbon bonds. The protein responsible for this feat performed more efficiently than any synthetic catalyst.

2020: Ingrida Šimonytė assumed office as the new Prime Minister of Lithuania, becoming the second woman to hold this position in the country's history. She appointed a cabinet that achieved gender balance.

November 26

783: Asturian queen Adosinda was placed in the San Juan de Pravia monastery, where she spent the rest of her life to prevent her relatives from reclaiming the throne from Mauregatus.

1748: Maria Gaetana Agnesi, an Italian mathematician, philosopher, theologian, and humanitarian, published *Instituzioni analitiche ad uso della gioventù italiana* (*Analytical Institutions for the Use of Italian Youth*). It was the first mathematics handbook written by a woman and aimed to systematically illustrate the various results and theorems of infinitesimal calculus. Agnesi was also the first woman appointed as a mathematics professor at a university, specifically at the University of Bologna, in 1750.

1894: Princess Alix of Hesse and by Rhine, a German noblewoman, became Alexandra Feodorovna upon her marriage to Tsar Nicholas II of Russia. She served as the last Empress of Russia before the Russian Revolution.

1910: A devastating fire broke out in a Newark, New Jersey building, which housed multiple factories. The fire claimed the lives of 24 women and girls employed by the Wolf Muslin Undergarment Company. This incident brought attention to the inadequate exits and fire hazards in similar buildings, raising concerns about the safety of factory workers.

1913: Phi Sigma Sigma, the first collegiate nonsectarian sorority, was founded at Hunter College in New York City. It was notable for its acceptance of women from diverse religious backgrounds.

1942: The film *Casablanca*, directed by Michael Curtiz and starring Humphrey Bogart and Ingrid Bergman, premiered at the Hollywood Theater in New York. The film went on to win the Academy Award for Best Picture in 1943.

2020: Somali-American model Halima Aden announced her decision to quit runway modeling due to conflicts with her religious beliefs. Aden gained recognition as the first *hijab*-wearing model to walk international runways and be signed by a major agency.

2022: Betssy Chávez was sworn in as the new Prime Minister of Peru following the resignation of Aníbal Torres.

November 27

1542: The Palace Women's Uprising occurred during the Ming dynasty in China. A group of palace women conspired to assassinate the Jiajing Emperor but were unsuccessful. The emperor, known as the "Daoist emperor," practiced divination and alchemy, including consuming a concoction from young virgin girls' menstrual blood. These girls, kept solely for this purpose, endured harsh conditions and were physically abused. The cruel treatment sparked the uprising, and Empress Fang ordered the execution of all palace women involved, including those who informed her of the plot.

1914: The first female police officers went on duty in Grantham, Lincolnshire.

1932: The Second Eastern Women's Congress (also known as Second General Congress of Oriental Women and Second Oriental Women's Congress), an international women's conference, began in Tehran, Iran, and ended December 2. It was arranged with royal support by Iran's leading women's rights organization, *Jam'iyat-e Nesvan-e Vatankhah*, under the leadership of Ashraf Pahlavi, with participants from the Arab World and Eastern Asia. Ashraf Pahlavi served as the honorary President of the Congress, and Sediqeh Dowlatabadi as its secretary. Šayḵ-al-Molk Owrang of Lebanon served as its President, and Fāṭema Saʿīd Merād of Syria, Ḥonayna Ḳūrīya of Egypt, and Mastūra Afšār of Persia belonged to the organization committee. Representatives from Afghanistan, Australia, China, Egypt, Greece, India, Indonesia, Iraq, Japan, Lebanon, Persia, Syria, Tunisia, Turkey, and Zanzibar participated in the Congress, which discussed the situation of women in their respective countries and debated issues were the dire situation of women in the Muslim world, specifically the illiteracy and the oppression within marriage of women.

1968: Penny Ann Early became the first woman to play professional basketball for the Kentucky Colonels in an ABA game against the Los Angeles Stars, making history in the sport.

1972: The album *Free To Be You and Me* was released. It featured non-sexist stories and songs aimed at promoting equality and inclusivity.

1981: Around three hundred migrant women workers, frustrated by the absence of Textile Workers' Union officials during a pay claim meeting, staged a strike at the Kortex textile factory in Brunswick, Australia. They demanded higher wages, removing the bonus system, more breaks, a canteen, restroom access, and an end to mandatory boss's birthday gift contributions. They faced opposition from management, the union, police, and hired thugs. After ten days, they won a substantial pay raise and returned to work.

1990: Women's suffrage was introduced in the last Swiss half-canton of Appenzell

Innerrhoden, granting women the right to vote in this region.

1990: Margaret Thatcher, the first female Prime Minister of the United Kingdom, resigned after serving for 11 years.

1999: Helen Clark became New Zealand's first elected female Prime Minister.

2009: Able Seaman Class 1 Kate Nesbitt was awarded the Military Cross for her bravery in tending to a soldier shot during a gun battle in Afghanistan. She received the medal at Buckingham Palace.

2015: Patricia Scotland, Baroness Scotland of Asthal, was appointed the sixth Secretary-General of the Commonwealth of Nations, becoming the first woman to hold this position in April 2016.

November 28

1881: The first organizational meeting was held for the predecessor group to the American Association of University Women (AAUW), an organization dedicated to advancing equity for women and girls through advocacy, education, and research.

1893: The women's suffrage movement in New Zealand concluded as women were able to vote for the first time in the general election. Activists like Kate Sheppard played a significant role in this achievement, with many women enrolling to vote and casting their ballots.

1919: The International Labour Organization (ILO) Convention established the principles of the first Maternity Protection Convention to ensure working women's well-being during pregnancy and after childbirth. The convention has been modified multiple times and sent for ratification by member states.

1919: Nancy Astor was elected as a Member of the Parliament of the United Kingdom, becoming the first woman to sit in the House of Commons.

1956: Brigitte Bardot gained public attention and became known as a "sex kitten" with the release of the drama film *And God Created Woman*, directed by Roger Vadim.

1967: Jocelyn Bell Burnell, while analyzing observations from a telescope she designed and constructed, discovered an anomaly in a tiny section of recorder paper, which was later identified as the first pulsar (PSR B1919+21, a pulsar with a period of 1.3373 seconds and a pulse width of 0.04 seconds), in the constellation of Vulpecula.

1989: Queen Latifah (Dana Elaine Owens) released her debut album titled *All Hail the Queen*, featuring the hit single "Ladies First."

1992: 4,000 women in London rallied against violence towards women. Because of a ban on using electricity, speakers were forced to scream into a megaphone.

2012: CNN published a list of the top 10 CNN Heroes of 2012, which included Pushpa Basnet, a social worker from Nepal, recognized for her efforts in supporting children living in prisons.

2014: Tuğçe Albayrak, who bravely defended two harassed women, died from injuries sustained during an attack on November 15. German police arrested the suspect.

2017: Jenny Durkan became Seattle's first female mayor since the 1920s and the second openly LGBTQ+ elected mayor in the city's history.

2020: Sarah Fuller, a player from Vanderbilt, became the first female athlete to participate in a Power Five college American football game.

2021: Iceland's Prime Minister Katrín Jakobsdóttir's second cabinet took office after reaching an agreement with the Left-Green Movement, the Independence Party, and the Progressive Party.

November 29

1767: As Queen of Hungary, Archduchess Maria Theresa of Austria issued an edict against the Romani people, commonly referred to as "gypsies." The decree imposed restrictions on their marriages and called for the government to take Romani children away from their families and raise them in white Christian families.

1949: Iriaka Matiu Rātana became the first woman to represent Māori in the New Zealand Parliament when she won the Western Māori electorate for Labour. She held the seat for twenty years until she retired.

1964: During the Simba rebellion in Congo, a group of rebels abducted 46 nuns from the Sisters of the Holy Family, a Roman Catholic convent in the village of Bafwabaka. Marie-Clémentine Anuarite Nengapeta, who oversaw the convent, was killed two days later. She was later beatified in 1985.

2016: The Israeli political party *Shas*, which primarily represents the Mizrahi ultra-Orthodox community, proposed a bill to restrict the mixed prayer area at the Western Wall. The bill aimed to place the site under the jurisdiction of the Chief Rabbinate and impose fines on those who engaged in certain prayer practices, such as male-female prayer or women wrapping themselves in the traditional *tallit* or laying *tefillin*.

2019: The government of Sudan repealed all laws that previously restricted women's freedom in terms of dress, movement, association, work, and study. Additionally, the former ruling party was dissolved. Sudanese Prime Minister Abdalla Hamdok publicly praised women on social media, condemning these laws as instruments of exploitation, humiliation, and violations of citizens' rights.

2020: President-elect Joe Biden and Vice President-elect Kamala Harris announced the first all-female Communications team for the White House.

2021: Magdalena Andersson was elected as the Prime Minister of Sweden by the *Riksdag*, the national Parliament of Sweden.

November 30

1882: Eagle Woman That All Look At (Lakota: Waŋblí Ayútepiwiŋ, also known as Matilda Picotte Galpin) signed a treaty jointly with the chiefs and headmen of the Sioux, becoming the first woman to sign a treaty with the U.S. government.

1913: The annual National American Woman Suffrage Association convention was held in Washington, D.C. Notable speakers at the convention included Anna Howard Shaw, Jane Addams, Helen Ring Robinson, Margaret Hinchey, and Rose Winslow.

1950: After the death of her husband, Rabbi William Ackerman, Paula Ackerman took over the leadership of the Temple Beth Israel in Meridian, Mississippi. Even though she was not ordained as a rabbi, she served as a de facto one until a new rabbi was picked in 1953.

1950: Luisa Moreno, a Guatemalan social activist and participant in the United States labor movement, was forced to leave the U.S. after the Immigration and Naturalization Service (I.N.S) conducted Operation Wetback to deport Mexicans and Mexican Americans forcibly. The operation targeted labor leaders in particular. Moreno's activism in the Congress of Industrial Organizations (C.I.O), organizing and unionizing workers and past membership in the Communist Party (in 1935) labeled her as a "dangerous alien." She was offered American citizenship for testifying against the union leader Harry Bridges. She refused, stating she didn't want to be "a free woman with a mortgaged soul." Together with her husband, she settled in Guatemala.

1976: The Anglican Church ordained its first six women priests.

2017: American producer Russell Simmons announced his resignation from his companies following a sexual assault allegation made by screenwriter Jenny Lumet against him. This announcement came as part of the broader "Weinstein effect," which shed light on sexual misconduct in the entertainment industry.

2020: President-elect Joe Biden announced the nomination of Janet Yellen for the position of U.S. Treasury Secretary. If confirmed, Yellen would become the first woman to hold this position in the history of the United States.

2021: Josephine Baker, an American-born entertainer, became the first American-born, first Black woman, and first entertainer to be honored at Paris' Panthéon, France's highest honor.

2021: Dame Sandra Mason was inaugurated as the first president of Barbados as the country transitioned from a constitutional monarchy to a republic within the Commonwealth of Nations.

DECEMBER

December 01

1767: Ahilya Bai Holkar became the Queen of the Maratha Empire in early-modern India after the death of her male relatives. She was well educated and trained in military affairs by Malhar Rao Holkar, and she established Maheshwar (in Madhya Pradesh) as the seat of the Holkar Dynasty.

1844: The first article by Margaret Fuller, a review of a collection of essays by Emerson, appeared in Horace Greeley's *New-York Tribune*, becoming the first full-time book reviewer in American journalism. In addition to reviewing American literature, she explored foreign works, covering concerts, lectures, and art exhibitions during her four-year tenure at the publication. She authored over 250 columns, many marked with an "*," where she discussed diverse topics, from art and literature to critical social issues like enslavement and women's rights.

1917: Annie Besant assumed the presidency of the Indian National Congress, a significant political organization in India's struggle for independence from British rule. She played an essential role in the Indian nationalist movement.

1919: Nancy Astor became the first woman to take her seat in the United Kingdom's House of Commons. She was elected as a Member of Parliament on November 28, following Constance Markievicz, the first woman elected to Parliament in 1918.

1922: Monica Cobb became the first female solicitor in the United Kingdom to address a court. She spoke at the Birmingham Assizes, where she prosecuted a man for bigamy. Cobb was admitted to the practice of law on November 17.

1924: The silent drama film *Romola*, featuring Lillian Gish, debuted at George M. Cohan's Theatre in New York City. The film was a meaningful achievement in Gish's career as a prominent actress during the silent film era.

1933: New law forced all German children older than ten to join one of the Nazi youth organizations. All girls had to join the Young Girl's League (*Jungmädelbund*, JM) or, if older than fourteen, the League of German Girls (*Bund Deutscher Mädel*, BDM). In 1938, a third section was added, Faith and Beauty (*Glaube und Schönheit*), which was voluntary and open to girls between 17 and 21 and intended to groom them for marriage, domestic life, and future career goals. The League used campfires, camps, folklore, and sports to indoctrinate girls into Nazi beliefs and prepare them for domestic roles.

1952: Christine Jorgensen was outed without her knowledge when *The New York Daily News* ran a front-page story, "Ex-GI Becomes Blonde Beauty," announcing (incorrectly) that Jorgensen had become the recipient of the first "sex change."

1955: Rosa Parks, an African-American civil rights activist, refused to give up her seat on a bus to a white person in Montgomery, Alabama. Her arrest sparked the

Montgomery bus boycott, a prominent civil rights protest that played a pivotal role in the modern civil rights movement in the United States.

1988: Israeli and Jewish-American women joined together in an attempt to pray as a group, including reading from the Torah scroll, at the Western Wall in Jerusalem. This event marked a significant moment in the ongoing struggle for gender equality and religious rights in Israel.

2012: Anastasiya Petryk from Ukraine won the Junior Eurovision Song Contest 2012 with her song *Nebo*, earning 138 points.

2019: Ursula von der Leyen assumed the office of the President of the European Commission, the executive branch of the European Union, as the first woman ever.

2019: Arsenal Women's football team broke the record for the most goals scored in an F.A. Women's Super League match, defeating Bristol City Women with a score of 11-1. Vivianne Miedema played a significant role in ten of Arsenal's eleven goals.

December 02

1948: Sister Rosetta Tharpe, a pioneering African-American singer, songwriter, and guitarist, recorded *Down by the Riverside*. This influential recording was selected for the National Recording Registry of the U.S. Library of Congress in 2004. The Registry recognized Tharpe's spirited guitar playing, unique vocal style, and significant influence on early rhythm-and-blues performers and her impact on gospel, jazz, and rock artists.

1969: Marie Van Brittan Brown, an African-American nurse from New York, was granted a patent for her innovative closed-circuit home security system. Her invention allowed homeowners to monitor visitors via a camera and view their images on a television monitor, contributing to the development of modern home security systems.

1988: Benazir Bhutto, a Pakistani politician and daughter of former Prime Minister Zulfikar Ali Bhutto, was sworn in as Prime Minister of Pakistan. She became the first woman to head the government of a Muslim-majority state.

2011: United States Secretary of State Hillary Clinton met with Aung San Suu Kyi, Burma's prominent pro-democracy activist. Their meeting aimed to promote democratic reforms and strengthen the relationship between the United States and Burma (now known as Myanmar).

2012: Anna Ushenina, a Ukrainian chess player, won the Women's World Chess Championship in 2012. The championship occurred in Khanty-Mansiysk, Russia, and Ushenina emerged victorious after defeating Antoaneta Stefanova from Bulgaria in rapid tie-breaks.

2013: French artist Laure Prouvost was awarded the prestigious Turner Prize in 2013. She won the prize for her video installation featuring a mock tea party, showcasing her innovative and thought-provoking artistic approach.

2020: Hong Kong activist Agnes Chow, along with two other activists, Ivan Lam and Joshua Wong, was sentenced to prison for their involvement in an "illegal assembly." Chow received a 10-month sentence, while Lam and Wong received seven months and 13 and a half months, respectively. These sentences reflected the challenging political environment in Hong Kong at the time and drew international attention to the ongoing pro-democracy movement in the region.

December 03

1326: Queen Isabella and Crown Prince Edward, acting on behalf of King Edward II, issued a writ to delay the opening of the English Parliament. This delay allowed the subsequent Parliament to approve the replacement of King Edward II by the Crown Prince, who assumed the title of "Keeper of the Realm." This event marked a significant political shift in England.

1910: Freda Du Faur, an Australian mountaineer, became the first woman to successfully summit Aoraki/Mount Cook, the highest peak in New Zealand. Her achievement broke gender barriers in mountaineering and inspired future generations of female climbers.

1926: Acclaimed detective novelist Agatha Christie mysteriously disappeared for eleven days, leading to a widespread search and media attention. Her disappearance remains the subject of intrigue and speculation to this day.

1962: Edith Spurlock Sampson was sworn in as the first Black female judge to be elected in Illinois.

1990: Mary Therese Winifred Robinson became the first woman to hold the office of President of Ireland.

2003: St Hilda's College, the last remaining all-female college at Oxford University, voted to remain single-sex. This decision ensured the preservation of a unique educational environment for women at the prestigious institution.

2003: During the Annual Meeting of the Radiological Society of North America (RSNA), researchers announced study results suggesting a connection between anorexia nervosa, a disorder primarily affecting young women, and emphysema. The study found that malnutrition associated with anorexia nervosa can lead to changes in the physical structure of the lungs, potentially contributing to the development of emphysema.

2012: Elizabeth Price, a British artist, was awarded the Turner Prize in 2012 for her video installation titled *The Woolworths Choir of 1979*. The artwork explored themes of consumerism, culture, and memory.

2020: Gitanjali Rao, at the age of 15, was named *TIME* magazine's first-ever "Kid of the Year" for her remarkable achievements in various fields, including science, technology, and social activism.

December 04

1829: Lord Bentinck, the Governor of India, promulgated Regulation XVII, officially deeming *Sati*—an ancient tradition in which widows immolate themselves upon their deceased husband's funeral pyre—illegal and subject to prosecution in criminal courts. The law was extended to Madras and Bombay in February 1830.

1913: The term "isotope" gained widespread usage when Frederick Soddy, a prominent figure in radiochemistry, published an article in *Nature*. The term was suggested to him by Margaret Todd, an Edinburgh physician and friend of Soddy. Isotopes refer to variations of a chemical element with the same number of protons but a different number of neutrons.

1938: Tehilla Lichtenstein gave her first sermon as the new Society of Jewish Science leader, titled *Harnessing Thought's Potential*. Jewish Science, developed by Rabbi Alfred Geiger Moses in the early 1900s, interprets Jewish philosophy in response to Christian Science and the New Thought Movement.

1942: Zofia Kossak-Szczucka and Wanda Filipowicz, Polish-Catholic activists, founded *Żegota*, the Polish Council to Aid Jews, with the Government Delegation for Poland. This underground Polish resistance organization played a crucial role in providing assistance and saving the lives of thousands of Polish Jews during World War II.

1961: The contraceptive pill was introduced, revolutionizing reproductive healthcare. The medication, which suppressed women's fertility using hormones such as progestogen or estrogen (or a combination), initially became available to married women only. However, its availability was extended to unmarried women in 1967, empowering women with greater control over their reproductive choices.

1966: A professional golfer, Kathy Whitworth, had a remarkable year on the LPGA Tour. She won nine tournaments and earned the prestigious Player of the Year title. Whitworth's exceptional performance led to her being voted female athlete of the year by 428 sportswriters and broadcasters.

1978: Following the tragic murder of Mayor George Moscone, Dianne Feinstein became San Francisco's first female mayor.

December 05

1718: Ulrika Eleonora, sister of Charles XII, declared herself the reigning Queen of Sweden following her brother's passing on November 30. After agreeing to sign a new Swedish constitution, the *Riksdag* of the Estates recognized her claim to the Swedish throne, officially making her the queen regnant of Sweden.

1858: Falakika Seilala became the *Lavelua* (monarch) of Uvea (on Wallis Island, Oceania) and ruled until February 19, 1869.

1898: During a General Meeting of the Royal Institute of British Architects, a discussion and voting took place to decide whether Ethel Mary Charles could be admitted as an associate member. Finally, her candidacy was agreed upon by 51 persons voting for and 16 against. The full membership was not obtained by a woman until 1938.

1900: Yoshioka Yayoi, a Japanese physician, educator, and women's rights activist founded the Tokyo Women's Medical University as the first medical school for women in Japan.

1906: The Woman's Hospital opened at a new location on 110th Street and Amsterdam Avenue in New York City. Four years later, a maternity service was established at the hospital, providing essential healthcare services for women.

1921: The English Football Association implemented a ban on women playing on association football (soccer) pitches. This decision effectively excluded women from the sport and relegated them to playing in backyards and public parks.

1935: Mary McLeod Bethune established the National Council of Negro Women, an organization dedicated to advocating for the rights and empowerment of African American women.

1941: Sister Elizabeth Kenny's innovative treatment for infantile polio-related paralysis was approved. Her principles of muscle rehabilitation became the foundation of modern physical therapy.

2016: HBO aired the documentary *The Trans List*, narrated by Janet Mock, in which eleven transgender people shared their stories. Caroline Cossey, Laverne Cox, Miss Major Griffin-Gracy, Caitlyn Jenner, Alok Vaid-Menon, and Bamby Salcedo were among them.

2017: A previously unpublished novel titled *The Saint's Second Front*, written by Leslie Charteris in the summer of 1941, resurfaced at a private auction. The book described a fictional military attack by Japan on America but was rejected for political reasons at the time and was believed to be lost.

2017: Austria's Constitutional Court ruled that the government could not discriminate against the right of same-sex couples to marry.

December 06

1741: Elizabeth of Russia became *Tsarina* following a palace coup that removed Empress Anna Leopoldovna from power. Elizabeth's reign would be marked by significant cultural and territorial expansion.

1774: Archduchess Maria Theresa, the ruler of Austria, Hungary, and Croatia, signed the General School Ordinance, which mandated education for male and female students and introduced compulsory education for children between the ages of six and twelve.

1849: Harriet Tubman, an African-American abolitionist and political activist, successfully escaped slavery in Maryland for the second and final time. Tubman would become a prominent figure in the Underground Railroad and a leader in the fight against slavery.

1894: Kate Chopin's feminist short story *The Story of an Hour* was published in the American magazine *Vogue*. It explores themes of female independence and autonomy within the constraints of marriage, making it a significant work in the early feminist movement.

1954: The French existentialist philosopher and writer Simone de Beauvoir received the prestigious *Prix Goncourt* prize in French literature. De Beauvoir is known for her influential feminist works, including *The Second Sex*, which examined the status of women in society.

1989: Marc Lépine, an anti-feminist and misogynist gunman, carried out the *École Polytechnique* massacre in Montreal, Canada. Lépine targeted and murdered fourteen young women at the École Polytechnique.

2010: A meeting took place at Temple Reyim in Newton, M.A., where Sara Hurwitz, along with other female rabbis, met to discuss their experiences as women in the rabbinate. This gathering included Amy Eilberg, the first Conservative female rabbi; Sally Priesand, the first Reform female rabbi; and Sandy Eisenberg Sasso, the first Reconstructionist female rabbi.

2017: *TIME* magazine named the "Silence Breakers," including those involved in the #MeToo movement, the 2017 TIME Person of the Year.

2018: Gladys West, an 87-year-old mathematician, received the Air Force Space and Missile Pioneers Award for contributing to the Air Force's space program. West was among the pioneering Hidden Figures, a group of African-American women mathematicians who played a crucial role in early space exploration.

2021: Aung San Suu Kyi, former leader of Myanmar, was sentenced to four years (later reduced to two) for charges of "inciting public unrest" and "breaching Covid-19 protocols."

December 07

1941: First Lt. Annie G. Fox, head nurse at Hickam Field Air Force Base in Honolulu, displayed bravery and leadership during the bombing of Pearl Harbor. She became the first woman to receive the Purple Heart for her actions during the attack.

1944: The Egyptian Feminist Union hosted the Arab Women's Congress of 1944 in Cairo, leading to the formation of the Arab Feminist Union. This event brought together women from different Arab countries to discuss women's rights.

1955: 350 people met in Hotel Theresa in Harlem, N.Y., to see off the Communist, feminist, and Black nationalist activist Claudia Jones, originally from Trinidad and Tobago, after she was imprisoned multiple times for "un-American activities" (due to the political persecution of Communists in the U.S.) and then finally deported from the U.S.A. She was granted residency in the United Kingdom on humanitarian grounds.

1956: Larisa Semyonovna Latynina, a Soviet gymnast, made her Olympic debut at the Melbourne Olympic Games. She won the gold medal in the all-around event and became the most decorated Olympic athlete in history, regardless of gender.

1972: Imelda Marcos, the First Lady of the Philippines, was stabbed and wounded by an assailant. The incident occurred during an assassination attempt on her husband, President Ferdinand Marcos.

1996: Wisława Szymborska, a Polish poet, was awarded the Nobel Prize in Literature "for her lyrical poetry that reflects a keen sense of irony and explores philosophical themes."

2006: 3,000 women at the Misr Spinning and Weaving complex in El-Mahalla El-Kubra, Egypt, protested unpaid bonuses, calling men to join them. Thousands gathered in solidarity nearby. Seventy workers occupied the factory, resisting eviction by riot police for four days. The government eventually conceded, agreeing to pay the bonus and protect the plant from privatization, sparking a nationwide strike wave.

2013: *The Tragedy of Mariam, the Fair Queen of Jewry* was performed on Shakespeare's Globe stage and directed by Rebecca McCutcheon, designed by Talulah Mason, playing Nicola Sangster, Kate Russell-Smith, Sarah Vevers, and Kate Russell-Smith. The play's author was Elizabeth Cary, Viscountess Falkland, an English poet, dramatist, translator, and historian, considered the first woman to have written and published an original play in English, in 1613.

2014: Alia Atkinson, a Jamaican swimmer, won Jamaica's first-ever gold medal at the World Short Course Championships, becoming the first Black woman to win a world swimming title.

2018: Annegret Kramp-Karrenbauer was elected as the new leader of Germany's Christian Democratic Union party, succeeding Angela Merkel. Kramp-Karrenbauer's election marked a transition of leadership within the party.

2019: Aung San Suu Kyi, the former leader of Myanmar, traveled to The Hague to face charges of genocide against her government for the atrocities committed against the Rohingya Muslim minority.

2021: Chile became the 31st nation to legalize same-sex marriage, granting equal marriage rights to same-sex couples.

December 08

1644: Christina of Sweden assumed the position of ruling queen upon reaching the age of maturity. She became one of Sweden's most notable monarchs, known for her intellectual pursuits and unorthodox behavior.

1660: Margaret Hughes or Anne Marshall, depending on historical accounts, became the first woman to appear on an English public stage, playing the role of Desdemona in a production of William Shakespeare's play *Othello*.

1881: Gabriela Zapolska debuted with *Jeden dzień z życia róży* (*One Day in the Life of a Rose*) novella, which was published in the *Gazeta Krakowska* magazine. Zapolska was a versatile Polish talent, excelling as a novelist, playwright, naturalist writer, feuilletonist, theatre critic, and stage actress. She created an extensive body of work, including 41 plays, 23 novels, 177 short stories, 252 pieces of journalism, a screenplay, and an impressive collection of over 1,500 letters. *The Morality of Mrs. Dulska*, a 'petty -bourgeois tragic-farce,' is regarded as a landmark of early modernist Polish drama.

1930: Agatha Christie's first play, *Black Coffee*, premiered at the Embassy Theatre in London. Christie, known for her detective novels, contributed significantly to the theater world.

1931: Hattie Caraway of Arkansas became a United States senator, succeeding her late husband, Thaddeus Caraway. She was the second woman to serve in the U.S. Senate but the first woman elected to that position.

1972: Tini "Whetu" Marama Tirikatene-Sullivan became New Zealand's first Māori woman cabinet minister.

1977: Rosalyn S. Yalow became the first American-born woman to receive the Nobel Prize in Physiology or Medicine. She was recognized for her work in developing radioimmunoassay, a technique for measuring tiny quantities of substances in the body.

2000: Tokyo Women's War Crimes Tribunal was held (until December 12). It was a private People's Tribunal organized by women's rights organizations and advocates from Japan, China, Indonesia, the Philippines, Taiwan, East Timor, Malaysia, and North and South Korea to make the tribunal a reality. During the proceedings, victims of the comfort system employed by the Japanese military in the 1930s and 1940s testified, as did lawyers and experts representing former comfort women from across East Asia and the Netherlands. For the first time, this tribunal named Emperor Hirohito as one of the defendants, accusing him of being complicit in the crimes committed against comfort women. Though invited, the Japanese government refused to send representatives for either the government or the emperor to the proceedings. Documents that implicated the Japanese government and emperor in the atrocities committed throughout the Japanese Empire against these women were presented - kidnapping, rape, sexual abuse, assault, and even murder ranked in the indictments. The judges presiding over the tribunal found that the Japanese government and Emperor Hirohito were guilty of crimes against humanity in the form of the military policy that was the comfort system; later, a more complete ruling was issued in 2001, which cemented the preliminary ruling.

2010: Marisela Escobedo Ortiz began a sit-in protest in front of the Government Palace of Chihuahua in Mexico to demand justice for the victims of femicide. She started her fight after her 16-year-old daughter, Rubí Marisol Frayre, was murdered.

2019: Sanna Mirella Marin was chosen to become the Prime Minister of Finland, making her the youngest person to hold that office in Finnish history at 34.

2019: The Ministry of Municipal and Rural Affairs of Saudi Arabia announced that gender-segregated restaurant entrances would be optional. However, this change was optional, and there have been no indications of similar adjustments in other public establishments.

2022: U.S. basketball player Brittney Griner was released in a prisoner swap with Russia involving arms dealer Viktor Bout.

2022: The U.S. House of Representatives passed the Respect for Marriage Act in a 258–169–1 vote. The act aims to enshrine same-sex and interracial marriage into federal law, providing legal recognition and protections at the national level.

December 09

1907: Emily Bissell, an American author, social worker, and activist, designed and printed the first Christmas seal as a fundraising tool for tuberculosis research. She introduced Christmas Seals to the United States, which have since become a popular way to raise funds for various charitable causes.

1931: Hattie Wyatt Caraway was appointed to the vacant senatorial seat in Arkansas by the state's governor following the death of her husband. She later became the first woman elected to serve a full term as a United States Senator, holding the position until 1945.

2002: Michele Norris, an award-winning journalist, became the first African American female regular co-host of National Public Radio's news magazine, *All Things Considered*.

2009: Elinor Ostrom, an American political economist, became the first woman to receive the Nobel Memorial Prize in Economic Sciences. She was recognized for her analysis of economic governance, particularly her work on how communities manage shared resources.

2015: Angela Merkel, the Chancellor of Germany, was named *TIME* magazine's Person of the Year for her leadership and influence on the European and global stage.

2017: The Marriage Amendment Bill received royal assent in Australia, officially legalizing same-sex marriage. Australia became the 26th nation to recognize same-sex marriage.

2022: Eva Kaili, a Greek Member of the European Parliament (MEP) and European Parliament vice-president, was arrested by the Belgian Federal Police. The arrest was made as part of an investigation into corruption linked to lobbying efforts supporting Qatar.

December 10

1869: Wyoming became the first U.S. territory to grant women the right to vote.

1870: Ellen Swallow Richards became the first woman admitted to the Massachusetts Institute of Technology (MIT). She paved the way for women in science and engineering and had a successful career as a pioneering scientist in sanitary engineering and domestic science.

1899: The National Jewish Hospital for Consumptives in Denver opened, thanks to the efforts of Frances Wisebart Jacobs. It was the first hospital in the world to exclusively treat destitute tuberculosis patients from anywhere in the country.

1902: Women in Tasmania, Australia, won the right to vote, making it the first state in Australia to grant women suffrage.

1905: Bertha von Suttner, an Austrian writer and pacifist, became the first woman to receive the Nobel Peace Prize for promoting peace and disarmament.

1909: Selma Lagerlöf, a Swedish author, became the first female writer to win the Nobel Prize in Literature for her outstanding contributions to Swedish literature.

1927: Grazia Deledda, an Italian author, was awarded the Nobel Prize in Literature for her poignant depictions of life in Sardinia.

1928: Nobel Prize in Literature was awarded to the Danish-born Norwegian novelist Sigrid Undset "principally for her powerful descriptions of Northern life during the Middle Ages."

1938: Pearl S. Buck, an American writer, received the Nobel Prize in Literature for her novel *The Good Earth*, which portrayed the struggles of Chinese peasants.

1945: Nobel Prize in Literature was awarded to Gabriela Mistral (Lucila Godoy Alcayaga)

> "for her lyric poetry, which inspired by powerful emotions, has made her name a symbol of the idealistic aspirations of the entire Latin American world."

1947: Gerty Cori, an American biochemist, became the first Jewish woman and American woman to win a Nobel Prize in the sciences. She received the Nobel Prize in Physiology or Medicine for her groundbreaking work on the metabolism of carbohydrates.

1968: Maria Telkes, a Hungarian-American scientist, patented a collapsible solar still with a water vapor permeable membrane, contributing to her extensive research on solar energy and solar-powered systems.

1992: Pung Chhiv Kek formed the rights group Cambodian League for the Promotion and Defence of Human Rights (LICADHO) to monitor the Khmer Rouge after a peace agreement. After graduating from medical school in France, Kek Galabru became the first Cambodian woman to qualify as a doctor. She was a dedicated advocate for women's rights in Cambodia and has played a pivotal role in shaping domestic violence legislation.

2009: Ada E. Yonath, an Israeli crystallographer, became the first Israeli woman to win the Nobel Prize in Chemistry for her pioneering research on the structure and function of ribosomes.

2013: Mary Barra became the first female CEO of a major automotive company as she assumed the position at General Motors.

2014: May-Britt Moser, along with Edvard Moser and John O'Keefe, was awarded the Nobel Prize in Physiology or Medicine for their discoveries of cells that constitute a positioning system in the brain, contributing to our understanding of spatial navigation.

2020: Journalist Malalai Maiwand, an activist for women's and children's rights in Afghanistan, was shot dead, along with her driver, in an attack claimed by the Islamic State Khorasan Province.

2021: Riding the Vortex, a mentorship program for African-American women architects, received the Whitney M. Young Jr. Award, recognizing their commitment to addressing social issues and promoting diversity in architecture.

December 11

1941: Mildred Gillars, also known as "Axis Sally," made her first propaganda broadcast to Allied troops during World War II. She worked as a radio broadcaster for the German government and aimed to demoralize American soldiers through her broadcasts.

1950: Cecil Powell received the Nobel Prize in Physics for his achievements using the photographic film method created by Marietta Blau and her assistant, Hertha Wambacher. Blau's work in 1932-1937 was crucial in further research in particle physics, as she pioneered the development of photographic emulsions capable of reliably and quantitatively imaging high-energy nuclear particles and events, including reactions induced by cosmic radiation. Both women were nominated for the Prize by Erwin Schrödinger (who continued to nominate her multiple times) but wholly ignored, and Blau's name was not mentioned. As a Jew, Marietta Blau had to escape Nazi Austria. She was forced to migrate to Oslo, Mexico City, and finally New York, unable to continue her research, while her discoveries were expropriated and her name erased.

1983: Three weeks after cruise missiles arrived at the Greenham military base in the UK, 50,000 women protested by encircling the base, holding mirrors to reflect the military's image back at itself symbolically. Towards the end of the day, some women began tearing down sections of the base's fence, leading to the arrest of hundreds by the police.

1992: U.S. President George H.W. Bush presented the Presidential Medal of Freedom to Audrey Hepburn, recognizing her contributions as an actress and humanitarian. Hepburn was known for her iconic roles in films such as *Breakfast at Tiffany's* and her work with UNICEF.

2009: The Ugandan Parliament passed a law banning the practice of female genital mutilation (FGM), acknowledging the harmful effects and human rights violations associated with the procedure.

2017: U.S. District Judge Colleen Kollar-Kotelly denied a request from the Trump administration to enforce a ban on transgender troops while the case was under appeal. The judge reaffirmed her order that required the U.S. military to accept transgender recruits starting January 1, 2018.

2019: Greta Thunberg, the Swedish climate activist, was named *TIME* magazine's Person of the Year for her influential role in raising awareness about the urgent need for action on climate change.

2020: The U.S. Food and Drug Administration (FDA) granted the Pfizer-BioNTech COVID-19 vaccine emergency use authorization. This vaccine, which utilizes mRNA technology, was developed by

BioNTech in collaboration with Pfizer under the oversight of Kathrin Jansen.

2021: Reckya Madougou, an opposition leader in Benin who previously held positions in the Boni Yayi cabinet, including Minister of Microfinance, Youth, and Women's Employment, and Minister of Justice, received a 20-year prison sentence for "financing terrorism." The verdict sparked controversy, with a judge involved in the case fleeing to France and publicly criticizing it as politically motivated.

2022: Mathea Allansmith became the oldest woman to complete a marathon at 92 years and 194 days old during the 2022 Honolulu Marathon in just 10 hours and 48 minutes, setting a new female Guinness record.

December 12

1474: Isabella of Castile and Aragon crowned herself queen, beginning her reign as the joint ruler of both kingdoms. Isabella played a significant role in the unification of Spain and sponsored Christopher Columbus's voyages to the Americas.

1901: Millicent Fawcett led the Ladies' Commission, a British government-appointed commission tasked with investigating the mistreatment of internees at concentration camps during the Second Boer War in South Africa. The commission corroborated the reports made by Emily Hobhouse regarding the harsh conditions in the camps.

1935: Irène Joliot-Curie and Frédéric Joliot-Curie, a married couple, were awarded the Nobel Prize in Chemistry for discovering artificial radioactivity. They successfully produced radioactive isotopes by bombarding stable elements with alpha particles.

1935: *Lebensborn* ("fount of life"), an SS-sponsored and state-supported association in Nazi Germany, was established. It aimed to increase the birth rate of children meeting Nazi criteria for Aryan purity and health, aligned with Nazi eugenic principles (referred to as "racial hygiene"). Established by Heinrich Himmler, *Lebensborn* assisted unmarried mothers, encouraged discreet births at their facilities, and facilitated adoptions by "racially pure" and healthy families, particularly SS members. The Cross of Honour of the German Mother was awarded to mothers with at least four Aryan children. While the Nazis legalized and promoted abortion for disabled and non-Germanic children, they severely punished others. Part of *Lebensborn*'s activity was kidnapping "Aryan-looking" children from occupied territories in Poland and Ukraine.

2009: Annise Parker was elected Mayor of Houston, Texas, becoming the first openly gay person to be elected mayor of a major U.S. city.

2012: Miriam Defensor Santiago became the first Filipina and the first Asian from a developing country to be a judge of the International Criminal Court.

2015: Saudi Arabia held its first-ever elections in which women were allowed to vote and stand as candidates, which was a significant step forward for women's rights in the country after a longstanding ban on women's participation in elections was lifted.

December 13

1923: The Equal Rights Amendment (ERA), drafted by Alice Paul, was introduced in the U.S. Congress for the first time. The ERA aimed to provide equal legal rights for all American citizens regardless of sex. Although the amendment was not ratified, it played a significant role in the women's rights movement and continues to be a subject of debate.

1974: Nyi Ageng Serang was awarded the National Heroine of Indonesia title for her leading role in wars against the Dutch colonizers. At first, she fought by her father's side; then, during the Diponegoro War (1825 – 1830), she led Javanese troops as an older woman from a stretcher and later acted as a war advisor to her son-in-law.

1981: Anna Pienkowska, an anti-communist Polish activist and a nurse at the shipyard in Gdańsk, was arrested and interned in multiple camps over the next two years. She was under surveillance for the following years.

1982: Martha Stewart's book, *Entertaining*, was released, beginning her successful career as an author and lifestyle guru. Stewart published numerous bestselling books on cooking, entertaining, and home decoration, becoming a prominent figure in the field.

1993: Susan A. Maxman became the first woman president of the American Institute of Architects (AIA), a prestigious professional organization in architecture.

2013: Beyoncé released her fifth album, *Beyoncé*. The album's release was a surprise as it came without any prior announcement or promotion. This unconventional approach to album releases significantly impacted the music industry, and the album debuted at number one on the Billboard 200 chart.

2020: Hoda Amid and Najmeh Vahedi, two women's rights activists, were sentenced to 15 years in prison by a court in Tehran, Iran. They were charged with "collaborating with the United States government against the Islamic Republic on the issue of women and the family."

December 14

1542: Princess Mary Stuart became the Queen of Scots at just one week old following the death of her father, James V of Scotland. Her reign was marked by political turbulence and conflicts, and she is a significant figure in Scottish history.

1847: Emily Brontë and Anne Brontë, sisters and talented writers, published their novels *Wuthering Heights* and *Agnes Grey* respectively, in England. The books were initially released as a 3-volume set under their pen names, Ellis Bell and Acton Bell. *Wuthering Heights* has since become a classic of English literature.

1911: Eleanor Davies-Colley became Britain's first female Fellow of the Royal College of Surgeons.

1935: Lillian Hellman's play *The Children's Hour* faced a ban in Boston for being deemed "indecent." The controversial play dealt with themes of homosexuality and scandal, which caused it to face censorship and restrictions in some areas.

1944: The film *National Velvet* was released in the United States, propelling Elizabeth Taylor into stardom. The movie, based on Enid Bagnold's novel, showcased Taylor's talent and charm, and she became one of the most iconic actresses of her time.

1961: The U.S. President's Commission on the Status of Women was established to examine gender discrimination against women and explore ways to eliminate it.

1985: Wilma Mankiller, a trailblazing Native American activist, took office as the first woman elected Principal Chief of the Cherokee Nation.

2017: The Supreme Court of Justice in Guatemala decided against permitting the usage of a manual by the Procuratorate of Human Rights for discussions and workshops on sexuality. The decision was influenced by the manual's stance on abortion, which is generally prohibited in Guatemala except in cases where the mother's life was at risk.

2022: Iran was expelled from the United Nations Commission on the Status of Women following the death of Mahsa Amini and the violent crackdown on protests advocating for women's rights in Iran. The expulsion was a response to human rights concerns and the treatment of women in the country.

December 15

1283: After her father's death, Catherine inherited his claims to the Latin throne of Constantinople and was recognized as Empress by the Latin states in Greece at the age of nine.

1911: British suffragettes employed a new tactic to draw attention to their cause by destroying mailboxes. One notable example was Emily Wilding Davison, who ignited a linen cloth soaked in paraffin and placed it in a public mail drop. The suffragettes later escalated their actions by setting fire to vacant buildings to raise awareness for women's suffrage.

1950: Celia Cruz recorded her first songs with the group Sonora Matancera, which was the beginning of a highly successful and enduring career. Cruz became one of the most iconic figures in Latin music, known as the "Queen of Salsa."

1973: The American Psychiatric Association voted 13–0 to remove homosexuality from its official list of psychiatric disorders in the Diagnostic and Statistical Manual of Mental Disorders. This step was instrumental in challenging stigmatization and advancing the understanding of sexual orientation.

1983: Grace Hopper, a pioneering computer scientist and naval officer, was promoted to commodore by a special presidential appointment. Hopper significantly contributed to computer programming languages and was crucial in developing early computers.

1997: Janet Jagan was elected President of Guyana, becoming the first American-born woman to be elected President of any country. Jagan was born in Chicago, Illinois, and played a significant role in Guyanese politics, particularly advocating for social and economic reforms.

2011: Zainab Alkhawaja, a prominent Bahraini blogger and activist, was detained by the police during a protest near the capital, Manama. Alkhawaja has been vocal in advocating for human rights and democracy in Bahrain.

2015: Brig. Gen. Diana Holland was appointed as the first female commandant of cadets at the U.S. Military Academy at West Point, New York.

2017: A Federal District Judge for Eastern Pennsylvania issued a temporary injunction, preventing the Trump administration from implementing new rules that modified the Obamacare contraceptive mandate. Several states, including California, Delaware, Maryland, Massachusetts, New York, Virginia, and Washington, filed lawsuits against the federal government regarding these rules.

December 16

1903: Selina Anderson, Vida Goldstein, Nellie Martel, and Mary Moore-Bentley became the first women to stand in Australian federal elections.

1913: Emma Goldman, a Jewish anarchist, defied police warnings and addressed members of the Industrial Workers of the World Union on "the spirit of anarchism in the labor struggle" in Paterson, New Jersey. Despite being forced off the platform by the police, her speech sparked a battle between the audience members and law enforcement.

1918: Following a National Woman's Party conference, 300 suffragists burned President Woodrow Wilson's speeches in protest at Lafayette Park in Washington, D.C. President Wilson had arrived in France on that date to promote democracy overseas, and the suffragists' action was a powerful statement demanding women's right to vote.

1938: In Nazi Germany, the Mother's Cross, officially known as the Cross of Honour of the German Mother (*Ehrenkreuz der Deutschen Mutter*), was established as a state decoration. It was awarded by the government of the German Reich between 1939 and 1945 to German mothers for their "exceptional contributions to the nation." The decoration had three classes: bronze, silver, and gold, and recipients were required to exhibit qualities such as integrity, exemplary motherhood, and raising at least four children. It embodied motherhood and ethnic nationalism during the era of National Socialism in Germany.

1985: The film *The Color Purple*, based on Alice Walker's novel and directed by Steven Spielberg, premiered in New York. The film, starring Whoopi Goldberg, explored themes of race, gender, and resilience, garnering critical acclaim and making a significant cultural impact.

1989: Lesléa Newman published the groundbreaking children's book *Heather Has Two Mommies*, which portrayed a same-sex family. The book played a significant role in representing diverse family structures and promoting inclusivity in children's literature.

2012: The brutal gang rape and murder of Jyoti Singh, a 22-year-old physiotherapy intern, occurred in Delhi, India, sparking widespread outrage and protests against gender-based violence. The incident, widely known as the Nirbhaya case, symbolized the urgent need for improved safety measures and justice for victims of sexual violence.

2013: Michelle Bachelet, a center-left candidate, was elected as the President of Chile for the second time, becoming the first leader in Chile to serve two terms since the end of military rule in 1990.

2014: Julia Morgan, an accomplished architect, became the first woman to receive the American Institute of Architects' highest honor, the AIA Gold Medal, posthumously.

2020: Sviatlana Tsikhanouskaya, the Belarusian opposition leader, appealed to the European Union for solidarity with protesters in Belarus during her acceptance speech upon receiving the Sakharov Prize.

December 17

769: The coronation of Irene of Athens took place. Irene served as the Byzantine empress consort to Leo IV, regent from 780 until 790, co-ruler from 792 until 797, and finally empress regnant and sole ruler of the Eastern Roman Empire from 797 to 802.

1663: Queen Ana Nzinga of the Kingdom of Ndongo and the Kingdom of Matamba, located in present-day Angola, passed away after a reign of 39 years in Ndongo and 32 years after conquering Matamba. Her sister, Barbara Mukambu Mbandi, assumed the throne and governed for less than three years.

1907: Ashi Tsundue Pema Lhamo became Bhutan's *Druk Gyaltsuen* ("Dragon Queen" - Queen consort).

1922: After dissolving the New Women's Association, Oku Mumeo, a Japanese feminist and politician, formed the Women's League.

1942: Friedl Dicker-Brandeis (with husband Pavel) was deported to Terezin, the "model ghetto." She was a Jewish-Austrian artist and educator who studied and then taught at the Weimer Bauhaus, working in textile design, printmaking, bookbinding, and typography. During her stay in Terezin, she gave art classes and helped organize secret education for children. Before she was transported to Auschwitz-Birkenau Nazi Camp, where she perished, she saved thousands of children's drawings now on display in Prague.

1947: Dorothy Fuldheim became television's first female news anchor.

1991: The Minnesota Court of Appeals established in the case *In re Guardianship of Kowalski*, Karen Thompson's partner as her legal guardian after Sharon Kowalski became incapacitated following an automobile accident. Kowalski's parents and family contested the case and excluded Thompson from visiting Kowalski for several years, claiming that Sharon wasn't a lesbian and against her wishes to live with Karen. This victory was celebrated as a win for LGBTQ+ rights by the gay community.

1993: Judith Rodin was named the President of the University of Pennsylvania, becoming the first woman to head an Ivy League institution.

2003: Sex work rights activists established December 17 as the International Day to End Violence Against Sex Workers ("D17"). This day aims to raise awareness about the violence and discrimination faced by sex workers and advocate for their rights and safety.

2008: South Korean actress Ok So-ri received an eight-month suspended prison sentence for adultery as the Constitutional Court upheld the law criminalizing such acts.

2013: Angela Merkel secured her third term as Chancellor of Germany through reelection, continuing her leadership role in the country.

2015: Arlene Foster became the first female leader of the Democratic Unionist Party in Northern Ireland.

2020: Israeli Justice Minister Avi Nissenkorn signed an extradition order to Australia for Malka Leifer, who was accused of child sex abuse. Leifer had previously been convicted of faking mental illness to evade extradition.

December 18

1894: Women in South Australia became the first in Australia to gain the right to vote and the first in the world with the right to be elected to Parliament. This law came into effect in 1895 after years of activism and advocacy by women.

1913: *The Jew's Christmas*, a silent film written by Lois Weber and directed by Weber and her husband, Phillips Smalley, premiered. It was the first American film to feature a rabbi as a character and explore themes of cultural assimilation, interfaith marriage, and the challenges immigrants face in abandoning their ancestral customs and traditions.

1965: Shirley Jackson's short story, *The Possibility of Evil*, was published in the *Saturday Evening Post*. The story went on to win the 1966 Edgar Allan Poe Award for Best Mystery Short Story.

1977: Björk Guðmundsdóttir, known as Björk, released her first studio album at the age of 11, showcasing the beginning of her musical career, as she would go on to become a highly influential and innovative artist.

1979: The United Nations adopted the Women's Bill of Rights, also known as the Convention on the Elimination of All Forms of Discrimination against Women (CEDAW).

1986: Patricia Era Bath, an ophthalmologist, inventor, humanitarian, and academic, patented a "Laser apparatus for surgery of cataractous lenses," the first of five medical patents she was issued throughout her career.

2007: Yulia Tymoshenko, a prominent figure in the Orange Revolution, regained parliamentary support and reclaimed her position as the Prime Minister of Ukraine.

2012: In response to the death of Savita Halappanavar, the Irish government introduced legislation to provide clear guidelines to doctors regarding abortion procedures when the mother's life was at risk.

2013: Prominent American sports figures, including tennis player Billie Jean King and ice hockey player Caitlin Cahow, represented the United States in the Sochi Olympics as a protest against the treatment of LGBTQ+ people in Russia.

December 19

1154: Eleanor of Aquitaine was crowned Queen Consort of England following her marriage to King Henry II. She was a powerful and influential queen known for her political understanding and involvement in the kingdom's affairs.

1799: Maria Dalle Donne, at 21, was deemed worthy of the Doctorate in Philosophy and Medicine. Since a young age, she studied Latin, humanities, and philosophy, and then – at the University of Bologna-anatomy, physiology, surgery, and obstetrics.

1933: Lotfia El Nadi participated in the international flight race from Cairo to Alexandria. Maintaining an average speed of 100 miles per hour, she guided her single-engine plane to victory, surpassing all competitors. She received a £E200 prize and congratulations from King Fuad. Huda Sha'arawi, a prominent feminist leader, also admired Elnadi's inspiring performance and organized a fundraising campaign to help her acquire her own aircraft.

1978: Indira Gandhi, the former Prime Minister of India, was arrested and jailed for a week for breach of privilege and contempt of Parliament.

1984: Chinese Premier Zhao Ziyang and British Prime Minister Margaret Thatcher signed the Sino-British Joint Declaration. This agreement outlined the transfer of Hong Kong from British rule to Chinese sovereignty, which took place in 1997.

1994: Sweden officially legalized civil unions for same-sex couples, becoming one of the first countries worldwide to recognize such partnerships.

1997: Janet Jagan became the first female President of Guyana. Before her presidency, she also served as Guyana's first female Prime Minister from March 17, 1997, to December 19, 1997. Janet Jagan was recognized for her contributions to Guyana and women's rights, receiving prestigious honors such as the Order of Excellence and the UNESCO Mahatma Gandhi Gold Medal.

2003: An Ontario court granted survivors' benefits to Canadians whose same-sex partners died after 1985 in a landmark class-action lawsuit.

2012: Park Geun-Hye won the South Korean presidential election, becoming the country's first female President.

December 20

1971: The first preview issue of *Ms.* magazine, founded by Gloria Steinem and Dorothy Pitman Hughes, was published in the United States. The magazine played a significant role in the women's liberation movement and focused on women's rights, social issues, and feminist perspectives.

1993: The Declaration on the Elimination of Violence Against Women (DEVAW) was adopted by the United Nations General Assembly through Resolution 48/104. It emphasized the urgent need to extend the rights and principles of equality, security, liberty, integrity, and dignity to all women. Within DEVAW, Articles 1 and 2 offer the widely accepted definition of violence against women.

2006: The European Institute for Gender Equality (EIGE) was founded by the European Union. Its mission was to monitor gender disparity and to support institutions and EU Member States in promoting equality and combating discrimination.

2007: Queen Elizabeth II became the oldest monarch in the history of the United Kingdom, surpassing the previous record held by Queen Victoria. On this day, she had lived for 81 years and 244 days, moving beyond Queen Victoria's lifespan of 81 years and 243 days.

2011: Thousands of Egyptian women took to the streets to protest against abuses by military police. This demonstration highlighted the concerns and demands of women during the political upheaval that followed the Arab Spring.

2013: The Supreme Court of Canada struck down anti-prostitution laws in the country, ruling that they violated sex workers' constitutional rights. The court decision recognized the importance of ensuring the safety and well-being of sex workers and opened up discussions about the regulation and decriminalization of prostitution in Canada.

2022: The Taliban, who regained control of Afghanistan, issued a decree banning university education for women. The ban, which came into effect immediately, represented a significant setback for women's rights and access to education in the country.

December 21

1507: Princess Mary of England, the 11-year-old daughter of King Henry VII, was betrothed to the 7-year-old Duke of Burgundy. This betrothal was part of political alliances and negotiations common among European royal families.

1788: German astronomer Caroline Herschel discovered the periodic comet 35P/Herschel-Rigollet. This comet has an orbital period of 155 years and was named after Herschel and Jean Rigollet, who independently rediscovered it in 1949.

1914: *Tillie's Punctured Romance*, a comedy film by Mack Sennett, premiered. It was the first feature-length film released through Keystone Studios and featured famous actors of the time, including Marie Dressler, Mabel Normand, Charlie Chaplin, and the Keystone Cops.

1919: American anarchist Emma Goldman was deported to Russia as a "radical alien." Goldman was a prominent activist and writer known for advocating anarchism, women's rights, and social issues.

1924: An exhibition showcasing the work of Russian avant-garde artist Lyubov Popova opened in Moscow. The show included various Popova works, such as paintings, books, posters, textile designs, and line engravings, providing a comprehensive view of her artistic contributions.

1934: The French film *Zouzou* premiered in Paris, starring Josephine Baker. Baker, an American-born entertainer, became the first Black woman to star in a major motion picture.

1966: Tsuneko Okazaki and her husband, Reiji, published an article, "Mechanism of DNA chain growth. I. Possible discontinuity and unusual secondary structure of newly synthesized chains," in the *Proceedings of the National Academy of Sciences Journal*, describing their findings on what would be called the "Okazaki fragments" - short sequences of DNA nucleotides which are synthesized discontinuously and later linked together by the enzyme DNA ligase to create the lagging strand during DNA replication.

1976: President Jimmy Carter appointed Patricia Roberts Harris as the Secretary of Housing and Urban Development, making her the first African-American woman to hold a U.S. cabinet position. Harris was a notable government official and diplomat, serving in various high-level positions throughout her career.

2008: Iranian police raided and closed the Children's Rights Support Association, founded by Nobel Peace Prize laureate Shirin Ebadi. The closure occurred just before a planned celebration of Human Rights

Day, reflecting the challenges faced by human rights activists in Iran.

2016: After a 17-year wait since its introduction, a bill protecting the rights of the LGBTQ+ community in the Philippines was up for debate in the legislature. The urgency for this bill arose from the killing of a transwoman in 2014, highlighting the need for legal protections and equal rights.

2020: Volha Khizhynkova, a former Miss Belarus winner, was released from prison after serving 42 days for participating in protests against President Alexander Lukashenko. The protests in Belarus were triggered by allegations of election fraud and demanded democratic reforms.

December 22

1891: Asteroid 323 Brucia became the first asteroid discovered using photography. It was named in honor of Catherine Wolfe Bruce, a prominent supporter of astronomy who provided funding for the construction of the telescope used by astronomer Max Wolf to make the discovery.

1898: Scientists Marie Skłodowska Curie and her husband Pierre Curie discovered radioactive radium. Their research on radioactivity led to groundbreaking contributions in physics. It earned Marie Curie two Nobel Prizes, making her the first woman to receive a Nobel Prize and the only person to win it in two scientific disciplines.

1984: Madonna's single *Like a Virgin* reached No. 1 on the music charts and stayed there for six weeks. The song became one of Madonna's signature hits and established her as a pop culture icon.

2010: President Obama signed the Don't Ask, Don't Tell Repeal Act of 2010, ending the policy prohibiting gay and lesbian individuals from serving openly in the United States military.

2019: NASA astronaut Jessica Meir, the fourth Jewish woman to travel to space, celebrated the first day of Chanukah on the International Space Station. She wore neon socks decorated with menorahs and Stars of David, bringing a festive touch to her time in space.

2022: The Scottish Parliament passed the Gender Recognition Reform (Scotland) Bill, amending the Gender Recognition Act 2004 of the United Kingdom. The Bill aimed to simplify the legal gender change process in Scotland.

2022: The Spanish Congress of Deputies passed a bill allowing individuals over 16 to change their gender on their national identity card legally. The bill was sent to the Senate for final approval.

2022: Nataša Pirc Musar was sworn in as the first female President of Slovenia.

December 23

583: Maya Queen Yohl Ik'nal, also known as Lady Kan Ik or Lady K'anal Ik'nal, was crowned ruler of Palenque. Yohl Ik'nal was the first recorded female ruler in Maya history and one of the few known female rulers with a full royal title.

1384: Maria Angelina Doukaina Palaiologina became the ruler of Epirus on the Greek island of Ioannina after allegedly orchestrating the death of her abusive husband. She used the title basilissa, the female form of basileus.

1815: Jane Austen's novel *Emma* was first published. *Emma* is one of Austen's most beloved works, exploring themes of love, matchmaking, and social class in Regency-era England.

1873: The Woman's Christian Temperance Union (WCTU) was organized in Hillsboro, Ohio. The WCTU became a prominent organization advocating for women's rights and social reforms, mainly focused on temperance and the prohibition of alcohol to better women's situation.

1919: The Sex Disqualification Act was passed in the United Kingdom, removing legal barriers that prevented women from entering secular public professions.

1970: Agatha Christie's play *The Mousetrap* reached its 7,511th performance in London's West End. *The Mousetrap* is the world's longest-running play, captivating audiences with its thrilling murder mystery storyline.

2009: Liberian President Ellen Johnson Sirleaf voluntarily imprisoned herself in Bella Yalla prison, a historic maximum security facility in the northern jungle. This symbolic act aimed to signify the end of torture in Liberia and promote the country's healing and rebuilding after years of civil war.

2013: Political activists Maria Alyokhina and Nadezhda Tolokonnikova, prominent members of the Russian band Pussy Riot, were granted amnesty shortly before the completion of their sentences. They had been convicted of "hooliganism motivated by religious hatred."

2015: The rate of twin births in the United States reached a historic high, as reported by the United States National Center for Health Statistics. Advancements in reproductive technology, such as in vitro fertilization and delayed childbirth, increased the likelihood of twins during this period.

December 24

1910: Italian operatic soprano Luisa Tetrazzini performed to a crowd of 250,000 people at Lotta's Fountain in San Francisco. The concert was held as a gesture of gratitude to the city for its support after the devastating earthquake and fire in 1906.

1919: An African-American inventor, Alice H. Parker, submitted a formal patent application for the modern central heating gas furnace, revolutionizing home heating systems.

1948: The "Dover Sun House," designed by architect Eleanor Raymond and sponsored by Amelia Peabody, became the first house in the United States to be entirely solar-heated.

2019: Alba Rueda was appointed the Undersecretary for Diversity Policies within Argentina's newly established Ministry of Women, Genders, and Diversity. Rueda became the country's first openly transgender politician to hold a senior governmental position, contributing to greater inclusivity and representation.

2020: Women's rights activist Freshta Kohistani and her brother were killed by gunmen on a motorbike in the Kohistan district of Kapisa province, Afghanistan. Kohistani's activism and dedication to advancing women's rights were met with violence, highlighting the ongoing challenges faced by activists in some regions.

2020: Maia Sandu was sworn in as the first female President of Moldova.

2022: The Taliban issued a decree banning female employees from working in Afghanistan's non-governmental organizations (NGOs). This restriction further limited women's participation in various sectors and raised concerns about erasing women's rights and freedoms under Taliban rule.

December 25

1252: Margaret Sambiria was crowned the Queen consort of Denmark. She later ruled as a regent after the death of her husband in 1259, which was the first time a woman was made a regent in Denmark.

1560: Queen Jeanne of Navarre publicly embraced the teachings of John Calvin and declared Calvinism the official religion of her kingdom, becoming the highest-ranking Protestant in France. She was announced as an opponent of the Counter-Reformation led by the Catholic Church. After introducing Calvinism in her domain, priests and nuns were expelled, Catholic churches were torn down, and Catholic rituals were forbidden. She arranged for the translation of the New Testament into Basque and Béarnese for the benefit of her subjects.

1951: Harriette V.S. Moore and her husband Harry T. Moore, early leaders of the Civil Rights Movement in the United States, were tragically killed when a bomb exploded at their home in Florida.

2002: Katie Hnida, a University of New Mexico player, became the first woman to play in an NCAA Division 1 football game.

2011: Faezeh Hashemi, the daughter of former President of Iran Akbar Hashemi Rafsanjani, stood trial on charges of making anti-regime propaganda.

2013: Tetiana Chornovol, a Ukrainian civic activist, journalist, and prominent leader of the *Euromaidan* movement, was violently assaulted by a group of men who forcibly pulled her out of her car. This incident was part of a series of targeted attacks against government critics during the Ukrainian political crisis.

2016: The movie *Hidden Figures* was released, depicting the untold story of African-American female mathematicians who worked at NASA during the Space Race. The film starred Taraji P. Henson as Katherine Goble Johnson, Octavia Spencer as Dorothy Vaughan, and Janelle Monáe as Mary Jackson.

December 26

1851: Queen Teriitaria II was removed from her office and banished by the French for her opposition to their colonial rule. She accompanied her niece, Pōmare IV, into exile on Raiatea during the Franco-Tahitian War (1844–1847). Teriitaria repelled a French invasion force at the Battle of Maeva in 1846, which secured the independence of the Leeward Islands. She was then banished from the island on March 18, 1854, for troubling the new government.

1898: Marie Curie, along with her husband Pierre Curie, publicly announced their discovery of a new element, which they named radium. This groundbreaking discovery marked a significant advancement in the field of radioactivity.

1907: The New York City Rent Strike or the East Side Rent Strike began in response to proposed rent increases in the wake of the Panic of 1907 financial crisis, which saw tens of thousands unemployed. Most organizers were Jewish immigrant women such as Pauline Newman (who was 16 and working in the Triangle Shirtwaist Factory). It spread to other parts of the city and lasted until January 8, 1908, when police, under the direction of the landlords, brutalized strikers after they had refused to disperse meetings.

1981: Massoumeh Shademani, also known as Mother Kabiri, was executed by the Khomeini regime in Iran for her opposition work.

2020: The statue of Breonna Taylor, a Black woman tragically killed by police during a raid at her home in March 2020, was destroyed in a racist assault. The statue, erected in Oakland, California, just two weeks prior, was vandalized and smashed.

December 27

1845: Crawford Long administered ether as an anesthetic during childbirth for the first time in Jefferson, Georgia, which was a significant advancement in medical history, as anesthesia revolutionized surgical procedures and provided pain relief.

1935: Regina Jonas became the first woman to be ordained as a rabbi in modern Judaism after undergoing a test by Rabbi Max Dienemann on behalf of the Liberal Rabbis' Association.

1944: Sára Salkaházi, who had saved numerous Jews during World War II, was betrayed and handed to the Hungarian pro-Nazi Arrow Cross Party. Along with the Jews she was hiding, she was lined up by the Danube River and shot to death.

1955: In the *Davis et al. v. The St. Louis Housing Authority* case, a significant class-action lawsuit challenging racial discrimination in public housing, the judgment was ruled in favor of the plaintiffs. Attorneys Frankie Muse Freeman and Constance Baker Motley played instrumental roles in this landmark case.

1956: Physicist Chien-Shiung Wu conducted experiments on the beta-decay of cobalt-60, which disproved the previously accepted "law" of conservation of parity.

2007: Benazir Bhutto, the former prime minister of Pakistan, was assassinated in a shooting incident. Her death marked a tragic event in Pakistani politics and had far-reaching consequences for the country's political landscape.

2012: Marzieh Vahid-Dastjerdi, the first and only female minister in the history of the Islamic Republic of Iran, was dismissed from her position following a disagreement with President Mahmoud Ahmadinejad.

2019: The office of Canadian Governor General Julie Payette announced that Anne Innis Dagg, a zoologist, feminist, and author of numerous books, had been appointed a Member of the Order of Canada. She was honored for her contribution to the modern scientific understanding of the giraffe and her work in animal behavior science.

December 28

1886: Josephine Garis Cochran was granted a patent for the dishwashing machine she designed, which was an essential advancement in household technology and automation.

1914: The film *Cinderella*, starring Mary Pickford, premiered. Directed by James Kirkwood Sr. and produced by Daniel Frohman, it was released by Famous Players Film Company and contributed to the early development of the film industry.

1918: Constance Markievicz, imprisoned, became the first woman elected as a Member of Parliament (M.P.) to the British House of Commons. However, as per Sinn Féin's abstentionist policy, she did not take her seat. Markievicz is also recognized as the first woman elected to the Irish *Dáil Éireann*.

1930: German dancer Mary Wigman made her highly anticipated American debut in New York City, performing to a sold-out audience at Chanin's 46th Street Theatre. Wigman was influential in the development of modern dance and left a lasting impact on the art form.

1931: Irene Joliot-Curie reported her discovery of gamma rays as a result of bombarding beryllium with alpha particles, expanding our understanding of radiation and its properties. Joliot-Curie's work contributed to the field of nuclear physics.

1967: Muriel Siebert became the first woman to own a seat on the New York Stock Exchange.

1981: Elizabeth Jordan Carr, the first American "test-tube baby," was born in Norfolk, Virginia. Her birth marked a significant breakthrough in the field of assisted reproductive technology.

1991: Naoko Takeuchi published the first installment of *Sailor Moon* in the shōjo manga magazine *Nakayoshi*. The series became one of the most popular and influential worldwide manga, particularly within the magical girl genre.

2011: An Egyptian court banned forced virginity tests on female detainees in military prisons, recognizing the violation of human rights and the need to protect women's dignity and bodily autonomy.

2015: Japan and South Korea reached an agreement to address the issue of Korean women, known as "comfort women," who were forced into sexual slavery by the Japanese military during World War II. The agreement aimed to resolve the longstanding dispute and included an apology from the Japanese prime minister and financial compensation.

2020: Women's rights activist Loujain al-Hathloul was sentenced to five years and eight months in prison in Saudi Arabia on charges related to activities prohibited by the anti-terrorism law.

December 29

1202: Yang became the empress consort of the Song dynasty when she married Emperor Ningzong of Song, ruling as a de facto co-ruler and consolidating power over the years.

1852: Emma Snodgrass was arrested in Boston for wearing pants (trousers), considered male attire at the time. Snodgrass argued that the laws prohibiting her from wearing such clothing were unconstitutional, highlighting gender inequality and societal norms.

1913: *The Adventures of Kathlyn*, the first serial film, premiered in Chicago. Starring Kathlyn Williams as the lead actress, the film marked a significant development in storytelling through multiple installments, a format that would become popular in subsequent years.

1918: After Poland regained independence and reunited, the two Leagues (League of Polish Women of the War Preparedness from the former Russian territory and the League of Women in Galicia and Silesia from the former Austrian and Prussian lands) were merged into a united national Polish Women's League on a conference in the new capital of Warsaw. The participants demanded equal opportunities in all official positions, gender equality and justice for children born out of wedlock, equal pay for equal work, and the end of legislative restrictions for women's work (such as night work or underground work). They also created several general political, social, and ethical statements. Maria Dulębianka became the first president.

1922: Aloha Wanderwell embarked on her journey in Nice, France, becoming the first woman to drive around the world. She completed her global journey in January 1927, documenting her adventures and capturing footage of various cultures and landscapes.

1955: Barbra Streisand, at 13, recorded her first song, *You'll Never Know*, which marked the beginning of her illustrious career as a singer and actress, eventually becoming one of the most successful entertainers in history.

2009: Shirin Ebadi, Iran's Nobel Peace Prize laureate, revealed that her sister Nooshin, a medical professor and human rights advocate, had been apprehended by authorities.

2021: Ghislaine Maxwell, a British socialite and associate of financier Jeffrey Epstein, was found guilty of sex trafficking charges by a court in New York City. The verdict marked a significant development in the Epstein case's legal proceedings and brought some accountability to those involved in his criminal activities.

December 30

1610: Hungarian aristocrat Elizabeth Báthory was arrested at Csejte Castle on suspicion of killing and torturing hundreds of young girls and women. The case of Elizabeth Báthory, often referred to as the "Blood Countess," remains infamous in history due to the allegations of her sadistic acts.

1917: Renowned opera singer Mary Garden debuted in the historical drama film *Thaïs*. Despite Garden's fame, the movie, directed by Hugo Ballin and Frank Hall Crane and released by Goldwyn Pictures, was a major box office flop.

1918: Rosa Luxemburg led an effort to rename the Spartacus League to the Communist Party of Germany. Alongside Karl Liebknecht, Clara Zetkin, and others, Luxemburg founded the organization. On January 1, 1919, they merged into the newly formed Communist Party of Germany (KPD) and ceased to exist independently.

1929: Sigma Gamma Rho, a historically African-American sorority and international community service organization, was officially incorporated. The sorority has since worked towards empowering women and serving their communities.

2010: Pezilet Ekber, a 19-year-old Uyghur student in northwestern China, was sentenced to death with a two-year suspension following a secretive trial on charges of participating in ethnic riots. Ekber became the second Uyghur woman to receive the death penalty for alleged involvement in the ethnic riots.

2010: North Korea's state-run television broadcasted *Bend It Like Beckham*, a 2002 sports comedy-drama film directed by Gurinder Chadha. It marked the first time a Western movie was shown on the country's television.

2020: Argentina legalized abortion following a Senate vote of 38 to 29, with one abstention, on the Voluntary Interruption of Pregnancy Bill. President Alberto Fernández supported and planned to enact the bill, solidifying its transition into law.

2022: A court in Myanmar sentenced the ousted leader, Aung San Suu Kyi, to seven years in prison, adding to her overall sentence of 33 years.

December 31

1225: Lý Chiêu Hoàng, the only Empress to rule Vietnam, married Trần Thái Tông, who became the first ruler of the Trần dynasty.

1903: The National Association for Women's Suffrage (*Landsföreningen för kvinnans politiska rösträtt*, LKPR) was established in Sweden, thanks to the organizing efforts of Anna Whitlock, Lydia Wahlström, and Signe Bergman.

1911: Marie Skłodowska Curie received her second Nobel Prize, this time in Chemistry, for her groundbreaking work with radioactivity.

1967: Anita Hoffman, her husband Abbie Hoffman, Nancy Kurshan, and others cofounded the Youth International Party (YIP), affectionately known as the Yippies. The Yippies were known for their countercultural activism and playful political stunts during the 1960s and 1970s.

1976: Mahnaz Afkhami, an Iranian women's rights activist, became Minister of Women's Affairs, a post that had not existed in Iran before, and the only other person holding such a position was Françoise Giroud in France. Afkhami stayed in the office until August 27, 1978.

1993: Barbra Streisand performed her first public concert in 20 years before a sell-out crowd of over 25,000 in Las Vegas.

2009: Amanda Simpson became the first transgender presidential appointee to a senior position. She was appointed Senior Technical Adviser in the Bureau of Industry and Security at the U.S. Department of Commerce.

Do you know of an event or some fascinating thing that occurred by or to women?
Should more people know about something that happened in your country or community?
Let me know! I will be happy to learn about it and include it in the next edition of this book.
I will include your name (if you want) in the acknowledgments to express my gratitude.

emma.rosen.books@gmail.com

BIRTH & DEATH ANNIVERSARIES

JANUARY

Births: **JANUARY 01**
1638 Antoinette du Ligier de la Garde Deshoulières
1769 Marie Lachapelle
1862 Georgina Pope
1868 Sophia Alice Callahan
1878? Josephine Casey
1884 Mary Hamilton Swindler
1914 Noor Inayat Khan
1939 Naomi Weisstein
1949 Gayle Rubin
Deaths:
1252 Saint Zdislava Berka
1910 Harriet Powers
1914 Alice Brady
1921 Mary Macarthur
1988 Clementine Hunter
1992 Grace Hopper

Births: **JANUARY 02**
1713 Marie Françoise Dumesnil
1847 Julia Lermontova
1895 Edith B. Jackson
1913 Mary Tift
1917 Zaynab al-Ghazali
1919 Beatrice Hicks
Deaths:
1818 Martha Christina Tiahahu

Births: **JANUARY 03**
1730 Rani Velu Nachiyar
1793 Lucretia Mott
1884 Mary Hamilton Swindler
1897 Pola Negri
1905 Anna May Wong
1905 Migishi Setsuko
Deaths:
1993 Leah Feldman d. 1993

Births: **JANUARY 04**
1800 Martha Christina Tiahahu
1870 Helena Willman-Grabowska
1883 Johanna Westerdijk
1887 Allie Mae Carpenter
1931 Ro Lala (Litia Cakobau Lalabalavu Katoafutoga Tuisawau)Phyllis
1947 Margaret Starkey
Deaths:
1911 Charlotte E. Ray

Births: **JANUARY 05**
1723 Nicole-Reine Lepaute
1869 Sissieretta Jones
1882 Dorothy Levitt
1890 Sarah Aaronsohn
1893 Elizabeth "Libba" Cotten
1895 Rebecca Lancefield
1895 Jeannette Piccard
1920 Rachel “Sarenka” Zilberberg
1935 Forugh Farrokhzad
Deaths:
1796 Anna Barbara Reinhart

Births: **JANUARY 6**
1256 Gertrude the Great
1412 Joan of Arc
1618 Margherita Gonzaga, Duchess of Ferrara

1809 Marie Durocher
1812 Melchora Aquino
1888 Anna Braude-Hellerowa
1894 Catherine Brieger Stern
1913 Loretta Young

Deaths:

1840 Fanny Burney
1929 Louisine Havemeyer
1944 Ida Minerva Tarbell
1945 Roza Robota
1945 Ala Gertner
1945 Regina Safirsztajn
1945 Rose Grunapfel Meth

Births: **JANUARY 7**

1774 Anna Bunina
1819 Theresa Pulszky
1876 Gertraud Rostosky
1877 Margarete von Wrangell
1891 Zora Neale Hurston
1918 Joan Maie Freeman

Deaths:

1536 Catherine of Aragon
1715 Mary Somerset
1912 Sophia Jex-Blake
1976 Miriam O'Brien Underhill
2010 Bruria Kaufman

Births: **JANUARY 8**

1618 Madeleine Béjart
1638 Elisabetta Sirani
1640 Elisabeth Dorothea of Saxe-Gotha-Altenburg
1859 Fanny Bullock Workman
1863 Ellen Churchill Semple
1867 Emily Greene Balch
1937 Shirley Bassey

Deaths:

1672 Elizabeth Hooton
1693 Marguerite de la Sablière
1705 Zipporah Potter Atkins
2007 Jane Bolin

Births: **JANUARY 9**

1624 Empress Meishō
1773 Cassandra Austen
1858 Elizabeth Gertrude Britton
1908 Simone de Beauvoir
1925 Carlene Allen "Cardy" Raper
1971 Angie Martinez

Deaths:

1367 Giulia della Rena
1514 Anne of Brittany
1848 Caroline Herschel
1963 Matilda Getrude Robbins (Tatiana Gitel Rabinowitz)

Births: **JANUARY 10**

1897 Amy Ashwood Garvey
1898 Katharine Burr Blodgett

Deaths:

1700 Louise de Bossigny
1957 Gabriela Mistral
1985 Mary Kenneth Keller

Births: **JANUARY 11**

1619 Diane de France
1657 Elizabeth van der Woude
1721 Anna Magdalena Godiche
1760 Zofia Potocka
1868 Shimizu Shikin (Shimizu Toyoko)
1885 Alice Paul
1895 Graciela Amaya de García
1897 Isabel Bassett Wasson
1901 Kwon Ki-ok (Quan Jiyu)
1921 Juanita M. Kreps
1936 Katie Webster
1971 Mary J. Blige

Deaths:

937 Empress Cao
1800 Kyra Frosini

Births: **JANUARY 12**

1673 Rosalba Carriera
1916 Ruth Mary Rogan Benerito
1923 Alice Miller

Deaths:

1976 Dame Agatha Christie

Births: **JANUARY 13**

1616 Antoinette Bourignon
1709 Mollie Sneden
1810 Ernestine Rose
1900 Gertrude Cox
1911 Phyllis Rountree
1926 Melba Liston
1970 Shonda Rhimes

Deaths:

703 Empress Jitō
1717 Maria Sibylla Merian
1929 Marie Andree-Eysn

Births: **JANUARY 14**

1273 Joan I of Navarre
1273 Catherine of Austria, Queen of Portugal

1841 Berthe Morisot
1900 Elfriede Paul
1912 Tillie Olsen
1927 Zuzana Růžičková
1938 Indira Nath
1939 Louise Fishman
1941 Mahnaz Afkhami

Deaths:

1044 Adelaide I, Abbess of Quedlinburg
1575 Barbara Uthmann

Births: **JANUARY 15**

1815 Bertha Wehnert-Beckmann
1826 Marie Pasteur
1842 Mary MacKillop
1850 Sofya Kovalevsky
1859 Paulina Kuczalska-Reinschmit

Deaths:

570 Íte of Killeedy
1919 Rosa Luxemburg

Births: **JANUARY 16**

1634 Dorothe Engelbretsdatter
1837 Ellen Russell Emerson
1855 Eleanor Marx
1896 Maria Ossowska
1898 Gerta Overbeck
1932 Diane Fossey
1944 Jill Tarter
1979 Aaliyah Dana Haughton

Births: **JANUARY 17**

1647 Elżbieta Heweliusz (Elizabeth Hevelius)
1774 Marie-Thérèse Figueur
1820 Anne Brontë
1853 Alva Erskine Belmont
1905 Peggy Gilbert
1910 Edith Starrett Green
1927 Eartha Kitt
1934 Gabriela Basařová
1955 Katalin Karikó

Deaths:

2019 Mary Oliver
2019 Fumiko Yonezawa

Births: **JANUARY 18**

1659 Damaris Cudworth Masham
1853 Alva Erskine Belmont
1910 Valentina Grizodubova

Deaths:

1122 Christina Ingesdotter
1213 Tamar the Great of Georgia
1906 Lucy N. Colman
1971 Nora Stanton Barney

Births: **JANUARY 19**

398? Aelia Pulcheria
1850 Alice Eastwood
1873 Hamida Ahmad bey qizi Javanshir
1943 Janis Joplin
1946 Dolly Rebecca Parton

Deaths:

1213 Queen Tamar of Georgia

Births: **JANUARY 20**

1758 Marie Anne Lavoisier
1772 Angélique Brûlon
1856 Harriot Stanton Blatch
1895 Eva Jessye
1914 Mufidah Abdul Rahman
1914 Amīnah al-Sa'īd
1944 Pat Parker

Deaths:

1029 Queen Heonae of the Hwangju Hwangbo clan
1993 Audrey Hepburn

Births: **JANUARY 21**

1638 Beata Rosenhane
1714 Anna Morandi
1804 Eliza Roxcy Snow
1840 Sophia Jex-Blake
1879 Helen Gwynne-Vaughan
1890 Hertha Spielberg
1895 Itō Noe
1928 Patricia A. Locke (Tawacin WasteWin)
1935 Raye Jean Montague
1936 Blu Greenberg
1948 Afërdita Veveçka Priftaj

Births: **JANUARY 22**

1816 Catherine Wolfe Bruce
1828 Dora d'Istria
1875 Astrid Cleve von Euler
1895 Eva Taylor
1906 Willa Brown Coffey
1909 Tikvah Alper

Deaths:

1901 Queen Victoria
2018 Ursula K. Le Guin

Births: **JANUARY 23**

1688 Ulrika Eleonora of Sweden
1889 Claribel Kendall

1896	Charlotte, Grand Duchess of Luxembourg
1897	Margarete Lihotzky
1918	Gertrude Belle Elion
Deaths:	
1252	Isabella, Queen of Armenia

Births:	**JANUARY 24**
1541	Magdalena Moons
1857	Kate Waller Barrett
1862	Edith Wharton
1880	Elisabeth Achelis
1904	Berta Karlik
1925	Elizabeth Marie Tallchief
1932	Éliane Radigue
Deaths:	
40 CE	Julia Drusilla
40 CE	Milonia Caesonia

Births:	**JANUARY 25**
1858	Lillie Eginton Warren
1882	Virginia Woolf
1896	Florence Mills
1896	Ruth Buxton Sayre
1903	Kaneko Fumiko
1938	Etta James
1941	Jane Richardson
Deaths:	
1214	Taira no Tokuko
1990	Ava Gardner

Births:	**JANUARY 26**
180	Lady Zhen (Empress Wenzhao)
1792	Eleanor (Nelly) Brennan
1839	Rachel Lloyd
1872	Julia Morgan
1882	Julia Anna Gardner
1892	Bessie Coleman
1892	Zara Cully
1935	Dame Maria Paula Figueiroa Rego
1941	Joan A. Steitz
1945	Jacqueline du Pré
1944	Angela Davis
1944	María Cristina Lugones
1965	Catherine Martin
Deaths:	
1938	Zitkála-Šá

Births:	**JANUARY 27**
1242	Margaret of Hungary
1569	Emilia Lanier (baptized)
1901	Lilly Becher
1903	Susie Walking Bear Yellowtail
1937	Renate Tölle-Kastenbein
1941	Beatrice Tinsley
1944	Mairead Maguire
Deaths:	
1890	Prudence Crandall
1922	Nellie Bly
1970	Marietta Blau

Births:	**JANUARY 28**
1864	Kathleen Lynn
1873	Colette
1903	Dame Kathleen Lonsdale
1929	Edith M. Flanigen
1933	Bolanle Awe
1971	Mickalene Thomas
Deaths:	
1993	Helen Sawyer Hogg

Births:	**JANUARY 29**
1499	Katharina von Bora
1797	Sibylle Mertens-Schaaffhausen
1850	Sarah Loguen Fraser
1866	Józefa Joteyko
1878	Mary Jobe Akeley
1939	Germaine Greer
1949	doris davenport
Deaths:	
1943	Tatiana Yosypivna Markus
2015	Colleen McCullough

Births:	**JANUARY 30**
59 BCE	Livia Drusilla
1590	Lady Anne Clifford
1874	Björg Þorláksdóttir
1912	Barbara W. Tuchman
1913	Amrita Sher-Gil
1914	Elizabeth McCord
1929	Lucille Teasdale-Corti
1937	Vanessa Redgrave
Deaths:	
680	Queen Balthild
1308	Margaret of Tyre
1971	Winifred Goldring

Births:	**JANUARY 31**
1723	Petronella Johanna de Timmerman
1859	Alice Bennett
1889	Aŋpétu Wašté Wiŋ (Ella Cara Deloria)
1896	Sofya Yanovskaya
1870	Susan Anderson

1873	Melitta Bentz
1909	Cornelia MacIntyre Foley
Deaths:	
39 BCE	Antonia Minor
876	Emma of Altdorf (Hemma)

FEBRUARY

Births:	**FEBRUARY 1**
1572	Ellen Marsvin
1882	Marie Majerová
1889	Gertrude Caton-Thompson
1905	Doris Lee
1918	Minnette de Silva
1946	Elisabeth Heath-Sladen
Deaths:	
525	Brigid of Kildare
1907	Kurmanjan Datka
1980	Toshiko Yuasa
1986	Alva Myrdal
2012	Wisława Szymborska
2014	Marie-Thérèse Assiga Ahanda

Births:	**FEBRUARY 2**
1494	Bona Sforza
1650	Eleanor Gwyn
1724	Amina I of the Maldives (Amina Kabafaanu)
1841	Sarah Hackett Stevenson
1935	Anne Raven Wilkinson
Deaths:	
1211	Adelaide of Meissen
1799	Dorothea Maria Lösch
1999	Marie Van Brittan Brown
2002	Ani Pachen

Births:	**FEBRUARY 3**
1338	Joanna of Bourbon
1821	Elizabeth Blackwell
1874	Gertrude Stein
1877	Janet Lane-Claypon
1898	Lil Hardin Armstrong
1909	Simone Weil
1974	Ayanna Soyini Pressley
Deaths:	
1094	Princess Teishi (Yōmeimon-in)

Births:	**FEBRUARY 4**
1868	Constance Markievicz
1913	Rosa Parks
1921	Betty Friedan
1827	Charlotte von Krogh
1899	Virginia M. Alexander
Deaths:	
1983	Karen Carpenter
2006	Betty Friedan

Births:	**FEBRUARY 5**
1626	Marie de Rabutin-Chantal, marquise de Sévigné
1892	Elizabeth Montague Ryan
1919	Cornelia Fort
Deaths:	
1912	Mary Greenleaf Clement Leavitt
1995	Ruth Smith Lloyd

Births:	**FEBRUARY 6**
1665	Anne, Queen of Great Britain
1839	Caroline Testman
1887	Florence Luscomb
1913	Mary Leakey
1917	Zsa Zsa Gabor (Sári Gábor)
1927	Eunice Xash-wee-tes-na Henry Bommelyn
Deaths:	
1135	Elvira of Castile, Queen of Sicily
2022	Lata Mangeshkar

Births:	**FEBRUARY 7**
1102	Empress Matilda (Maude)
1693	Empress Anna Ioannovna
1867	Laura Ingalls Wilder
1918	Ruth Sager
1923	Martha Holmes
1956	Eva Ayllón
Deaths:	
1127	Ava (Frau Ava, Ava of Göttweig, Ava of Melk)

Births:	**FEBRUARY 8**
1831	Rebecca Lee Crumpler
1850	Kate Chopin
1869	Maud Slye
1871	Lucy Minnigerode
1876	Paula Modersohn-Becker
1888	Edith Evans
1944	Harmony Hammond
Deaths:	
1587	Mary, Queen of Scots
1987	Papusza

Births:	**FEBRUARY 9**
1619	Queen Inseon

1819 Lydia Pinkham
1826 Ruth Ke'elikolani Keanolani Kanahoahoa
1854 Aletta Henriëtte Jacobs
1911 Bessie Stringfield
1942 Carole King
1944 Alice Walker
1979 Zhang Ziyi

Deaths:
1869 Charlotte Murchison

Births: **FEBRUARY 10**
1758 Amalia Holst
1806 Emma Catherine Embury
1842 Agnes Mary Clerke
1878 Jennie Smillie Robertson
1883 Edith Clarke
1886 Hiratsuka Raichō
1888 Eliza Amy Hodgson
1894 Mãe Menininha do Gantois
1932 Vivienne Malone-Mayes
1937 Roberta Flack

Deaths:
1050 Ingegerd Olofsdotter of Sweden (Anna/Saint Anna)
1660 Judith Leyster

Births: **FEBRUARY 11**
1466 Elizabeth of York
1715 Margaret Cavendish-Bentinck
1802 Lydia Maria Child
1847 Ada Kepley
1855 Ellen Day Hale
1869 Else Lasker-Schüler
1872 Hannah Mitchell
1916 Florynce Kennedy
1934 May Wykle

Deaths:
1275 Urania of Worms
1310 Marguerite d'Oingt
1963 Sylvia Plath
2005 Mary Jackson
2012 Whitney Houston

Births: **FEBRUARY 12**
661 Princess Ōku
1855 Fannie Barrier Williams
1890 Nina Hamnett
1914 Johanna Neumann
1921 Kathleen Rita Antonelli

Deaths:
1517 Catherine, Queen of Navarre
1865 Elizabeth Carrington Morris
2007 Peggy Gilbert

Births: **FEBRUARY 13**
1838 Annetta Seabury Dresser
1882 Katherine Von Madaler
1912 Antonia Pozzi
1926 Fay Ajzenberg-Selove

Deaths:
1906 Mary Emilie Holmes
1967 Forugh Farrokhzad
2015 Faith Bandler

Births: FEBRUARY 14
1632 Elizabeth, Lady Wilbraham
1820 Kutti Kunju Thankachi (Lakshmy Pilla)
1835 Emmy Carolina Rappe
1847 Anna Howard Shaw
1871 Marion Mahony Griffin

Deaths:
2013 Mary Brave Bird

Births: **FEBRUARY 15**
1638 Zeb-un-Nissa
1795 Rebecca Cox Jackson
1850 Sophie Bryant
1910 Irena Sendler
1931 Maxine Singer

Deaths:
1641 Sara Copia Sullam
2014 Thelma Estrin

Births: **FEBRUARY 16**
1574 Juliana Morell
1870 Leonora O'Reilly
1880 Kono Yasui
1883 Elizabeth Josephine Craig
1906 Vera Francevna Mencikova
1918 Patty Andrews
1920 Anna Mae Hays

Deaths:
902 Mary the Younger
1636 Tokuhime
1943 Mildred Harnack
1997 Chien-Shiung Wu

Births: **FEBRUARY 17**
624 Empress Wu Zetian
1827 Elisabeth Blomqvist
1858 Margaret Warner Morley
1875 Dulah Marie Evans
1877 Isabelle Marie Eberhardt
1909 Gertrude Abercrombie

1917 Whang-od Oggay
1948 Hung Liu
Deaths:
1694 Antoinette du Ligier de la Garde Deshoulières
2009 Conchita Cintrón

Births: **FEBRUARY 18**
1516 Mary Tudor I ("Bloody Mary")
1878 Blanche Ames
1889 Birleanna Blanks
1931 Toni Morrison
1933 Yoko Ono
1934 Audre Lorde
1944 Margaret H. Wright
Deaths:
1876 Charlotte Cushman

Births: **FEBRUARY 19**
1865 Franciszka Arnsztajnowa
1877 Gabriele Münter
1946 Karen Gay Silkwood
1952 Marcia Kemper McNutt
1964 Jennifer Anne Doudna
Deaths:
1989 Rosa Slade Gragg
2002 Sylvia Rivera

Births: **FEBRUARY 20**
1630 Josefa de Óbidos (baptized)
1805 Angelina Grimké
1875 Mary Barbour
1893 Elizabeth Holloway Marston
1902 Katharine "Kay" Way
1941 Buffy Sainte-Marie
Deaths:
922 Empress Theodora
1778 Laura Bassi
1869 Queen Falakika Seilala

Births: **FEBRUARY 21**
1878 Mirra Alfassa
1906 Agnes Yewande Savage
1914 Juliette Hampton Morgan
1915 Claudia Vera Cumberbatch Jones
1933 Nina Simone
1936 Barbara Jordan
1954 Cynthia Kenyon
Deaths:
1919 Mary Edwards Walker
1996 Zahra Rajabi
2000 Constance Cummings-John

Births: **FEBRUARY 22**
1829 Princess Sumiko
1855 Grace Annie Lockhart
1876 Ita Wegman
1876 Zitkála-Šá
1899 Katharine Lane Weems
Deaths:
845 Empress Dowager Wang
1911 Frances E.W. Harper
1913 Empress Dowager Longyu

Births: **FEBRUARY 23**
1879 Agnes Arber
1901 Ruth Nichols
1951 Deborah "Debbie" Friedman
Deaths:
1679 Anne Conway

Births: **FEBRUARY 24**
1876 Martha Cunz
1935 Hasna Begum
1942 Gayatri Chakravorty Spivak
Deaths:
1931 Fanny Cook Gates
1943 Helene Stöcker
2006 Octavia Estelle Butler

Births: **FEBRUARY 25**
1657 Agathe de Saint-Père
1670 Maria Margaretha Kirch
1842 Idawalley Zoradia Lewis
1871 Larysa Petrivna Kosach-Kvitka (Lesya Ukrainka)
1881 Lady Mabel Marguerite Annesley
1885 Princess Alice of Battenberg
1896 Ida Noddack
1896 Ida Cox
1904 Adelle Davis
1905 Iriaka Matiu Rātana
Deaths:
777/9 Saint Walpurga

Births: **FEBRUARY 26**
1858 Lavinia Lloyd Dock
1886 Mihri Müşfik Hanım
1900 Else Ida Pauline Kienle
Deaths:
1839 Sybil (Sibbell) Ludington
1939 Rahmah el Yunusiyah

Births: **FEBRUARY 27**
1859 Bertha Pappenheim
1869 Alice Hamilton

1890 Mabel Keaton Staupers
1932 Elizabeth Taylor
1956 Meena Keshwar Kamal
Deaths:
1984 Anna J. Cooper

Births: **FEBRUARY 28**
1261 Margaret of Scotland, Queen of Norway
1813 'Aimata Pōmare IV Vahine-o-Punuatera'itua
1920 Jadwiga Piłsudska
Deaths:
1903 Emily Warren Roebling

Births: **FEBRUARY 29**
1736 Ann Lee
1828 Emmeline B. Wells
1892 Augusta Savage
1916 Dinah Shore
1920 Michèle Morgan
1932 Reri Grist
Deaths:
1976 Florence P. Dwyer

MARCH

Births: **MARCH 1**
1717 Catharina Helena Dörrien
1860 Theresa Bernstein
1865 Elma Danielsson
1877 Mary Elizabeth Price
1889 Kanoko Okamoto
1921 Catharine McClellan
1945 Arlene Blum
1983 Lupita Amondi Nyong'o
Deaths:
1201 Shikishi
1585 Amalia of Cleves
1935 Sarah Schenirer
1938 Gauri Ma

Births: **MARCH 2**
1860 Susanna M. Salter
1916 Matilda J. Clerk
1950 Karen Carpenter
1951 Nancy Segal
1955 Dale Bozzio
Deaths:
1286 Empress Fujiwara no Ariko
1949 Sarojini Naidu
1995 Suzanne Basdevant Bastid
2007 Tsai-Fan Yu
2016 Berta Cáceres

Births: **MARCH 3**
1743 Izabela Czartoryska
1913 Margaret Allison Bonds
1949 Bonnie Dunbar
1931 Eva Jiřičná
Deaths:
1990 Charlotte Sitterly

Births: **MARCH 4**
1819 Narcyza Żmichowska
1946 Gloria Arellanes
1951 Theresa Hak Kyung Cha
1971 Berta Cáceres
Deaths:
1943 Marianne Joachim
1986 Ding Ling
2011 Alenush Terian

Births: **MARCH 5**
1224 Kinga of Poland (Saint Kinga)
1362 Empress Renxiaowen
1842 A. Viola Neblett
1856 Emma Steghagen
1871 Rosa Luxemburg
1885 Pauline Sperry
1885 Louise Pearce
1897 Soong Mei-ling
1912 Velma Bronn Johnston
1931 Geraldyn (Jerrie) Cobb
1938 Lynn Margulis

Births: **MARCH 6**
1906 Nora Stanton Blatch
1907 Katharina Jacob
Deaths:
1986 Georgia O'Keeffe

Births: **MARCH 7**
150 Lucilla
1869 Abby Lillian Marlatt
1938 Janet Guthrie
1940 Angela Carter
Deaths:
1489 Princess Yi Gu-ji
1913 E. Pauline Johnson
1942 Lucy Gonzalez Parsons

Births: **MARCH 8**
1702 Anne Bonny

1721 Elizabeth Pierrepont, Duchess of Kingston-upon-Hull
1892 Juana de Ibarbourou
1905 Dolores Prat Coll
1909 Beatrice Shilling
1923 Lydia Rapoport

Deaths:
1126 Queen Urraca of León and Castile
1365 Queen Noguk of Korea

Births: **MARCH 9**
1787 Josephine Kablick
1910 Sue Lee
1928 Graciela Olivarez

Deaths:
1847 Mary Anning
1895 Rebecca Lee Crumpler
1952 Alexandra Kollontai

Births: **MARCH 10**
1822 Rosa Bonheur
1850 Hallie Quinn Brown
1870 Ester Rachel Kamińska
1876 Anna Hyatt Huntington
1896 Nancy Cunard
1961 Laurel Blair Salton Clark

Deaths:
1913 Harriet Tubman

Births: **MARCH 11**
1811 Lady Katherine Sophia Kane
1829 Sarah Adamson Dolley
1914 Élisabeth Boselli

Deaths:
1950 Cora Reynolds Anderson
2016 Doreen Barbara Massey

Births: **MARCH 12**
1862 Jane Delano
1883 Ethel Collins Dunham
1923 Johnnie Mae Young
1968 Ladda Tammy Duckworth

Births: **MARCH 13**
963 Anna Porphyrogenita
1453 Mary Stewart, Countess of Arran
1774 Rose Fortune
1900 Queen Sālote Tupou III
1916 Ina Ray Hutton
1938 Erma Franklin
1941 Dana Meadows

Deaths:
1385 Katherine Berkeley
1906 Susan B. Anthony
1995 Odette Sansom

Births: **MARCH 14**
1523 Helena Magenbuch
1618 Nadira Banu Begum
1688 Anna Maria Garthwaite
1833 Lucy Hobbs Taylor
1851 Anna C. Maxwell
1868 Emily Murphy
1918 Dickey Chapelle
1947 Judith Plaskow
1997 Simone Biles

Deaths:
968 Matilda of Ringelheim
1765 Elżbieta Drużbacka

Births: **MARCH 15**
601 Empress Zhangsun (Empress Wendeshunsheng or Wende)
1758 Magdalene Sophie Buchholm
1825 Harriet E. Wilson
1838 Alice Cunningham Fletcher Grace
1868 Chisholm Young
1933 Ruth Bader Ginsburg
1938 Lynn Margulis

Births: **MARCH 16**
1750 Caroline Herschel
1799 Anna Atkins
1822 Rosa Bonheur
1943 Ursula Goodenough

Births: **MARCH 17**
1849 Cornelia Maria Clapp
1863 Anna Wessels Williams
1873 Margaret Grace Bondfield
1886 Alice Austen
1961 Kalpana Chawla

Deaths:
1912 Anna Filosofova
1956 Irène Joliot-Curie
1965 Nancy Cunard

Births: **MARCH 18**
1634 Marie-Madeleine de La Fayette
1883 Josephine Verstille Nivison (Jo Hopper)
1919 G. E. M. Anscombe
1935 Rosemary A. Stevens
1964 Bonnie Blair
1970 Dana Elaine Owens (Queen Latifah)

Deaths:
1980 Tamara de Lempicka

Births: **MARCH 19**
1841 Jeannette Wilkinson
1844 Minna Canth
1890 Nancy Elizabeth Prophet
1893 Gertrud Dorka
1921 Xie Xide
1923 Betty Roodish Goodwin
1947 Glenn Close
Deaths:
1612 Sophia Olelkovich Radziwill
1896 Pa Upoko Takau Ariki
1947 Carrie Chapman Catt

Births: **MARCH 20**
1263 Yolande of Dreux
1612 Anne Bradstreet
1845 Lucy Wright Mitchell
1879 Maud Menten
1890 Elizabeth Rona
Deaths:
1280 Empress Chabi
1572 Mary Basset

Births: **MARCH 21**
1467 Caritas Pirckheimer
1474 Angela Merici
1486 Imperia Cognati (Imperia La Divina)
1821 Graceanna Lewis
1835 Maria Magdalena Mathsdotter
1902 Regina Jonas
1920 Emīlija Gudriniece
Deaths:
1062 Richeza of Lotharingia
1617 Pocahontas (Rebecka Rolfe)

Births: **MARCH 22**
1470 Lucrezia Maria Romola de' Medici
1615 Katherine Jones, Viscountess Ranelagh
1846 Rita Cetina Gutiérrez
1880 Eleonora Noll-Hasenclever
1912 Agnes Martin
1917 Zuzanna Polina Gincburg (Ginczanka)
1920 Katsuko Saruhashi
1929 Yayoi Kusama
1932 Frances Allen
Deaths:
1882 Anna Murray Douglass
1948 Mileva Marić
2020 Frances Allen

Births: **MARCH 23**
1614 Jahanara Begum
1706 Anna Maria Barbara Abesch
1882 Emmy Noether
1906 Lea Grundig
190? Joan Crawford
1924 Jane Beverley Drew
1937 Judith D. Sally
1942 Ama Ata Aidoo
1948 Bracha Lichtenberg Ettinger
1953 Yvette Marie Stevens (Chaka Khan)
Deaths:
59 CE Agrippina the Younger
1914 Rafqa Pietra Choboq Ar-Rayès
2022 Madeleine Albright

Births: **MARCH 24**
1826 Matilda Joslyn Gage
1827 Candace Wheeler
1884 Chika Kuroda
1911 Jane Beverley Drew
1912 Dorothy Irene Height
Deaths:
1968 Alice Guy-Blaché

Births: **MARCH 25**
1347 Caterina di Jacopo di Benincasa (Catherine of Siena)
1594 Maria Tesselschade Visscher
1625 Ann, Lady Fanshawe
1723 Catharina Mulder
1776 Sophie Blanchard
1842 Susan Augusta Pike Sanders
1897 Emma Barrett (Sweet Emma)
1921 Mary Douglas
1934 Gloria Steinem
1942 Aretha Franklin
1967 Debi Thomas
Deaths:
1931 Ida B. Wells
2020 Soledad "Chole" Alatorre

Births: **MARCH 26**
1633 Mary Beale
1819 Louise Otto-Peters
1821 Amalie Dietrich
1824 Julie-Victoire Daubié
1863 Bertha Van Hoosen
1888 Elsa Brändström

1894 May Farquharson
1930 Sandra Day O'Connor
1940 Nancy Pelosi
1944 Diana Ross
1957 Shirin Neshat

Deaths:

1091 Wallada bint al-Mustakfi
1326 Alessandra Giliani
2011 Geraldine Ferraro

Births: **MARCH 27**

1676 Maria Clara Eimmart
1724 Jane Colden
1852 Anna Antoinette Weber-van Bosse
1857 Ella Hepworth Dixon
1873 Ollie Josephine Bennett
1880 Ruth Hanna McCormick
1883 Marie Under
1905 Elsie MacGill
1924 Sarah Vaughan
1924 Margaret Butler
1945 Annie Mae Aquash

Deaths:

1962 Augusta Savage
1977 Shirley Graham Du Bois

Births: **MARCH 28**

1515 Teresa of Ávila (Teresa Sánchez de Cepeda Dávila y Ahumada, Saint Teresa of Jesus)
1886 Clara Lemlich
1888 Regina Fleszarowa
1904 Margaret Lilardia Tucker
1912 Marina Raskova
1959 Bernardine Evaristo

Deaths:

1533 Katerina Lemmel
1941 Virginia Woolf

Births: **MARCH 29**

1843 Frances Wisebart Jacobs
1893 Dora Carrington
1920 Alene B. Duerk
1928 Joan Kelly
1968 Lucille Frances Ryan (Lucy Lawless)

Deaths:

1906 Slava Raškaj
1976 Mary Pickford
1985 Janet Vida Watson

Births: **MARCH 30**

1858 Gabriela Zapolska
1863 Mary Whiton Calkins
1882 Melanie Klein
1935 Cecilia Berdichevsky

Deaths:

1430 Joan of Arc
1842 Élisabeth Louise Vigée Le Brun
1911 Ellen Swallow Richards

Births: **MARCH 31**

356 Aelia Flaccilla
1577 Empress Nur Jahan
1865 Anandi Gopal Joshi
1882 Alexandra Kollontai
1895 Lizzie Miles
1928 Joan Feynman
1929 Jay DeFeo

Deaths:

1495 Cecily Neville
1876 Elizabeth Greenfield
2016 Dame Zaha Hadid

APRIL

Births: **APRIL 1**

1776 Marie-Sophie Germain
1882 Florence Aby Blanchfield
1897 Lucille Bogan
1940 Wangarĩ Muta Maathai
1963 Aprille J. Ericsson-Jackson

Deaths:

1984 Alma Clavering Howard Rolleston Ebert

Births: **APRIL 2**

1566 Bartholda van Swieten
1614 Jahanara Begum
1647 Maria Sibylla Merian
1788 Wilhelmine Reichard

Births: **APRIL 3**

1461 Anne of France
1791 Anne Lister
1817 Mathilde Franziska Anneke
1934 Jane Goodall

Deaths:

1915 Mary Elizabeth Garrett
2013 Ruth Prawer Jhabvala

Births: **APRIL 4**

1802 Dorothea Dix

1819 Queen Maria II of Portugal
1822 Grisell Baillie
1868 Philippa Fawcett
1869 Mary Colter
1873 Benita Asas Manterola
1891 Lidija Liepiņa
1911 Stella Walsh
1914 Marguerite Duras
1928 Maya Angelou

Births: **APRIL 5**
1170 Isabella of Hainault
1447 Catherine of Genoa
1751 Maria Lullin
1804 Mary Philadelphia Merrifield
1848 Emma Paterson
1863 Ida Freund
1901 Hattie Elizabeth Alexander
1908 Bette Davis
1910 Bracha Zefira
1975 Caitlin Moran
Deaths:
1205 Isabella I of Jerusalem
1970 Harriet Margaret Bolus
1992 Molly Picon

Births: **APRIL 6**
1863 Kate Macy Ladd
1867 Kate Campbell Hurd-Mead
1878 Abastenia St. Leger Eberle
1882 Rose Schneiderman
1917 Mary Leonora Carrington
Deaths:
1760 Charlotte Charke
1832 Queen Tripurasundari
1914 Lillian M. N. Stevens
1944 Rose O'Neill

Births: **APRIL 7**
1782 Marie-Anne Libert
1803 Flora Tristan
1872 Marie Equi
1874 Charlotte Maxeke (Manye)
1889 Gabriela Mistral
1890 Marjory Stoneman Douglas
1891 Martha May Eliot
1900 Gertrude Morgan
1915 Billie Holiday
1917 Irene Ayako Uchida
1930 Jane Priestman
Deaths:
1976 Mary Margaret McBride
2010 Graciela

Births: **APRIL 8**
1408 Jadwiga of Lithuania
1912 Mary Dee
1913 Erna Diez
1914 María Félix
1941 Vivienne Isabel Westwood
Deaths:
1993 Marian Anderson
2013 Margaret Hilda Thatcher

Births: **APRIL 9**
1773 Marie-Anne Victoire Gillain Boivin
1860 Emily Hobhouse
1876 Dorothy Hahn
1887 Florence Price
1904 Queen Sisowath Kossamak
1923 Sonja Ashauer
Deaths:
1302 Constance II of Sicily, Queen of Aragon

Births: **APRIL 10**
1825 Phoebe Lankester
1838 Lucy Higgs Nichols
1855 Jadwiga Olszewska
1861 Rachel ("Ray") Frank
1880 Frances Perkins
1882 Cora Reynolds Anderson
1930 Dolores Huerta
Deaths:
1922 Luisa Capetillo

Births: **APRIL 11**
1492 Marguerite de Navarre
1749 Adélaïde Labille-Guiard
1864 Johanna Elberskirchen
1908 Jane Bolin
1910 Annie Dodge Wauneka
Deaths:
1956 Zilphia Horton
2013 Maria Tallchief

Births: **APRIL 12**
1116 Richeza of Poland
1898 Clare Leighton
1933 Montserrat Caballé
1934 Yayori Matsui
1955 Sandy Hill
1964 Amy Ray
Deaths:
1912 Clara Barton

Births: **APRIL 13**
1350 Margaret III, Countess of Flanders
1519 Catherine de' Medici
1869 Isabel Maddison
1916 Edna Regina Lewis
1929 Yvonne Y. Clark
Deaths:
1622 Katharina Kepler

Births: **APRIL 14**
1331 Jeanne-Marie de Maille
1740 Anna Strong
1866 Anne Sullivan
1868 Annie Maunder
1910 Zilphia Horton
1919 Shamshad Begum
1937 Lucy R. Lippard
1940 Julie Christie
Deaths:
1935 Amalie Emmy Noether
1944 Mary Adela Blagg
2021 Joye (Hummel) Murchison Kelly

Births: **APRIL 15**
1858 Millicent Shinn
1863 Ida Freund
1865 Olga Helena Karolina Boznańska
1870 Mina Benson Hubbard
1892 Mary Harris Thompson
1892 Cornelia Arnolda Johanna "Corrie" ten Boom
1894 Bessie Smith
1896 May Edward Chinn
1926 Norma Merrick Sklrek
1915 Elizabeth Catlett
1952 Emma Thompson
Deaths:
628 Empress Suiko
1757 Rosalba Carriera
1999 Grace Zia Chu

Births: **APRIL 16**
1755 Élisabeth Vigée Le Brun
1845 Mary Eliza Mahoney
1855 Mary Ellen Britton
1892 Dora Rudolfine Richter
1921 Marie Maynard Daly
1939 Dusty Springfield
Deaths:
1090 Sikelgaita, Lombard duchess of Apulia
1689 Aphra Behn

Births: **APRIL 17**
1845 Isabel Hayes Barrows
1868 Zdeňka Wiedermannová-Motyčková
1912 Marta Eggerth
1912 Jo Ann Robinson
1916 Sirimavo Bandaranaike
1929 Mariama Bâ
Deaths:
1629 Catherine de' Medici, Governor of Siena
1794 Angélique Marguerite Le Boursier du Coudray
1913 Agnes McLaren
2013 Fatima binti Baraka

Births: **APRIL 18**
1480 Lucrezia Borgia
1619 Taj Bibi Bilqis Makani
1853 Ana Roqué de Duprey
1872 Ann Preston
1877 Bird Margaret Turner
1898 Ruth Bunzel
1917 Mamie Phipps Clark
1922 Alina Margolis-Edelman
1959 Susan Faludi
Deaths:
1076 Beatrice of Bar
1605 Marie de Brimeu
1618 Marie of the Incarnation
1942 Gertrude Vanderbilt Whitney

Births: **APRIL 19**
626 Eanflæd
1806 Sarah George Bagley
1856 Anna Sarah Kugler
1892 Germaine Tailleferre
Deaths:
843 Judith of Bavaria
1539 Katarzyna Weiglowa

Births: **APRIL 20**
1869 Mary Agnes Chase
1887 Margaret Newton
1891 Mary Phelps Jacob
1939 Gro Harlem Brundtland
Deaths:
1704 Agnes Block
1708 Damaris Cudworth Masham Laura
1898 Smith Haviland
2008 Monica Lovinescu

Births: **APRIL 21**
1816 Charlotte Brontë
1830 Clémence Royer
1841 Jennie Kidd Trout
1866 Josefa Toledo de Aguerri
1879 Raden Adjeng Kartini (Raden Ayu Kartini)
1912 Mary McCarthy
1912 Eve Arnold
Deaths:
1163 Héloïse
1994 Félicité Niyitegeka
2003 Nina Simone

Births: **APRIL 22**
1450 Queen Isabella I of Castile
1873 Ellen Glasgow
1909 Rita Levi-Montalcini
1912 Kathleen Ferrier
1937 Patricia Goldman-Rakic
1949 Elizabeth Ann Warren
Deaths:
2006 Henriette Avram

Births: **APRIL 23**
1522 Catherine of Ricci
1835 Uemura Shōen
1850 Agda Montelius
1876 Mary Ellicott Arnold
1899 Grace Zia Chu
1907 Lee Miller
1910 Sheila Scott Macintyre
1916 Sinah Estelle Kelley
1933 Annie Jean Easley
Deaths:
1554 Gaspara Stampa
1971 Dolores Cacuango

Births: **APRIL 24**
1847 Susan Dimock
1889 Lyubov Sergeyevna Popova
1911 Irene Sanger-Bredt
1937 Grace Oladunni Taylor
1959 Yvonne Cagle
Deaths:
2000 Vera Atkins
2020 Taneko Suzuki

Births: **APRIL 25**
1872 Henrietta Dozier
1884 Toshiko Tamura (Toshi Satō)
1885 Queen Emma of Hawaii
1905 Martha Sharp
1917 Ella Jane Fitzgerald
Deaths:
1566 Louise Charlin Perrin Labé

Births: **APRIL 26**
1875 Natalie Curtis Burlin
1886 Gertrude "Ma" Rainey
1905 Lily Parr
1909 Margaret Blackwood
Deaths:
1967 María de los Ángeles Cano Márquez
2005 Elisabeth Domitien

Births: **APRIL 27**
1759 Mary Wollstonecraft
1837 Queen Cheorin
1847 Emma Irene Åström
1912 Zohra Sehgal
1953 Ellen S. Baker

Births: **APRIL 28**
1652 Magdalena Sibylla of Hesse-Darmstadt
1701 Madeleine-Françoise Basseporte
1786 Elizabeth Andrew Warren
1844 Katarina Milovuk
1854 Phoebe Sarah Ayrton
1882 Frances Elliott Davis
1896 Na Hye-sŏk (Jeongwol)
1912 Odette Sansom
1926 Nelle Harper Lee
1929 Renate Mayntz

Births: **APRIL 29**
1871 Yoshioka Yayoi
1876 Empress Zewditu
1894 Marietta Blau
1896 Minnie Lucinda Fisher
1927 Betsy Ancker-Johnson
Deaths:
1380 Catherine of Castile

Births: **APRIL 30**
1662 Mary II of England
1758 Jane West
1864 Maria Ogilvie Gordon
1883 Elsinore Justinia Robinson
1904 Rosa Slade Gragg
1920 Gerda Lerner
1945 Rita Coolidge
1954 Elizabeth Jane Campion

Deaths:

535 Amalasuintha
783 Queen Hildegard
1948 Martha Beatrice Webb

MAY

Births: **MAY 1**

1689 Martha Fowke
1831 Emily Stowe
1847 Hildegard Björck
1852 Calamity Jane
1881 Mary MacLane
1910 Raya Dunayevskaya (Raya Shpigel, later Rae Spiegel)
1948 Patricia Hill Collins

Deaths:

1118 Matilda of Scotland, queen of England
1256 Mafalda of Portugal
1539 Isabella of Portugal
1911 Queen Makea Takau Ariki
1928 Xiang Jingyu

Births: **MAY 2**

1729 Catherine the Great
1856 Helene von Druskowitz
1872 Ichiyō Higuchi
1896 Helen of Greece and Denmark,
1902 Queen Mother of Romania
Mabel Hampton

Deaths:

1786 Petronella Johanna de Timmerman
1997 Queen Mother Moore

Births: **MAY 3**

1839 Anna Etheridge
1844 Sarah Warren Keeler
1849 Bertha Benz
1865 Martha M. Simpson
1898 Golda Meir
1901 Estelle Massey Osborne
1912 May Sarton
1930 Luce Irigaray
1987 Raffi Freedman-Gurspan

Deaths:

678 Princess Tōchi
1944 Margaret Eliza Maltby

Births: **MAY 4**

1559 Alice Spencer, Countess of Derby, Baroness Ellesmere and Viscountess Brackley
1804 Margaretta Riley
1842 Marietta Bones
1853 Marie Robinson Wright
1884 Agnes Fay Morgan
1898 Joy Bright Hancock
1904 Umm Kulthum
1922 Eugenie Clark

Deaths:

1138 Queen Arwa al-Sulayhi
1678 Anna Maria van Schurman
1912 Nettie Stevens
1924 E. Nesbit
1980 Elizabeth Muriel Gregory "Elsie" MacGill

Births: **MAY 5**

1775 Marie-Anne Calame
1837 Anna Maria Mozzoni
1852 Lydia Folger Fowler
1892 Dorothy Garrod
1921 Dorothy Louise Taliaferro "Del" Martin
1938 Lynn Margulis
1959 Kimberlé Crenshaw
1988 Adele

Deaths:

1138 Queen Arwa al-Sulayhi
1565 Queen Munjeong

Births: **MAY 6**

1757 Veronika Gut
1812 Madame Restell
1882 Ann Haven Morgan
1929 Rosemary Cramp

Deaths:

1275 Marie of Brienne
1942 Lilian Sheldon
1952 Maria Montessori

Births: **MAY 7**

1747 Judith van Dorth
1818 Juliet Hopkins
1842 Isala Van Diest
1845 Mary Eliza Mahoney
1952 Jacqueline Barton

Births: **MAY 8**

1869 Flora Murray
1910 Mary Lou Williams

Deaths:
1891 Helena Petrovna Blavatsky
1896 Vera Yevstafievna Popova
1944 Ethel Smyth

Births: **MAY 9**
1555 Jerónima de la Asunción
1842 Mary Bassett Mumford
1893 Regina Quintanilha
1921 Sophie Scholl
1951 Joy Harjo-Sapulpa

Births: **MAY 10**
1888 Lucy Wills
1900 Cecilia Helena Payne
1919 Ella Rosa Grasso
1946 Birutė Mary Galdikas
1953 Ellen Ochoa
Deaths:
1403 Katherine Swynford

Births: **MAY 11**
1838 Isabelle Bogelot
1875 Harriet Quimby
1894 Martha Graham
1899 Sára Salkaházi
1906 Jacqueline Cochran
1916 Farangis Yeganegi
Deaths:
1749 Catharine Cockburn d. 1749
1971 Lilian Bland d. 1971

Births: **MAY 12**
1756 Maria Pellegrina Amoretti
1820 Florence Nightingale
1849 Matilda Coxe Stevenson
1872 Eleanor Rathbone
1883 Hazel Harrison
1907 Katharine Hepburn
1921 Lily Renée
Deaths:
1986 Alicia Moreau de Justo
1991 Laudelina de Campos Melo

Births: **MAY 13**
1573 Empress Taj Bibi Bilqis Makani
1804 Janet Taylor
1888 Inge Lehmann
1899 Pelageya Polubarinova-Kochina
1947 Diane Noomin
1953 Sabina Chebichi
Deaths:
1934 Jeannette Elizabeth Brown

Births: **MAY 14**
1851 Anna Laurens Dawes
1856 Julia Dempsey
1955 Marian Croak
1969 Cate Blanchett
Deaths:
1881 Mary Jane Seacole
1940 Emma Goldman

Births: **MAY 15**
1689 Lady Mary Wortley Montagu
1759 Maria Theresia von Paradis
1857 Williamina Fleming
1900 Ida Rhodes
Deaths:
1886 Emily Dickinson
2014 Remedios Gomez-Paraiso (Kumander Liwayway)

Births: **MAY 16**
1626 Andrea Carlone
1718 Maria Gaetana Agnesi
1804 Elizabeth Peabody
1862 Margaret Fountaine
1898 Tamara de Lempicka
1925 Nancy Grace Roman
1929 Adrienne Rich
1947 Cheryl Clarke
1966 Janet Jackson
Deaths:
1163/4 Héloïse

Births: **MAY 17**
1665 Élisabeth Jacquet de La Guerre
1801 Lovisa Åhrberg
1858 Mary Adela Blagg
1873 Dorothy Richardson
1903 Lena Levine
1929 Jill Johnston
1938 Marcia Freedman
Deaths:
528 Empress Dowager Hu of Northern Wei
1395 Maria of Anjou, Queen of Hungary

Births: **MAY 18**
1917 Jacqueline Shohet Kahanoff
1926 Jane C. Goodale
1937 Suzanne Corkin
1938 Janet Fish
Deaths:
1910 Eliza Orzeszkowa
1990 Margaret Sylvia Gilliland

Births: **MAY 19**
1759 María Rita de Barrenechea y Morante
1812 Charlotte Guest
1834 Catherine Furbish
1856 Nadezhda Ziber-Shumova
1903 Ruth Ella Moore
1913 Morrnah Nalamaku Simeona
1941 Nora Ephron
Deaths:
1623 Mariam-uz-Zamani
1917 Belva Ann Lockwood

Births: **MAY 20**
1803 Ann Walker
1882 Sigrid Undset
1935/7 Hanna Krall
1946 Cherilyn Sarkasian (Cher)
Deaths:
1896 Clara Schumann
1921 Antoinette Brown
1961 Nannie Helen Burroughs

Births: **MAY 21**
1632 Feodosia Morozova
1780 Elizabeth Fry
1864 Stéphanie of Belgium
Deaths:
1911 Williamina Stevens Fleming
2016 Katherine Dunham

Births: **MAY 22**
1832 Laura Gundersen
1844 Mary Cassatt
1863 Josephine Cecilia Diebitsch Peary
1943 Betty Williams
1956 Helen James
Deaths:
1799 Toypurina
1959 Yoshioka Yayoi

Births: **MAY 23**
1810 Margaret Fuller
1831 Teriimaevarua
1841 Queen Teri'i-maeva-rua II
1842 Maria Konopnicka
1879 Elizabeth Gunn
1908 Annemarie Schwarzenbach
1910 Margaret Wise Brown
1934 Willie Hobbs Moore

Births: **MAY 24**
1335 Margaret of Bohemia
1789 Betsi Cadwaladr
1826 Marie Goegg-Pouchoulin
1870 Ynés Mexía
1878 Lillian Moller Gilbreth
1898 Helen B. Taussig
1899 Suzanne Flore Lenglen
Deaths:
1940 Olga Guramishvili-Nikoladze

Births: **MAY 25**
1849 Louise Hammarström
1854 Clara Louise Burnham
1886 Leta Stetter Hollingworth
1895 Dorothea Lange
1943 Mirriam Johnson (Jessi Colter)
1970 Octavia Spencer
Deaths:
1693 Marie-Madeleine Pioche de La Vergne, Comtesse de La Fayette
1899 Rosa Bonheur
1919 Madam C.J. Walker

Births: **MAY 26**
1895 Dorothea Lange
1948 Stevie Nicks
1966 Helena Bonham Carter
1975 Lauryn Hill
Deaths:
1091 Wallada bint al-Mustakfi

Births: **MAY 27**
1564 Margherita Gonzaga, Duchess of Ferrara
1652 Elizabeth Charlotte, Madame Palatine
1709 Margaret Lloyd
1818 Amelia Bloomer
1849 Alzina Stevens
1861 Victoria Earle Matthews
1870 Anna Magdalena Stecksén
1877 Isadora Duncan
1907 Rachel Louise Carson
1959 Donna Theo Strickland

Births: **MAY 28**
1831 Eliza Ann Gardner
1871 Queen Ari'i-'Otare Teri'i-maeva-rua III Pomare
1892 Margaret Frances Skinnider
1899 Irena Krzywicka
1912 Ruby Payne-Scott
1920 Pearl Prescod

Deaths:
1509 Caterina Sforza
1893 Queen Maerehia of Ra'iatea and Taha'a
1946 Lyda Conley
1974 Ángela Loij

Births: **MAY 29**
1876 Helen W. Atwater
1892 Mona Wilson
Deaths:
2008 Paula Gunn Allen

Births: **MAY 30**
1808 Caroline Chisholm
1926 Christine Jorgensen
1959 Claudia Joan Alexander
1963 Helen Patricia Sharman
Deaths:
375 Emmelia of Caesarea
1431 Joan of Arc
1472 Jacquetta of Luxembourg
2011 Maria Vasilyevna Klenova

Births: **MAY 31**
1725 Ahilyabai Holkar
1827 Kusumoto Ine
1887 Ethel Mary Doidge
1896 Hilda Margaret Lyon
1912 Chien-Shiung Wu
1947 Margaret Sloan-Hunter

JUNE

Births: **JUNE 1**
1776 Marie-Sophie Germain
1888 Iris Runge
1919 Judith Ethel Graham Pool
1926 Marilyn Monroe
1940 Katerina Gogou
1953 Liv Ragnheim Arnesen
Deaths:
847 Empress Xiao (Tang Dynasty)
1310 Marguerite Porete

Births: **JUNE 2**
1663 Anne-Marguerite Petit du Noyer
1899 Lotte Reiniger
1907 Dorothy West
1913 Barbara Pym
1913 Elsie Tu
1923 Béatrice Saada (Slama)
1978 Yi So-yeon
Deaths:
1701 Anna Stanisławska
1945 Agnes Baden-Powell
1970 Lucía Sánchez Saornil

Births: **JUNE 3**
1664 Rachel Ruysch
1799 Elisabetta Fiorini Mazzanti
1919 Elizabeth Duncan Koontz
Deaths:
1991 Catherine Joséphine "Katia" Krafft

Births: **JUNE 4**
1394 Philippa of England
1866 Miina Sillanpää
1870 Elizabeth Hesselblad
1925 Nurjahan Begum
1944 Holly Michelle Gilliam (Michelle Phillips)
Deaths:
1849 Marguerite Gardiner, Countess of Blessington
1997 Katherine Esau

Births: **JUNE 5**
1646 Elena Cornaro Piscopia
1887 Ruth Fulton Benedict
1930 Alifa Rifaat
1937 Hélène Cixous
1941 Martha Argerich
Deaths:
1832 Ka'ahumanu
2000 Bibi Titi Mohammed

Births: **JUNE 6**
1826 Sarah Parker Remond
1842 Elida Barker Fowle
1872 Alexandra Feodorovna
1942 Elma González
Deaths:
2014 Lorna Wing

Births: **JUNE 7**
1772 Aurora Liljenroth
1831 Amelia B. Edwards
1843 Susan Blow
1848 Dolores Jiménez y Muro
1909 Virginia Apgar
1909 Jessica Tandy
1917 Gwendolyn Brooks
1933 Tsuneko Okazaki

1950 Mosadi Seboko

Deaths:

1967 Dorothy Parker

Births: **JUNE 8**

1621 Anne de Xainctonge

1803 Amalia Assur

1858 Charlotte Angas Scott

1895 Dora Gordine

1900 Lena Baker

1907 Wilhelmina Goodson (Billie Pierce)

1930 Monique Andrée Serf

1940 Nancy Sinatra

Deaths:

62 CE Claudia Octavia

1290 Beatrice Portinari

1913 Emily Davison

1956 Marie Laurencin

Births: **JUNE 9**

1836 Elizabeth Garrett Anderson

1887 Gertrude Muller

Deaths:

1842 Maria Dalle Donne

1952 Alice Austen

Births: **JUNE 10**

1822 Lydia White Shattuck

1847 Gina Krog

1893 Hattie McDaniel

1904 Lin Huiyin (Phyllis Lin, Lin Whei-yin)

1912 Mary Lavin

1973 Faith Evans

1984 Shiva Nazar Ahari

Deaths:

1982 Margaret Manning

Births: **JUNE 11**

1815 Julia Margaret Cameron

1827 Natalie Zahle

1847 Millicent Fawcett

1860 Mary Jane Rathbun

1939 Rachael Heyhoe Flint

1941 Darshan Ranganathan

Deaths:

1297 Queen Jangmok

2001 Darshan Ranganathan

Births: **JUNE 12**

1802 Harriet Martineau

1879 Carolyn Van Blarcom

1883 Margaret Haig Thomas, 2nd Viscountess Rhondda

1895 Eugénie Brazier

1899 Anni Albers

1902 Daisy Yen Wu

1912 Eva Crane

1918 Georgia Louise Harris Brown

1929 Anne Frank

Deaths:

918 Æthelflæd

1697 Ann Baynard

2012 Elinor Ostrom

Births: **JUNE 13**

1643 Queen Myeongseong

1852 Anna Whitlock

1863 Lucy Christiana, Lady Duff-Gordon

1927 Aoki Yayoi

1937 Eleanor Holmes Norton

1954 Ngozi Okonjo-Iweala

Deaths:

1550 Veronica Gambara

1925 Ada Kepley

Births: **JUNE 14**

1839 Alice Fisher

1868 Anna B. Eckstein

1969 Steffi Graf

Deaths:

1928 Emmeline Pankhurst

1950 Katharine Glasier

Births: **JUNE 15**

1479 Lisa del Giocondo

1549 Elizabeth Knollys

1808 Juana Manuela Gorriti

1873 Leonora Cohen

1945 Miriam Defensor Santiago

1953 Ana Castillo

Deaths:

991 Theophanu

2016 Lois Duncan Steinmetz

Births: **JUNE 16**

1332 Isabella de Coucy

1850 Elizabeth Chambers Morgan

1885 Lilly Reich

1892 Ellen Schulz Quillin

1902 Barbara McClintock

Deaths:

1913 Mary Seney Sheldon

Births: **JUNE 17**
1610 Birgitte Thott
1865 Susan La Flesche Picotte
1902 Marion Hilliard
1922 Toshiko Takaezu
Deaths:
1889 Lozen
1918 Henrietta Augusta Dugdale

Births: **JUNE 18**
1913 Sylvia Porter
Deaths:
1164 Elisabeth of Schönau
1858 Queen Rani Lakshmibai
1996 Josefina Guerrero
2014 Stephanie Louise Kwolek
2016 Truus Menger-Oversteegen

Births: **JUNE 19**
1282 Gwenllian ferch Llywelyn
1838 Mary Cole Walling
1928 Joyce D. Miller
1940 Shirley Muldowney
Deaths:
1282 Eleanor de Montfort
1864 Sarah Rosetta Wakeman

Births: **JUNE 20**
1779 Dorothy Ann Thrupp
1896 Ellen Louise Mertz
1931 Constance Abernathy
Deaths:
1912 Voltairine de Cleyre

Births: **JUNE 21**
1851 Lillias Horton Underwood
1870 Clara Immerwahr
1927 Ye Shuhua
Deaths:
2012 Anna Jacobson Schwartz
2021 Ruth Leach Amonette

Births: **JUNE 22**
1427 Lucrezia Tornabuoni
1707 Elizabeth Blackwell (baptized)
1728 Princess Anna Paulina Jabłonowska
1876 Gwen John
1918 Cicely Saunders
1939 Ada E. Yonath
1949 Meryl Streep
1953 Cyndi Lauper
196? Erin Brockovich
Deaths:
1664 Katherine Philips

Births: **JUNE 23**
1751 Gregoria Apaza
1810 Fanny Elssler
1867 Augusta Kirchhoff
1879 Huda Sha'arawi
1889 Anna Akhmatova
1913 Helen Humes
1940 Wilma Rudolph
1957 Joanne Shenandoah
Deaths:
679 Queen Æthelthryth
1222 Constance of Aragon
1404 Eleanor of Arborea
1576 Levina Teerlinc

Births: **JUNE 24**
1871 Beatrice Tonnesen
1893 Suzanne La Follette
1914 Cecile Pearl Witherington Cornioley
1929 Carolyn Shoemaker
1941 Julia Kristeva
Deaths:
1933 Sissieretta Jones

Births: **JUNE 25**
617 Lady K'awiil Ajaw
1371 Queen Joanna II of Naples
1568 Gunilla Bielke, Queen of Sweden
1726 Anne Monson
1932 Aiono Fanaafi Le Tagaloa
Deaths:
2014 Ana María Matute

Births: **JUNE 26**
1854 Maria Pavlova
1900 Else Kienle
1911 Babe Didrikson Zaharias
Deaths:
1265 Anne of Bohemia, Duchess of Silesia
1339 Aldona Ona

Births: **JUNE 27**
1878 He Xiangning
1880 Helen Keller
1958 Maria Zuber
Deaths:
1786 Harriet Martineau
1837 Marie-Sophie Germain

1960	Lottie Dod

Births:	**JUNE 28**
1458	Charlotte, Queen of Cyprus
1641	Marie Casimire Louise de La Grange d'Arquien ("Marysieńka")
1891	Esther Forbes
1893	Florence Henri
1906	Maria Goeppert Mayer
Deaths:	
548	Theodora
1900	Harriet E. Wilson

Births:	**JUNE 29**
1475	Beatrice d'Este
1758	Clotilde Tambroni
1856	Maria Cederschiöld
1867	Emma Azalia Hackley
1930	Maryly Van Leer Peck
Deaths:	
1984	Audrey I. Richards

Births:	**JUNE 30**
1162	Empress Yang (or Gongsheng)
1702?	Elizabeth Timothy
1943	Florence Ballard
Deaths:	
1337	Eleanor de Clare
2012	Joyce D. Miller

JULY

Births:	**JULY 1**
1725	Rhoda Delaval
1804	George Sand
1873	Alice Guy-Blaché
1899	Doris Reynolds
1908	Estée Lauder
1971	Missy Elliott
Deaths:	
1589	Lady Saigō
1888	Chana Rachel Verbermacher (Maiden of Ludomir)
1912	Harriet Quimby

Births:	**JULY 2**
1559	Margareta Brahe
1876	Harriet Brooks
1911	Dorothy M. Horstmann
1923	Wisława Szymborska
1951	Sylvia Rivera
1984	Elise Marie Stefanik
Deaths:	
260	Cao Jie
1919	Anna Howard Shaw
1997	Shamsi Hekmat (Šamsi Morādpur Hekmat)
2020	Betsy Ancker-Johnson

Births:	**JULY 3**
1590	Lucrezia Orsina Vizzana
1832	María Ruiz de Burton
1860	Charlotte Perkins Gilman
1873	Frances Stern
1901	Ruth Crawford Seeger
1912	Elizabeth Taylor
1913	Dorothy Kilgallen
1957	Poly Styrene

Births:	**JULY 4**
68 CE	Salonia Matidia
1473	Matilda of Hesse
1844	Mary Edmonia Lewis
1868	Henrietta Swan Leavitt
1885	Lucy Diggs Slowe
1911	Elizabeth Peratrovich
1926	Berta Bensusen Özgün (Brudo)
1927	Gina Lollobrigida
1955	Polly E. Apfelbaum
Deaths:	
1336	Elizabeth of Portugal
2014	Hanna von Hoerner

Births:	**JULY 5**
1750	Elizabeth Philpot
1806	Blanka Teleki
1857	Clara Zetkin
1879	Wanda Landowska
1894	Margarita Nelken
2002	Zara Rutherford

Births:	**JULY 6**
1823	Sophie Adlersparre
1865	Mina Miller Edison
1887	Annette Kellermann
1907	Frida Kahlo y Calderón
1912	Molly Yard
1914	Viola Desmond
1934	Lobsang Dolma Khangkar
1952	Ann Tsukamoto
Deaths:	
1992	Marsha P. Johnson

Births: **JULY 7**
611 Eudoxia Epiphania
1207 Elizabeth of Hungary
1768 María Pascuala Caro Sureda
1851 Lillien Jane Martin
1861 Nettie Maria Stevens
1921 Helen Rodríguez Trías
Deaths:
1944 Elsinore Justinia Robinson
2007 Dame Anne Laura Dorinthea McLaren

Births: **JULY 8**
1593 Artemisia Gentileschi
1899 Audrey Richards
1862 Käthe Kollwitz
1898 Marie Jeanne (May) Picqueray
1926 Elisabeth Kübler-Ross
1972 Angela Warnick Buchdahl
Deaths:
900 Asma bint Khumarawayh ibn Ahmad ibn Tulun (Qatr al-Nada)
1967 Vivien Leigh
2020 Flossie Wong-Staal

Births: **JULY 9**
1764 Ann Radcliffe
1832 Martha Waldron Janes
1922 Kathleen Booth
1929 Eula Bingham
1936 June Jordan
Deaths:
1977 Alice Stokes Paul

Births: **JULY 10**
1724 Eva Ekeblad
1875 Mary Jane McLeod Bethune
1877 Hélène Dutrieu
1891 Edith Hinkley Quimby
1905 Millie Benson
1910 Mary Bunting
1931 Alice Ann Munro
Deaths:
1613 Kusumāsana Devi, Queen of Kandy

Births: **JULY 11**
1846 Gertrude Abbott
1901 Gwendolyn Lizarraga
1929 Heather Ashton
1939 Clara Adams-Ender
1974 Kimberly Denise Jones (Lil' Kim)
Deaths:
969 Olga of Kyiv
2002 Irene Bernard
2022 Gloria Lim

Births: **JULY 12**
1653 Elizabeth Walker
1730 Anna Barbara Reinhart
1780 Juana Azurduy de Padilla
1895 Kirsten Malfrid Flagstad
1912 Aoua Kéita
1913 Mildred Cohn
1939 Esther Eillam
Deaths:
1913 Ynés Enriquetta Mexía
1926 Gertrude Bell
1940 Augusta Kirchhoff
1979 Olive Morris

Births: **JULY 13**
1619 Birgitta Durell
1863 Margaret Murray
1938 Helga Königsdorf
Deaths:
1853 Jane Wells Webb Loudon
1952 Marie Equi

Births: **JULY 14**
1858 Emmeline Pankhurst
1862 Florence Bascom
1868 Gertrude Bell
1871 Gertrude Buck
1911 Gertrude Scharff Goldhaber
1914 Wim Hora Adema
Deaths:
1498 Gentile Budrioli
2017 Maryam Mirzakhani

Births: **JULY 15**
1455 Queen Yun
1793 Almira Hart Lincoln Phelps
1883 Eleanora Knopf
1892 Milena Rudnytska
1904 Dorothy Fields
1919 Jean Iris Murdoch
1938 Carmen Callil
1943 Jocelyn Bell Burnell
Deaths:
1884 Almira Hart Lincoln Phelps
1907 Qiu Jin
1919 Mana Sitti Habib Jamaladdin
1932 Bahíyyih Khánum

Births: **JULY 16**
1194 Clare of Assisi

1828 Abby Howland Woolsey
1862 Ida B. Wells
1882 Violette Neatley Anderson
1903 Irmgard Flügge-Lotz
1947 Assata Olugbala Shakur

Deaths:
1200 Empress Li Fengniang (or Cixian)
2001 Janina Oyrzanowska -Poplewska
2003 Celia Cruz

Births: **JULY 17**
1819 Eunice Newton Foote
1898 Berenice Abbott
1917 Margarete Mitscherlich-Nielsen
1921 Toni Stone

Deaths:
1399 Queen Jadwiga of Poland
1989 Mary Winifred Parke
2001 Katharine Graham

Births: **JULY 18**
1861 Kadambini Bose Ganguly
1869 Maria von Linden
1925 Shirley Strickland

Births: **JULY 19**
1817 Mary Ann Ball
1862 Ellen Beata Sandelin
1875 Alice Dunbar Nelson
1941 Carole Jordan
1954 Sophia Hennion Eckerson
1972 Zanele Muholi

Deaths:
379 Macrina the Younger

Births: **JULY 20**
1870 Margaret Ethel MacDonald
1896 Ellen Louise Mertz
1939 Judy Chicago
1959 Pamela Sklar

Deaths:
1980 Maria Montoya Martinez
2013 Helen Thomas

Births: **JULY 21**
1462 Queen Jeonghyeon
1837 Helen Appo Cook
1856 Louise Bethune
1944 Buchi Emecheta
1966 Sarah Ann Waters
1976 Cori Bush

Deaths:
710 Empress Wei
710 Shangguan Wan'er
1863 Josephine Ettel Kablick
2020 Joan Feynman

Births: **JULY 22**
1849 Emma Lazarus
1894 María Sabina
1898 Miriam O'Brien Underhill

Births: **JULY 23**
1503 Anne of Bohemia and Hungary
1880 Emma Perry Carr
1892 Icie Hoobler
1899 Ruth Charlotte Ellis
1902 Rosa Lee Ingram
1928 Vera Cooper Rubin
1931 Dame Te Atairangikaahu
1946 Felicia "Flames" Elizondo

Deaths:
1497 Barbara Fugger
1999 Emma Tenayuca
2011 Amy Weinhouse
2012 Sally Ride

Births: **JULY 24**
1866 Mary Bartelme
1868 Princess Srivilailaksana
1897 Amelia Earhart
1900 Zelda Fitzgerald
1914 Frances Oldham Kelsey
1920 Bella Savitzky Abzug
1940 Cynthia Moss
1960 Catherine Destivelle
1969 Jennifer Lopez
1976 Rashida Tlaib

Deaths:
661 Empress Kōgyoku
1115 Matilda, margravine of Tuscany
1912 Emma Cons

Births: **JULY 25**
1871 Margaret Floy Washburn
1873 Anne Morgan
1912 Ann Gregory
1920 Rosalind Elsie Franklin
1927 Eleanore Mikus
1940 Lourdes Grobet Argüelles
1956 Frances Hamilton Arnold

Deaths:
1190 Sibylla, queen of Jerusalem
1195 Herrad of Landsberg
1954 Mary Bartelme
1980 Martha Euphemia Haynes

Births: **JULY 26**
1817 Lucy N. Colman
1872 Maria Johanna Dahl
1902 Antonia Brico
1906 Irena Iłłakowicz
1925 Ana María Matute
1945 Helen Mirren
1945 Betty Davis
1973 Lenka Kotková
Deaths:
1937 Gerda Taro
1978 Mary Blair

Births: **JULY 27**
1740 Jeanne Baret
1841 Linda Richards
1898 Queen Mother Moore
1920 Belva Cottier
1927 Gisèle Halimi (Zeiza Gisèle Élise Taïeb)
1930 Shirley Brittain Williams
Deaths:
1924 Mohtaram Eskandari

Births: **JULY 28**
1609 Judith Jans Leyster (baptized)
1839 Isabelle Gatti de Gamond
1855 Louisine Havemeyer
1866 Beatrix Potter
1879 Lucy Burns
1884 Aida de Acosta

Births: **JULY 29**
1838 Shah Jahan Begum of Bhopal
1851 Jane Dieulafoy
1859 Karin Arosenius
1952 Ana María Sanzetenea
Deaths:
1994 Dorothy Mary Crowfoot Hodgkin

Births: **JULY 30**
1818 Emily Brontë
1857 Lucy Bacon
1893 Fatima Jinnah
1898 Poldi Fuhrich
1898 Friedl Dicker-Brandeis
1920 Marie Tharp
1926 Betye Irene Saar
1947 Françoise Barré-Sinoussi
1961 Sediqeh Dowlatabadi

Births: **JULY 31**
1909 Jenny Rosenthal Bramley
1916 Louise Smit
Deaths:
54 BCE Aurelia Cotta
2004 Virginia Grey

AUGUST

Births: **AUGUST 1**
1818 Maria Mitchell
1905 Helen Battles Sawyer Hogg
1910 Gerda Taro (Gerta Pohorylle)
1911 Jackie Ormes
1920 Henrietta Lacks
1963 Laura Janner-Klausner

Births: **AUGUST 2**
1894 Bertha Lutz
1902 Mina Spiegel Rees
1917 Catherine (Ginette) Dior
1942 Isabel Allende
1959 Shula Keshet
1963 Alysa Stanton
Deaths:
1911 Arabella Mansfield
1994 Hilde Radusch

Births: **AUGUST 3**
1486 Imperia Cognati (Imperia La Divina)
1704 Catherine-Nicole Lemaure
1821 Graceanna Lewis
1902 Regina Jonas
1920 Emīlija Gudriniece
Deaths:
925 Empress Dowager Cao

Births: **AUGUST 4**
1470 Lucrezia Maria Romola de' Medici
1880 Eleonora Noll-Hasenclever
1897 Anbara Salam Khalidi
1932 Frances Allen
Deaths:
1113 Gertrude of Saxony
1882 Anna Murray Douglass
1948 Mileva Marić
2020 Frances Allen

Births: **AUGUST 5**
1565 Paola Massarenghi
1823 Eliza Tibbets
1837 Anna Filosofova

1876	Mary Ritter Beard
1877	Ruth Wheeler
1905	Josefina Guerrero
1908	Miriam Louisa Rothschild
Deaths:	
1962	Marilyn Monroe
2013	Ruth Aiko Asawa
2019	Toni Morrison

Births:	**AUGUST 6**
1619	Barbara Strozzi (baptized)
1848	Susie King Taylor
1886	Inez Milholland
1919	Frances Adams Le Sueur
1930	Abbey Lincoln
1954	Lorna Dee Cervantes
Deaths:	
1676	Weetamoo

Births:	**AUGUST 7**
1735	Claudine Picardet
1890	Elizabeth Gurley Flynn
1933	Elinor Ostrom
1938	Helen Mary Caldicott
1947	Lydia Villa-Komaroff
1953	Margaret Profet

Births:	**AUGUST 8**
1640	Amalia Catharina
1814	Esther Morris
1850	Ruth Homan
1863	Florence Merriam Bailey
1879	Queen Tehaapapa III
1899	Eunice Thomasina Thomas Miner
1914	Sarla Thukral
Deaths:	
2005	Monica Sjöö

Births:	**AUGUST 9**
800	Irene of Athens
1869	Annie Turnbo Malone
1878	Eileen Gray
1894	Kathleen Lockhart
1908	Mary G. Ross
1914	Tove Marika Jansson
1919	Leona Harriet Woods
1922	Conchita Cintrón
Deaths:	
803	Empress Irene of Athens

Births:	**AUGUST 10**
1491	Queen Janggyeong
1658	Susanne Maria von Sandrart
1850	Ella M. S. Marble
1858	Anna J. Cooper
Deaths:	
30 BCE	Cleopatra
1241	Eleanor, Fair Maid of Brittany

Births:	**AUGUST 11**
1834	Orie Moon
1873	May Wilson Preston
1939	Val Plumwood
1965	Viola Davis
1941	Elizabeth Holtzman
Deaths:	
1253	Clare of Assisi
2009	Eunice Mary Kennedy Shriver

Births:	**AUGUST 12**
1831	Helena Blavatsky
1880	Radclyffe Hall
1887	María de los Ángeles Cano Márquez
1907	Gladys Bentley
1919	Eleanor Margaret Burbidge
Deaths:	
1895	María Ruiz de Burton
1898	Maria Vasilyevna Klenova
2017	Fatima Ahmed Ibrahim

Births:	**AUGUST 13**
1616	Plautilla Bricci
1880	Mary Macarthur
1890	Lydia Zvereva
1905	Anita Brenner
1927	Frances Sarnat Hugle
Deaths:	
587	Radegund
612	Fabia Eudokia
1910	Florence Nightingale

Births:	**AUGUST 14**
1814	Charlotte Fowler Wells
1848	Margaret Lindsay, Lady Huggins
1901	Mercedes Comaposada
1911	Ethel L. Payne
1928	Lina Wertmüller
Deaths:	
1912	Octavia Hill

Births:	**AUGUST 15**
1858	E. Nesbit
1892	Kathleen Maisey Curtis
1896	Gerty T. Cori
1906	Suzanne Basdevant Bastid

1912 Julia Child
1984 Ayọ (Opal) Tometi
1990 Jennifer Lawrence

Births: **AUGUST 16**
1594 Queen Inyeol
1776 Amalia von Helvig
1859 Anna Ancher
1865 Dame Mary Jean Gilmore
1899 Maria Wittek
1912 Wendy Hiller
1958 Angela Bassett
Deaths:
79 CE Empress Ma
1852 Táhirih (Fatimah Baraghani)
2001 Anna Mani

Births: **AUGUST 17**
1828 Maria Deraismes
1893 Mae West
1895 Caroline Haslett
1900 Vivienne de Watteville
1908 Papusza
1912 Elsie Locke
1936 Margaret Hamilton
1938 Trina Robbins
1954 Ingrid Daubechies
1958 Belinda Carlisle

Births: **AUGUST 18**
1629 Agneta Horn
1770 Dorothea von Rodde-Schlözer
1859 Anna Ancher
1874 Nora Lilian Alcock
1902 Margaret Thomas Murie
1911 Amelia Boynton Robinson
1911 Maria Ulfah Santoso
1912 Josephine Barnes
1912 Elsa Morante
1940 Joan Joyce
1959 Winona LaDuke
Deaths:
1942 Marianne Baum

Births: **AUGUST 19**
1883 "Coco" Chanel

Births: **AUGUST 20**
1565 Margaretha van Valckenburch
1893 Lotte Cohn
1938 Isabel Morgan
1967 Mika Yamamoto

Births: **AUGUST 21**
1844 Edith Jemima Simcox
1874 Eleanor Davies-Colley
1912 Natalia Dudinskaya
1915 Ismat Chughtai
1917 Esther Cooper Jackson
1947 Margaret Chan Fung Fu-chun
1967 Carrie-Anne Moss
Deaths:
1762 Mary Wortley Montagu

Births: **AUGUST 22**
1816 Jeanette Berglind
1867 Minnie "Maud" Powell
1882 Baroness Raymonde de Laroche
1893 Dorothy Parker
Deaths:
251 Empress Zhen
1664 Maria Cunitz (Cunitia)

Births: **AUGUST 23**
1720 Sybilla Masters
1876 Agnes Cleve-Jonand
1911 Betty Robinson
1915 Graciela
1924 Elaine Frances Sturtevant
1942 Patricia McBride
Deaths:
1335 Heilwige Bloemardinne
1777 Clelia Grillo Borromeo
1989 Katharina Jacob
2006 Marie Tharp

Births: **AUGUST 24**
1552 Lavinia Fontana (baptized)
1559 Sophia Brahe
1617 Rose of Lima
1663 Catherine Bernard
1707 Selina Hastings, Countess of Huntingdon
1829 Emanuella Carlbeck
1841 Anna Hierta-Retzius
1856 Rosa Welt-Straus
1862 Zonia Baber
1919 Tosia Altman
1942 Hazel Ying Lee
1945 Marsha P. Johnson
Deaths:
1261 Ela of Salisbury
2022 Lily Renée

Births: **AUGUST 25**
1588 Elizabeth Poole

1876	Eglantyne Jebb
1927	Althea Gibson
Deaths:	
1298	Queen Gongwon
1995	Edith Kristan-Tollmann

Births:	**AUGUST 26**
1702	Judith Madan
1827	Nathalie Lemel
1892	Elizebeth Smith Friedman
1918	Katherine Johnson
1920	Alberte Pullman
1945	Jo Freeman (Joreen)
Deaths:	
1462	Catherine Zaccaria
1788	Elizabeth Pierrepont, Duchess of Kingston-upon-Hull

Births:	**AUGUST 27**
1875	Katharine McCormick
1937	Alice Coltrane
1941	Cesária Évora
1946	Flossie Wong-Staal
Deaths:	
923	Queen Ageltrude
1949	Uemura Shōen
2011	Eva Schönbeck-Temesy

Births:	**AUGUST 28**
1938	Ramona Bennett
1952	Rita Dove
Deaths:	
630	Fāṭima bint Muḥammad
770	Empress Kōken (Shōtoku)
1616	Queen Raja Hijau
1941	Nguyễn Thị Minh Khai
2012	Shulamith Bath Shmuel Ben Ari Firestone

Births:	**AUGUST 29**
1899	Christina Cruikshank Miller
1915	Ingrid Bergman
1923	Truus Menger-Oversteegen
1924	Dinah Washington
1947	Mary Temple Grandin
1955	Diamanda Galás
Deaths:	
1982	Ingrid Bergman

Births:	**AUGUST 30**
1627	Margaretha van Godewijk
1684	Marguerite de Launay, baronne de Staal
1906	Olga Taussky-Todd
1912	Nancy Wake
1922	Regina Resnik
1935	Sylvia Earle
1969	Sara Ahmed
1973	Amy Sherald
Deaths:	
1979	Jean Seberg

Births:	**AUGUST 31**
1675	Elizabeth Thomas
1775	Agnes Bulmer
1842	Mary Putnam Jacobi
1861	Jessie Brown Pounds
1870	Maria Montessori
1880	Wilhelmina of the Netherlands
1903	Helen Irene Battle
1913	Helen Levitt
Deaths:	
1056	Theodora Porphyrogenita
1944	Maria Dimadi

SEPTEMBER

Births:	**SEPTEMBER 1**
504	Lady (Queen) of Tikal
1789	Marguerite Gardiner, Countess of Blessington
1815	Emma Stebbins
1854	Anna Botsford Comstock
1895	Hertha Sponer
1927	Soshana Afroyim
1949	Leslie Feinberg
Deaths:	
2022	Diane Noomin

Births:	**SEPTEMBER 2**
1838	Queen Lili'uokalani
1840	Emilia Dilke
Deaths:	
1941	Kei Okami

Births:	**SEPTEMBER 3**
1629	Lady Mary Dering
1803	Prudence Crandall
1836	Sara Allen Plummer
1854	Anna Sandström
1868	Mary Parker Follett
1891	Bessie Delany
1905	Nechama Leibowitz
1910	Dorothy Maynor

1963	Paula Therese Hammond
Deaths:	
1912	Josephine Silone Yates
1996	Emily Kame Kngwarreye
2010	Rajeshwari Chatterjee

Births:	**SEPTEMBER 4**
1895	Xiang Jingyu
Deaths:	
1199	Joan of England, queen of Sicily
2014	Joan Delano Aiken

Births:	**SEPTEMBER 5**
1500	Maria of Jever
1867	Amy Marcy Cheney Beach
1897	Cornelia Ponse
1976	Sarab Abu-Rabia-Queder
Deaths:	
1782	Gregoria Apaza
1964	Elizabeth Gurley Flynn
2018	Freddie Nanda Dekker-Oversteegen

Births:	**SEPTEMBER 6**
1620	Isabella Leonarda
1761	Marie-Gabrielle Capet
1829	Marie Zakrzewska
1860	Jane Addams
1916	Kathleen Basford
1923	Nada Dimić
1925	Freddie Nanda Dekker-Oversteegen
Deaths:	
1951	Winifred Edgerton Merrill
1966	Margaret Sanger
2017	Katherine Murray Millett

Births:	**SEPTEMBER 7**
1533	Elizabeth I, the Virgin Queen
1633	Catharina Regina von Greiffenberg
1859	Margaret Crosfield
1885	Jovita Idar
1975	Marie-Agnès Gillot
1933	Tomoko Ohta

Births:	**SEPTEMBER 8**
1413	Catherine of Bologna
1652	Luisa Roldán
1934	Margaret Caroline Heagarty
Deaths:	
1882	Sarah Mapps Douglass
1959	Elsinore Justinia Robinson
1969	Alexandra David-Néel

Births:	**SEPTEMBER 9**
1806	Sarah Mapps Douglass
1868	Mary Hunter Austin
1892	Tsuru Aoki
1899	Theodora Mead Abel
1914	Marjorie Lee Browne
1919	Maria Lassnig
1934	Sonia Sanchez
1945	Elena Cándida Quinteros Almeida
Deaths:	
803	Irene of Athens
1282	Ingrid of Skänninge

Births:	**SEPTEMBER 10**
1880	Laura Cornelius Kellogg
1890	Elsa Schiaparelli
1907	Dorothy Hill
1909	Tránsito Amaguaña
1910	Reva Stern Stetten Gornbein
1917	Ena Collymore-Woodstock
1935	Mary Oliver
1938	Roxanne Dunbar-Ortiz
1982	Misty Danielle Copeland
Deaths:	
1749	Emilie du Châtelet
2011	Dame Bernice Lake

Births:	**SEPTEMBER 11**
1762	Joanna Baillie Mercedes
1804	Marín del Solar
1847	Mary Watson Whitney
1859	Kei Okami
1875	Edith Ellen Humphrey
Deaths:	
1161	Melisende, Queen of Jerusalem
1990	Myrna Mack Chang

Births:	**SEPTEMBER 12**
1788	Charlotte Heidenreich von Siebold
1840	Mary Jane Patterson
1867	Justyna Budzińska-Tylicka
1894	Dorothy Maud Wrinch
1897	Irène Joliot-Curie
1953	Nancy Goldin
Deaths:	
640	Queen Sak K'uk' of Palenque
1949	Izabela Textorisová

Births:	**SEPTEMBER 13**
64 CE	Julia Flavia
1546	Isabella Bendidio
1775	Laura Secord

1819	Clara Josephine Schumann
1856	Maria Louise Baldwin
1886	Amelie Hedwig Boutard-Beese
1977	Fiona Apple
Deaths:	
1931	Lili Elbe (Lili Ilse Elvenes)

Births:	**SEPTEMBER 14**
1401	Maria of Castile, Queen of Aragon
1810	Caroline Rosenberg
1843	Lola Rodríguez de Tió
1879	Margaret Sanger
1934	Kate Millett
1983	Amy Winehouse
Deaths:	
1982	Grace Kelly
2017	Klara Perahya

Births:	**SEPTEMBER 15**
1505	Mary of Hungary
1857	Anna Winlock
1870	Rahel Hirsch
1879	Anna Essinger
1977	Chimamanda Ngozi Adichie
Deaths:	
1173	Petronilla, queen of Aragon
1396	Queen Sindeok

Births:	**SEPTEMBER 16**
10 CE	Julia Drusilla
1725	Anna Barbara Gignoux
1846	Anna Kingsford
1885	Karen Horney
1887	Louise Arner Boyd
1887	Nadia Boulanger
1902	Mildred Harnack
1920	Hannie Schaft
1921	Ursula Franklin
1933	Dame Vera Stephanie "Steve" Shirley
Deaths:	
1977	Maria Callas

Births:	**SEPTEMBER 17**
1783	Nadezhda Durova
1888	Michiyo Tsujimura
1931	Anne Bancroft
Deaths:	
1179	Hildegard of Bingen

Births:	**SEPTEMBER 18**
1587	Francesca Caccini (La Cecchina)
1905	Greta Garbo
1905	Agnes de Mille
1907	Agathe van Beverwijk
Deaths:	
1918	Susan La Flesche Picotte

Births:	**SEPTEMBER 19**
1865	Rosetta Sherwood Hall
1839	Mary Anna Draper
1883	Mabel Vernon
1911	Jane Oppenheimer
1917	Amalia Hernández
1932	Stefanie Zweig
Deaths:	
961	Helena Lekapene
1039	Empress Fujiwara no Genshi

Births:	**SEPTEMBER 20**
1888	Susan S. Dauser
1890	Rachel Bluwstein
1910	Dorothy Jean Johnson Vaughan
1948	Adrian Piper
Deaths:	
1933	Annie Besant
1947	Jantina "Tine" Tammes
1978	Lilly Becher

Births:	**SEPTEMBER 21**
1552	Barbara Longhi
1851	Susan Macdowell Eakins
1898	Frances Mary Albrier
1902	Marie Germinová
1917	Phyllis Nicolson
1917	Sara Little Turnbull
1921	Tatiana Yosypivna Markus
1947	Marsha Norman
Deaths:	
1931	Hazrat Babajaan

Births:	**SEPTEMBER 22**
1664	Catherine Jérémie
1829	Emeline Horton Cleveland
1891	Alma Thomas
1939	Junko Tabei
1953	Julianne Marie Malveaux
Deaths:	
1840	Anne Lister
1948	Florence Augusta Merriam Bailey

Births:	**SEPTEMBER 23**
1569	Tachibana Ginchiyo
1838	Victoria Woodhull
1839	Helen A. Shafer
1843	Emily Warren Roebling

1851 Ellen Hayes
1863 Mary Church Terrell
1917 Asima Chatterjee
1923 Anita Cornwell
1970 Ani DiFranco

Deaths:

1869 Eleonora Ziemięcka

Births: **SEPTEMBER 24**

1825 Frances Ellen Watkins Harper
1861 Bhikaiji Cama (Madam Cama)
1862 Winifred Edgerton Merrill
1919 Teresa Rebull (Soler i Pi)
1946 María Teresa Ruiz
1963 Mary Agnes Chase
1978 Ida Noddack

Deaths:

1418 Anne of Cyprus

Births: **SEPTEMBER 25**

1621 Mary Sidney
1867 Katharine Glasier
1904 Olive Beech
1917 Chajka Klinger
1952 bell hooks

Deaths:

1900 Elizabeth Van Lew
2011 Wangari Maathai

Births: **SEPTEMBER 26**

1832 Zsófia Torma
1876 Edith Abbott
1877 Bertha De Vriese
1920 Domina Eberle Spencer
1942 Gloria Evangelina Anzaldúa

Births: **SEPTEMBER 27**

1657 Sophia Alekseyevna
1953 Mātā Amritānandamayī Devī

Deaths:

1939 Jadwiga Szeptycka

Births: **SEPTEMBER 28**

1856 Kate Douglas Wiggin
1887 Beulah Louise Henry
1893 Hilda Geiringer
1947 Sheikh Hasina Wazed
1959 Margarita del Val

Deaths:

782 Leoba
1992 Johanna Piesch

Births: **SEPTEMBER 29**

1683 Elizabeth Elstob
1927 Barbara Mertz
1944 Anne Briggs

Deaths:

2001 Mabel Fairbanks

Births: **SEPTEMBER 30**

1847 Wilhelmina Drucker
1883 Nora Stanton Barney
1911 Ruth Gruber

Deaths:

1888 Eunice Newton Foote
2019 Victoria A. Braithwaite

OCTOBER

Births: **OCTOBER 1**

1814 Josefina Deland
1847 Annie Besant
1859 Clarissa Thompson Allen
1860 Mary Eileen Ahern
1893 Marianne Brandt
1912 Kathleen Ollerenshaw
1930 Julie Andrews

Deaths:

1126 Morphia of Melitene
1854 Anne Royall
1864 Rose O'Neal Greenhow

Births: **OCTOBER 2**

1718 Elizabeth Montagu
1755 Hannah Adams
1889 Margaret Jessie Chung
1907 Ria Deeg

Deaths:

1775 Fukuda Chiyo-ni

Births: **OCTOBER 3**

1648 Elisabeth Sophie Chéron
1858 Eleonora Amalia Duse
1885 Sophie Treadwell
1916 María de los Ángeles Alvariño González
1920 Philippa Foot
1925 Simone Segouin
1931 Denise Scott Brown
1983 Tessa Thompson

Deaths:

1953 Florence Rena Sabin
1993 Katerina Gogou

2015	Anneliese Sitarz

Births:	**OCTOBER 4**
1843	Marie-Alphonsine Danil Ghattas
1924	Eulie Chowdhury
1942	Pung Chhiv Kek
1946	Susan Sarandon
1982	Ilhan Omar
Deaths:	
1582	St. Teresa of Ávila
1951	Henrietta Lacks
2020	Lee Hyo-jae

Births:	**OCTOBER 5**
1524	Queen Rani Durgavati
1643	Zinat-un-Nissa
1884	Zhang Mojun
1932	June Almeida
1975	Kate Winslet
Deaths:	
2000	Ruth Charlotte Ellis
2008	Beth A. Brown
2015	Grace Lee Boggs

Births:	**OCTOBER 6**
1565	Marie de Gournay
1729	Sarah Crosby
1839	Catherine Louisa Pirkis
1864	Jadwiga Szczawińska-Dawidowa
1887	Marie Jedličková (Maria Jeritza)
1897	Florence Barbara Seibert
1900	Ethel Edith Mannin
1907	Salome Gluecksohn-Waelsch
1917	Fannie Lou Hamer
Deaths:	
404	Empress Aelia Eudoxia

Births:	**OCTOBER 7**
1675	Rosalba Carriera
1845	Marie Heim-Vögtlin
1845	Edith Pechey
1891	Louisa Gould
Deaths:	
1904	Isabella Bird
2021	Myriam Paula Sarachik

Births:	**OCTOBER 8**
1807	Harriet Taylor
1826	Emily Blackwell
1872	Mary Engle Pennington
1881	Evelyn Cheesman
1936	B. Rosemary Grant
1956	Janice Voss
Deaths:	
1910	Maria Konopnicka
1978	Bertha Parker Pallan

Births:	**OCTOBER 9**
1862	Fatma Aliye Topuz
1884	Helene Deutsch
1888	Julie Reisserová
1895	Frances Beatrice Bradfield
1901	Alice Lee Jemison
1924	Eva Hodgson
1949	Fan Chung
1950	Jody Williams

Births:	**OCTOBER 10**
1853	Jeanne Immink
1915	Édith Piaf
1928	Marylise Ben Haïm
Deaths:	
1827	Nandi Bhebhe
1971	Margaret Frances Skinnider
1977	Lea Grundig

Births:	**OCTOBER 11**
1871	Harriet Boyd Hawes
1872	Emily Wilding Daviso
1884	Eleanor Roosevelt
1885	Alicia Moreau de Justo
Deaths:	
1905	Isabelle Gatti de Gamond

Births:	**OCTOBER 12**
1818	Elizabeth Van Lew
1840	Helena Modjeska (Modrzejewska)
1859	Diana Abgar
1904	Ding Ling
1904	Laudelina de Campos Melo
1912	Alice Childress
1919	Wignuke Waste Win
1939	Carolee Schneemann
Deaths:	
1914	Margaret E. Knight

Births:	**OCTOBER 13**
1320	Perenelle Flamel
1613	Luisa María Francisca de Guzmán y Sandoval
1856	Eliza Ruhamah Scidmore
1862	Mary Kingsley
1901	Edith Sampson
1906	Aloha Wanderwell
1989	Alexandria Ocasio-Cortez

Births:	OCTOBER 14
1856	Vernon Lee (Violet Paget)
1888	Katherine Mansfield
1888	Hanayo Ikuta
1894	Victoria Drummond
1897	Dorothy Wright Liebes
1906	Hannah Arendt
1914	Liliana Lubińska
1939	Callista Roy

Births:	OCTOBER 15
1831	Isabella Bird
1859	Augusta Dejerine-Klumpke
1880	Marie Stopes
1917	Marion Donovan
Deaths:	
958	Toda Aznárez of Pamplona
1173	Petronilla of Aragon
1240	Razia Sultana (Raziyyat-Ud-Dunya Wa Ud-Din)
1904	Anna Magdalena Stecksén

Births:	OCTOBER 16
1867	Kazimiera Bujwidowa
1912	Maidie Norman
1915	Nancy Bird Walton
1928	Mary Daly
1935	Umpeleya Marsema Balinton (Sugar Pie DeSanto)
1959	Pamela C. Rasmussen
Deaths:	
1793	Marie-Antoinette-Josèphe-Jeanne d'Autriche-Lorraine
1868	Nakano Takeko
1908	Eugénie Le Brun (Madame Rushdi)

Births:	OCTOBER 17
1517	Amalia of Cleves
1720	Maria Teresa Agnesi
1720	Marie Geneviève Charlotte Thiroux d' Arconville
1847	Chiquinha Gonzaga
1854	Queenie Newall
1864	Queen Yaa Asantewaa
1868	Sophia Hayden
1915	Concha Pérez Collado
1917	Niuta Tajtelbaum
1956	Mae Jemison
Deaths:	
33 CE	Agrippina the Elder
1271	Steinvör Sighvatsdóttir
1891	Sarah Winnemucca Hopkins
1921	Queen Yaa Asantewaa

Births:	OCTOBER 18
1523	Anna Jagiellon
1849	Sarah Tyson Rorer
1881	Elizabeth Bagshaw
1887	Pauline Newman
1898	Lotte Lenya
1903	Karoline Radke-Batschauer
1921	Beatrice Helen Worsley
1947	Laura Nyro
1984	Esperanza Emily Spalding
Deaths:	
1480	Eowudong
1891	Sarah Winnemucca Hopkins

Births:	OCTOBER 19
1835	Amanda Jones
1850	Annie Smith Peck
1908	Zofia Lissa
1909	Marguerite Perey
1909	Marguerite Catherine Perey
1932	Joan Semmel
1936	Aleida March

Births:	OCTOBER 20
1820	Mary F. Eastman
1889	Suzanne Duchamp
1922	Kathryn Hach-Darrow
1937	Wanda Jackson
1942	Christiane Nüsslein-Volhard
Deaths:	
460	Aelia Eudocia
2016	Junko Tabei

Births:	OCTOBER 21
1628	Úrsula Micaela Morata
1861	Maria Dulębianka
1911	Mary Blair
1921	Jane Briggs Hart
1929	Ursula K. Le Guin
1956	Carrie Fisher
1967	Julia Roberts
1973	Lera Auerbach
Deaths:	
1808	Maria Christina Bruhn
1944	Hilma af Klint
2017	Denise P. Barlow

Births:	OCTOBER 22
1844	Sarah Bernhardt
1865	Borghild Holmsen
1875	Harriet Chalmers Adams
1912	Frances Drake
1919	Doris Lessing

1925 Violet Rosemary Strachan Hutton

Births: **OCTOBER 23**

1727 Empress Xiaoyichun
1752 Maria Anna Adamberger
1844 Sarah Bernhardt
1881 Adelina Otero-Warren
1906 Gertrude Ederle
1907 Sofka Skipwith

Births: **OCTOBER 24**

1621 Serafina of God
1732 Cristina Roccati
1764 Dorothea von Schlegel
1830 Belva Ann Lockwood
1830 Marianne North
1859 Jane Walker
1885 Rachel Katznelson-Shazar
1895 Oku Mumeo
1896 Marjorie Stewart Joyner
1924 Evangelina Villegas

Deaths:

1911 Idawalley Zoradia Lewis
1913 Cornelia Cole Fairbanks
2005 Rosa Parks
2021 rita bo brown

Births: **OCTOBER 25**

1750 Marie Le Masson Le Golft
1887 Emma Rowena Gatewood (Grandma Gatewood)
1900 Funmilayo Ransome-Kuti
1921 Marian Koshland
1972 Esther Duflo
1975 Zadie Smith

Deaths:

1989 Mary McCarthy

Births: **OCTOBER 26**

1862 Hilma af Klint
1881 Dolores Cacuango
1902 Beryl Clutterbuck Markham
1902 Henrietta Swope
1911 Mahalia Jackson
1929 Cleofé Elsa Calderón
1935 Ora Mendelsohn Rosen
1947 Hillary Rodham Clinton

Deaths:

1555 Olympia Fulvia Morata
1631 Catherine de Parthenay
1879 Angelina Grimké
1902 Elizabeth Cady Stanton
1989 Mabel Hampton

Births: **OCTOBER 27**

1561 Mary Sidney
1885 Sigrid Hjertén
1898 Hélène Cazès-Benatar
1910 Margaret Hutchinson Rousseau
1927 Lee Krasner
1930 Gladys Mae West
1932 Sylvia Plath

Deaths:

1441 Margery Jourdemayne
1603 Irina Godunova
1968 Elise Meitner
2016 Susan Lee Lindquist

Births: **OCTOBER 28**

1816 Mary Frame Myers
1842 Anna Elizabeth Dickinson
1867 Sister Nivedita
1879 Luisa Capetillo
1891 Maria José de Castro Rebello Mendes
1897 Edith Head
1965 Miyako Yoshida

Deaths:

1412 Margaret I of Denmark
1997 Marian Elliott Koshland

Births: **OCTOBER 29**

1629 Agneta Block
1711 Laura Maria Caterina Bassi Veratti
1808 Caterina Scarpellini
1837 Harriet Powers
1881 Marion Phillips
1908 Louise Bates Ames
1930 Omara Portuondo
1938 Ellen Johnson-Sirleaf
1948 Kerstin Jeppsson
1960 Fabiola Gianotti

Deaths:

1707 Maria Clara Eimmart
1804 Sarah Crosby
1939 Margaret Floy Washburn

Births: **OCTOBER 30**

1741 Angelica Kauffmann
1872 Louisa Martindale
1889 Anne-Marie Durand-Wever
1939 Grace Barnett Wing (Grace Slick)
1939 Emily Howell Warner

Deaths:

1953 Alice Eastwood
2012 Samina Raja

Births: **OCTOBER 31**
1618 Mariana de Jesús de Paredes
1711 Laura Bassi
1768 María Isidra de Guzmán y de la Cerda
1860 Juliette Gordon Low
1874 Mary Swartz Rose
1876 Natalie Clifford Barney
1883 Marie Laurencin
1903 Joan Violet Robinson
1918 Genoa Keawe
1937 Casey Hayden
1980 Alondra de La Parr
Deaths:
1214 Eleanor of England, Queen of Castile
1984 Indira Priyadarshini Gandhi

November

Births: **NOVEMBER 1**
1526 Catherine Jagiellon
1848 Caroline Still Anderson
1874 Salima Machamba, Sultan of Mohéli
1910 Nguyễn Thị Minh Khai
1972 Toni Collette
Deaths:
1892 Queen Tamaeva IV

Births: **NOVEMBER 2**
1154 Constance, Queen of Sicily
1582 Elizabeth Jane Weston
1890 Moa Martinson
1913 Beryl Eugenia McBurnie
1936 Rosemary Radford Ruether
Deaths:
1261 Bettisia Gozzadini
1996 Toni Stone

Births: **NOVEMBER 3**
1474 Isabella d'Este
1659 Hui-bin Jang
1836 Elena Arellano Chamorro
1869 Ester Almqvist
1877 Rosalie Barrow Edge
1880 Avra Theodoropoulou
1890 Yamakawa Kikue
1905 Loïs Mailou Jones
1912 Marie-Claude Vaillant-Couturier
Deaths:
1112 Anna Vsevolodovna
1324 Petronilla de Meath
1526 Katherine Briçonnet

Births: **NOVEMBER 4**
1829 Hanna Hammarström
1853 Anna Bayerová
1889 Elna Kiljander
1897 Edavalath Kakkat Janaki Ammal
1922 Kanitha Wichiencharoen
1923 Sulamith Goldhaber
1924 Lee Hyo-jae
1929 Mary Sherman Morgan
1942 Patricia Era Bath
1954 Condoleezza Rice
Deaths:
604 Queen Yohl Ik'nal of Palenque
1130 Margaret Fredkulla
1360 Elizabeth de Clare

Births: **NOVEMBER 5**
1607 Anna Maria van Schurman
1641 Empress Xiaohuizhang
1770 Sarah Guppy
1833 Georgeanna Woolsey
1900 Ethelwynn Trewavas
1913 Vivien Leigh
1917 Jacqueline Auriol
1921 Marianne Joachim
1945 Elouise Pepion Cobell (Yellow Bird Woman)
1960 Tilda Swinton
1974 Susana Chávez
Deaths:
1957 Olive Dennis

Births: **NOVEMBER 6**
10 CE Agrippina the Younger
1479 Joanna of Castile
1874 Helen Thompson Woolley
1901 Juanita Hall
1903 Hilde Radusch
1936 Barbara Morgan (Sparkle Moore)
1945 Lani Hall Alpert
1946 Sally Field
Deaths:
1908 Cut Nyak Dhien (Tjoet Nja' Dhien)
1954 Atalie Unkalunt
1975 Annette Kellerman

Births: **NOVEMBER 7**
1867 Marie Skłodowska-Curie

1943 Roberta Joan Anderson (Joni Mitchell)

Births: **NOVEMBER 8**
1456 Queen Gonghye
1720 Madeleine de Puisieux
1833 Alice Bunker Stockham
1857 Kate Sessions
1862 Signe Hornborg
1875 Qiu Jin (Ch'iu Chin)
1878 Dorothea Bate
1884 Margaret Watkins
1920 Felicitas Svejda
1952 Alfre Woodard
Deaths:
1246 Berengaria of Castile
1258 Grzymisława of Łuck
1832 Marie-Jeanne-Amélie Le Francais de Lalande

Births: **NOVEMBER 9**
1805 Harriot Kezia Hunt
1868 Marie Dressler
1871 Florence Sabin
1913 Hedy Lamarr
1914 Cywia (Zivia) Lubetkin
1923 Alice Coachman
1946 Martha Settle Putney
Deaths:
1333 Empress Saionji Kishi
1978 Thérèse Tréfouël

Births: **NOVEMBER 10**
1697 Louise Hippolyte, Princess of Monaco
1884 Zofia Nałkowska
1957 Oyèrónkẹ́ Oyěwùmí
Deaths:
1293 Isabella de Forz, Countess of Devon
1705 Justine Siegemund
1941 Carrie Matilda Derick
2008 Zensi Miriam Makeba

Births: **NOVEMBER 11**
990 Gisela of Swabia
1852 Clorinda Matto de Turner
1866 Martha Annie Whiteley
1876 Ellen Pyle
1886 Alice Huyler Ramsey
1896 Shirley Graham Du Bois
1915 Anna Jacobson Schwartz
1922 Mary Belle Allen
1926 Maria Teresa de Filippis
1930 Mildred Dresselhaus
1933 Miriam Tlali
Deaths:
875 Teutberga, queen of Lotharingia
1130 Teresa of León, Countess of Portugal
1917 Maria Firmina dos Reis
2006 Jeanne A. Smith

Births: **NOVEMBER 12**
1559 Princess Yaza Datu Kalaya
1606 Jeanne Mance
1630 Catherine Duchemin
1648 Juana Inés de la Cruz
1666 Mary Astell
1815 Elizabeth Cady Stanton
1905 Louise Thaden
1917 Dahlov Ipcar
1917 Jo Elizabeth Stafford
1926 Taneko Suzuki
Deaths:
1946 Elisa Acuña Rossetti
1959 Dolores Ibárruri

Births: **NOVEMBER 13**
1715 Dorothea Erxleben
1806 Emilia Plater
1845 Marta Abreu
1869 Helene Stöcker
1885 Sonia Delaunay
1897 Tilly Edinger
1906 Eva Zeisel
1924 Sarah Jackson
1938 Jean Seberg
Deaths:
1462 Anne of Austria, Landgravine of Thuringia
1939 Florence Lois Weber

Births: **NOVEMBER 14**
1860 Isabel Bevier
1864 Claribel Cone
1954 Condoleezza Rice
Deaths:
1687 Eleanor Gwyn
1817 Policarpa Salavarrieta
1847 Fanny Mendelssohn

Births: **NOVEMBER 15**
1607 Madeleine de Scudéry
1873 Sara Josephine Baker
1887 Georgia O'Keeffe

1891 Anna Regina Feuerstein
1913 Riek Schagen
1916 Bouena Sarfatty Garfinkle
1923 Miriam Schapiro
1932 Petula Clark
1968 Deborah Jin

Deaths:
1908 Dowager Empress Cixi
1942 Annemarie Schwarzenbach
2014 Sylvia Anita Edlund

Births: **NOVEMBER 16**
1775 Jane Austen
1862 Ida Alexander Gibbs Hunt
1866 Cornelia Sorabji
1869 Esther Pohl Lovejoy
1889 Anna Kéthly
1913 Dora de Pedery-Hunt
1946 Barbara Smith
1949 Pattie Santos
1985 Sanna Marin

Deaths:
1093 Margaret, queen of Scotland
1131 Dobrodeia Eupraxia Mstislavna of Kiyv
1625 Sofonisba Anguissola

Births: **NOVEMBER 17**
1650 Joanna Koerten
1715 Dorothea Erxleben
1719 Marie Marguerite Bihéron
1882 Germaine Dulac
1903 Ema Řezáčová
1903 Ruth Harriet Bleier

Deaths:
1447 Euphemia of Münsterberg
1998 Sultana Daoud (Reinette l'Oranaise)
2013 Doris May Lessing
2015 Irma M. Wyman

Births: **NOVEMBER 18**
1825 Amanda Akin Stearns
1924 Anna Elisabeth Østergaard
1931 Barbara McMartin
1945 Wilma Pearl Mankiller

Deaths:
1990 Beatrice Shilling

Births: **NOVEMBER 19**
1828 Queen Rani Lakshmibai
1845 Agnes Giberne
1876 Tatyana Afanasyeva
1910 Gladys Lounsbury Hobby
1956 Eileen Marie Collins
1957 Bat-Sheva Ofra Haza
1970 Loung Ung

Deaths:
1299 Mechtilde
1515 Claudine, Lady of Monaco
1963 Carmen Amaya
2013 Mavis Lilian Batey

Births: **NOVEMBER 20**
1797 Mary Buckland
1815 Maria Cederschiöld
1827 Emily Howland
1838 Hedvig Raa-Winterhjelm
1858 Selma Lagerlöf
1910 Pauli Murray
1919 Haika Grossman
1927 Miriam Akavia
1963 Ming-Na Wen
1995 Olive Dennis

Deaths:
1230 Nicola de la Haye
1242 Queen Narchat

Births: **NOVEMBER 21**
1700 Charlotta Elisabeth van der Lith
1834 Hetty Green
1868 Martha Wollstein
1902 Phoebe Omlie
1933 Jean Shepard
1940 Natalia Makarova

Deaths:
2011 Olivia Hooker

Births: **NOVEMBER 22**
1828 Lydia Shackleton
1860 Maud Morgan
1861 Ranavalona III
1925 Geraldine Lois Fredritz (Jerrie Mock)
1990 Maria Toorpakai Wazir

Deaths:
2021 Joanne Shenandoah

Births: **NOVEMBER 23**
1798 Klementyna Hoffmanowa
1857 Katharine Coman
1897 Ruth Etting
1912 Virginia Prince
1924 Josephine "JoJo" D'Angelo
1930 Geeta Dutt
1934 Rita Colwell

Deaths:
1535 Beatriz Galindo
1612 Elizabeth Jane Weston (Alžběta Johana Vestonie)
1856 Manuela Sáenz
1985 Concepción Mendizábal Mendoza

Births: **NOVEMBER 24**
1685 Kate Gleason
1891 Maria Pawlikowska-Jasnorzewska
1896 Rosa Henderson
1933 Marie Desma Wilcox
Deaths:
1642 Walatta Petros

Births: **NOVEMBER 25**
1274 Catherine I (Catherine of Courtenay)
1454 Catherine Cornaro, Queen of Cyprus, Jerusalem and Armenia
1493 Osanna of Cattaro
1545 Ana de Jesús
1848 Margaret Abigail Cleaves
1865 Kate Gleason
1914 Bessie Blount Griffin
Deaths:
1944 Hazel Ying Lee

Births: **NOVEMBER 26**
1653 Empress Xiaochengren
1792 Sarah Moore Grimké
1814 Luise Aston
1822 Lilly Martin Spencer
1832 Mary Edwards Walker
1907 Ruth Myrtle Patrick
1939 Anne Mae Billock (Tina Turner)
1948 Elizabeth Helen Blackburn
Deaths:
1504 Queen Isabella I of Castile
1883 Sojourner Truth
1998 Gyo Fujikawa

Births: **NOVEMBER 27**
1635 Françoise d'Aubigné, Marquise de Maintenon
1809 Fanny Kemble
1863 Olha Kobylianska
1873 Ellen Newbold LaMotte
1875 Elsie Clews Parsons
1882 Elsinore Justinia Robinson
1932 Elsa Guðbjörg Vilmundardóttir
Deaths:
450 Galla Placidia
1198 Constance, Queen of Sicily
1655 Anna Ovena Hoyer
1884 Fanny Elssler
1939 Leta Stetter Hollingworth
1976 Sarah Elizabeth Stewart

Births: **NOVEMBER 28**
1682 Elizabeth "Betty" Parris
1698 Charlotta Frölich
1896 Asta von Mallinckrodt-Haupt
1919 Faye Schulman
1932 Ethel Ennis
1944 Rita Mae Brown
Deaths:
1982 Queen Helen of Greece and Denmark

Births: **NOVEMBER 29**
1759 Jemima Wilkinson
1832 Louisa May Alcott
1835 Empress Dowager Cixi
1843 Gertrude Jekyll
1912 Viola Smith
Deaths:
320 Saint Illuminata
1872 Mary Somerville

Births: **NOVEMBER 30**
1843 Martha G. Ripley
1874 Lucy Maud Montgomery
1919 Jane Cooke Wright
1924 Shirley Chisholm
1927 Martha Cowles Chase
1946 Marina Abramović

DECEMBER

Births: **DECEMBER 1**
1083 Anna Komnene
1813 Ann Preston
1882 Nina Vedeneyeva
1913 Mary Ainsworth
1985 Janelle Monáe

Births: **DECEMBER 2**
1501 Queen Munjeong
1745 Queen Jeongsun
1885 Susan Stebbing
1995 Mária Telkes

Births: **DECEMBER 3**
1766 Barbara Fritchie
1797 Margaretta Morris
1838 Octavia Hill
1842 Ellen Swallow Richards
1847 Christine Ladd-Franklin
1895 Anna Freud
1909 Dana Suesse
1912 Alice Bunker Stockham

Births: **DECEMBER 4**
1822 Frances Power Cobbe
1884 Dewi Sartika
1899 Barbara Brukalska
1915 Ellinor Catherine Cunningham van Someren
1945 Roberta Bondar
1964 Dionne Farris

Births: **DECEMBER 5**
1806 Anne Pratt
1912 Kate Simon
Deaths:
902 Ealhswith
1730 Alida Withoos (burial)
1784 Phillis Wheatley Peters
1926 Felicia Adetowun Omolara Ogunsheye

Births: **DECEMBER 6**
1863 Margaret Morse Nice
1888 Libbie Hyman
1912 Paloma Efrón
1916 Katya Budanova
1927 Patsy Matsu Mink
1944 Akasha Gloria Hull
Deaths:
1788 Nicole-Reine Lepaute

Births: **DECEMBER 7**
1578 Okaji no Kata
1831 Rachel Bodley
1878 Yosano Akiko
1890 Katharine Densford
1893 Paula Ackerman
1896 Yoshiko Yuasa
1924 Mary Ellen Rudin
Deaths:
1979 Cecilia Payne-Gaposchkin
2008 Marlyn Meltzer

Births: **DECEMBER 8**
1626 Queen Christina of Sweden
1854 Anna Maria Bilińska-Bohdanowiczowa
1878 Marie Mattingly Meloney
1805 Adeline Blanchard Tyler
1907 Gwendolyn Wilson Fowler
1919 Kateryna Yushchenko
1919 Julia Hall Bowman Robinson
1926 Azar Andami
Deaths:
1418 Queen Jeonghui
1431 Hedwig Jagiellon
1444 Charlotte, Queen of Cyprus

Births: **DECEMBER 9**
1779 Sarah "Tabitha" Babbitt
1823 Rosalie Olivecrona
1870 Ida Sophia Scudder
1895 Dolores Ibárruri
1900 Margaret Brundage
1906 Grace Hopper
1934 Judith Olivia Dench

Births: **DECEMBER 10**
1815 Augusta Ada King (née Byron), Countess of Lovelace
1830 Emily Elizabeth Dickinson
1856 Karolina Widerström
1866 Louise de Hem
1891 Nelly Sachs
Deaths:
1875 Ōtagaki Rengetsu

Births: **DECEMBER 11**
1813 Clemence S. Lozier
1863 Annie Jump Cannon
1879 Gertrude Weil
1888 Božena Laglerová
1926 Willie Mae Thornton (Big Mama Thorton)
1968 Emmanuelle Marie Charpentier
Deaths:
1950 Leslie Comrie
2002 Marvin Breckinridge

Births: **DECEMBER 12**
1826 Martha Coston
1900 Mária Telkes
1919 Olivia Barclay
1925 Elizabeth "Betita" Martínez
1928 Helen Frankenthaler
1938 Concetta Rosamarie Franconero (Connie Francis)
1942 Micere Githae Mugo

Deaths:
1912 Susan Tolman Mills
1981 Queen Khamphoui of Laos
1988 June Tarpé Mills

Births: **DECEMBER 13**
1818 Ana Néri
1871 Emily Carr
1903 Ella Josephine Baker
Deaths:
1075 Empress Xuanyi (Xiao Guanyin)

Births: **DECEMBER 14**
1631 Anne Conway
1705 Queen Seonui
1771 Regina von Siebold
1784 Hortense Haudebourt-Lescot
1789 Maria Szymanowska
1817 Sophia Wilkens
1832 Ana Betancourt
1863 Marie Louise Bottineau Baldwin
1885 Ethel Browne Harvey
1908 Doria Shafik
1960 Catherine Coleman
Deaths:
1077 Agnes of Poitou
1963 Marie Marvingt

Births: **DECEMBER 15**
1584 Queen Inmok
1861 Clara Driscoll
1896 Eslanda Robeson
1900 Hellé Nice
1913 Muriel Rukeyser
Deaths:
1673 Margaret Cavendish, Duchess of Newcastle-upon-Tyne
1934 Maggie L. Walker
2021 bell hooks

Births: **DECEMBER 16**
1624 Queen Jangnyeol
1630 Mary Somerset, Duchess of Beaufort
1777 Madame Clicquot Ponsardin
1850 Betzy Akersloot-Berg
1868 Agnes Baden-Powell
1878 Gertrud Woker
1901 Margaret Mead
1906 Raquibunnesa Mahmuda Khatun Siddiqua
1907 Frances Hamerstrom
1938 Liv Ullmann
Deaths:
705 Empress Wu-hou (Wu Zetian)
999 Adelaide of Italy
2013 Inés Lucia Cifuentes

Births: **DECEMBER 17**
1706 Émilie du Châtelet
1900 Mary Lucy Cartwright
1913 Mary Kenneth Keller
Deaths:
1559 Irene di Spilimbergo
1562 Eleonora di Toledo
1663 Queen Nzinga Mbande
1879 Maria W. Stewart
1970 Parashqevi Qiriazi
2018 Anne Raven Wilkinson

Births: **DECEMBER 18**
1783 Mary Anne Whitby
1847 Augusta Holmès
1862 Hedda Maria Emerence Adelaide Elisabeth Ekman
1881 Gladys Dick
1922 Esther Lederberg
1937 Karen DeCrow
1980 Christina Aguilera
Deaths:
1645 Emperess Nur Jahan
1888 Eagle Woman
2006 Mollie Orshansky

Births: **DECEMBER 19**
1291 Margareta Ebner
1778 Marie Thérèse of France
1820 Mary Livermore
1831 Bernice Pauahi Bishop
1875 Mileva Marić Einstein
1895 Grace Marie Bareis
1895 Ingeborg Refling Hagen
1908 Yvette Cauchois
1915 Édith Piaf
1924 Cicely Tyson
1932 Lola Hendrics
1969 Aziza Mustafa Zadeh
Deaths:
739 Samthann
1091 Adelaide of Susa
1588 Esther Handali
1848 Emily Jane Brontë
1957 Ida Alexander Gibbs Hunt

Births: **DECEMBER 20**
1808 Laura Smith Haviland

1812 Laura M. Hawley Thurston
1827 Lydia Sayer Hasbrouck
1851 Thérèse Schwartze
1861 Ivana Kobilca
1904 Yevgenia Ginzburg
1948 Mitsuko Uchida
1954 Sandra Cisneros

Deaths:

1812 Sacagawea
2007 Lydia Mendoza

Births: **DECEMBER 21**

1744 Anne Vallayer-Coster
1846 Julia Lermontova
1866 Maud Gonne
1884 María Cadilla
1892 Rebecca West (Dame Cicily Isabel Fairfield)
1905 Käte Fenchel
1916 Emma Tenayuca
1920 Adele Goldstine
1920 Alicia Alonso
1922 Cécile DeWitt-Morette
1926 Ellen Lanyon
1937 Jane Fonda
1959 Florence Griffith Joyner

Deaths:

1921 Gabriela Zapolska
1937 Violette Neatley Anderson
1950 Hattie Ophelia Caraway

Births: **DECEMBER 22**

1853 Teresa Carreño
1853 Sarada Devi
1868 Katharina "Käthe" Paulus
1873 Lilian Helen "Lily" Montagu
1907 Peggy Ashcroft
1944 Mary Doreen Archer

Deaths:

1880 George Eliot
1915 Rose Talbot Bullard
1925 Amelie Beese
1959 Gilda Gray
1986 Mary Burchell

Births: **DECEMBER 23**

1828 Mathilde Wesendonck
1857 Helen Abbott Michael
1865 Anna Farquhar Bergengren
1867 Clotilde Apponyi
1898 Taki Fujita
1912 Anna Jane Harrison
1917 Sophie Masloff
1952 Ulrike Beisiegel

Deaths:

1304 Matilda of Habsburg
1754 Queen Alliquippa
1805 Geneviève Thiroux d'Arconville
1912 Lotten von Kræmer
1918 Thérèse Schwartze
2022 Margaret Heagarty

Births: **DECEMBER 24**

1520 Martha Eriksdotter Leijonhufvud
1632 Gabrielle Suchon
1843 Lydia Koidula
1887 Lucrezia Bori (Lucrecia Borja y González de Riancho)
1900 Hortense Powdermaker
1920 Stormé DeLarverie

Deaths:

1660 Mary, Princess Royal and Princess of Orange
1813 Empress Go-Sakuramachi
1964 Claudia Jones
2015 Adriana Olguín

Births: **DECEMBER 25**

1820 Susan Hayhurst
1821 Clara Barton
1870 Helena Rubinstein
1886 Malak Hifni Nasif
1911 Louise Joséphine Bourgeois

Deaths:

304 Saint Anastasia

Births: **DECEMBER 26**

1424 Margaret Stewart, Dauphine of France
1526 Rose Lok
1618 Elisabeth of the Palatinate
1636 Justine Siegemund
1665 Lady Grizel Baillie
1780 Mary Somerville
1870 Virginia Bolten
1872 Helena Rubinstein
1883 Hana Meisel
1929 China Machado
1954 Susan Butcher

Deaths:

1395 Elisabeth, Countess of Neuchâtel
1796 Queen Velu Nachiyar
1941 Frances Hardcastle
1952 Margrethe Mather
2018 Sulagitti Narasamma

Births: **DECEMBER 27**

1000 Emma of Blois
1797 Manuela Sáenz
1913 Elizabeth Smart
1924 Jean Bartik

Deaths:

1557 Queen Dangyeong
2001 Helen Rodríguez Trías
2007 Benazir Bhutto
2011 Helen Frankenthaler
2016 Carrie Fisher

Births: **DECEMBER 28**

1722 Eliza Lucas
1774 Mary Birkett Card
1920 Loretta Ford

Deaths:

1394 Maria Angelina Doukaina Palaiologina
1566 Margaret Paleologa
1694 Mary II of England
2004 Susan Sontag

Births: **DECEMBER 29**

1704 Martha Daniell Logan
1709 Elizaveta Petrovna Romanova, Empress of Russia
1721 Madame de Pompadour
1841 Rosalie Ingeborg Karolina Fougelberg
1879 Florence Mary Taylor
1867 Annie Montague Alexander
1923 Yvonne Choquet-Bruhat

Deaths:

721 Empress Genmei

Births: **DECEMBER 30**

159 Empress Dowager Bian
1855 Katharine J. Bush
1906 Josephine Elizabeth Butler
1912 Pasha Angelina
1912 Peggy Glanville-Hicks
1929 Rosalinde Hurley
1977 Helen Tracy Parsons
2012 Rita Levi-Montalcini

Births: **DECEMBER 31**

1872 Tui Manu'a Matelita
1878 Elizabeth Arden
1903 Fumiko Hayashi
1905 Helen Prince
1919 Recy Taylor
1925 Daphne Oram
1930 Odetta

Deaths:

1916 Alice Augusta Ball
1958 Gudrun Marie Ruud

❦ ❦ ❦

NOBEL PRIZE AWARDED TO WOMEN

❦ ❦ ❦

Year	Name	Category	Rationale
1903	Marie Skłodowska -Curie	Physics	"in recognition of the extraordinary services they have rendered by their joint researches on the radiation phenomena discovered by Professor Henri Becquerel"
1963	Maria Goeppert Mayer	Physics	"for their discoveries concerning nuclear shell structure"
2018	Donna Strickland	Physics	"for groundbreaking inventions in the field of laser physics" | "for their method of generating high-intensity, ultra-short optical pulses."
2020	Andrea Ghez	Physics	"for the discovery of a supermassive compact object at the centre of our galaxy"
2023	Anne L'Huillier	Physics	"for experimental methods that generate attosecond pulses of light for the study of electron dynamics in matter"
1911	Maria Skłodowska -Curie	Chemistry	"in recognition of her services to the advancement of chemistry by the discovery of the elements radium and polonium, by the isolation of radium and the study of the nature and compounds of this remarkable element"
1935	Irène Joliot-Curie	Chemistry	"in recognition of their synthesis of new radioactive elements"
1964	Dorothy Crowfoot Hodgkin	Chemistry	"for her determinations by X-ray techniques of the structures of important biochemical substances"
2009	Ada E. Yonath	Chemistry	"for studies of the structure and function of the ribosome"
2018	Frances H. Arnold	Chemistry	"for the directed evolution of enzymes"

Year	Name	Category	Rationale
2020	Jennifer A. Doudna Emmanuelle Char-pentier	Chemistry	"for the development of a method for genome editing"
2022	Carolyn R. Bertozzi		"for the development of click chemistry and bioortho-gonal chemistry"
1947	Gerty Theresa Cori	Physiology or Medicine	"for their discovery of the course of the catalytic conversion of glycogen"
1977	Rosalyn Yalow		"for the development of radioimmunoassays of peptide hormones"
1983	Barbara McClin-tock		"for her discovery of mobile genetic elements"
1986	Rita Levi-Montalcini		"for their discoveries of growth factors"
1988	Gertrude B. Elion		"for their discoveries of important principles for drug treatment"
1995	Christiane Nüsslein-Volhard		"for their discoveries concerning the genetic control of early embryonic development"
2004	Linda B. Buck		"for their discoveries of odorant receptors and the organization of the olfactory system"
2008	Françoise Barré-Sinoussi		"for their discovery of human immunodeficiency virus"
2009	Carol W. Greider Elizabeth H. Blackburn		"for the discovery of how chromosomes are protected by telomeres and the enzyme telomerase"
2014	May-Britt Moser		"for their discoveries of cells that constitute a positio-ning system in the brain"
2015	Tu Youyou		"for her discoveries concerning a novel therapy against Malaria"
2023	Katalin Karikó		"for their discoveries concerning nucleoside base modi-fications that enabled the development of effective mRNA vaccines against COVID-19"
1909	Selma Ottilia Lovi-sa Lagerlöf	Literature	"in appreciation of the lofty idealism, vivid imagination and spiritual perception that characterize her writings"
1926	Grazia Deledda		"for her idealistically inspired writings which with pla-stic clarity picture the life on her native island and with depth and sympathy deal with human problems in general"

Year	Name	Category	Rationale
1928	Sigrid Undset	Literature	"principally for her powerful descriptions of Northern life during the Middle Ages"
1938	Pearl Buck		"for her rich and truly epic descriptions of peasant life in China and for her biographical masterpieces"
1945	Gabriela Mistral		"for her lyric poetry which, inspired by powerful emotions, has made her name a symbol of the idealistic aspirations of the entire Latin American world"
1966	Nelly Sachs		"for her outstanding lyrical and dramatic writing, which interprets Israel's destiny with touching strength"
1991	Nadine Gordimer		"who through her magnificent epic writing has – in the words of Alfred Nobel – been of very great benefit to humanity"
1993	Toni Morrison		"who in novels characterized by visionary force and poetic import, gives life to an essential aspect of American reality"
1996	Wisława Szymborska		"for poetry that with ironic precision allows the historical and biological context to come to light in fragments of human reality"
2004	Elfride Jelinek		"for her musical flow of voices and counter-voices in novels and plays that with extraordinary linguistic zeal reveal the absurdity of society's clichés and their subjugating power"
2007	Doris Lessing		"that epicist of the female experience, who with scepticism, fire and visionary power has subjected a divided civilisation to scrutiny"
2009	Herta Müller		"who, with the concentration of poetry and the frankness of prose, depicts the landscape of the dispossessed"
2013	Alice Munro		"master of the contemporary short story"
2015	Svetlana Alexievich		"for her polyphonic writings, a monument to suffering and courage in our time"
2018	Olga Tokarczuk		"for a narrative imagination that with encyclopedic passion represents the crossing of boundaries as a form of life"
2020	Louise Glück		"for her unmistakable poetic voice that with austere beauty makes individual existence universal"
2022	Annie Ernaux		"for the courage and clinical acuity with which she uncovers the roots, estrangements and collective restraints of personal memory"

Year	Name	Category	Rationale
1905	Baroness Bertha Sophie Felicita von Suttner	Peace	"for her audacity to oppose the horrors of war"
1931	Jane Addams		"for their assiduous effort to revive the ideal of peace and to rekindle the spirit of peace in their own nation and in the whole of mankind"
1946	Emily Greene Balch		"for her lifelong work for the cause of peace"
1976	Mairead Corrigan Betty Williams		"for the courageous efforts in founding a movement to put an end to the violent conflict in Northern Ireland"
1979	Mother Teresa		"for her work for bringing help to suffering humanity"
1982	Alva Myrdal		"for their work for disarmament and nuclear and weapon-free zones"
1991	Aung San Suu Kyi		"for her non-violent struggle for democracy and human rights"
1992	Rigoberta Menchú Tum		"in recognition of her work for social justice and ethno -cultural reconciliation based on respect for the rights of indigenous peoples"
1997	Jody Williams		"for their work for the banning and clearing of anti-personnel mines"
2003	Shirin Ebadi		"for her efforts for democracy and human rights. She has focused especially on the struggle for the rights of women and children"
2004	Wangari Muta Maathai		"for her contribution to sustainable development, democracy and peace"
2011	Tawakkol Karman Leymah Gbowee Ellen Johnson Sirleaf		"for their non-violent struggle for the safety of women and for women's rights to full participation in peace-building work"
2014	Malala Yousafzai		"for their struggle against the suppression of children and young people and for the right of all children to education"
2018	Nadia Murad		"for their efforts to end the use of sexual violence as a weapon of war and armed conflict"
2021	Maria Ressa		"for their efforts to safeguard freedom of expression, which is a precondition for democracy and lasting peace"
2023	Narges Mohammadi		"for her fight against the oppression of women in Iran and her fight to promote human rights and freedom for all"

Year	Name	Category	Rationale
2009	Elinor Ostrom	The Sveriges Riksbank Prize in Economic Sciences in Memory of Alfred Nobel	"for her analysis of economic governance, especially the commons"
2019	Esther Duflo		"for their experimental approach to alleviating global poverty"
2023	Claudia Goldin		"for having advanced our understanding of women's labour market outcomes"

Printed in Great Britain
by Amazon